HARVARD ECONOMIC STUDIES

I. The English Patents of Monopoly. By William H. Price. 8vo.

II. The Lodging House Problem in Boston. By Albert B. Wolfe. 8vo.

III. The Stannaries: A Study of the English Tin Miner. By George R. Lewis. 8vo.

IV. Railroad Reorganization. By Stuart Daggett. 8vo.

V. Wool-Growing and the Tariff. By Chester W. Wright. 8vo.

VI. Public Ownership of Telephones on the Continent of Europe. By Arthur N. Holcombe. 8vo.

VII. The History of the British Post Office. By J. C. Hemmeon. 8vo.

VIII. The Cotton Manufacturing Industry of the United States. By M. T. Copeland. 8vo.

IX. The History of the Grain Trade in France. By Abbott Payson Usher. 8vo.

X. Corporate Promotions and Reorganizations. By A. S. Dewing. 8vo.

XI. The Anthracite Coal Combination in the United States. By Eliot Jones. 8vo.

XII. Some Aspects of the Tariff Question. By F. W. Taussig. 8vo.

XIII. The Evolution of the English Corn Market from the Twelfth to the Eighteenth Century. By N. S. B. Gras. 8vo.

XIV. Social Adaptation: A Study in the Development of the Doctrine of Adaptation as a Theory of Social Progress. By L. M. Bristol. 8vo.

XV. The Financial History of Boston, from May 1, 1822, to January 31, 1909. By C. P. Huse. 8vo.

XVI. Essays in the Earlier History of American Corporations. By J. S. Davis. 8vo. 2 volumes.

XVII. The State Tax Commission. By H. L. Lutz. 8vo.

XVIII. The Early English Customs System. By N. S. B. Gras. 8vo.

XIX. Trade and Navigation between Spain and the Indies in the time of the Hapsburgs. By C. H. Haring. 8vo.

XX. The Italian Emigration of Our Times. By R. F. Foerster. 8vo.

XXI. The Mesta: A Study in Spanish Economic History, 1273–1834. By Julius Klein. 8vo.

XXII. Argentine International Trade under Inconvertible Paper Money: 1880–1900. By J. H. Williams. 8vo.

XXIII. The Organization of the Boot and Shoe Industry in Massachusetts before 1875. By Blanche E. Hazard. 8vo.

XXIV. Economic Motives. By Zenas C. Dickinson. 8vo.

XXV. Monetary Theory before Adam Smith. By Arthur E. Monroe. 8vo.

XXVI. Canada's Balance of International Indebtedness 1900–1913. By Jacob Viner. 8vo.

XXVII. The History of the United States Post Office to the Year 1829. By W. E. Rich. 8vo.

XXVIII. The Theory of International Prices. By James W. Angell. 8vo.

XXIX. Forests and Sea Power. By Robert G. Albion. 8vo.

XXX. Banking Theories in the United States before 1860. By Harry E. Miller. 8vo.

XXXI. Karl Marx's Interpretation of History. By Mandell Morton Bober. 8vo.

XXXII. Grain Growers' Cooperation in Western Canada. By Harald S. Patton. 8vo.

HARVARD UNIVERSITY PRESS
CAMBRIDGE, MASS., U. S. A.

HARVARD ECONOMIC STUDIES

PUBLISHED UNDER THE DIRECTION OF THE DEPARTMENT OF ECONOMICS

VOL. XXXII

LONDON : HUMPHREY MILFORD
OXFORD UNIVERSITY PRESS

GRAIN GROWERS' COÖPERATION IN WESTERN CANADA

BY

HARALD S. PATTON, PH.D.

CAMBRIDGE
HARVARD UNIVERSITY PRESS
1928

PRINTED AT THE HARVARD UNIVERSITY PRESS
CAMBRIDGE, MASS., U. S. A.

PREFACE

THIS study was first undertaken during the latter part of four years' teaching at the University of Alberta. The term of association coincided with the acute period of post-war agricultural depression, and with the beginning of the wheat pool movement. The subject of the study was discussed with Professor Carver of Harvard University during a visit of the latter to Edmonton early in 1923, and was pursued under his advice and general direction. The present work reproduces in part the doctoral thesis presented by the writer at Harvard University at the end of 1925. The significant developments since that date, in connection with the wheat pools, and in the interrelations of pools, grain growers' companies, and farmers' associations, have involved very considerable additions to the original matter, which were made during a return sojourn in Western Canada in the summer of 1927.

The comparative geographic isolation of the Prairie Provinces, lying between the Laurentian wilderness of New Ontario and the Rocky Mountains, and the general concentration on grain growing throughout that region, have tended to develop a solidarity of interest and action among the growers of the three provinces, which have found expression in coöperative organization of a distinctively indigenous character. The history of the Canadian Grain Growers' Movement from the beginning of the present century, following the twofold course of organization for the securing of protective and advantageous legislation, and for business coöperation, exhibits a notable continuity and progressive adaptability. This study is mainly concerned with the origins, growth, experiences, and interrelations of those coöperative institutions whereby prairie grain growers have successively assumed wider and more inclusive functions in the marketing of their product, until today the Canadian Co-operative Wheat

Producers, as the world's largest wheat exporting agency, deals more or less directly with consumers in overseas markets. The study also involves an examination of the functions demanded of, and assumed by, governmental agencies, in connection with the marketing of Canada's major export commodity, and a consideration of the dynamically changing relations between private middleman agencies, public institutions, and farmers' coöperative organizations.

In addition to the helpful counsel and encouragement of Professor Carver, I wish to acknowledge especially my indebtedness to Professor D. A. MacGibbon, Professor of Political Economy at the University of Alberta, and a member of the Royal Grain Inquiry Commission of 1923–24, whose critical judgment in the reading of draft sections of the study has been a most valuable aid.

The work of revision and amplification during the summer of 1927 was greatly helped through the facilities placed at my disposal and the courtesies extended by Mr. George F. Chipman, whose editorial leadership of the *Grain Growers' Guide* has played so influential a part in the Grain Growers' Movement; by Mr. W. A. MacLeod, Director of the Department of Publicity and Statistics of the Canadian Co-operative Wheat Producers, by whom the chapters dealing with pool operations and policies were read; and by Mr. W. J. Healey, Provincial Librarian of Manitoba and former Secretary of the Ottawa Press Gallery. I also wish to express my appreciation for personal information and courteous assistance received from Mr. R. S. Law, Secretary of the United Grain Growers, Limited; from Mr. W. C. Mills, Secretary (later, President) of the Saskatchewan Co-operative Elevator Company; from Mr. E. B. Ramsay, Secretary of the Canadian Co-operative Wheat Producers; and from Mr. Andrew Cairns, Mr. H. S. Fry, and Mr. J. T. Hull, the respective educational directors of the Alberta, Saskatchewan, and Manitoba wheat pools.

While periodic files, documents, reports, and statutes have constituted the tangible raw material of the study, a love of the Canadian prairie country and cherished contacts with men in many parts who have furrowed its responsive soil, and with many of the leaders who have labored to build up a coöperative agricultural commonwealth in Western Canada, have been ingredients which have served to make my task something more than a matter of mere academic research.

HARALD S. PATTON

UNIVERSITY OF CINCINNATI
November, 1927

CONTENTS

PART I

THE STRUGGLE FOR FREE MARKETING

1900–10

INTRODUCTORY

CHAPTER I

CHAPTER II

CHAPTER III

CHAPTER IV

CHAPTER V

CHAPTER VI

PART II

THE FARMERS' CO-OPERATIVE ELEVATOR COMPANIES

CHAPTER VII

THE ELEVATOR ISSUE IN MANITOBA

CHAPTER VIII

ORIGIN OF SASKATCHEWAN CO-OPERATIVE ELEVATOR COMPANY

CHAPTER IX

THE ALBERTA FARMERS' CO-OPERATIVE ELEVATOR COMPANY

CHAPTER X

THE GRAIN GROWERS AND THE TERMINALS

CHAPTER XI

AMALGAMATION: THE UNITED GRAIN GROWERS, Ltd.

CHAPTER XII

PART III

THE MOVEMENT FOR COLLECTIVE MARKETING 1919–27

CHAPTER XIII

THE WHEAT BOARD MOVEMENT, 1919–23

CHAPTER XIV

INCEPTION OF THE WESTERN WHEAT POOLS, 1923–24

CHAPTER XV

THE POOLS AND THE CO-OPERATIVE ELEVATOR COMPANIES

CHAPTER XVI

POOL POLICIES AND OPERATIONS

PART IV

RESULTS AND TENDENCIES IN THE GRAIN GROWERS' COÖPERATIVE MOVEMENT

CHAPTER XVII

EXPERIENCES IN COÖPERATIVE SUPPLY

CHAPTER XVIII

BUSINESS RESULTS OF GRAIN GROWERS' COÖPERATIVE ORGANIZATIONS

CHAPTER XIX

COÖPERATIVE POLICIES AND RESULTS

CHAPTER XX

SOLIDARITY OF THE GRAIN GROWERS' MOVEMENT

CONCLUSION

APPENDICES

PART I

THE STRUGGLE FOR FREE MARKETING

1900–10

INTRODUCTORY

RISE OF GRAIN GROWING IN WESTERN CANADA

WHEAT growing in Western Canada had its beginning as far back as 1812, when Lord Selkirk's Highland settlers made their first abortive sowing of winter seed-wheat brought from Scotland by way of Hudson Bay, in hoe-broken plots along the banks of the Red River, where the grain metropolis of Winnipeg now stands. Despite murderous attacks and expulsions in the first years by the Northwest Company, which resented the establishment of a civilized settlement across its main fur-trading routes, and despite the early ravages of frost, hail, grasshoppers, mice, and flood, wheat has been planted annually in the Red River Valley ever since the first arrival of the Selkirk settlers. For nearly three quarters of a century, however, such crops as were raised in this region were milled locally, and their market was limited to supplying the flour requirements of the Red River Colony itself and of the trading posts of the Hudson's Bay Company.[1]

It was necessary that four distinct developments should come to pass before the Canadian Northwest could become a factor in the world's wheat trade. First, the status of the land itself had to be converted from the territorial monopoly of a fur-trading company to that of an organized federal territory available for general settlement. Second, the suitability of the environment for the production of varieties of wheat desired by the milling trade had to be demonstrated. Third, transportation facilities for the shipment of prairie-grown wheat to the distant seaboard at non-prohibitive rates had to be provided. Fourth, even with the preceding conditions realized, no considerable extension of wheat growing in Western Canada was likely to take place until the more accessible wheat lands of the United States should show signs of being fairly well appropriated, and the economic justifi-

[1] See A. H. R. Buller, *Essays on Wheat*, chap. 1.

cation of a further expansion of the margin of extensive cultivation should be indicated by the behavior of world wheat prices.

The first condition was brought about in the decade of the eighteen-seventies. The purchase in 1869 of the proprietary rights of the chartered Hudson's Bay Company in the immense inland empire comprised in Prince Rupert's Land and the North-West Territory, as one of the first acts of the newly formed Canadian Confederation, prepared the way for the conversion in 1870 of the southeastern portion of the Hudson's Bay territory, containing the Red River Settlement, into the Province of Manitoba. The total population of the Settlement at that time, including whites, Indians, and half-breeds, was but 12,000, and the land under cultivation was still confined to riverside farms near the junction of the Red and the Assiniboine.

At the outset the Lieutenant-Governor of Manitoba was also the Administrator of the North-West Territories. In 1875, however, provision was made for a separate resident Lieutenant-Governor for the Territories, and for a species of Crown Colony Council, whose personnel was to be nominative at first, but supplemented by elective members as settlement warranted. The organization in 1873 of the Royal North-West Mounted Police, following the Riel half-breed insurrection of 1869, laid the basis of justice, order, and protection, and of friendly relations with the Indians in the newly acquired federal territory. These conditions were further assured through the negotiation of various treaties with the Indian tribes, marking off the reserve areas from the regions destined for settlement, and equitably defining the rights and compensations of the aboriginal occupants. Successive surveys gradually blocked off the prairie empire into ranges, townships, and sections based on "prime meridians" of which the first was taken through Winnipeg. The eighteen-seventies was thus a period of preparation and organization in anticipation of agricultural settlement, for which, however, adequate economic inducement did not yet exist.

Development of Red Fife Wheat. — The wheat-growing experiences of the early Red River settlers had afforded abundant demonstration of the high fertility of the black loam of that valley, and of the rapidity of plant growth during the long daylight hours of the northern summer season. Climatic conditions on the whole, however, had not proved encouraging. The persistence of late spring frosts precluded the sowing of winter wheat, and the frequency of early autumn frosts made even the growing of the ordinary spring wheat varieties decidedly precarious. In Red Fife wheat, however, which appears to have been introduced into Manitoba by way of Wisconsin and Minnesota about 1870,[1] a variety was found whose hardiness made it well adapted to the Manitoba environment, and whose yields proved exceptionally favorable in the productive loam of the Red River Valley. But while Red Fife was well suited to prairie-growing conditions, it did not originally enjoy favor with millers, since its flinty kernels made it difficult to produce a fine and uniform white flour by the usual grist-mill processes. The introduction in the seventies, however, of the La Croix purifier (for separating branny particles from middlings), and of the gradual reduction process, involving the substitution of chilled iron rollers for the traditional millstones, brought about a veritable milling revolution.[2] Millers were now able to produce a spring wheat flour that was "strong" and highly glutenous, and at the same time even in texture and uniformly white in color. Thus hard spring wheats became the preferred instead of the ill-favored wheats of the miller and baker for bread-making purposes, and Red Fife in particular rose to premium rank.

[1] This hard and hardy grain had been accidentally introduced into Ontario in 1842, through the observation and preservation by David Fife, a Peterborough County farmer, of the distinctive yield from apparently a single grain contained in an otherwise abortive spring sowing of a sample of wheat from Danzig, sent to Fife by a friend in Glasgow. Dr. Charles Saunders, late Dominion Cerealist, has established the identity of Red Fife with Galician wheat, so that David Fife's revolutionary kernel in all likelihood found its haphazard way to Ontario from Central Europe by way of Scotland. After its successful introduction into Ontario, Red Fife passed into the spring-wheat region of the United States, from which it entered Manitoba. The various versions of the origin of Red Fife are related in Buller's *Essays on Wheat*, pp. 206–218.

[2] The commercialization of these processes is associated with the names of Christian, Washburn, and Pillsbury, whose enterprise contributed to making Minneapolis the centre of the milling revolution of the seventies. See Wm. Edgar, *The Story of a Grain of Wheat*, pp. 156–166.

The Transportation Factor. — However excellent the yield and milling quality of Red River Fife, its cultivation could not be profitably extended until the means of transporting it economically to eastern milling and export centres should become available. The Red River Valley lies near the centre of the North American continent, with over four hundred miles, mostly through rock and forest, separating it from the head of Lake Superior. Lord Selkirk's settlers had reached it from the north by way of Hudson Bay, the Nelson River, and Lake Winnipeg. The Northwest Company's traders had made use of a devious but fairly continuous canoe route, from their western base at Fort William to Lake Winnipeg, by way of Rainy Lake, Lake of the Woods, and the Winnipeg River. Considerable sums were spent by the government of Canada in developing the amphibious Dawson route — five hundred miles of combined water stretches and wagon route — as a colonization road between Thunder Bay and Fort Garry (Winnipeg).

The arduous character, however, of this all-Canadian route (traversed with great hardship by the Wolseley Expedition during the Red River Rising in 1870) caused it to be abandoned. The natural highway to the Manitoba colony was down the Red River from the south through American territory. During the eighteen-sixties and seventies St. Paul, Minnesota, was the established "jumping-off place" for the Fort Garry settlement. The intervening 450 miles were covered, first by ox-cart train, then by subsidized stage line, and later by Red River steamers.[1] Finally, in 1878, a government railway line was completed along the Red River, from St. Boniface (East Winnipeg) to Emerson on the Minnesota boundary, where connection was made with the St. Paul and Pacific Railway. While the rail service thus established greatly facilitated the transportation of settlers and

[1] The Hudson's Bay Company's steamers at first carried only company supplies, until competition was introduced in 1872, when James J. Hill's "Selkirk" commenced operations as a common carrier. Competition soon led to amalgamation and the formation of the Red River Transportation Company, which at one time operated seven steamers between Winnipeg and Fisher's Landing, Minnesota, where rail connection was made with St. Paul. H. A. Innis, *History of the Canadian Pacific Railway*, p. 93.

supplies into the new province, it did not bring the Manitoba farmer within competitive range of the Minneapolis spring-wheat market, so long as the intermediate territory was still in process of conversion to spring-wheat cultivation.

If Manitoba wheat was to find an outlet, it must be in and through Eastern Canada. Such a movement was of course an object of Canadian national policy. The Red River railway line had been constructed merely as a provisional line of communication, pending the completion of the all-Canadian railway to the Pacific in fulfilment of the Confederation pact with British Columbia. In 1883 the abandoned Dawson project of a colonization route from Thunder Bay to Red River was restored in improved form, with the completion of the Canadian Pacific main line between Port Arthur and Winnipeg. In the same year that railway erected the first of the great series of grain elevators that has arisen on the shores of Thunder Bay. By 1884 Manitoba spring wheat was moving by rail and boat to Eastern Canada,[1] and by 1886 the all-rail route by the Canadian Pacific main line along the north shore of Lake Superior became available for winter transportation. Western wheat growing no longer needed to be confined to supplying the needs of Hudson's Bay traders, Mounted Police detachments, freighters, and railway construction gangs.

The year 1886, which marked the restoration of order and security following Riel's second rebellion, the inauguration of the Canadian Pacific transcontinental service, and the institution of federal grain inspection at Winnipeg, thus found Western Canada with three of the preliminary conditions for development as a wheat-growing region at least initially realized. Vast fertile tracts, traversed by an all-Canadian transcontinental railway, were provincially or federally organized, police patrolled, and

[1] While the regular movement of grain from Western Canada dates from 1884, the first shipment of wheat actually made from Manitoba appears to have been a parcel of 857 bushels of Red River Fife, consigned to a Toronto seed merchant by way of Fisher's Landing on the Red River and Duluth in 1876, when the Red Fife crop in Ontario failed. Thus Manitoba repaid its indebtedness to Ontario for Red Fife seed. C. C. James, "Canadian Wheat History," in *Grain Growers' Guide*, June 7, 1916.

available for occupation, either by homestead entry or by purchase at low prices from the Canadian Pacific, Hudson's Bay Company, or various colonization companies.[1] The productivity and high milling qualities of Manitoba Red Fife had already been demonstrated, and sale on the basis of government grade certificate was now established. Lakehead terminals were rising as the necessary medium of transfer of export grain from box car to lake carrier.[2]

Reasons for Tardiness of Settlement. — With all these facilities the development of settlement and grain-growing on the prairies made slow headway. Despite the Manitoba land boom during the construction of the C. P. R., the census of 1891 showed that the total population of Manitoba and the North-West Territories had grown during the decade, from 118,706 to but 251,473 (of whom over one-fifth were Indians). Within the same period the population of the Territory of Dakota alone had increased from 135,000 to 510,000. While homestead entries to the number of 37,397 were taken up during the census decade, a great many were allowed to lapse. In 1890, a year of record crop yields, government inspection of wheat accounted for but 6,630,000 bushels.

[1] Settlement during the eighteen-eighties was undoubtedly retarded to some extent by frequent changes in land-grant regulations by the federal government, whose policy oscillated between the desire to encourage rapid colonization and the disposition to finance the Pacific railroad out of the proceeds of western lands rather than of eastern taxes. Thus, while the even-numbered sections in each surveyed township were opened for free homestead entry (on the model of the United States Homestead Act of 1862), the odd-numbered sections for 24 miles on each side of the railway line were reserved as lands from which the C. P. R. might select its 25,000,000 contractual acres, as earned and as desired. At the outset the railway company offered farms to settlers for $2.50 an acre, with a rebate of $1.25 for every acre broken and put under cultivation. Outside the railway belt the odd-numbered sections were largely "blocked off" to land and colonization companies at a dollar an acre, conditional on the introduction of a specified number of settlers. By the terms of the deed of surrender of 1869 the Hudson's Bay Company was entitled to one twentieth of all land subsequently set out for settlement in the fertile belt (south of the North Saskatchewan, between Lake Winnipeg and the Rockies).

[2] Between 1883 and 1902 five terminal elevators were erected by the C. P. R. at Fort William.

Agricultural settlement in Western Canada lagged, despite the potential opportunities and basic facilities offered by the country, because the economic inducement was not yet sufficiently strong to stimulate any movement of large proportions. In the United States the extension of the agricultural frontier had proceeded fairly continuously, from the post-Revolutionary movement across the Alleghenies to the post-Civil War migration beyond the Mississippi and Missouri to the borders of the semi-arid territory west of the 100th meridian. In Canada the southern sweep of the great pre-Cambrian shield imposes an 800-mile barrier of rock and forest between the older settled portion of Ontario and the western plains. The population of Eastern Canada was not sufficiently large to permit any considerable overflow of native stock to the west, even if there had been no geographic barrier to surmount. Nor had the Canadian West become as yet an alluring prospect or object in the eyes of emigrants from Europe, or even from the British Isles. The United States, with its earlier national momentum, with its more accessible resources and more attractive climate, and with its high tide of enterprise and expansion following the Civil War, dominated the calculations of the great majority of European people desirous of seeking opportunities in the New World. The surveyed homestead areas of Western Canada were bound to remain relatively vacant until the free and more accessible wheat land of the American Northwest had become fairly completely appropriated.

Emergence of the West. — It was not until the very turn of the century that the fourth basic condition for the free development of wheat-growing in Western Canada began to be realized. The persistent downward trend of world wheat prices after 1873 reached its lowest (annual average) level in 1894, after which a general steadiness became apparent, passing into a gradual upward movement after 1903.[1] In part the advancing price of wheat was in sympathy with the general rise in international

[1] In 1894 the index number of the annual average Gazette price of British wheat was 84 (1900 = 100), the lowest point of the century. Only twice after 1900 did the annual index number fall below 104, the figures for 1901 and 1903 being 99. See W. T. Layton, *Introduction to the Study of Prices*, p. 114.

price levels, accompanying the substantial additions to the world's gold stocks from the South African and Klondike fields during this period. Wheat prices advanced, however, independently as well as sympathetically,[1] as the rate of expansion of the wheat-growing acreage of the United States began to slacken, and the exportable surplus of both that country and Russia began to diminish in response to the increasing consumptive requirements of their rapidly growing populations.[2]

The combination of better prices for wheat with the availability of free virgin farm lands in Western Canada constituted an economic conjuncture in which the aggressive immigration policy inaugurated by the Laurier administration, which came into office in 1896, began to yield conspicuous results. The process of rapid colonization was further promoted by the no less aggressive efforts of the remarkable partnership of William Mackenzie and Donald Mann, who in the same pivotal year constructed in northwestern Manitoba the first hundred miles of track that shortly developed into the Canadian Northern Railway, providing a second outlet to Lake Superior, and opening up the fertile basin of the Saskatchewan west to Edmonton. Under these conditions, immigrants from the British Isles as well as from the Continent of Europe began to seek in the Canadian prairies the free homesteads which were no longer available in the United States. The westward migration from Eastern Canada began also to attain impressive proportions, while rising farm-land values in the American Middle West and Northwestern states sent farmers' sons northward over the border in increasing numbers, and led many American farm owners to realize the increment on their improved property, and take up free or cheap

[1] For the decade 1896–1905 the average all-commodity price index number for the United Kingdom was 90.3 (1900 = 100). For the same period and the same base the average price index of British wheat was 104.7. Layton, *loc. cit.*

[2] The peak of American wheat acreage (pre-war) was reached in 1899, when 52,589,000 acres were harvested. The maximum proportion of the crop to be exported was realized in 1892, when 38.6 per cent was shipped to foreign consumers. For the decade 1896–1905 the proportion exported averaged 25.3 per cent. — U. S. Dept. Agric. *Year-book*, 1923. In 1872 Russia's wheat exports to Great Britain amounted to 4,108,000 quarters. By 1900 they had decreased to 1,030,000 quarters.

land in Canada, with a view to reproducing their pioneering methods and gains in a new, yet not strange environment.[1]

The census of 1901 showed the population of Manitoba and Territories to have increased from 251,473, in 1891 to 414,151 in 1901, the gain being principally in the last half of the decade. The expansion in crop acreage was in greater proportion, the 3,600,000 acres of 1901 being two and a half times the number under crop in 1891. Approximately 65 per cent of this acreage was in wheat, of which the production in 1901 amounted to 63,000,000 bushels, representing an average yield of 25 bushels per acre.

The turn of the century thus marked the real emergence of Western Canada as a natural field for agricultural immigration and as a definite factor in the world's wheat trade. During the last quarter of the nineteenth century the four preliminary conditions for the development of its wheat-growing potentialities had been slowly realized. The number of wheat growers was now increasing each year at an accelerated rate. For the next quarter of a century the problem was to be primarily one of controlling the marketing of the ever-increasing crop to the greatest advantage of the producers. In the grievances entertained by settlers in respect to the handling of their crops now moving in increasing commercial volume, the Grain Growers' Movement had its birth. The nature of those initial grievances must next be considered in some detail.

[1] The advance wave of American immigration came in 1896, when 142 homestead entries were made by residents of the United States. By 1901 it was estimated that there were 50,000 Americans located in Western Canada. J. W. Dafoe, *Economic History of Prairie Provinces, in Canada and its Provinces*, XX, 304.

CHAPTER I

EARLY GRIEVANCES OF WESTERN GRAIN GROWERS

While the early grievances of western grain growers were focussed chiefly upon the railway and line-elevator companies, their basis was primarily geographic. The climate of Western Canada is more favorable to the production than to the marketing of grain. The same northerly conditions that stimulate rapid development during the brief growing season, and produce wheats of high gluten content,[1] conspire to induce congestion in the harvesting, threshing, and shipping of grain. Spring sowing in high latitudes means a late harvesting period, and late harvesting involves risks of early frosts. Consequently the operations of cutting and threshing have to be rushed, lest the kernels become frosted and thereby lowered in grade. Late threshing leaves but a limited period for grain to be marketed, inspected, and moved to terminal storage before the lakehead ports become icebound. Lake shipping insurance premiums usually rise by daily increments after the first of December, and owners of grain that has not been shipped out before the close of navigation must either bear the higher cost of all-rail shipment to seaboard or of all-winter storage until the reopening of lake navigation. Consequently, between the end of September and the beginning of December there is a general feverish rush to move grain from farm to lakehead, which imposes a tremendous seasonal strain upon transportation and storage facilities, particularly in years of heavy yields and late harvests.

[1] "Climatic conditions influence the quality of the wheat through the vegetative processes by shortening or lengthening the time which elapses between the formation of the kernel and its maturity — the shorter the period, the higher the protein content within certain limits. High temperature, long days, and absence of excessive moisture during the ripening process, hasten the maturation of the grain and increase its percentage of gluten. These are the conditions that prevail in the northwestern wheat areas in those seasons which give the largest proportion of first quality wheat." F. T. Shutt, Dominion Chemist; cited in Rutter, *Wheat Growing in Canada, the United States and the Argentine*, p. 21.

Difficulties in Crop Movement. — The stimulated settlement and rapid expansion of grain acreage, especially in the North-West Territories, during the eighteen-nineties, subjected the Canadian Pacific Railway to the increasing pressure, not only of greater volumes of grain to be moved, but also of longer hauls during the acute shipping season. The construction of 3000 miles of line through a scarcely inhabited country proved such a strain upon the finances of a company whose capital was raised entirely by issuing stock instead of bonds, and whose lands were of largely speculative value, that very great difficulty was experienced in the early years in providing rolling stock adequate to meet the seasonal demands of the western crop movement. Moreover, practically the entire exportable crop had to be moved over the single line of steel between Winnipeg, where inspection was concentrated, and the terminals at Fort William. Thus, while the dimensions of the western grain-hopper expanded as the wheat frontiers extended westward and northward, the increased volume of grain had still to flow through a single pipe line of unenlarged bore.[1]

The shipping difficulty was not merely a question of adequate rolling stock and trackage, but also one of initial storage. The pioneer grain grower, with a granary on his own farm, was the exception. The C. P. R., as we have noted, undertook at the very outset to provide terminal storage. It lacked the capital, however, even if it had had the disposition, to erect warehouses at local shipping points. Hence the farmer who could not load his grain directly on cars usually had to haul it to some railway point where a private dealer had erected a flat warehouse. Here he might sell his grain to the warehouse owner, or store it until he had accumulated sufficient to make a carload or part-carload consignment to a Winnipeg commission dealer. As the number of grain growers multiplied, and as the scale of individual operations expanded, the inadequacy of these flat warehouses became acutely apparent. A few wagonloads flooded their shallow bins,

[1] In 1886 the C. P. R. carried 10,900,000 bushels of grain; in 1890, 20,200,000 bushels were moved; in 1896, 32,500,000 bushels; and in 1899, 42,700,000 bushels. Innis, *History of the Canadian Pacific Railway*, p. 144.

while the slow process of loading cars by truck [1] necessarily restricted the velocity of car circulation.

The C. P. R. and the Elevators. — Similar conditions had been met in the American wheat belt by Peavey's invention of the endless cup conveyor, making possible the handling of grain in bulk and the utilization of its flowing properties in binning and loading, through the substitution of the elevator for the flat warehouse. With a view to relieving the acute seasonal strain on its limited rolling stock, the C. P. R. decided to offer inducements to attract capital and enterprise into the provision of a more adequate and expeditious system of initial storage and loading. Accordingly the company made it known that to any individual or company erecting at any shipping point a "standard" elevator of not less than 25,000 bushels' capacity equipped with steam or gasoline engine and cleaning machinery, special concessions would be extended in the form of a free lease of site on the railway's property, and of an agreement not to allow cars to be loaded through flat warehouses, or direct from farmers' wagons, or otherwise than through such elevators.

The Farmer and the Elevators. (*a*) The Carload Shipper. — The offer of such monopoly privileges and the rising volume of western grain production promptly led to the springing up of standard elevators at every shipping point of importance, the majority of them belonging to a few line companies or milling concerns.[2] The additional storage capacity, the elimination of the cost and trouble of bagging the grain, the facilities for cleaning and bulk weighing, and the expeditious loading of cars by gravity, constituted an immense improvement over previous methods of handling at country points. In the farmers' eyes, however, the undoubted technical advantages possessed by the

[1] Before the advent of the line elevators, western growers usually bagged their grain, which was then weighed on ordinary scales, and handled through the flat warehouse by hand trolleys and trucks. R. Magill, *Grain Inspection in Canada* (Dept. of Trade and Commerce, Ottawa, 1914), p. 11.

[2] The Royal Grain Commission of 1899 reported that 447 standard elevators were doing business in the Canadian West at the close of the century; of these 206 were owned by three elevator syndicates and 75 by two large milling companies.

standard elevators over the old flat warehouses were more than offset by the disadvantages associated with their privileged conditions of operation. The grower could no longer order and load his own car of grain for sale on track, for consignment to a Winnipeg commission agency, or for terminal storage. He must either store his grain with the local elevator under its own conditions, or else sell his load to the operator or other street buyer on the latter's own terms.

In the former case he had to pay one and a half cents per bushel for handling, cleaning and fifteen days' storage. The charge for the same services at the terminal elevator where his grain could be sold as "spot" was three fourths of a cent a bushel (one half a cent after 1899). By being compelled to ship through the standard elevator, instead of being free to load his own car over shipping platform, the farmer suffered an apparent loss of three fourths of a cent to a cent a bushel, provided he did not take into account the trouble of securing his own car, and the time and labor of direct loading. Even if he did not consider the elevator handling charges unreasonable, he was rarely able to obtain "special binning" accommodation, by which the identity of his wagon deliveries might be preserved until he had accumulated a carload in storage, as he had been accustomed to do through the flat warehouse. Under the bulk method of storage his grain would be binned with that of other growers, to whom the operator had issued "graded storage tickets" bearing the same grade. While this system made for economy in storage, and while it was easier to obtain bank advances on the security of graded warehouse receipts, it meant that the farmer had to accept the grade given by the elevator operator, instead of being able to obtain the inspector's official grading on his own identical grain.

(*b*) The Street Seller. — The grain growers strongly resented the alliance of the railway and the line-elevator companies, which enabled the latter to exercise their monopoly in the storing and shipping of grain at country points, but they resented more their activities as dealers in grain. Elevator owners had learned that an elevator involving the capital outlay necessary to conform to "standard" requirements could not operate profitably as a warehouse alone unless it were filled at least three times in a season.[1] The possibility of realizing such a turnover in a given elevator depended, of course, upon the size of the tributary crop, the degree of local competition, and the conditions of car supply. As the requisite turnover could not ordinarily be counted on with any degree of regularity, most elevators had come to combine the function of merchandising with that of warehousing, and to supplement storage revenues by speculative profits on grain purchased under conditions of post-harvest selling pressure. The farmer whose marketable surplus was not sufficiently large to fill a car of his own,[2] and who found himself under the immediate necessity of converting his crop into cash, had to deal with the elevator operator as a "street" buyer instead of as a warehouseman. As his entire cash income for the year often depended on these wagonload sales, it was not surprising that he was disposed to regard with suspicion the middleman through whom that income was mediated.

At points where but a single elevator existed, the seller of street wheat had virtually no alternative but to accept the price the operator chose to offer, the grade he saw fit to allow, and whatever "dockage" he set.[3] At larger shipping points the farmer's selling alternatives might be less restricted. It was generally believed, however, that the local prices to be paid for "street" grain were determined by a conference of line-elevator representatives at Winnipeg, which wired quotations for the day that were more or less unanimously requoted by dealers at local buying points. The farmer's experience, at any rate, was that a plurality

[1] C. B. Piper, *Principles of Grain Trade of Western Canada*, pp. 81–83.

[2] The minimum weight for carload grain shipment on Canadian railways is 60,000 lbs., or 1000 bushels, the equivalent of about 20 to 25 ordinary wagonloads.

[3] "Dockage" represents the unacceptable portion of a farmer's delivery, consisting of weed seeds, dirt, or broken kernels mixed with his grain. The precise dockage could be determined by taking the difference between the gross weight and the net weight after cleaning. During the rush season, however, there was rarely time to do the cleaning on delivery, and the usual method of arriving at the dockage was by weighing that portion of a sample pound which came through a cleaning sieve. Not a few operators frequently employed the still speedier method of "setting" the dockage by cursory inspection. *Report of Grain Commission of 1899–1900*, p. 4.

of buyers did not ensure competition in buying. Even where a little higher price or a better grade might be offered by one dealer, it was suspected, and not always without foundation, that the buyer contrived to compensate himself by overdocking or short-weighing.

Farmers' Elevators. — Here and there discontented farmers formed local companies and erected elevators of their own. The necessity of constructing these in conformity with standard elevator requirements, as a condition of obtaining the railway's concessions, involved, however, a capital investment which limited their number largely to older and more prosperous settlements. Confining themselves, as they generally did, merely to storing farmers' grain for carload shipment, these local elevators were of little service to the seller of street wheat, and were at a distinct financial disadvantage in competing with the line elevators, whose revenue was derived more largely from trading operations on the Grain Exchange than from local storage charges. The companies, or elevator pools, were capable, moreover, of putting farmers' elevators out of business by cutting charges at competing points. At the close of the century there were but twenty-six farmers' elevators, all in more or less precarious operation, in Manitoba and the Territories.[1]

The Economic Basis of Grain Growers' Grievances. — All these conditions and abuses, actual or suspected, combined to produce intense irritation and resentment among prairie grain growers. Where knowledge of the actual facts was not accessible, and where ignorance of the technicalities of grain marketing and of price-determining conditions prevailed, suspicion was bound to be rampant and the most extreme accusations were most likely to be accepted. The farmer was acutely aware of the fact that, because of the agreement between railway and elevator companies, he had no alternative but to ship his grain through, or sell his crop to the latter, who had come to form a more or less complete combine.[2]

[1] *Report of Grain Commission*, Sessional Paper, No. 81, 1900, pp. 7–9.

[2] "A hard and fast elevator monopoly existed, and the grievance existed that every producer of grain was compelled not by law, but in practice, to deal with

Under these circumstances he was prone to believe that he was being victimized at every turn, and to attribute unsatisfactory returns for his crop directly to the manipulations of the railway and the elevator trust. While the expressions of indignation and recrimination that were voiced with rising intensity in meetings of agricultural societies, in farmers' letters to the press, and in speeches of farmer representatives in the Manitoba legislature, in the Council of the North-West Territories, and finally in the Federal Parliament, were inclined to be hyperbolic in tone, the basis of grievance was undoubtedly present, and called for reform.

The underlying factor in the situation in Western Canada in the closing years of the last century was that the area and the volume of grain production had increased much more rapidly than the physical facilities for shipping and handling it. The box car and the elevator were the limiting factors in the case. Their strategic importance was accentuated, moreover, by the peculiar seasonal and geographic conditions governing the marketing and transportation of the grain crop of Western Canada. Little capital and slight organization were required to file on a homestead and commence raising wheat on the virgin prairie. Much capital and considerable organization were needed to provide the means of efficient transportation, storage, and handling of a bulk commodity thinly produced over an ever-expanding area in the interior of a young country. The Canadian government had found it necessary to offer monopoly privileges to bring the Pacific railway into being. The Canadian Pacific Railway in turn had found it necessary to offer monopoly concessions to have its grain-shipping points equipped with standard elevators as a means of relieving the seasonal strain upon its limited rolling stock. Since the majority of the country elevators were owned by a few line companies, combination among them was not difficult to effect. On account, therefore, of the limited and indispensable nature of facilities supplied by the railway and elevator companies, and because of the monopolistic or semi-monopolistic basis on which

that hard and fast elevator monopoly." Hon. Walter Scott, *Regina Leader*, Feb. 7, 1911; cited by W. A. Mackintosh in *Agricultural Coöperation in Western Canada*, p. 11.

they had been brought into being, they found themselves in a position to make practically their own terms with the unorganized grain growers.

The farmer was, indeed, in very much the same economic position as the unorganized, unskilled laborer in relation to a great industrial corporation. In all such cases, where economic power is unbalanced, friction and strife are bound to arise and persist until a new equilibrium is established. On the one side, strategic domination affords almost irresistible temptations to arrogance and abuse, even where no such deliberate intent exists. On the other side, the sense of dependence, and ignorance of the risks and responsibilities involved in highly organized undertakings, induce an attitude of inflamed suspicions and immoderate antagonism. The very secrecy of the dominating interests, and their unwillingness to lay before the aggrieved parties the economic facts determining their policies and methods, inevitably aggravate the friction. In default of a voluntary taking of the interested public into confidence, there are two other means by which these facts may be learned by the latter. One is by compulsory government investigation. The other is by the dissatisfied individuals organizing and undertaking themselves the functions whose performance by other interests they have claimed to be prejudicial. The grain growers of Western Canada resorted to both of these alternatives.

CHAPTER II

THE BEGINNINGS OF GRAIN TRADE REGULATION

The Grain Growers' Case in Parliament. — The grievance of the western grain growers in regard to the shipping of their grain were projected into the Federal Parliament when Mr. James Douglas, member for East Assiniboia (North-West Territories) introduced, in the session of 1898, a "bill to regulate the shipping of grain by railway companies in Manitoba and the North-West Territories." Its main features called for a legal recognition of the right of farmers to ship grain through flat warehouses and to obtain cars for direct loading from the wagon. Although the bill failed to emerge from the Railway Committee of the House, the right of the C. P. R. to refuse cars to farmers had been publicly challenged in the legislature from which that railway had derived its charter. At the same time, the Manitoba government was negotiating with the Northern Pacific Railway for the joint operation of an alternative grain-carrying route from Emerson (where the Red River enters Manitoba) to Duluth.[1]

The threat of federal regulation, the determined attitude of the Manitoba government backed by strong public opinion, and the competitive activities of Mackenzie and Mann in Manitoba, were not without effect upon the C. P. R. Before the 1898 crop began to move, the company announced that it would furnish cars to farmers who wished to load direct. This service was, of course, subject to conditions of car supply, and the elevators still enjoyed an effective priority in distribution. If a farmer obtained a car, it was by favor of the company, not by virtue of an enforceable

[1] The emergence at this time of Messrs. Mackenzie and Mann as railway builders in Manitoba (see *supra*, p. 10) led to the substitution of an agreement by which the Manitoba government leased the Northern Pacific of Manitoba to the Canadian Northern, and guaranteed the bonds of the latter for the construction of a line to Port Arthur through the Rainy River district, on condition of a freight rate of ten cents a bushel between Winnipeg and Port Arthur. The completion of this line in 1901 provided a second spout to the western grainhopper. See S. J. McLean, in *Canada and its Provinces*, vol. XX, *passim*.

right. At the best the concession was of advantage only to farmers living sufficiently near to the railway to be able to load the assigned car within the twenty-four hours before demurrage began to accrue. Without the right to order cars to flat warehouses where long-haul wagonloads could be accumulated, the company's announcement meant little to the more removed homesteader. A great many shipping points, moreover, were not equipped with loading platforms, and there was no obligation on the part of the railway to furnish them.

The belated action of the C. P. R. did not forestall, therefore, the reintroduction of Mr. Douglas's bill in the following session, with an added clause calling for the appointment of a government inspector to supervise the shipment and handling of grain between country points and terminals. The discussion of the western members' representations before a special committee of the House revealed such a conflict of fact and opinion, and suggested such far-reaching implications, that the Laurier ministry became convinced of the necessity of a fuller and closer investigation of the question than was possible within the committee rooms of the House. Accordingly, before the close of the 1899 session, the government announced the appointment of a Royal Commission on the Shipment and Transportation of Grain in Manitoba and the North-West Territories. In constituting this, the first of the four federal royal commissions which have been created from time to time to investigate the complaints of western grain growers,[1] the government followed the policy of appointing representative Manitoba farmers to investigate the western grain-growers' grievances, under the chairmanship of an eastern judge.[2]

[1] The second commission was appointed in 1906, under the chairmanship of Mr. John Millar of Indian Head, Sask. Its report led to extensive amendments to the Manitoba Grain Act in 1908. The third commission, under Mr. Justice Hyndman, was appointed in 1920 by the Meighen government. Its investigations were arrested through an injunction sought by the United Grain Growers, and upheld by the Supreme Court of Canada. The fourth commission, under Mr. Justice Turgeon, was appointed by the King government in 1923, and presented its report in 1925.

[2] The three farmer commissioners were W. F. Sirett, William Lothian, and C. C. Castle. Judge E. J. Senkler of St. Catharines, Ontario, was appointed chairman, but died before the completion of the commission's labors, being succeeded by

Royal Grain Commission of 1899–1900. — The three general complaints which the commissioners were instructed to investigate were the following:

1. That a vendor of grain is at present subjected to an unfair and excessive dockage of his grain at the time of sale.
2. That doubts exist as to the fairness of the weight allowed or used by owners of elevators.
3. That owners of elevators enjoy a monopoly in the purchase of grain by refusing to permit the erection of flat warehouses where standard elevators are situated, and are able to keep the price of grain below its true market value, to their own benefit and the disadvantage of others who are specially interested in the grain trade, and of the public generally.[1]

During the winter of 1899–1900 hearings were held at twenty-two points throughout the west, from Fort William to Edmonton. Every facility was given for local farmers to present their grievances and for grain-trade interests to state their cases. Two of the members of the commission also visited Minnesota grain centres, to investigate the system of railway and warehouse regulation in effect in that state.

In the report of the Commission, which was presented in March, 1900, the legitimacy of the western farmers' grievances was generally recognized, and definite recommendations were made for their relief. So long as the grain grower was not free to ship or market his grain except through the regular elevators, he was bound to be more or less at the mercy of the latter. The Commission found that

as a result of the refusal of railway companies to take grain from flat warehouses (which resulted in driving many small buyers out of the market) and of their refusal until 1898 to furnish cars to farmers desirous of doing their own shipping, and of the consequent necessity of shipping through elevators or of selling to the operators thereof, and of lack of competition between buyers, the elevator owners have had it in their power to depress prices below what in our opinion farmers should realise for their grain. It would naturally be to their interest to depress prices, and when buying to dock as much as possible. We consider, therefore, that the proper relief from the possibility of being compelled to sell under the value, and of being

---

A. E. Richards (afterwards Mr. Justice Richards) of Winnipeg. Mr. Chas. N. Bell, a Winnipeg grain man, acted as secretary.

[1] *Sessional Papers*, Nos. 81–81b, 1900, p. 2.

unduly docked for cleaning, is only to be had by giving the fullest obtainable freedom in the way of shipping and selling grain. So long as any farmer is hampered in, or hindered from, himself shipping to terminal markets, he will be more or less at the mercy of elevator operators.[1]

As a means of ensuring such freedom in shipment the commissioners deemed it necessary that provision should be made for the optional erection of flat warehouses and the compulsory construction of loading platforms, where the demand for such was duly established. These facilities would, of course, be of advantage to the farmer only if assured of equality in car distribution. "Though the furnishing of cars to farmers has been given as a privilege," ran the report, "they should, with proper restrictions, enjoy it as a legal right." [2]

Investigation of the system of regulation carried out by the Railroad and Warehouse Commission of the State of Minnesota led to the inclusion of recommendations for an adaptation of that system to the grain trade of Western Canada. "There being no rules laid down for the regulation of the grain trade other than those made by the railway companies and the elevator owners, we think it of great importance that laws should be enacted and that rules should be made under power given by such laws which will properly regulate the trade." [3] It was felt that while the existing proportions of the latter hardly warranted the immediate creation of a statutory board of commissioners, the appointment of at least a warehouse commissioner was imperative, to supervise the operations of both country and terminal elevators, and to receive and investigate complaints of alleged infractions of the proposed regulation.

Provisions of Manitoba Grain Act. — The Manitoba Grain Act, which emerged from the session of 1900, on the eve of a general election, substantially followed the recommendations of the farmer commissioners. The act provided that its administration should be placed in the hands of a Warehouse Commissioner, with headquarters at Winnipeg. His duties were to see that all owners and operators of both country and terminal elevators were duly licensed and bonded under the provisions of the act; to supervise

[1] *Sessional Papers*, Nos. 81–81b, p. 7. [2] *Ibid.*, p. 8. [3] *Ibid.*

the handling and storage of grain in and out of elevators and cars; and to investigate all complaints made under oath of undue dockage, improper weighing or grading, refusal or neglect on the part of railways to furnish cars within reasonable time, or any fraud or oppression in connection with the handling of grain. In order that farmers should not be deterred from obtaining their full rights under the act through fear of legal expense, the Commissioner was empowered to institute proceedings at government expense "whenever he considered a case proper therefor." [1] The Warehouse Commissioner, in short, was to function as an attorney-general for the grain growers.

With a view to affording the farmer greater competitive freedom in the shipment and selling of his grain, railways were required to supply cars without discrimination for loading over platform or through flat warehouse as well as through elevators. In order that growers should not lack the facilities for direct shipment, the provision of standard loading platforms was made obligatory upon the railway, whenever written application from ten or more farmers resident within twenty miles of the nearest shipping point was received and approved by the Warehouse Commissioner. Such platforms were to be constructed at the expense of the railway and were to be available for farmers' use free of charge.[2] Twenty-four hours might be taken by a farmer to load a car allotted to him. To meet the case of growers located too far from the railway to be able to fill cars within such time, it was further provided that on the request of ten or more farmers living within forty miles of any shipping point, the Commissioner might authorize the erection of a flat warehouse of not less than 3000 bushels capacity at such point. Five clear days were allowed the shipper to fill his bin in the warehouse.[3] Thus, it was intended, the outlying farmer might accumulate his carload at trackside at a lower handling charge than that made by the standard elevators, while at the same time preserving the identity of his grain.

Not only were the elevator companies thus deprived of their

[1] Stat. of Canada, 63–64 Vic., c. 39, 1900, sec. 4.

[2] Ibid., sec. 42.

[3] Ibid., sec. 41.

former monopoly of shipping and storage, but they were also required to comply with a number of specific regulations which could be disregarded only at the risk of prejudicing their licenses. Schedules annexed to the act prescribed compulsory standard forms for grain-purchase tickets, graded-storage tickets, "special bin" receipts, and flat-warehouse receipts. In the case of stored grain, elevators must guarantee both the grade and weight shown on the ticket. If the farmer was not satisfied with the dockage given by the operator, he could require a sample of his delivered grain to be selected in his presence and forwarded to the Chief Inspector at Winnipeg, whose certificate would be final as between the farmer and the elevator.[1] Finally, country elevators were required to furnish returns of grain handled and stored, of grades and weights in and out, and so forth, on demand of the Warehouse Commissioner.[2] Terminal elevators were under obligation to file weekly returns of the quantity of each grade in store, and were forbidden to mix grades.[3]

The Manitoba Grain Act, it will thus be seen, not only imposed at a single step a far-reaching system of regulation of railways and elevators in the interests of grain growers, but also provided for a permanent administrative officer to whom farmers might forward complaints directly. In appointing an official to execute the exacting and highly responsible duties of Warehouse Commissioner, the government selected one of the members of the Royal Commission itself, in the person of Mr. C. C. Castle, who had investigated the Minnesota system of regulation and who had participated most largely in the drafting of the Commission's report. Thus it came about that a farmer, and not a lawyer, was constituted "attorney-general for the grain growers." It was a farmer, however, who had enjoyed a unique opportunity of studying the western grain trade in all its functions and aspects.

Federal Character of Canadian Grain-Trade Regulation. — The legislation arising out of the report of the Commission of 1899–1900 was largely based, it has been noted, on the Railroad and Warehouse Commission Act of Minnesota. The latter, however, was merely state-wide in its scope, whereas the Manitoba Grain

[1] Stat. of Canada, 63–64 Vic., c. 39, 1900, sec. 36.

[2] Ibid., sec. 38. [3] Ibid., sec. 24.

Act, despite its provincial designation,[1] was a federal measure, federally administered. In the United States, regulation of the grain trade and standardization and inspection of grades developed under the independent initiative and jurisdiction of the states most directly concerned, such as Illinois, Minnesota, and the Dakotas. It was only in 1916 that federal standardization and inspection of grain in interstate commerce was established, with the passing of the United States Grain Standards Act. In Canada, on the other hand, legislative regulation of the grain trade was from the first federal in its origin and operation. The reasons for this distinctive development in Canada are partly geographical, partly constitutional, and partly historical.

In the case of Minnesota, extensive grain-growing areas, a central grain market, a dominating milling centre, and the principal lake terminal, are all found within the boundaries of the same state. The state legislature was thus competent to deal with both country and terminal elevators, and with railway service between them. In Western Canada, on the other hand, the Province of Manitoba and the North-West Territories formed a continuous grain-growing area, for which the only existing outlet was the Thunder Bay ports in the Province of Ontario. Winnipeg, the point of concentration and of official inspection, as well as the seat of the dominating Grain Exchange, was separated by over four hundred miles and an interprovincial boundary line from the terminal warehouses. The interprovincial character of the western grain trade, and the further fact that the Territories were administered by the Dominion government, predetermined, therefore, the federal character of any comprehensive system of grain-trade regulation.[2]

A second cause is to be found in the status of the Canadian Pacific Railway, whose arbitrary policy in respect to car distri-

[1] The Manitoba Grain Act was so called because it applied to the Manitoba Inspection Division which had been created by an act of the previous year. See *infra*, p. 28. The general revision and consolidation of grain legislation, in 1912, was embodied as the Canada Grain Act; see *infra*, p. 140.

[2] Under Section 91 of the British North America Act, the exclusive legislative authority of the Parliament of Canada extends to all matters coming within "the regulation of trade and commerce."

bution had been chiefly responsible for bringing about the legislation of 1900. Any regulation effectively binding that railway had necessarily to emanate from the Federal Parliament which had incorporated it, which had entered into a national contract with it, and which had conditionally granted to it the land on which elevators, flat warehouses and loading platforms must of necessity be erected.[1]

Evolution of Federal Regulation.—A third factor in the Canadian situation was the precedent of a quarter of a century of grain standardization and inspection under the Federal Department of Inland Revenue. Prior to Confederation the United Provinces of Upper and Lower Canada had passed acts in 1853 and 1863 establishing official measures, marks, and grades for grains and other staples, and providing for the appointment of grain inspectors in designated cities.[2] As Ontario and Quebec were the principal grain-producing provinces at the time of Confederation, it was natural that the acts of the old Province of Canada should be extended to the Dominion of Canada as a whole. This was effected by the General Inspection Act of 1874.[3] As grain from Western Canada began to find its way to eastern ports, amending orders-in-council established separate grades for western spring wheat, and in 1886 government inspection was inaugurated at Winnipeg and Port Arthur. From time to time amendments had been added in response to representations from western grain interests. Thus in 1889 provision was made for a separate Western Standards Board, whose grade standards should govern inspection in all parts of Canada so far as wheat grown west of Lake Superior was concerned.[4]

In the very year in which the Royal Grain Commission had been appointed, yet another amendment to the General Inspection Act[5] had been placed on the statute book in response to

[1] Under Section 92 of the British North America Act, the provincial legislatures are specifically excluded from making laws governing lines of railways connecting one province with any other.

[2] Stat. of Canada, 16 Vic., c. 118, 1853, and 26 Vic., c. 3, 1863.

[3] Stat. of Canada, 37 Vic., c. 45, 1874. Rev. Stat. of Canada, c. 99, 1886.

[4] Stat. of Canada, 52 Vic., c. 16, 1889.

[5] Stat. of Canada, 62–63 Vic., c. 25, 1899.

resolutions forwarded from the Winnipeg Grain Exchange, demanding that inspection at Winnipeg of all grain in transit to terminals should be compulsory. This was with a view to making it possible to secure reinspection at Fort William in the case of cars whose owners were not satisfied with the official grade, before the identity of the shipment was submerged in the terminal bins. The Act of 1899 created the separate Inspection District of Manitoba, comprising not merely the province of that name, but also the North-West Territories and that portion of Ontario west of and including Port Arthur and Fort William.[1]

It will thus be seen that by the close of the century a considerable tradition of federal grain legislation had been created in Canada. The early acts, however, had arisen out of the inspection of weights and measures, under the Department of Inland Revenue, and so far as the grain trade was concerned, had to do chiefly with the definition and inspection of grades and the inspection of elevator scales. While of advantage to the producer in marketing, these government functions were more immediately in the interests of grain dealers; and most amendments to the General Inspection Act had been made in response to middlemen's representations. The Manitoba Grain Act, however, instituted a comprehensive regulation of grain middlemen, and of the entire movement of grain in commerce.[2] Its enactment was essentially the outcome of representations by the grain growers themselves. Its provisions embodied quite literally the recom-

[1] On early Canadian grain legislation, see D. A. MacGibbon, "Grain Legislation Affecting Western Canada," in *Journal of Political Economy*, 1912, pp. 224–226.

[2] The Manitoba Grain Act was administered at the outset by the Department of Inland Revenue. In 1902, however, its administration was placed under the Department of Trade and Commerce; while in 1904 the latter ministry was also entrusted with the administration of a separate Grain Inspection Act.

"The supervision of the grain trade grew up under the Inland Revenue Department which has within its scope the arrangement of weights and measures. Out of the inspection of weights and measures grew the determination of grain standards and then the inspection also of grades. Thus government control over the grain trade began in a purely nominal way in connection with the excise system of the country, rather than as a deliberate attempt to build up and control an industry. It is the logic of circumstances that has shifted the emphasis and placed the grain trade under the care of the Department of Trade and Commerce." MacGibbon, *op. cit.*, p. 235.

mendations of a commission composed chiefly of Manitoba farmers. Its administration, moreover, was entrusted to an experienced farmer as Warehouse Commissioner.

The Canadian system of grain regulation has both its disadvantages and its merits. Ottawa is far removed from the Prairie Provinces, and the federal legislative machinery is naturally less directly responsive to western agrarian opinion than the legislatures of the grain-growing provinces themselves. On the other hand, the national character of the Canadian grain trade calls for national control. The uniformity of regulations governing elevator, shipping and inspection practices in all the grain-growing provinces is of immense value both to growers and the trade, while shipment under federal government grade certificate gives a unique standing to Canadian wheat in foreign markets. Furthermore, the very necessity of bringing considerable pressure to bear in order to effect legislative amendments to the Grain Act has contributed a certain desirable stability to the system, and helped to ensure that the need for changes should be substantially demonstrated before they are put into effect.

CHAPTER III

THE BEGINNINGS OF GRAIN GROWERS' ORGANIZATION

The Manitoba Grain Act was hailed by western grain growers as a veritable agrarian Magna Charta. The system of regulation which it provided was indeed comprehensive in intent. Its workability and enforcability were, however, yet to be demonstrated. Its main purpose was to give the farmer greater freedom in the shipping and marketing of his grain, and make him less dependent upon the privileged elevator companies. Much had been expected from the provisions governing the construction and use of flat warehouses, as an alternative to shipment through standard elevators.[1] As a matter of fact, very few flat warehouses were built after 1900, and every year saw more of the older ones close down or disappear.[2] The technical superiority of the standard elevator over the flat warehouse in the bulk handling of grain, and the limitation of the owners of the latter to mere warehousing operations[3] placed the old flat warehouse at a competitive disadvantage, even with the railway's discrimination against them removed by law. Greater freedom in platform loading, and greater facilities and protection in the storing and shipping of grain through elevators, made the farmer himself less desirous of using the flat warehouse. The elaborate provisions of the act with respect to them offered, therefore, a means of potential competition rather than an effective alternative to elevator patronage.

The Problem of Car Distribution. — The real alternative to marketing through elevators was loading over platform, which

[1] The clauses relating to flat warehouses had been considered by Mr. Douglas as the most vital in the bills introduced by him in 1898 and 1899. See L. A. Wood, *Farmers' Movements in Canada*, pp. 163–168.

[2] In 1900 there were 97 flat warehouses in operation; by 1915 the number had decreased to 28. W. C. Clark, *The Country Elevator in the Canadian West*, p. 15.

[3] The Manitoba Grain Act (sec. 41, sub-sec. 8) had prohibited operators of flat warehouses from storing or shipping grain of their own. While this clause was repealed in 1902, it made little difference, as flat warehouse owners lacked the integrated marketing facilities of the line elevator company.

enabled the grower with one or more carloads to save country elevator charges,[1] to obtain official government grade and dockage, and to sell on the basis of Grain Exchange spot prices, either to a local track buyer or through a Winnipeg commission house. Alternatively, he might hold his grain in terminal storage and sell when the market suited him. The legal right to load over platform was of little advantage to the shipper, however, unless the railway supplied cars as well as platforms when and where they were needed. The crop of 1901 exceeded all previous western records,[2] and the strain upon the railways was correspondingly acute. Elevator companies as well as farmers were embarrassed by the car shortage. The latter complained, however, that the elevators invariably obtained the preference in the allotment of such cars as were locally available. The exasperation of the grain growers against the railway and elevator companies was intensified by the organization at this time of the North-West Elevator Association, which was regarded by the farmers as an organization of line companies to neutralize the regulations imposed by the Manitoba Grain Act, and to fix the prices of street grain by secret agreement.[3]

Irritation was particularly acute among Territorial growers, who in general produced on a larger scale than their Manitoba neighbors, while their grain had a longer distance to move to market. In Manitoba, moreover, the activity of the provincial government in encouraging new or competitive railroad building, and the enterprise of the builders of the Canadian Northern, had

[1] At 1¾ cents a bushel the saving on a carload amounted to about 18 dollars.

[2] The western wheat crop of 1901 amounted to 62,820,000 bushels; the largest production previous to that year had been 35,000,000 bushels in 1895. When navigation closed in the first week of December, 1901, half the crop was still in the farmers' hands. *Report of Warehouse Commissioner to Dept. of Trade and Commerce*, 1901–02.

[3] The North-West Elevator Association, reorganized in 1903 as the Northwest Grain Dealers' Association, was in fact a coöperative organization of elevator companies, organized partly for the joint purchase of elevator supplies, but principally for reducing telegraphic expense, by having daily closing prices wired to local agents who communicated them to members entitled to receive them at their respective points. While the indicated street price was not binding on members, it more or less governed local buying. See evidence of F. C. Fowler, Secretary, Northwest Grain Dealers' Association, before Royal Grain Commission, Nov. 23, 1906.

resulted in some measure of transportation relief for farmers, at least, in certain districts, of that province.

The town of Indian Head, some forty miles east of Regina on the main line of the C. P. R., enjoys a twofold distinction in the history of Western grain growing. As the seat of one of the original five Dominion Experimental Farms established in 1886, it was conspicuously associated with the adaptation of Red Fife to Territorial growing, and it was through this station that in 1907 Dr. Charles Saunders' revolutionary Marquis wheat was successfully introduced to the prairies.[1] In the second place it was in a fanning mill factory of Indian Head that the organized Grain Growers' Movement in Western Canada had its birth on December 18, 1901.

Informal indignation gatherings and conferences of neighboring farmers had led to the issue of a written summons by W. R. Motherwell and Peter Dayman, who had farmed at Abernethy since 1883, for a meeting at the above time and place of local grain growers, to discuss action. The occasion was well chosen, for a large crowd had assembled in Indian Head on that date to hear a public debate in the evening between Premier Roblin of Manitoba and Premier Haultain of the North-West Territories on the mooted annexation of East Assiniboia to the Province of Manitoba.[2] The formal debate between the western premiers is a forgotten incident in the history of Western politics; but the afternoon gathering of Qu'Appelle Valley farmers, which preceded it, proved to be the genesis of a movement whose subsequent proportions and manifestations were little suspected by the two pioneer neighbors who sent out the summons.[3]

[1] See Buller, *Essays on Wheat*, pp. 157–160.

[2] A number of Assiniboia farmers had been agitating for such a transfer in the hope that incorporation with Manitoba, with its provincial autonomy and aggressive railway policy, might bring about better transportation services and rates and improve their marketing position generally. Premier Roblin, desirous of expanding the boundaries and taxable capacity of his province, sought to show what advantages would accrue to the farmers of Assiniboia from such annexation. Premier Haultain, on the other hand, pointed out that real solution lay in the translation of the Territories into a second prairie province. *Manitoba Free Press*, Dec. 19, 1901.

[3] The initiation of the Grain Growers' movement is dramatically described by Hopkins Moorhouse in *Deep Furrows*, Toronto, 1917.

Initiation of Territorial Grain Growers' Association Dec., 1901. — Although W. R. Motherwell was destined to become, a few years later, Minister of Agriculture in the new Province of Saskatchewan, and eventually political head of the federal Department of Agriculture, it was no political solution which he proposed to the grain growers at Indian Head. He had witnessed the political miscarriage of the short-lived Patrons of Industry movement in the West in the early eighteen-nineties,[1] and in sending out, with Dayman, the joint call to the meeting he had associated himself with a member of the opposite political party. He had become convinced, moreover, that legislation in itself was inadequate as a remedy for the grain growers' disabilities, unless they possessed a permanent organization of their own to see that such legislation was rendered effective, and to protect their interests in general. His purpose in convening the Indian Head meeting is best indicated in the words of a speech made by him on a subsequent occasion.[2]

The harvest of 1901 was very heavy, and as the result of a terrific traffic congestion all over the country, indignation meetings were held everywhere, both by business men in the towns and by the farmers. A deluge of resolutions and protests were showered upon the heads of railway and government officials. For two years or more previous to this I had been very much impressed with the necessity of a permanent organization amongst the farmers, to represent the special requirements of the grain-growing interests of the country. All branches of agriculture had their distinctive organizations in our various provinces, such as the Livestock Association, but in the West, or in any part of the Dominion, there was no distinct organized body of farmers to look after the grain interests, which after all were, and are still likely to be, of paramount importance in Saskatchewan. With the farmers righteously indignant over their inability to dispose of the 1901 crop, the time seemed to be ripe for the commencement of a movement looking towards a permanent organization whose duty it would be to press persistently and insistently for an improvement in marketing con-

---

[1] The Patrons of Industry movement, which originated at Port Huron, Michigan in 1887, and flourished vigorously for a time in Ontario, was carried to Manitoba in 1891. It reached its climax in the West in 1895, when 330 lodges were reported, with a membership of about 5,000. For some years the Patrons' Commercial Union carried on a coöperative farmers' supply business. Political candidacies and quarrels between hot-headed leaders brought about the disintegration of the order in the West about 1898. See Wood, *Farmers' Movements in Canada*, chap. 11.

[2] Quoted by N. P. Lambert in *Grain Growers' Guide*, June 26, 1918.

ditions, transportation, warehousing, and for the introduction of new or amended legislation from time to time as the rapidly changing character of the country seemed to warrant it.

The outcome of the well-conceived preliminary to the Roblin–Haultain debate was the unanimous decision to organize a "Territorial Grain Growers' Association," and to name provisional officers and directors. It was planned to proceed at once with the organization of local associations at all points where an interest could be created, and to hold at the earliest practicable date a convention of delegates from such locals, which might elect a permanent central executive.

Mid-winter organization work was carried on entirely by volunteers; but so energetically did they canvass, and so ripe for action were the dissatisfied farmers, that twelve local branches and four agricultural societies[1] were represented at the convention — the first Grain Growers' convention in Western Canada — which gathered in Indian Head six weeks later, on February 1, 1902. W. R. Motherwell and John Millar of Indian Head were confirmed as president and secretary, respectively, and a representative directorate elected. Of the various resolutions passed the following were typical and significant:

That section 42 of the Manitoba Grain Act be amended to empower the Warehouse Commissioner to compel all railway companies to erect every loading platform approved by the said Commissioner within thirty days after said approval is given, and in default the Commissioner shall have power to impose penalties on such defaulting railway, and collect same through the courts, and that this amendment come into force on May 1, 1902.

That railway companies be compelled to provide farmers with cars to be loaded direct from vehicles, at all stations, irrespective of there being an elevator, warehouse or loading platform at such station or not.

That the Grain Act be amended making it the duty of the railway agent, when there is a shortage of cars, to apportion the available cars in the order in which they are applied for, and that in case such cars are misappropriated by applicants not entitled to them, the penalties of the act be enforced against such parties.[2]

These resolutions, whose explicit, business like character contrasted significantly with the vague and spacious declarations of

[1] See *infra*, p. 36.

[2] Territorial Grain Growers' Association, 1902.

the old Patrons' lodges, were carried to Ottawa, where the western grain blockade was the subject of an all-day debate in Parliament.[1] The government was impressed, and the Grain Growers' resolutions were incorporated, in almost the very language of the petitioners, in amendments to the shipping clauses of the Manitoba Grain Act, introduced by the Minister of Trade and Commerce,[2] and passed before the close of the 1902 session.[3]

The Sintaluta Test Case, 1902. — Once again, however, it became apparent that mere legislative enactment did not bring relief. The crop of 1902 exceeded the record one of the preceding year, and the C. P. R. exhibited either incapacity or disinclination to carry out the amended car-distribution clauses. Loading platforms were of little use to farmers if the elevators got such cars as were available.[4] This time, however, there was an alert organization to see that the farmers' shipping rights, which Parliament had recognized, should not be disregarded with impunity by the great railway corporation. Messrs. Motherwell and Dayman, acting for the Territorial Grain Growers, proceeded to Winnipeg and intimated to the C. P. R. officials that, unless the car-distribution clauses were interpreted differently by the company, the Association would take action to ensure their fulfilment. When railway headquarters' promises failed to be translated into local performances, the Association laid a formal complaint before Warehouse Commissioner Castle against the C. P. R. agent at Sintaluta, for infraction of the Grain Act in his allotment of cars at that point.

The test character of the case caused intense interest throughout the country. Mr. Castle was accompanied by T. G. Mather of the Federal Department of Justice, and the C. P. R. counsel, Mr. J. A. M. Aikins (later Lieutenant-Governor of Manitoba) admitted the facts, and confined the argument to the legal construc-

[1] *Commons' Debates*, March 17, 1902.

[2] To whose department the administration of the Act was transferred from the Department of Inland Revenue at this time. See *supra*, p. 28, n. 2.

[3] Stat. of Canada, 2 Edw. VII, c. 19, 1902.

[4] "The plain provisions of the car-distribution clause are disregarded at every shipping point, I believe, in the West. . . . Of 67 'spotted' cars at Sintaluta only 7 have been assigned to farmers." W. R. Motherwell to T. G. G. A., 1902.

tion of the act. The magistrates at Sintaluta found the defendant guilty of violating the priority clause in the act, and imposed a fine of fifty dollars and costs. This decision was later sustained in an appeal before the Supreme Court. The railway company fairly accepted the situation, and instructed its agents to distribute cars strictly in order of application in the car-order book. The relief meant much to Territorial grain growers, and the Association felt that it had won a victory for western farmers that justified its organization.

Character of Grain Growers' Organization. — Prior to the inauguration of the Territorial Grain Growers' Association the only existing local farmers' organizations in the West were agricultural societies. These were concerned primarily with problems and methods of production and with agricultural fairs, and were promoted largely through the Manitoba and Territorial Departments of Agriculture. The latter had manifested considerable interest in the grain growers' fight for free shipment, and the Deputy Minister, Mr. C. W. Peterson, had been instructed to attend the ratification meeting of the Territorial Growers' Association in January, 1902, and to lend his assistance in the work of organization. At his suggestion the constitution had been so drafted as to permit the inclusion of agricultural societies as local units, wherever these were prepared to subscribe formally to the aims of the Association. He had also offered his services as secretary for the central body. The grain growers, however, preferred to keep the executive control entirely within their own hands, and declined this offer of official assistance. As the work of organization proceeded, it was found that the agricultural societies did not show any general inclination, as units, to identify themselves with the new movement. On the other hand grain growers as a class showed themselves eager to form distinct local organizations for the purpose of realizing the protective aims of the Association. At the first Territorial convention, therefore, the constitution was amended to exclude agricultural societies as affiliated locals.[1] The raisons d'être of the agricultural societies and of the grain growers' locals were in fact quite different. The former were gov-

[1] See Wood, *op. cit.*, pp. 174, 175.

ernment promoted and concerned with the technique of farm management; the latter were class-conscious organizations, and interested primarily in problems of marketing and protective legislation.

Formation of Manitoba Grain Growers' Association, 1903.—The securing of the Grain Act amendments of 1902 and the winning of the Sintaluta test case led to a rapid accession of membership in the Territorial Association, and made considerable impression upon the farmers of western Manitoba. Just a year after the historic gathering summoned by Motherwell at Indian Head, the Agricultural Society of Virden, Manitoba, appointed a committee to take steps toward calling a district meeting, for the purpose of organizing the first grain growers' association in Manitoba. Mr. Motherwell was invited to address this gathering, and with his experienced assistance, a strong local association was formed at Virden on January 3, 1903, under the presidency of J. W. Scallion. The Virden leaders realized that little could be accomplished unless local associations were organized throughout the province, and these united in purpose and effort through a central provincial organization, as in the case of the Territorial Association. Accordingly, during the following months, Mr. Scallion wrote letters to every place where complaints were being expressed, and urged organization for self-defence on the lines of the Virden Association. The exasperated farmers through the province were quick to respond to such a lead. Within two months of the Virden meeting a provincial convention was held at Brandon (March 3–4, 1903), attended by one hundred delegates representing twenty-six local associations. The constitution of the Manitoba Grain Growers' Association substantially reproduced that of the Territorial Association. It was decided that no one but an actual grain grower should be eligible for the Association's executive. In J. W. Scallion as president and Roderick McKenzie of Brandon as secretary-treasurer, the Manitoba Association was led by farmers of long experience in the province, who knew quite definitely what they wanted. The Patrons' lodges of the eighteen-nineties had been projected into the West from Supreme Association headquarters in Michigan.

The Grain Growers' Associations of the new century were indigenously generated.

The Grain Growers and the Government. — Although the two associations were not at this time organically related, their leaders were not slow to recognize the advantages of joint conferences and action in matters of common interest and protection. Additions and improvements to the Grain Act were the favorite subjects of resolution at Grain Growers' conventions. As the number of western farmers affected by its provisions increased, and as each season's operation revealed defects to be remedied, ambiguities to be clarified, fresh irregularities or evasions to be controlled, or new complexities of the expanding grain trade to be regulated, the act was subject to continual criticism and amending resolutions. By making representations jointly to the federal government, the two organizations were generally able to obtain favorable consideration of changes upon which the solidarity of grain-grower opinion was manifest.

The shipping amendments of 1902 had been somewhat hastily enacted to meet emergency conditions, and it was largely on account of their incomplete and ambiguous wording that the C. P. R. had been disposed to test their validity. After the season of 1902 there was a strong desire by all interested parties to have this and other unsatisfactory sections of the Grain Act more clearly and fully defined. Accordingly, during the session of 1903, Messrs. Motherwell and Gillespie of the Territories and Messrs. McCuaig and Henders of Manitoba were sent to Ottawa on behalf of the western grain growers, to confer with representatives of the grain dealers and of the railways in regard to further amendments. Hon. Clifford Sifton, as Minister of the Interior, had undertaken to submit to Parliament an amending bill embodying such changes as the representatives of the interests concerned could agree upon.[1] The shipping amendments of 1903, which replaced those of 1902, were thus given a virtual assurance of workability and acceptability, before being sanctioned by Parliament, and the grain growers' representatives had the satisfaction of participating directly in the drafting of legislation em-

[1] *Commons' Debates*, 1903, p. 7294.

bodying their most cherished resolutions in respect to farmers' shipment of grain.

Issue of Fight for Direct Shipment. — The amendments of 1903 set forth with precision the procedure to be followed in the allotment of cars, and included numerous safeguards for the protection of farmer shippers.[1] At each shipping point, railway agents were required to keep car-order books of a form approved by the Warehouse Commissioner. Each applicant, whether elevator company or individual farmer, was to be given a number in the book in the order of application. Where an applicant required two or more cars, he was required to make two or more applications as the case might be. Cars were to be allotted strictly in order of application, and no applicant could obtain a second car until all preceding applicants had received one. To guard against pressure or inducement being brought by elevators to get farmers to turn over to them cars applied for in the farmer's name, it was stipulated that, if any applicant did not take his car, it should be assigned to the next in order, while heavy penalties were prescribed for selling or transferring the right to a car. All railway agents were further required to post daily a record showing the name and application number of each shipper to whom cars had been allotted during the preceding twenty-four hours.

By 1903 the fight for direct shipment and equality in car distribution had been substantially won.[2] Much bitterness and recrimination had attended the struggle. With the grievance of discrimination removed, however, the grain growers, through the educative process of conference and legislative participation, were more disposed to appreciate the tremendous transportation prob-

[1] Stat. of Canada, 3 Edw. VII, c. 33, sec. 21.

[2] As a matter of fact, the car-distribution clauses of the Grain Act benefit the carload grain shipper somewhat at the expense of the small grower who sells his grain on the street. The fact that the elevator can apply for only one car at a time, regardless of the amount of street grain it has to ship, has a tendency to widen the spread between street and track prices whenever car supply is restricted, or the close of navigation approaches. The Royal Grain Inquiry Commission of 1923–24 recommended that, in the interests of street sellers, the car-distribution clause of the Canada Grain Act be modified so as to allow country elevators the privilege of shipping two cars instead of one in rotation. *Dom. Sess. Papers*, No. 35, 1925, p. 14.

lem with which railways were confronted during the seasonal rush to the head of the lakes, from a continually expanding area of grain production. Legislative regulations and organized vigilance were needful to ensure equitable treatment to the farmer in the distribution of such cars as were available. The real solution lay, however, in more railroad building and more rolling stock. In this the steadily improving financial position and cumulative experience of the C. P. R., the aggressive enterprise of the Canadian Northern Railway, the advent of the Grand Trunk Pacific,[1] and the rapid multiplication of elevators were serving to reduce the transporation stringency which never again attained as relatively acute proportions as during the memorable "wheat blockade" of 1901–02.

[1] The Canadian Northern extended its system into the Territories at Kamsack in 1903. By 1905 its main line had reached Edmonton. Work on the prairie section of the Grand Trunk Pacific began in 1906.

CHAPTER IV

THE BEGINNINGS OF BUSINESS COÖPERATION

New Objectives of Organized Grain Growers. — The Territorial Grain Growers' Association, it has been seen, arose as a protective organization, with the object of countering, through the united action of the grain producers, the centralized control enjoyed by the grain-handling interests. Its initial efforts had been concentrated in the removal of the farmer's disabilities at the local shipping point. By determined recourse to press, Parliament, and law courts, the effective right to greater freedom in shipping and marketing had been substantially secured within the first two years of organization. While this relieved what was perhaps the grain growers' most acute grievance, it marked, however, but the beginning of their organized efforts to secure greater control over the marketing of their staple product. Beyond the local shipping point, with its country elevators and loading platforms, with its street buyers and track buyers, stood the Winnipeg Grain Exchange with its speculative machinery, the Northwest Grain Dealers' Association with its suspected manipulations, and the Inspection Department with its decisive authority. And beyond the dominating Winnipeg market stood the lakehead terminals, where the farmers' strictly graded grain was believed to be secretly mixed for export sale by terminal operators. At Grain Growers' meetings discussion and resolution centered increasingly about questions of grading and terminal handling, of Grain Exchange operations, and of the factors and agencies determining the spread between country prices and terminal prices.

In response to representations from the Grain Growers' Association, the Territorial Department of Agriculture arranged in 1903, and again in 1904, to have milling and baking tests made by an expert of the Ontario Agricultural College, of samples of wheat from the Indian Head district, bearing grades from No. 1 Hard to Feed, as determined by the Chief Inspector. The expert's report indicated quite conclusively that the difference in the bread-making properties of the flours from the various grades was by no means commensurate with the spread in grade prices.[1] The result of these experiments intensified the grain growers' demand for a change in the basis and method of grading, while many farmers began to agitate for the establishment of a sample market.

Royal Grain Commission of 1906–07. — In 1904, in response to representations from both grain growers and the grain trade, the somewhat confused legislation governing grain inspection had been clarified, by the consolidation in a separate Grain Inspection Act,[2] to be administered by the Department of Trade and Commerce, of those portions of the old General Inspection Act [3] which had to do with grain standards and inspection, together with the numerous amendments which had been successively grafted upon it as the western grain trade developed. While useful as a co-ordinating measure, the Grain Inspection Act did not make any appreciable changes in the existing grading system; and the belief persisted among grain growers that they were subject to more exacting grade requirements than were shippers at the terminals. In 1906, therefore, another grain growers' deputation appeared at Ottawa, to discuss before the Agricultural Committee of the House the subject of grading and inspection and other unsatisfactory aspects of the grain trade. So many contentious points and issues arose in these discussions that the government found it expedient to accede to the grain growers' request for the creation of a new grain inquiry commission. In the appointment of this commission the government departed from the usual procedure of naming a judge as chairman, and appointed as Senior Commissioner Mr. John Millar of Indian Head, who had been associated with W. R. Motherwell in the organization of the Territorial Grain Growers' Association, and had acted as its first secretary. The commissioners were authorized (*a*) to investigate complaints made by farmers in respect to the disposal of their grain, and (*b*) to make recommendations to Parliament as

[1] See Moorhouse, *op. cit.*, pp. 68–70.

[2] 4 Edw. VII, c. 15.

[3] This act, which was administered by the Department of Inland Revenue, governed the sale and inspection, not only of grain, but also of such other staples as meal, flour, provisions, meat, fish, hides, etc. See *supra*, p. 28.

to changes in the Grain and Inspection acts, if it was found necessary to do so, in order to meet better the requirements of grain producers.[1]

Project of a Farmers' Grain Company.—Meanwhile a group of Territorial grain growers had been conducting an unofficial investigation of the grain trade on their own account. One of the most active units in the Territorial Association was the local at Sintaluta, where the farmers' action against the C. P. R. station agent had first revealed the temper of the organized grain growers. At the request of the Sintaluta local, the Territorial Department of Agriculture had sent an official (W. H. Gaddes) at the end of 1904, to observe for a fortnight the grading of farmers' cars at the Winnipeg inspection yards. Certain members, however, determined to supplement this official observation by the more intimate and direct probings of one of their own number. The man selected and financed as "scout" by the Sintaluta grain growers was E. A. Partridge, who had farmed in the Qu'Appelle Valley since 1883. Partridge was a man of intense nature and challenging disposition, whose subsequent activities revealed a combination of pronounced democratic idealism with impetuous organizing energy.[2]

Partridge carried no credentials, and had no *entrée* to the Winnipeg grain trade. In most quarters the inquiries of the intrusive farmers' representative were resented or given scant consideration, and this lack of frankness did not tend to allay preconceived suspicions. Partridge pertinaciously pursued his investigations for a month, and obtained what he regarded as ample evidence of connivance among the larger elevator companies and exporters, and of concerted fixing of country prices. In regard to the government inspection and grading of grain, he was disposed to attribute any inconsistencies to the system rather than to the officials.[3] In

[1] *Commons' Debates*, 1906, p. 5615.

[2] "More ideas have originated with him affecting the farmers' social and economic welfare than with any other dweller in the grain country." L. A. Wood, *op. cit.*, p. 183.

[3] In the opinion of both Partridge and of W. H. Gaddes, the inspection system attached undue importance to the superficial factors of color and plumpness. T. G. G. A., 1905.

the Grain Exchange, however, he decided that the real exploiters of the farmers were organized.

The conclusion to which Partridge's observations led him was that the only effective way in which the farmers could intelligently learn what actual reforms were necessary and possible in the grain trade, was to form a grain company of their own and establish themselves competitively upon the central market. Such a coöperative company, moreover, would operate for the benefit of the growers, both through the dividends which it might earn and the superior service which it might render, and through the financial aid which it might bring to the Grain Growers' Associations in their efforts to improve the producers' marketing position.[1]

On his way back to Sintaluta, Partridge addressed the third annual convention of the Manitoba Grain Growers' Association at Brandon, reporting on his Winnipeg observations and propounding his idea of a farmer-owned grain company. The convention as a whole was not responsive to Partridge's scheme. Many of the members had memories of the inauspicious trading experiences of earlier Patrons' organizations in Manitoba, or in their former homes in Ontario or the States. From the first the grain growers had declared for the policy of keeping their organization "non-partisan, non-political, non-trading."[2] The convention contented itself, therefore, with appointing a committee under the chairmanship of Partridge to investigate the possibilities of a farmers' grain-marketing organization, and to report at the next convention of the association. In laying his observations

[1] The preamble to the resolution to form a coöperative company, drafted by Partridge, indicates that the educational objective was uppermost in his mind. The preamble runs in part: "Whereas such an enterprise would be immediately profitable without financial risk, would afford protection from crooked practices, and at the same time would enable the shareholders to gain an insight into, and a valuable knowledge of, the whole grain business, equipping the farmers for greater enterprises, and enable them to deal intelligently with such problems as a sample market, grades, inspection, hospital, sorting and mixing, and terminal elevators and legislation pertaining thereto, and whereas such a company, loyally supported, would, in addition to paying a dividend, provide a surplus to be used in investigating conditions," etc. Sask. G. G. A., 1906.

[2] Man. G. G. A., 1903.

and projects before the convention of the Territorial Association held shortly afterwards at Moose Jaw, Partridge again found a general distrust of any proposal to identify the association with commercial ventures. The Territorial convention did not even respond to the extent of appointing a committee to consider the scheme.

Initiation of the Grain Growers' Grain Company. — Among his own friends at Sintaluta, however, Partridge found both enthusiasm and support for his ideas. At a well-organized meeting of local farmers, held in the town hall of Sintaluta on January 27, 1906, the aims and objects of the prospective farmers' grain company were thoroughly discussed and unanimously approved. It was agreed that at the outset at least, the company should not seek to build or acquire elevators, nor buy grain on its own account, but should limit itself to doing a commission business, in which a minimum of capital was required, and in which the risks were relatively slight. While the company was to be on a joint-stock basis, coöperative principles were to prevail in its control and operations. Stockholders were to be composed of farmers exclusively, and no person might hold more than four shares. In order that membership should be reasonably accessible to small farmers, shares were to be issued at $25, with 10 per cent payable on application. With a view to ensuring against possible concentration of control, it was agreed that no shareholder might have more than one vote, that proxy voting should not be allowed, and that shares should not be transferable except by vote at annual meetings. Before the Sintaluta farmers left the town hall, the first two hundred shares of "The Grain Growers' Grain Company, Limited," had been subscribed, and a strong organization committee chosen to prosecute a stock-selling campaign among Grain Growers' Association members.

The Organization Campaign. — Although the Grain Growers' Grain Company had been launched at Sintaluta, where Partridge's personal influence was strong, the intention of its promoters was not to limit its scope to Saskatchewan farmers, but to secure the coöperation of the Manitoba Grain Growers' Association in organizing a farmers' grain commission company, in which membership should be based, not on a territorial, but on an occupational basis. While, however, the 1906 convention of the Manitoba Grain Growers' Association adopted the report of the committee of reference appointed at the previous convention, and put itself on record as favoring the idea of a farmers' coöperative grain company, the delegates were not prepared to authorize any formal or financial participation in the project by the association. A separate meeting of interested farmer delegates was held, however, during the convention. Here the plans of the Sintaluta promoters were discussed and endorsed, and arrangements made for a joint organization meeting at Winnipeg in April. At this latter gathering, which brought together the Saskatchewan and Manitoba enthusiasts, several Manitoba members were added to the Sintaluta organization committee,[1] and plans formulated for an active stock-selling canvass to raise the necessary funds for incorporation and purchase of a seat on the Winnipeg Grain Exchange. The canvassers either worked voluntarily among the farmers in their own neighborhood, or campaigned further afield, receiving their bare expenses. Despite their gratuitous labors, the motives of the canvassers were subject to considerable suspicion on the part of many farmers. Despite, too, the smallness of the subscription instalment of $2.50, the greatest difficulty was experienced in securing bona-fide subscribers. Western grain growers, especially in the spring of the year, were not as a class very familiar with cash, and many of those who did subscribe regarded their shares as experimental donations rather than as investments. The very coöperative features of the enterprise, which restricted the field of canvass to farmers, and limited the size of individual share allotments and subscription payments, added indeed greatly to the labor of accumulating the initial capital. On the other hand, the very efforts which the organization committee had to put forth to sell stock in the Grain Growers' Grain Company served to ensure that the original shareholders were more or less coöperatively converted, and so disposed to support the company loyally and intelligently.

[1] The most active Manitoba member of the committee was John Kennedy of Swan River, who is credited with having sold three quarters of the shares subscribed in Manitoba during the winter campaign. L. A. Wood, *op. cit.*, p. 186.

While the organization work might have been considerably facilitated had the two Grain Growers' associations officially identified themselves with the enterprise, such participation would inevitably have raised the question of control, with all its divisive implications. Although Partridge had originally appealed to the two Grain Growers' conventions for the endorsement of his coöperative business project, it was not his idea that the associations as such should engage in trading operations. He realized that the company would be more likely to succeed if it were not subject to the control of a large regional association organized for quite different purposes; and that the associations would be more effective in securing desired grain legislation if they were not themselves commercially identified with the grain trade.[1]

The voluntary canvass of the Grain Growers' Grain Company organizers in eastern Saskatchewan[2] and western Manitoba was carried on through the spring and early summer months of 1906, with results that were the reverse of spectacular. By midsummer less than a thousand shares had been sold. In June an unexpected and disconcerting difficulty developed in the refusal of the department of the Secretary of State at Ottawa to grant the application of the farmers' company for a federal charter, on the technical ground that the shares of a company with an authorized capital of $250,000 could not be issued at less than $100 per share par value. When the urgent representations of the organization committee's solicitor failed to obtain a reversal of the depart-

[1] "I have repeatedly stated that it is not desirable for the Association to engage in trade. . . . The Association has many important functions to perform in connection with the securing of legislative enactments required in the farmers' interests, and it would weaken them in their request for legislation to be a trading concern, as they could then hope for no greater recognition from legislative bodies than would be accorded to any other corporation. . . . It is in the interest of the farmers to establish a trading company separate and distinct from the Association, which, by actual experience obtained in the world's markets, would secure an intimate knowledge of conditions surrounding the trade that would be of incalculable service in disclosing to the farmers what legislative remedies were requisite to enable them to secure the full returns for their labor." E. A. Partridge in *Manitoba Free Press*, Jan. 29, 1907.

[2] The provinces of Saskatchewan and Alberta had been organized in 1905, and the Territorial Grain Growers' Association changed its name in 1906 to the Saskatchewan Grain Growers' Association.

mental ruling, the promoters suspected that secret obstructive influences were at work In this dilemma it was decided, on Kennedy's suggestion, to apply to the Manitoba authorities for incorporation, although the powers of the company, contemplating, as it had, interprovincial operation, would be necessarily more restricted under a provincial charter.[1] Commencement of business during the current crop season, even if in a limited way, was deemed by the committee to be preferable to the expensive and uncertain alternative of further pursuing its claims for federal incorporation. Under the Manitoba charter, which was promptly obtained, the company could begin operations with a provisional directorate of five members. As the harvest season was now close at hand, it was decided to take advantage of the large attendance of farmers at the Winnipeg Exhibition to hold a meeting of such shareholders as should be present, to elect a provisional directorate and officers, and thus place the company in a legal position to begin business. Accordingly, in a tent on the Exhibition ground, provisional organization was duly effected on July 26,[2] and the temporary directors concentrated their efforts during exhibition week upon securing from visiting grain growers new stock subscriptions, and assurances of consignment patronage for the farmers' commission company when the crop would begin to move.

Initial Operations. — Harvesting was now under way, and a seat on the Grain Exchange, for which the price was $2,500, had still to be acquired. Organization, publicity, incorporation, and legal expenses left for this purpose only about $1,000 in the treasury. A second call on farmer stock subscribers during the harvesting and threshing season offered slight prospect of bringing in the necessary funds within the necessary time. On the other hand, failure to be in a position to handle farmers' grain during the current crop season would probably mean the subsidence of the whole enterprise. In this emergency the president appealed

[1] For example, a provincially incorporated company could not sue for debts in another province without being registered in such province, which might involve payment of fees as great as those for incorporation.

[2] The following provisional officers were elected: President, E. A. Partridge (Sintaluta, Sask.); Vice-President, John Kennedy (Swan River, Man.); Secretary-Treasurer, John Spencer.

to some of his associates at Sintaluta. Five of the more substantial Sintaluta shareholders demonstrated their faith in Partridge's enterprise by giving their personal notes to the bank for the requisite $1,500. The seat on the Exchange was purchased forthwith in the name of E. A. Partridge, and the little farmers' company prepared to compete with the established trade on the most highly organized market in Western Canada.

The risks and complexities of the grain-handling business were not underestimated, however, and the necessity of securing an experienced manager was fully realized by the provisional directors. Such a position in an unproved and weakly financed farmers' company, whose patronage was uncertain, and whose competition was not likely to be cherished by the regular grain trade, offered little inducement to a manager of the type desired. An experienced manager was eventually secured, however, in Thomas Coulter of the Independent Grain Company, who had been one of the few grain men to show consideration to Partridge when the latter had come to Winnipeg as the scouting representative of the Sintaluta farmers. Under these conditions the Grain Growers' Grain Company opened its two-roomed top-floor office for business on September 5, 1906, and awaited the arrival of bills of lading for the first consigned cars. The long, heart-breaking canvass had not been in vain, however, and cars began to arrive at accelerating rate, so that by the end of the month the daily receipts were averaging fifteen cars, and larger office premises had to be secured. The initial expectations of the directors were being more than realized.[1]

[1] The circumstances under which the Grain Growers' Grain Company was launched are vividly described from the growers' viewpoint by Moorhouse.

CHAPTER V

THE GRAIN GROWERS AND THE GRAIN EXCHANGE

Suspension of the Grain Growers' Grain Company by the Exchange. —The auspicious trend of the first six of weeks commission operations by the farmers' company was abruptly arrested when, at the height of the grain movement, the president of the Grain Growers' Grain Company was summoned to appear before the council of the Grain Exchange, to answer the charges of having "offended against the honor and dignity of the Exchange" through the issue of certain pamphlets "reflecting on the methods adopted by certain members of the trade"; and of having violated the commission rule of the Exchange.[1] The unrestrained denunciation of the Grain Exchange and its methods, which Partridge had made before the Manitoba and Territorial Grain Growers' conventions after his Winnipeg "observations" in 1905, and the strong language employed in describing the abuses of the "elevator combine," in the campaign to win farmers' participation in the Grain Growers' Company, had not passed unnoticed by members of the Grain Exchange; nor had the increasing consignment of farmers' cars to the newly launched company been viewed with indifference. Undoubtedly there were a good many members of the Exchange who were disposed to welcome any pretext for embarrassing, if not indeed driving out of business, the aggressive company headed by Partridge.

The occasion for disciplinary action was the issue of a circular by the Grain Growers' Company indicating its intention of distributing the net profits of the season's business to farmer shippers on a patronage basis. This was interpreted by the council of the Exchange as being tantamount to "splitting the commission with the shipper," and therefore in violation of the commission rule, which established a uniform commission charge of one cent

[1] See evidence of E. A. Partridge and C. N. Bell before Royal Grain Commission, *Manitoba Free Press*, Nov. 22, 1906.

a bushel for handling grain for non-members.[1] Under the prevailing constitution and by-laws of the Winnipeg Grain and Produce Exchange,[2] member firms or corporations had to hold seats in the name of one of their chief executive officers or partners. The company represented by a member was allowed, if found in good standing, to be registered by resolution of the council, thereby entitling such company to full trading privileges on the Exchange. In case of complaints being laid against any member firm for breach of the rules of the Exchange, and satisfactory explanation or repudiation not being offered by its representative when summoned before the council, the latter might rescind registration of such company by resolution, thereby automatically depriving it of trading privileges.[3]

Although the president of the Grain Growers' Grain Company pointed out to the Grain Exchange council that the by-laws of his company contained no provision for patronage distribution of profits, and challenged the members to prove that any such distribution had ever been made, the intimation contained in the company's circular, and Partridge's defiant refusal to summon his directors and obtain a repudiation of the announced policy, were deemed by the council sufficient cause to rescind the registration of the Grain Growers' Grain Company. A few days later (November 8, 1906) notice was posted to all members of the Exchange, calling attention to the expulsion of the Grain Growers' Grain Company from all trading privileges, and declaring that any firm dealing with such company would be subject to penalties.[4] This meant that the latter could not dispose of its patrons' grain

[1] The relevant section of the commission by-law was as follows: "Any member charged with violating or offering to violate the rule relating to the established rates of commission, either by direct charging of less than such rates or rebating any portion of the same, shall, when such charge is made in writing to the Complaint Committee, and on such complaint being made proper by such committee, be summoned to appear before the Council," etc. Winnipeg Grain and Produce Exchange, By-Law 19, rule 4.

[2] Incorporated by special act of Manitoba legislature, 54 Vic., c. 31, 1891.

[3] Evidence of C. N. Bell, secretary, Winnipeg Grain Exchange, before the Royal Grain Commission, Nov. 21, 1906.

[4] Statement of C. N. Bell before Justice Phippen in King *v.* Gage *et al. Manitoba Free Press*, April 24, 1907.

through the Exchange without itself paying the full commission charge of one cent per bushel.

Under these conditions the increasing flow of consigned cars was an occasion of embarrassment instead of encouragement to the young company. Farmer shippers expected an advance of 75 per cent on their bills of lading, and a prompt remittance of the balance as soon as the inspection and out-turn certificates were received by the company. To delay settlement with shippers, or to notify its shareholders and patrons to suspend consignment of further grain, would mean the speedy termination of the company's existence. With no opportunity of making sales on the Exchange, therefore, except on terms which permitted no margin, the Grain Growers' overdraft at the bank began to assume extremely embarrassing proportions. When in December the company's indebtedness to the bank reached the figure of $356,000, the closing out of the account was prevented only by the three officers, Partridge, Kennedy, and Spencer, giving their personal bond without limit.[1]

Some measure of relief was obtained by making several large sales in Eastern Canada, and shipping directly from Fort William. Without the opportunity of selling to millers and exporters on the Winnipeg Exchange, however, and without any established connections in the East, the cost of such transactions cut heavily into the profits of the struggling company. It was a premium, however, which had to be paid for the very continuance of its existence. It was during this crisis that the struggling farmers' co-operative company obtained substantial relief through another much older and more powerful coöperative company. For the Winnipeg representative of the Scottish Co-operative Wholesale Society, on learning of the Grain Growers' predicament, decided to risk the disapproval of the Grain Exchange and support the newly formed western producers' coöperative, not only by buying a large portion of its wheat, but also by allowing it the regular commission of a cent a bushel. This instance of coöperation between coöperatives proved an occasion of distinct encouragement and appreciation on the part of the farmers' officers, and of distinct

[1] G. G. G. Co., *Farmers in Business, 1900–1916*, p. 6.

relief on the part of the manager of the Grain Growers' bank, who had first suggested the transaction.

Intervention of Manitoba Grain Growers' Association. — While the farmers' company was thus struggling desperately to handle its patrons' grain and preserve its commercial existence, even if excluded from the floor of the Exchange, determined efforts were being made on its behalf by the Manitoba Grain Growers' Association, not only to bring about the reinstatement of the company, but also to have the Grain Exchange and the Northwest Grain Dealers' Association brought under drastic control. It was seen now that, while the Grain Growers' Association had not been willing to assume organic or financial responsibility for the Grain Growers' Company, it was prepared to use its organized strength and powerful provincial influence in supporting the latter against what it conceived to be the malicious discrimination of the Grain Exchange.

In seeking relief for the Grain Growers' Company and regulation for the Grain Exchange the Manitoba Association appealed both to the courts and to the legislature. Facts adduced at the sittings held at Winnipeg during November (1906) by the Royal Grain Commission, under the chairmanship of Mr. J. A. Millar, for the specific purpose of hearing charges against the Northwest Grain Dealers' Association, led the president of the Manitoba Grain Growers, D. W. McCuaig, to lay a formal charge against three members of the council of the Winnipeg Grain Exchange,[1] of having "unlawfully conspired, combined or arranged with each other, to restrain or injure trade or commerce in relation to grain."[2] While the charges were laid against the individuals named, the case was essentially one against the rules and practices of the Grain Exchange and the Grain Dealers' Association.[3]

[1] J. C. Gage, John Love, and J. G. McHugh. Mr. Gage was president of the Exchange at the time, Mr. Love had been president in 1905, and Mr. McHugh had laid the complaint against Mr. Partridge before the Complaint Committee of the Exchange. Evidence of C. N. Bell in King *v.* Gage *et al.* *Manitoba Free Press*, April 24, 1907.

[2] *Ibid.*, Dec. 4, 1906.

[3] In a jointly signed letter to the press, appearing Jan. 28, 1907, Hon. Mr. Motherwell and Chairman J. A. Millar deprecated Mr. McCuaig's resort to law as

At the preliminary hearing on January 10, 1907, an indictment of thirteen points was obtained, and the case became one for crown prosecution in the Assize Court.

Shortly before the indictment of the three Grain Exchange councillors, the Grain Growers' Grain Company had appealed to the Manitoba government to insist on a revision of the rules of the Exchange or to amend its charter.[1] Although Premier Roblin wrote to the Exchange advising reconsideration of the case of the Grain Growers' Company, and expressing doubt as to whether the Exchange was acting within its charter powers,[2] that body took no other action than to maintain the legality of its position. The Manitoba Grain Growers' Association thereupon carried the issue further by sending a deputation to demand before the House Committee on Agriculture that the charter of the Grain Exchange be amended forthwith. They asked that the Exchange be not allowed to limit the number of its members; that the purchase of a seat should automatically entitle the firm for which it was acquired to full trading privileges; that arbitrary interference by the council with the business methods of member firms be prohibited; that penalties and disabilities against those failing to observe the common rules be abolished; that the expulsion of no member should be considered final unless assented to by the Minister of Agriculture; and that all by-laws should receive the approval of the Lieutenant-Governor in Council before becoming legal and binding. In short the Grain Growers' deputation demanded that the Exchange should be deprived of the power of regulating the practices of its members, and that it should itself be subjected to the regulation of the government. The only reason, they claimed, that the Exchange had admitted the Grain Growers' Grain Company, was that it might have the farmers' company under its discipline.

The Grain Exchange representatives replied vigorously before

indiscreet and untimely, in view of the fact that the Royal Commission investigating the charges against the Grain Dealers' Association had not completed its findings. President McCuaig's action was endorsed, however, by the Manitoba Grain Growers' convention in February. M. G. G. A., 1907.

[1] G. G. G. Co., to Premier Roblin, Dec. 20, 1906.

[2] Roblin to Grain Exchange, Dec. 26, 1906, *Manitoba Free Press*, Jan. 9, 1907.

the Agricultural Committee, to the charges and demands of the Grain Growers' Association, maintaining that their rules and disciplines were in the interests of uniformity of practice, integrity of dealing, and equality of treatment. If deprived of such powers of self-regulation, they declared, they would demand the complete cancellation of their charter, and go out of business altogether. As a deadlock appeared imminent, Premier Roblin found it expedient to accept a suggestion from President McCuaig for reference of the whole issue of grain handling in the province to a conference to be attended by representatives of the Grain Growers, the Grain Exchange, the government, reeves of municipalities, the railroads, and the banks. Mr. Roblin pledged his government to give legislative effect at the next session of the legislature to such resolutions as the proposed conference should agree upon.

Conditional Reinstatement of Grain Growers' Company.— While the Manitoba Grain Growers were thus carrying on the fight against the Grain Exchange, before both the courts and the government, the directors of the Grain Growers' Company were reconsidering their policy in regard to patronage distribution of profits. It was manifest that the council of the Exchange would not consent to reinstate the company unless this method were formally repudiated. While the government was professedly sympathetic, its intervention could be effective only through the uncertain and indefinite legislative procedure of charter amendment. Meanwhile every day's exclusion from the trading floor meant loss to the company. Legal consultation revealed, furthermore, that distribution of profits otherwise than for the benefit of shareholders was contrary not only to the rules of the Winnipeg Grain and Produce Exchange, but also to the provisions of the Manitoba Joint Stock Companies Act, under which the Grain Growers' Grain Company held its charter.[1] It was realized, moreover, that the distribution of such net profits as might be available, in the form of stock dividends rather than of patronage dividends, would be of greater advantage both to the shareholders and to the company itself. Accordingly, at a directors' meeting

[1] It was not until 1916 that the Coöperative Associations Act was placed on the Manitoba statute book.

held on December 22 (1906) a resolution was passed cancelling the patronage distribution proposal contained in the circular to which the Exchange had taken such uncompromising exception.[1] Notification to the Grain Exchange Council of such action and application for reinstatement failed, however, to bring about a lifting of the ban, the council demanding notification of formal repudiation by the shareholders of the company. Although the directors' resolution was endorsed at a special meeting of the Grain Growers' Grain Company (February 5, 1907), reinstatement was still withheld.

The continued refusal of the Exchange to readmit the farmers' company, even when notified of the formal abandonment of the proposed practice which had been made the occasion of exclusion, was regarded by the farmers as convincing proof that the real purpose of the Exchange was to wreck the Grain Growers' Grain Company. Finally, on March 22, President McCuaig of the Grain Growers' Association carried the latest letter of refusal from the Grain Exchange to the acting premier (Hon. Robert Rogers), whereupon Mr. Rogers promptly called upon the president of the Grain Exchange to render explanation. Upon the latter merely intimating that the Grain Growers' Grain Company had the right to appeal from the council's refusal to the general body of the Exchange, the acting premier forwarded the following peremptory communication:

> The action of your council in refusing trading privileges to the Grain Growers' Grain Company cannot be regarded by the government other than as an arbitrary and unjustifiable exercise of the powers conferred upon you through your charter by the Legislative Assembly of Manitoba, and unless remedied by the fifteenth of this month, the government will call the legislature together for the purpose of remedying this and other grievances by legislative amendments.[2]

During the following week several informal conferences took place between representatives of the government, the Exchange, and the farmers' company. As the council still showed itself unwilling to reinstate the latter, so long as its seat was held by one so distinctly *persona non grata* as Partridge, it was finally arranged

[1] G. G. G. Co., to Grain Exchange Council. *Manitoba Free Press*, Jan. 9, 1907.

[2] Published correspondence. *Manitoba Free Press*, April 24, 1907.

that the company should make fresh application in the name of John Spencer (the secretary-treasurer), to whom Partridge's membership should be transferred. On the last day of the ultimatum period a general meeting of the Exchange was held, at the conclusion of which the following intimation was forwarded to the acting premier:

> As the Grain Growers' Grain Company have written the Exchange admitting that they violated the rules (for which violation their trading privileges had been withdrawn), and that their system of rebating profits under the co-operative plan has recently been discontinued and annulled by a general meeting of their shareholders (which removes the cause for which their privileges were cancelled), and the company having today presented an application in which it expressly agrees to observe faithfully and to be obligated by all the by-laws, rules and regulations of every nature now existing, or to be hereafter adopted by the Exchange, a general meeting held today granted them registration, which it is hoped will satisfactorily remove all difficulties in connection with this matter.[1]

In the same communication the president of the Exchange advised the government that the clause of the commission by-law which prohibited any member of the Exchange from employing track buyers except on a salary basis of not less than $50 a month, had been rescinded that day by a general meeting of the Exchange, on the recommendation of a special committee. This rule which, had originally been inserted through the influence of the elevator companies,[2] had been particularly resented by the Grain Growers' Association as tending to limit buying competition at smaller points. Among Exchange members themselves the regulation had never been acceptable to the independent dealers and commission firms, including the Grain Growers' Grain Company, since it served to preclude their securing cars at places where the volume of business did not warrant the employment of full-time buyers. The repudiation of this objectionable rule was the result, therefore, of internal as well as of external pressure.

Issue of the Contest with the Exchange. — A week after the readmission of the Grain Growers' Grain Company to the privileges of the Exchange, the crown case against the three indicted council-

[1] *Manitoba Free Press*, April 24, 1907. [2] *Ibid.*

lors came before Mr. Justice Phippen in the Assize Court. The principal practices which the crown prosecutor sought to show, as being in violation of section 498 of the Criminal Code,[1] were the concerted fixing of prices at country points through the Northwest Grain Dealers' Association; the restrictive operation of the commission by-law; the limitation by agreement of the amount of street wheat purchased by elevators; and the pooling of receipts among elevator companies. The defence maintained that the joint telegrams sent out daily to country points by the Grain Dealers' Association merely indicated prices to members, and that there was no agreement or penalty against exceeding such prices.[2] The uniform commission charge of one cent a bushel was the smallest margin, it was claimed, which would enable a member to remain in business, and its maintenance was in the interest of the farmer, by permitting greater competition in the handling of his grain. It was admitted that in 1905 an agreement had been made among elevator companies to limit the amount of grain purchased so as not to exceed 5,000 bushels on hand at any time in country elevators. This was justified as being necessary by the car-distribution clauses of the Grain Act. The elevator could not purchase grain freely where it stood on the same basis as the individual farmer in the allotment of cars. This agreement, however, had been abandoned.[3] It was also admitted that, as a means of maintaining elevators at points where a great deal of grain was shipped over platform, several elevator companies had agreed during the two preceding seasons to pool receipts above the assigned quotas at a margin of two cents a bushel. This too had not been found satisfactory and had been discontinued.[4]

In reviewing the case, Mr. Justice Phippen declared that in his reading of section 498 of the Criminal Code, conspiracy was proved only where restraints were shown to be "undue and

[1] This section deals with conspiracy and combination in restraint of trade and competition.

[2] See also evidence of F. O. Fowler before Royal Grain Commission, *Manitoba Free Press*, Nov. 24, 1906.

[3] Evidence of T. Holchard in Rex *v.* Gage *et al.*, *Manitoba Free Press*, May 9, 1907.

[4] *Ibid.;* see also evidence of J. C. Gage before Royal Grain Commission, *Ibid.*, Jan. 25, 1907.

merely malicious, unconnected with any business relations of the accused." Taking the view that "the evidence offered assumed the form of an investigation into the conditions governing the grain trade of the west, rather than a trial of the charges specified in the indictment," the judge found the various practices discussed to be necessary and reasonable safeguards for the protection of those engaged in the grain trade, and concluded: "With all the evidence before me I am forced to the opinion that not only was no undue restraint of trade disclosed, but that the very acts complained of, taken in connection with their surrounding conditions, made on the whole for a more stable market at the fullest values and so for the public good." [1] The Grain Growers were much dissatisfied with the decision. The Provincial Court of Appeal, however, completely upheld the judgment of the Assize Court.

The same charges of restraint and combination had been investigated some months previously by the Royal Grain Commission. That body also concluded that no "undue" restraint of trade had been proved, but recommended that the pooling of receipts or earnings by elevators should be prohibited.[2] It pointed out that the most effective safeguard against combination by elevators was to be found in more adequate car supply, and in the freedom of the grower to load his own car and consign it to a commission firm.[3]

In June, 1907, the government convened the provincial conference on the grain trade, whose resolutions Premier Roblin had undertaken to implement by legislation.[4] The curbing of the Grain Exchange at once asserted itself as the dominating issue; and when a resolution was passed, at the instance of the Grain Growers' Association, declaring that no by-law, rule, or regulation of the Exchange should become effective until approved by the Lieutenant-Governor in Council, the Grain Exchange representatives withdrew from further participation in the conference.[5]

[1] 6 *Western Law Reporter* 19 (1907).

[2] The Manitoba Grain Act was amended accordingly, by 7–8 Edw. VII, c. 45, sec. 44.

[3] *Report of Royal Grain Commission of 1906–1907*, p. 17.

[4] See *supra*, p. 55.

[5] *Manitoba Free Press*, June 6, 1907.

Premier Roblin had pledged himself, however, to amend the Grain Exchange charter, and when the legislature opened in January, 1908, the government forced through a bill, on the threat of resignation, which made the by-laws of the Exchange subject to the supervision of the Court of King's Bench, and prohibited restrictions as to membership or trading commissions.[1] On finding its protests unavailing, although supported by unanimous resolution of the Winnipeg Board of Trade, the Exchange suspended operations on February 26, and for several months no organized trading was conducted. Finally, in September, the Exchange, having applied for cancellation of its charter, reorganized as a voluntary association,[2] on which basis it has continued to operate ever since.

During 1907 the Grain Exchange had been subject to the triple inquisition of a Royal Commission, a crown prosecution, and a legislative hearing. So far at least as the investigations of a judicial character were concerned, the Exchange had on the whole succeeded in justifying its rules and practices, while renouncing such methods as the prohibition of employment of track buyers on a commission basis, pooling of receipts, and limitation of street grain purchases.[3] Although many farmers considered the court decision tantamount to a justification of any combination or restraints so long as these could not be proved to be "malicious restraints, unconnected with any business relations of the accused," the concurrent federal, provincial, and judicial investigations had on the other hand served to clarify, and to some extent to render reasonable in the minds of many other farmers, regulations and practices of the Grain Exchange which had hitherto been merely objects of dark suspicion. In any event, the Exchange had been placed on the defensive and compelled to justify publicly its every rule and act. Undoubtedly the public animus against the Exchange was greatly intensified by its action in expelling the Grain Growers' Grain Company from trading privileges. The very justi-

[1] Stat. Manitoba, 7–8 Edw. VII, c. 79.

[2] *Manitoba Free Press*, Nov. 26, 1908.

[3] The evidence and findings of the Royal Commission and the court case are jointly analysed in W. A. Mackintosh, *Agricultural Coöperation in Western Canada*, pp. 27–31.

fication of that action under the rules of the Exchange led to the demand for government regulation of its powers and operations. While the Grain Growers' Grain Company was readmitted only upon its formal undertaking to abide by all the rules of the Exchange, and to transfer its membership to an officer who was *persona grata* with that body, the course of events makes it appear doubtful if the company would have been reinstated without the intervention of the Grain Growers' Association and the government. The right of the farmers' company to participate in the organized grain trade had been sustained. At the same time it had been obliged to conform to the recognized rules of that trade. The grain growers had gained an established place in the trading system as the outcome of the struggle of 1906–07. The system itself, however, remained substantially unchanged.

CHAPTER VI

EARLY STRUGGLES AND PROGRESS OF THE GRAIN GROWERS' GRAIN COMPANY

Effect of Grain Exchange Episode upon Farmers' Company. — The suspension of the Grain Growers' Grain Company by the Grain Exchange had a twofold effect upon the fortunes of the farmers' infant concern. In the first place, the company's spirited fight for reinstatement and survival, and the evident intent of certain grain interests to crush it, not only evoked the intervention of the organized Grain Growers' Association and the Manitoba government, but also gave it a publicity that attracted the business patronage of farmers who recognized in the Grain Growers' Grain Company the champion of their right to a competitive place in the organized grain trade. In their minds it became a cause as well as a trading venture. In its ten months of operation during the 1906–07 crop year, the company had handled 2,300,000 bushels of grain, and was able to show, after restoring one third of the capital expended on organization, a modest profit of $790, which permitted a dividend of 7 per cent on a paid-up capital of $11,000.[1] That such a report could be shown in spite of the inexperience of the company, and in spite of the fact that all its sales had to be made outside the Exchange during six months (October 23 to April 15) of the active trading period, was an indication both of resourceful management and of substantial patronage. The financial results of the first year's business were, however, far less significant than the prestige which the company gained among the farmers through the very efforts of elevator interests to destroy it.

In the second place, the suspension of the company had been terminated only upon its formal repudiation of its original intention to distribute patronage as well as share dividends. While this involved a relaxation of orthodox coöperative principles, it

[1] First Annual Report, G. G. G. Co., 1907.

did not make the company any less a bona-fide farmers' enterprise. Partridge's primary purpose in originating a farmers' grain company had been educational even more than commercial. In his mind the direct knowledge of the technique of grain marketing which such participation would afford was even more important than the immediate realization of dividends. Without active membership on the Exchange, and free enjoyment of its trading privileges, neither the fullest knowledge of the trade nor the largest financial returns could be realized. Neither the existing rules of the Exchange nor the provisions of the provincial Companies' Act recognized distribution of earnings on a patronage basis. If the farmers' company was to do business at all, it must conform to the laws and regulations of the system which it sought to enter. It was more important that the company should be in a position to function freely and to earn substantial profits, than to determine beforehand the particular form in which prospective profits should be distributed to farmers. A pro-rating of net profits on a patronage basis at the outset of the company's career would not only have retarded the growth of its subscribed capital, through lessening the dividend inducement, but would also have limited, if not prevented, the accumulation of reserve funds. Subsequent developments were to demonstrate the advantage, not only to the company, but to the grain growers in general, of the policy of capitalizing instead of rebating net earnings. As the action of the Grain Exchange in expelling the Grain Growers' Company rallied the farmers to the support of the latter, so its insistence on the repudiation of the principle of patronage distribution as the condition of reinstatement served to make the company become all the stronger a competitor.

New Leadership in the Company. — The provisional directorate chosen at the Winnipeg Exhibition in the previous July had been continued in office (with two directors added) for the remainder of the year by vote of the shareholders at the general meeting held in February to consider the directors' resolution regarding the disavowal of patronage distribution.[1] For some time, however, E. A. Partridge had contemplated resignation from the

[1] See *supra*, p. 56.

presidency. He had succeeded in getting the farmers' company definitely launched. His motives had been so frequently questioned by Grain Growers' officers,[1] as well as by suspicious farmers, and he had so antagonized the council of the Grain Exchange, that he felt that it would be better for the company if he occupied a less conspicuous position in its direction. The company's membership in the Exchange had been transferred from Partridge's to Spencer's name, it has been noted, as a condition of its readmission. It was only through the pressure of his associates that he agreed to continue in the presidency until the annual meeting. In considering a possible successor he and Kennedy had been observing for some time, with growing confidence, a young and active shareholder of the company at Russell, Manitoba.

Thomas Alexander Crerar, whose family had migrated to Western Manitoba from Perth County, Ontario, in 1881, had obtained a collegiate education at Portage la Prairie and Winnipeg by means of the meagre earnings of country school-teaching. As a grain grower on a Hudson's Bay Company quarter-section near Russell, he had experienced the disabilities suffered by the farmer in the marketing of his grain before the organization of the Grain Growers' Associations. Later, as manager of a farmers' elevator at Russell, he had been one of the first local subscribers to the Grain Growers' Grain Company, and had been able to secure the consignment of a number of Russell farmers' cars during its first months of operation. At the shareholders' meeting in February in connection with the Manitoba Grain Growers' convention, he had attracted not a little attention by his thoughtful and practical suggestions, particularly in his emphasis on the advisability of keeping the trading company's directorate independent of that of the association.

Although Crerar had disregarded a letter from Partridge after this meeting, suggesting that he should consider nomination for the next directorate, the conviction was growing in the minds of Partridge and Kennedy that the young elevator manager at

[1] See joint letter of W. R. Motherwell and J. A. Millar, *Manitoba Free Press*, Jan. 28, 1907.

Russell, who continued to send in business and occasional written suggestions, possessed both the vision and judgment, as well as the youth and energy, needed for permanent leadership of the farmers' commercial enterprise. Accordingly at the annual meeting in July, Partridge nominated Crerar for the new directorate, to which he was promptly elected. And when the directors met the same night to elect their officers, Crerar unexpectedly and protestingly found himself elected to the presidency of the company — a position which he has continued to hold ever since Partridge's nominating manœuvre in the midsummer of 1907.[1]

The Second Year's Operations.—One of the first difficulties which the new executive was called on to face was created by the receipt of a notification from the Bank of British North America that it was desired to close out the account of the Grain Growers' Grain Company. As the company had fully retired its overdraft, and had been able to regain its trading privileges and declare a 7 per cent dividend on its first year's business, the directors' inference was that this sudden shutting off of credit, just as the new crop was about to move, represented another move of the opposing interests to embarrass the farmers' company. This time, however, the embarrassment proved of short duration. The Winnipeg manager of the Bank of British North America, Mr. W. H. Machaffie, had always been sympathetic to the Grain Growers' Company, and shortly after the receipt of the headquarters notification, he resigned from that bank to undertake the Winnipeg management of the Home Bank, an eastern institution which had evolved from a loan and savings company into a chartered bank, and was now seeking to establish itself in the expanding Western field. Machaffie at once sought the Grain Growers' account for the new bank, and the company's line of credit was assured for the new crop movement.

The financial arrangements between the young bank and the young grain company were soon carried beyond the mere relations of lender and borrower. The Home Bank was anxious to increase the number of its Western shareholders. The Grain

[1] The circumstances of the "discovery" and election of Crerar are dramatically related by Moorhouse, *op. cit.*, chap. 8.

Growers' Grain Company, on the other hand, was desirous of securing some measure of control in a bank which was known to be less directly identified with the larger capitalistic interests. It was felt that a bank in which farmers were substantial stockholders might reasonably be expected to show greater consideration to the credit requirements of both the farmers' company and individual farmers. Accordingly arrangements were subsequently made by which the Grain Growers' Grain Company invested a considerable portion of its capital funds in Home Bank stock,[1] and was appointed agent to sell shares of the bank on commission to farmers, workingmen, and small merchants in the West. While the Grain Growers' identification with the Home Bank was later to be an occasion of considerable loss to many Western farmers, and of embarrassment to Mr. Crerar's position, the arrangement was undoubtedly advantageous to the company in its early financing.

With its membership on the Exchange in good standing and its bank credit assured, the second year's operations caused considerably less anxiety to the directors then the first season's struggle for survival. The dramatic fight with the Exchange proved the most effective sort of publicity for the farmers' company, and the loyalty, as well as the rising confidence of the grain growers, was reflected in a doubling of the grain consignments to five million bushels, and in an increase in the number of farmer shareholders from less than 400 when the company began business, to nearly 3,000 at the close of the second year.[2] The year's profits of

[1] About 1,000 shares of Home Bank stock were acquired by the G. G. G. Co. in 1908 and 1909. John Kennedy, and later T. A. Crerar, were appointed western directors of the Home Bank. Evidence of T. A. Crerar before Commission on the Home Bank, May 5, 1924.

[2] When, a few years later, Partridge, becoming dissatisfied with the policy of the G. G. G. Co. under Crerar's leadership, sought to obtain trading privileges on the Exchange for a new farmers' grain company under the name of "The Square Deal Grain Company," members of the Exchange council, in conferring with Crerar, pointed out the impossibility of granting registration to a company whose name implied dishonesty on the part of all other Exchange members. Crerar's reply was: "If you want to rally every grain grower to the support of Partridge's new company, refuse it registration. If you grant it trading privileges without protest, it won't last a year." His advice was followed, and his judgment vindicated. (Personal information.)

$40,190 were equivalent to nearly 150 per cent on the paid-up capital, which was substantially augmented by the declaration of a 40 per cent stock dividend.[1] The financial results served to justify Partridge's judgment that the safest and most advantageous point of entry for the farmers into the organized grain trade was the commission business. Already, however, the directors were feeling their way toward the export field. The exigencies of the first year's trading off the floor of the Exchange had forced the company prematurely into placing shipments directly in the East. During the second year several small cargoes were sold, by way of experiment, to exporters in eastern cities. The larger credit requirements of such long-range transactions were facilitated by the new relations with the Home Bank, and while these terminal shipments were conducted at first in a limited way, they permitted a larger margin of profit than the straight commission operations.

It was found, indeed, that during a considerable portion of the 1908–09 season, Fort William prices were from 8 to 12 cents a bushel below the level justified by overseas quotations. This was attributed mainly to seasonal credit stringency, which made it difficult for exporters to finance purchases.[2] As a result of this experience, the company, whose own capital and credit reserves were steadily increasing, decided to enter more actively into the export business, with the direct object of becoming a factor in keeping Fort William prices, on which farmers' returns were directly based, nearer the true export value of wheat.[3] In the third year 2,200,000 bushels were shipped by the company to eastern seaboard exporters. In the following year 6,000,000 bushels were so disposed of, and steps were taken to establish connections with overseas exporters.[4]

[1] G. G. G. Co., 1908.

[2] The rapid growth of grain production in Western Canada at this time placed a heavy seasonal strain upon the chartered banks. Largely as an outcome of the stringency of 1907–08, the Bank Act was amended in 1908 to permit banks to increase their note circulation to the extent of 15 per cent of their combined paid-up capital and reserve during the crop-moving period, Oct. 1 to Jan. 31. In the grain revision of the Bank Act in 1913, this period was extended from Sept. 1 to the end of Feb.

[3] G. G. G. Co., 1910, 1913.

[4] G. G. G. Co., 1910.

Establishment of Claims and Sampling Departments. — With a view to rendering greater marketing service to its patrons, as well as earning profits for its farmer shareholders, the company early inaugurated a Claims Department and a Sampling Department. The purpose of the former was to assist farmer shippers in the devious operations of collecting claims from the railroads for losses of grain in transit. To establish such claim, it was necessary to prove substantial discrepancy between the quantity of grain loaded on car and the official weight recorded on the terminal out-turn certificate. Where grain was loaded over platform, the precise initial weight could not be ascertained, and railway agents always signed bills of lading for approximate weights only. A claim could not usually be collected, therefore, unless it could be shown that a car was in a leaking condition on arrival. Although the government inspection staff at the terminals advised shippers or shippers' agents of the condition as well as the out-turn of their cars, the individual farmer was rarely in a position to collect such a claim. Through its Claims Department the company now undertook, on receipt of report from the Inspection Department indicating loss from leakage in any consigned car, to advise the shipper of the evidence he must supply, and then to enter and follow through the claim with the railway company on his behalf. Claims for freight overcharge were also handled through the department.[1]

Dissatisfaction with grades received on farmers' cars had been one of the principal factors, it will be recalled, which led the Territorial Department of Agriculture, at the request of the Grain Growers' Association, to send an official in 1904 to observe the work of the Inspection Department at Winnipeg, and which later led Sintaluta farmers to send Partridge as their own confidential "observer." [2] Now that a farmers' company was handling farmers' cars on the central market, its directors felt that an additional service could be rendered to shippers by checking the government grades. There was no sample market in Winnipeg, and

[1] During the crop year 1913–14 the company collected 525 claims, amounting to $30,195, on behalf of its customers. *Farmers in Business, 1906–1916*, p. 11.

[2] See *supra*, p. 43.

no commercial sampling bureaus such as were to be found at Minneapolis, where millers rather than exporters are the principal buyers. On the Winnipeg market, therefore, government grades not only were final, but were also the only basis of trading. There appeared to be no reason to question the conscientiousness of the hard-worked government officials, but where grading was based on a purely physical examination of hastily probed samples from cars in the railway yards,[1] the possibility of individual error or variation in inspection during the height of the grain rush, was by no means negligible. If the shipper was not satisfied with grade received on his inspection certificate, there was rarely time for him, acting individually, to obtain reinspection before the identity of his shipment was submerged in the terminal bins.

The Grain Growers' Company, therefore, secured the services of a former official of the government Inspection Department to take charge of a Sampling Department of its own. At first the company employed men to follow up the government sampling crews in the Winnipeg yards, and take duplicate samples against which the official grades could be checked. Later, this practice had to be discontinued when other grain firms sought to do the same for their customers, and the railway companies, concerned lest cars should be unduly delayed in transit thereby, withdrew the privilege altogether.[2] The Grain Growers' Sampling Department continued, however, to check the government grades, by comparing the filed samples at the Winnipeg Inspection office with the inspection certificate for each car. Whenever in the opinion of their expert the car was entitled to higher grade, reinspection or survey was immediately called for. Shippers were encouraged to notify the company of the grade they expected when sending in their bill of lading, although the company's officials generally used their own judgment in applying for reinspection.[3] Thus, in regard both to railway claims and grading, the Grain Growers' Company was able to look after the interests of its patrons in a

[1] The method of insepction and reinspection is fully described in R. Magill, *Grain Inspection in Western Canada*.

[2] Evidence of J. R. Murray (United Grain Growers) before Royal Grain Inquiry Commission, Winnipeg, March 10, 1924.

[3] *Farmers in Business*, pp. 10, 11.

way that was impossible to the individual shipper. As competition led other concerns seeking consignment of farmers' cars, to reproduce the services initiated by the Grain Growers' Company, the benefits became gradually generalized.

The Genesis of the Grain Growers' Guide. — In the effort to increase the number of its farmer shareholders and enlarge its patronage, the Grain Growers' Company had issued a number of pamphlets and prospectuses. In the minds of the directors the need was being increasingly felt for a medium of regular contact with farmers, which might educate them in the organization and technique of grain marketing and of the part played in it by the farmers' company; which might answer criticisms and misrepresentations circulated by those interested in discrediting it; and which might carry on the necessary educational preparation for the various subsidiary coöperative enterprises contemplated. At the same time, the provincial Grain Growers' organizations, which in 1907 had united to form an Interprovincial Council,[1] had for some time been discussing the establishment of an organ of their own. Their claims and declarations might find periodic expression in the resolutions of annual conventions, and, under emergency, in the more insistent presentations of deputations to the provincial or federal governments. It was felt by the leaders, however, that the full advantages of organization could not be realized without some medium of continuous contact between the officers and the rank and file of the membership, through which intelligent as well as united action might be developed.

The Grain Growers' Company was in a better position to finance such an organ than the provincial associations. On the other hand, it was felt by President Crerar and most of his fellow directors that the proposed publication would carry much more representative weight and fill a much broader function if it were issued as the official organ of the Grain Growers' Associations. After considerable discussion and conference, a joint committee of directors of the Grain Growers' Company and the Manitoba Grain Growers' Association was appointed, which decided to publish a monthly

[1] The constituent bodies were the Manitoba Grain Growers' Association, the Saskatchewan Grain Growers' Association, and the Alberta Farmers' Association.

under the name of the *Grain Growers' Guide*, to appear as the official organ of the Manitoba Association, but to be financed and managed by the Grain Growers' Company. Partridge, who was appointed provisional editor by the committee, desired to amalgamate the *Guide* with the *Voice*, the official organ of the Western labor unions, and in the first number, which appeared in June, 1908, he set forth its aims in the following terms:

> The purpose of the *Guide's* publication is to aid in the discussion of the economic and social problems which confront us, to assist in unifying opinion among our farmers and other workers as to what it is necessary to do in order that they and we may come to enjoy to the full the fruits of our labors, and having thus unified us in opinion, to serve as a trumpet in marshalling our forces for the accomplishing of whatever has been decided is best to be done.

In this statement are apparent the visionary social aims and propagandist purpose of Partridge,[1] and his desire to join hands with Labor. This latter concept of the *Guide's* function was not shared, however, by the majority of his associates, and Partridge, burdened with other duties in the Grain Growers' movement, and ever resentful of non-concurrence with his views, resigned after the first issue. The July number never appeared. A temporary editorial successor was found, however, in Roderick McKenzie, who had been secretary of the Manitoba Grain Growers' Association since its inauguration in 1903. In the second year, it was decided to issue the *Guide* as a weekly, and an associate editor was appointed in the person of George F. Chipman, a journalist of Nova Scotia farm origin, who as legislative reporter of the *Manitoba Free Press* had shown an intelligent sympathy with the Grain Growers' movement. In 1910 Chipman was appointed to full editorial responsibility, in order to permit McKenzie to devote his whole attention to his expanding duties as secretary of the Manitoba Grain Growers' Association.[2]

Relation of the Guide to the Grain Growers' Movement. — The Interprovincial Council of Grain Growers' Associations at a meet-

[1] Partridge's views on "the coöperative commonwealth" find characteristic expression in a volume published by him in 1926, entitled *A War on Poverty*.

[2] McKenzie continued as secretary of the M. G. G. A. until 1916, when he resigned to become secretary of the Canadian Council of Agriculture. G. F. Chipman has edited the *Guide* continuously since 1910.

ing in May, 1908, had endorsed the action of the Grain Growers' Company in undertaking "to finance a non-political paper," which would deal independently "with economic and social questions affecting the farmers' well-being." Shortly after the *Guide's* appearance, the Saskatchewan Grain Growers' Association and the Alberta Farmers' Association followed the Manitoba Association in adopting it as their joint official organ. Thereafter a special department was reserved in each issue for organization news of the three provincial associations, conducted by their respective secretaries. Deficits incurred in publication, which were fairly heavy at first, were absorbed by the Grain Growers' Company, whose directors regarded this as one form in which the trading profits might be distributed for the benefit of Western farmers as a whole. In 1909 the company decided to establish its own publishing plant. This involved the incorporation of the Public Press Limited, as the first of several subsidiary enterprises which the Grain Growers' Grain Company was soon to establish and control. With facilities for engaging in commercial printing as well as publishing the Grain Growers' organ, the Public Press was placed in a position where it might become self-financing within a reasonable time.

The serviceability of the *Guide* as a publicity arm of the Grain Growers' Company was demonstrated on at least two somewhat conspicuous occasions during the second year of its existence. In the fall of 1909 a series of letters, purporting to be from a farmer writing under the name of "Observer," began to appear in two Winnipeg newspapers and three farm journals. It soon became apparent that the aim of these letters was to create suspicion among farmers as to the motives and methods of those directing the farmers' company. Chipman's journalistic instinct promptly detected the hand of a press agent working in the interests of the "elevator combine." Concentrating on certain clues, he succeeded in identifying the pseudo-farmer "Observer" and establishing the terms of his publicity contract with certain elevator owners, together with the fact that the publication of the letters had been paid for at advertising rates. Through the columns of the *Guide*, Chipman published a complete exposé of the "conspiracy," with the photographs of those concerned. So great was the indignation of farmer readers, that cancellation of subscriptions to the papers which had published the "Observer" letters reached disturbing proportions, and the publication of the articles was discontinued.[1] It was evident that those interested in disrcediting the Grain Growers' Company must henceforth reckon with the *Guide*.

Suspension of Commission Rule by the Exchange. — The loyalty of farmers to their own trading company was presently exposed to a much more searching test than the disruptive influence of press innuendoes. This arose out of the decision of the Grain Exchange, at the instance of the elevator interests, to suspend the commission rule during the crop year of 1909–10. Under the successive amendments to the Manitoba Grain Act designed to increase the facilities and safeguards for shipping grain over platform on consignment, the line elevator companies were experiencing an increasing diversion of farmers' grain to track buyers and commission firms.[2] As the latter operations did not require any appreciable capital investment, beyond the purchase price of a seat on the Exchange, entrance into the field was fairly easy and profitable, as Partridge had shrewdly discerned. As noted elsewhere, it had been with a view to limiting the competition of the commission men that the rule prohibiting the employment of local buying or soliciting agents, except on a salary basis of not less than $50 a month, had been inserted in the commission by-law through the influence of the elevator interests.[3] The rescinding of that clause in 1907 had been due to the pressure of the commission members of the Exchange, as well as of the Grain Growers' Association and the Manitoba government.

So persistently had the commission rule been criticized both

[1] See *G. G. Guide*, 10th Anniversary Number (June 26, 1918), p. 2.

[2] The amendments to the Grain Act, passed in 1908 in accordance with the Royal Grain Commission Report of 1907, further stimulated this tendency. During the crop year 1907–08, 22 per cent of all wheat inspected had been shipped over platform. In the months immediately following the 1908 legislation, the Warehouse Commissioner gave orders for the construction or enlargement of 100 loading platforms. Statement of C. C. Castle, Warehouse Commissioner, 1908.

[3] See *supra*, p. 57.

without and within the Exchange, and so frequent were the suspected cases of evasion by members sharing the one cent commission with local agents, that the elevator and milling company interests on the reorganized Exchange succeeded in carrying through a resolution in 1909 to suspend the commission rule altogether for a "trial" period of one year, and to put trade on a "free for all" basis. Since the line elevator companies derived revenue, not only from commission operations, but also from trading in street grain and from storage both at country houses and controlled terminal elevators, they could afford to handle farmers' cars for half a cent a bushel, or even for nothing; whereas the commission firms, like the Grain Growers' Company, had to depend entirely on their commissions for their income.

Attitude of Grain Growers' Company. — The menace involved in the suspension of the commission rule was at once apprehended by the officers of the Grain Growers' Company. They could not continue to do business unless they received their regular commissions. If the willingness of the elevator companies to handle farmers' grain for a few dollars less a car should prove too strong a present inducement for grain growers to resist, not only would their company be forced out of business, but they would be reduced to their former dependence on the line companies, who could then restore the regular handling charge. The only hope of retaining the loyalty of their shareholders and patrons appeared to lie in placing the facts and implications fully and frankly before them. A spirited circular exposing "the conspiracy of the Elevator Combine" was mailed to each shareholder, and a referendum submitted on three questions:

1. Should the old rate be maintained by the company in spite of the action of the Exchange?
2. Should the commission rate be reduced by the company?
3. Should the matter be left to the discretion of the directors?

The contents of the referendum pamphlet were effectively supplemented by the editorials of the *Guide*, which vigorously took up the cudgels against the "elevator combine," supporting its charges with reports of Grain Exchange proceedings and with interviews and statements of elevator officials and representative grain men, while farmers' letters were freely published. Seventy-five per cent of the company's shareholders replied to the referendum. Of these over 98 per cent expressed themselves in favor of either retaining the regular commission charge or leaving the matter to the discretion of the directors.[1] On the strength of these assurances the directors announced that they would maintain the regular one-cent rate on wheat, while reducing the charge to three-quarters of a cent on barley and one-half cent on oats.

The result of the year's trading during the suspension of the commission rule fully justified the directors' confidence in the loyalty of their shareholders. Whereas in 1908–09 the company had handled 7,643,146 bushels, its turnover in this year of "free for all" trading amounted to 16,332,645 bushels, approximately 15 per cent of the total number of cars inspected in Western Canada during the crop year 1909–10. The profits for the year exceeded $95,000.[2]

Significance of the Episode. — At the end of the year the Exchange voted to restore the commission rule. In so far as its suspension may have been calculated to eliminate or embarrass commission firms like the Grain Growers' Company, it had reacted to the advantage instead of the detriment of the latter, thanks in no small measure to the value of the *Guide* as an auxiliary arm. In so far, however, as the action of the Exchange members had been contemplated as a means of demonstrating the desirability of the commission rule, their object was effectively accomplished. Under the conditions of "free for all" trading, the commission men discovered the extent to which a uniform commission rule was in their interest. Two years previously the Manitoba Grain Growers had appealed to the court against the commission rule as an undue agreement in restraint of competition, and had pressed the Manitoba legislature to neutralize it by amending the charter of the Exchange. Now the Grain Growers' Company and the *Grain*

[1] *Farmers in Business*, p. 6. The nature of the shareholders' response is reflected by the following comment accompanying one farmer's ballot: "I will pledge myself to ship every bushel of grain I grow to the Farmers' Company, even though the directors find it necessary to charge me five cents per bushel, coin." Cited by Moorhouse, *op. cit.*, p. 155.

[2] G. G. G. Co., 1910.

Growers' Guide were found appealing to farmers to uphold the rule in the interests of fair competition. As members of a grain trading company on the Exchange, the farmers had become firm advocates of a rule which as growers they had formerly denounced as being monopolistic in intent and effect. Perhaps to even a greater extent than Partridge had anticipated, participation in the organized grain trade was proving educative as well as remunerative to the farmers' company.

PART II

THE FARMERS' CO-OPERATIVE ELEVATOR COMPANIES, 1911–1923

CHAPTER VII

THE ELEVATOR ISSUE IN MANITOBA

I. Agitation for Government Ownership of Elevators

The early efforts of the organized Grain Growers, we have seen, were immediately concerned with combatting the monopolistic control of the line elevators over the marketing of grain at country points. The fight for flat warehouses, loading platforms, equality in car-distribution, and a regulating Warehouse Commissioner with progressively widened powers, had been prosecuted primarily with a view to securing for the grain grower alternative methods of shipping and selling that would make him less dependent on the elevator companies. The extension of these facilities under the administration of the Manitoba Grain Act with its successive amendments, and under the competitive multiplication of railway shipping points, had resulted in a marked increase in the number and business of commission and track buying firms. It was the very keenness of this competition which had led the elevator interests to secure the amendment of the commission rule of the Grain Exchange, and, later, to bring about its temporary suspension.[1] With the establishment of the Grain Growers' Grain Company farmers could not merely ship direct to the Winnipeg market, but could also have their shipments handled on that market by their own company, whose profits they might share.

Basis of Grain Growers' Demands for Government Ownership of Elevators. — While the increase in the proportion of grain shipped over platform was very marked during these years, the essential utility of the standard elevator as a factor in grain marketing could not be disregarded. Even under the special protection afforded by the Grain Act, the flat warehouse was disappearing as a competitive medium.[2] Loading over platform was not con-

[1] See *supra*, pp. 73, 74.

[2] See *supra*, p. 30.

venient for farmers who had long distances to haul their grain; nor did this method permit grain to be weighed or cleaned before loading. Its use, moreover, generally involved the hiring or procuring of extra teams and labor in order to load the car within the twenty-four hours allowed. Economically, the elevator offered the advantages of permitting the gradual accumulation of carload quantities in storage, of providing weighing and cleaning facilities, and of greatly abridging the labor of handling and shipping. Where a grower could secure special bin accommodation, by which the identity of his grain could be preserved, and official grade and dockage obtained, he generally found it more advantageous to pay the elevator handling and storage charges of $1\frac{3}{4}$ cents a bushel than to load his own car over platform. From the warehouseman's viewpoint, however, special binning was not favored, since it permitted less grain to be stored in proportion to the potential capacity of the elevator than did the method of graded storage. It was only exceptionally, therefore, that the grower was able to obtain special bin storage from line elevators.

Although the regulation imposed by the Manitoba Grain Act under the administration of the Warehouse Commissioner, and the competition afforded by direct shipment, had tended to limit the more palpable grievances of grain growers in regard to the operation of country elevators, most farmers felt that abuses were bound to persist so long as elevators were interested in buying and selling grain on their own account as well as in handling farmers' stored grain. Where the same operator was a grain buyer and private warehouseman as well as a public warehouseman, he was inevitably more or less under pressure, it was contended, to promote the interests of elevator owners at the expense of elevator patrons. Where, moreover, the majority of country elevators, and a large proportion of terminal storage as well, were owned by a few line companies and millers, it lay within the power of such concerted interests to determine the spread on street grain, since they alone controlled the facilities for handling it. It was on these premises that increasing support was developing in Grain Growers' organizations for the principle—of which Partridge was the leading exponent — of government ownership and operation of elevators as public utilities, with country buyers in the same position as farmer shippers in respect to binning accommodation. If an elevator monopoly were inevitable, a government monopoly was preferred. Provincial operation of elevators at initial shipping points, and federal operation of terminal and transfer elevators, was the solution proposed in the "Partridge Plan."

A request that the government of Manitoba should adopt the principle of public ownership and operation of country elevators had been coupled with the demand for legislative amendment of the charter of the Grain Exchange at the time of the exclusion of the Grain Growers' Company. At the provincial conference held in June, 1907, to which these matters were referred, a resolution was passed, after the withdrawal of the protesting Grain Exchange representatives,[1] urging the provincial government "to acquire and operate a complete system of storage elevators throughout the province."[2] At the 1908 convention of the Manitoba Grain Growers a detailed scheme of "Provincial Ownership and Operation of a System of Line Elevators," prepared mainly under Patridge's inspiration, was presented and endorsed.[3] The initial issue of the *Grain Growers' Guide*[4] was largely devoted to the propagation of the plan.

Interprovincial Character of Agitation. — In the demand for public ownership of elevators the Manitoba Grain Growers did not stand alone. In Saskatchewan, which was now rapidly overtaking Manitoba's lead in wheat production,[5] and in which elevator competition was as yet less developed, the principle of government ownership had been approved by the 1907 convention of the Saskatchewan Grain Growers' Association, in the form of a resolution calling on the federal government to take over the terminal elevators and construct interior storage elevators.[6] In Al-

[1] See *supra*, p. 59.
[2] *Manitoba Free Press*, June 7, 1907.
[3] M. G. G. A., 1908 (appendix).
[4] June, 1908, the only number edited by Partridge; see *supra*, p. 71.
[5] Saskatchewan definitely passed Manitoba in wheat acreage and production in 1909.
[6] S. G. G. A., 1907. Interior storage elevators were demanded primarily with a view to the establishment of a sample market at Winnipeg. The scheme was adversely reported on by the Royal Grain Commission of 1906–07.

berta, where spring wheat-growing was now beginning to assume significant proportions, the Alberta Farmers' Association had also declared itself in favor of a government interior storage elevator at Calgary.[1] The Interprovincial Council of Grain Growers' and Farmers' Associations, formed in 1907, gave special consideration to the subject, and in 1908 urged the executives of the three provincial associations to wait upon their respective governments and obtain a declaration of policy. General endorsment of the "Partridge Plan" was registered at the three conventions in 1908, and committees appointed to draft a detailed scheme.

In view of the concurrent demands in three prairie provinces, a conference of the three Western premiers[2] was held at Regina in May (1908), on the initiative of Mr. Roblin, to consider joint action in regard to the joint demands of their insistent farmer electors. A counter proposal,[3] that the three provincial governments should use their efforts to influence the railways to build loading elevators with special binning facilities for farmers, having been rejected as "totally inadequate" by the Interprovincial Council, the three premiers, after meeting directly with the Grain Growers' representatives at Regina in November, undertook to make a joint reply after cabinet consultation. The Grain Growers hoped that this might lead to uniform public ownership legislation and that the three provincial governments would unite in urging the federal authorities to take over the terminal elevators.

Constitutional Aspects. — In their written reply to the Interprovincial Council at the end of January (1909), the three premiers took the view that the Grain Growers' demands involved the creation of a government monopoly in the storage, weighing, and handling of grain, which, "in addition to being extra-territorial in effect, would be dealing with some of the matters as to which the Parliament of Canada has exclusive jurisdiction." The finan-

[1] See *infra*, p. 118.

[2] Hon. Rodmond Roblin (Manitoba); Hon. Walter Scott (Saskatchewan); and Hon. A. C. Rutherford (Alberta).

[3] Mediated through Mr. George Langley, who occupied a seat in the Saskatchewan legislature, as well as on the directorate of the S. G. G. A. *Manitoba Free Press*, Jan. 30, 1909.

cial as well as the constitutional difficulties were emphasized, the estimated cost of acquiring the 1334 licensed country elevators being placed at between seven and ten million dollars — a formidable commitment, especially for the newly erected provinces of Saskatchewan and Alberta. The communication closed with the specious assurance that

> upon the procurement of the necessary amendments to the British North America Act, giving the provinces powers to completely establish and control a public monopoly in storage, handling, and inspection of grain, we are quite willing to endeavour, subject to the approval of our respective assemblies, to frame a scheme, financially safeguarded for giving effect to the desire of your executive.[1]

In conformity with this declaration the premiers of Manitoba and Alberta introduced resolutions in their respective assemblies that the Governor-General in Council be memorialized in regard to the elevator question and asked to provide government ownership and operation, or to have the necessary powers to deal with the storage, transportation, and grading of grain conferred upon the provinces by special Dominion or Imperial legislation.[2] It was thus sought to place the onus of the elevator issue upon the federal authorities.

The Grain Growers' executives refused to be silenced, however, by the alleged constitutional difficulties. The Interprovincial Council replied that it did not ask the governments to assume a complete monopoly of grain handling, but merely to acquire sufficient storage to provide growers at each shipping point with the desired facilities under public operation. The preference of farmers for such a system would ensure the patronage necessary to safeguard the financial commitments of the provinces, without the assumption of a legal monopoly.[3] In the legal opinion rendered by R. A. Bonnar, the Grain Growers' counsel, it was claimed that each province could handle the ownership problem separately without infringing on federal prerogatives.[4]

[1] *Manitoba Free Press*, Jan. 30, 1909.

[2] Journal, Legislative Assembly of Alberta, Feb. 24, 1909; Journal, Legislative Assembly of Manitoba, March 4, 1909.

[3] *Manitoba Free Press*, March 1, 1909.

[4] *G. G. Guide*, Aug. 3, 1909.

In endeavoring to meet the premiers' constitutional objections, the Grain Growers had virtually declared for a modified provincial scheme. The joint negotiations between the Interprovincial Council and the "Premiers-in-Council" were succeeded therefore by the efforts of the three provincial associations to obtain action from their respective governments independently. The "diplomatic unity" of the Western premiers was also terminated when Premier Scott notified Mr. Roblin and Mr. Rutherford, as the provincial legislatures were about to assemble, that he deemed it advisable that each government should settle the elevator problem in its own way.[1] The separate solutions worked out in Manitoba, Saskatchewan, and Alberta were to prove of very considerable significance to Western grain growers. The nature and course of the experiments followed in each province will be considered in turn in the remainder of this chapter and in the two following.

II. The Manitoba Government Elevator System

Elevator Policy of Roblin Government. — By the end of 1909 the Roblin administration in Manitoba, which in the previous year had embarked on government ownership of telephones, decided to give government ownership of elevators a trial.[2] On December 16 the Minister of Education in the Roblin cabinet appeared at the seventh annual convention of the Manitoba Grain Growers' Association at Brandon, and announced that the government of Manitoba "has adopted the policy and accepted the principle laid down by the Grain Growers' Association of establishing a line of internal elevators as a public utility, owned and operated by the public," and "is prepared to coöperate with your association in working out a plan to that end."[3] For this purpose the association was invited to name representatives "to discuss the proposition in all its details with the government." This unexpected announcement was received with great enthusiasm by the

[1] *G. G. Guide*, Dec. 29, 1909.

[2] This decision was, doubtless, influenced by the result of a by-election at Birtle, in which a Grain Grower candidate had been returned mainly on the issue of government ownership of elevators.

[3] *Manitoba Free Press*, Dec. 17, 1909.

convention. Second consideration suggested, however, the possible danger of too great a government interest in the enterprise announced. By way of defining its position clearly, the convention adopted a resolution declaring "that the administration of such a system of elevators should be by a commission completely independent of political influence and control, and responsible directly to the people." [1] The directors of the association, together with President Crerar and Vice-President Kennedy of the Grain Growers' Company, were authorized to represent the Grain Growers in the elaboration of details with the government.[2]

Attitude of Manitoba Grain Growers. — On January 5 (1910) the Grain Growers' representatives submitted a memorandum to the government. Their plan laid upon the government the responsibility of providing the necessary funds (estimated at between two and three million dollars) for the acquisition or construction of adequate storage accommodation at each shipping point, existing elevators to be purchased "upon a fair valuation of their actual business worth as public utilities, as determined by the commission." [3] Control of the system should be vested in an independent commission of three members, nominated by the Grain Growers' Association and appointed by the government. Commissioners would be removable only by a two-thirds vote of the legislature, or by decision of the provincial Court of Appeal. Elevators acquired or built would be operated purely as public warehouses, and as far as possible on a special binning basis. Operators would be required to take and preserve samples of each wagonload of grain delivered, and where requested to do so by the owner, to forward another identified sample to a sample room to be maintained by the commission at Winnipeg, from which sales might be made on buyers' inspection, as an alternative to sale by government grade. The commission would be responsible for delivery of grain in conformity with sample preserved and weights entered into cars at initial points. Country buyers of street grain would be in the same position as farmer shippers in

[1] *G. G. Guide*, Dec. 29, 1909; M. G. G. A., 1909.
[2] *G. G. Guide*, Jan. 12, 1910.
[3] Text of memorandum in *Grain Growers' Guide*, Jan. 12, 1910.

the allotment of binning space. The Grain Growers' scheme thus placed the financial responsibility upon the government, and the control in the hands of a commission named by, but not responsible to, themselves. The advantages of the services and guarantees provided by the system were deemed to be sufficient to assure the patronage necessary to make it self-supporting.

When the government's draft bill [1] appeared, it revealed divergence from the Grain Growers' scheme in three significant respects. In the first place, it provided that the powers conferred on the commission in respect to the acquisition and construction of elevators should be exercised under the direction of the Minister of Public Works, and that the commissioners should "only be removable by order of the Lieutenant-Governor-in-Council, made for cause." It was provided in the second place, that where the commission and the owner of an elevator should be unable to arrive at a purchase price by agreement, valuation should be determined under the proceedings of the Manitoba Expropriation Act. Thirdly, it contained a local option provision whereby no purchase, lease, or construction of an elevator would be undertaken by the commission, unless it had previously received a petition to do so, "signed by at least sixty per cent of the growers contributory to such proposed elevator." In the case of elevators to be constructed, a pledge of patronage was also required from the petitioners.

These features were strongly opposed by the Grain Growers, through deputation, through the *Guide*, and through their legal adviser, Mr. Bonnar, during the committee stage of the bill's progress. Objection was specially pronounced in regard to the principle of a cabinet-controlled commission as opposed to a commission answerable to the legislature.[2] The government insisted, however, that in assuming the financial responsibility for the scheme, it must, in accordance with the principle of ministerial responsi-

[1] Text in *Manitoba Free Press*, Feb. 25, 1910.

[2] "We say control should be in the legislature; your bill says it is in the government. . . . If you are fully determined to carry out your scheme, while we are very sorry to say so, we cannot assume the responsibility in connection with it, because we feel it would be a failure." R. A. Bonnar to House Agricultural Committee, March 10, 1910.

bility, retain control of a commission expending public moneys. The supervision of the Minister of Public Works over the acquisition of elevators was criticized as tending to involve political considerations in purchase negotiations, while the arbitration provision was objected to as likely to favor the elevator owners.[1] The sixty-per-cent petition clause, it was claimed, would necessitate organized campaigns in each locality. The government insisted, however, that in view of the fact that the Grain Growers' membership did not include more than a fifth of the farmers of the province,[2] it would be justified in acquiring or building elevators only at points where the desire of local farmers for publicly owned elevators was sufficiently manifest to give assurance of patronage. With certain minor concessions these three features were retained in the act, which became law on March 16, 1910.[3]

Appointment of Manitoba Elevator Commission. — Although seriously disappointing the farmers in its policy of commission control, the government solicited the coöperation of the Grain Growers' Association by inviting that body to submit four names for the consideration of the cabinet in the appointment of the commissioners. On receiving this invitation the Elevator Committee of the Grain Growers' Association expressed its attitude in the following resolution:

> That while this committee still adheres to the principle declared in its former resolutions, believing that they are principles consistent with good government and necessary, irrespective of party, for the highest standard of efficiency in the administration of public affairs, we accept the invitation of the government to this committee to nominate commissioners, and urge all grain growers and farmers of the province to coöperate to secure the greatest possible success under the present act.[4]

---

[1] "Eventually it would be left to a judge of the court to appoint the third (arbitrator). He would very likely select some corporation manager or financial man, and that would mean, we think, that you would have two elevator interests against one farmer interest." R. A. Bonnar to House Agricultural Committee, March 10, 1910.

[2] The membership of the M. G. G. A. was reported at the 1909 convention as approximately 7,000. The number of occupied farms in Manitoba according to the 1906 census was 36,141.

[3] Statutes of Manitoba, 10 Edw. VII, c. 27.

[4] *G. G. Guide*, March 30, 1910.

When the personnel of the Commission was finally announced on May 17, two of the Grain Growers' nominees were found to be included.[1] General surprise was created, however, by the appointment as chairman of D. W. McCuaig, President of the Manitoba Grain Growers' Association. Such acceptance involved a repudiation of the "self-denying ordinance" embodied in the Grain Growers' draft bill,[2] and in a self-imposed resolution of the directors. By this astute move in persuading the leader of the Grain Growers' campaign for public ownership of elevators to assume the chairmanship of the Commission, the government evidently sought to place the chief responsibility in the public mind, for the outcome of the scheme upon the Grain Growers themselves.

Between the appointment of the Commission and the commencement of the 1910 crop movement, requests for petition forms (under the local option clause) were received from 240 stations, or 80 per cent of the grain-shipping points in the province — a significant indication of the generality of the farmers' demand for publicly owned elevators. Before the end of the year 163 elevators had been purchased throughout the province, being financed from the proceeds of twenty-year 4 per cent debentures. Forty petitions were received for the construction of new elevators. Of these the Commission erected ten, in which liberal provision was made for special binning. The total investment was slightly in excess of one million dollars.[3]

Failure of the Government Scheme. — The financial results of the operations of the Manitoba Elevator Commission proved nothing short of disastrous. The report covering the crop year 1910–11 showed a total deficit (after providing for maintenance and interest) of $84,145, revenue covering only 55 per cent of operating

[1] The four names submitted by the M. G. G. A. were (in order of preference) John Kennedy, Vice-President G. G. G. Co.; F. B. MacLennan, grain merchant; E. S. Estlin, elevator engineer; and W. C. Graham, manager Farmers' Mutual Hail Insurance Co. Messrs. MacLennan and Graham were appointed by the government. *Manitoba Free Press*, May 18, 1910.

[2] "No present or future director of the said Grain Growers' Association shall be eligible for appointment as commissioner unless he shall have ceased to be a member of the Association for a period of one year prior to the appointment." Quoted, *Manitoba Free Press*, May 18, 1910.

[3] Report of Manitoba Elevator Commission, *Sessional Paper*, No. 13, 1911.

expenses and fixed charges.[1] Official returns for 1911–12 were never published, but the deficit, for the two years, on operation and upkeep alone, without any provision for capital charges, was announced as $19,066.[2] In the debate on the first year's report in the legislature, Premier Roblin laid the responsibility for the unfavorable results upon the Grain Growers themselves:

> The Grain Growers sent a large delegation here, and said they spoke for the farmers of Manitoba. I took the voice of the demagogue for the voice of the public, and consequently I made a mistake. The Elevator Commission is controlled by the man who was president of the organization which led the agitation and made me believe the public wanted government-owned elevators. Experience has shown that the farmers as a whole never wanted them, for they do not patronize them. We have elevators which cost us nearly $12,000 where only nine cars were shipped up to January, 31 1912. The farmers used the loading platforms instead of putting their grain through our elevators. The policy of government is to build or buy no more elevators.[3]

The Grain Growers on their part attributed the poor showing of the public elevators to the government's disregard of their representations in respect to the independence of the Commission, and the method of acquisition. Their contention of political interference with the work of the Commission was supported by the leader of the Opposition in the legislature, who claimed that, after the commissioners had acquired the first few elevators on reasonable terms, the Minister of Public Works took over the purchasing, acquiring properties of dubious utility and resorting to arbitration.[4] Political interference was also cited in the appointment of local operators, and was given as the cause of the resignation of the only experienced grain man on the Commission (Mr. MacLennan) after the first year's operation.[5]

[1] *Manitoba Free Press*, March 13, 1912.

[2] *Ibid.*, Jan. 29, 1913.

[3] *Ibid.*, April 4, 1912.

[4] "The first government elevators were purchased on a basis of 12½¢ per bushel capacity; later on they were paid for at the rate of 20¢ per bushel capacity. In Griswold the government had purchased for $4,000 the oldest elevator in the town. About two weeks afterwards two more Griswold elevators were bought. To date, the government has paid from $15,000 to $16,000 for elevators in Griswold, from which there had been shipped up to the end of August last, 23,000 bushels of wheat." Speech of T. C. Morris in Manitoba Legislature, *Manitoba Free Press*, April 4, 1912.

[5] *G. G. Guide*, April 10, 1912.

There is little doubt that the Manitoba government elevators as a whole were overcapitalized. It would have been an exceptional experience indeed if the entry of a government body in the field as a purchaser on an extensive scale had not resulted in advancing purchase prices, even under arbitration. The Commission's own report showed that the average price for the fifteen elevators acquired by direct negotiation was 12.24 cents per bushel capacity, whereas the price for those purchased by arbitration averaged 20 cents.[1] A number of elevators also appear to have been superfluous or unsuitable. Only 97 of the Commission's 174 elevators were in use during the whole of the first season, while some were never operated at all.[2] The further fact that these 174 elevators were distributed over no more than 100 shipping points is on the face of it indicative of a measure of local duplication.[3]

While political interference and overcapitalization are more or less familiar features of government-owned enterprises in general, the statutory conditions under which the Manitoba elevator system was established were such as to make losses in its operation more or less inevitable. If a monopoly could have been constitutionally vested in the government, and if such powers had been used to acquire all the essential initial elevators on a strictly public utility valuation, it is possible that, with competition removed, they might under reasonably efficient management have paid their way as public warehouses from storage and handling revenues. But the government system enjoyed neither a monopoly nor competitive equality with line companies. The latter could supplement their storage earnings with their profits on street purchases and their selling commissions. Where they owned terminal elevators as well, the country houses could be operated primarily as "feeders," and the main profit be derived from terminal storage charges, and from merchandising, with or without "mixing." Still less was the government system in a position

[1] *Manitoba Sessional Paper*, No. 15, 1911. The prices for all elevators purchased from line companies were arrived at by arbitration.

[2] *Ibid.*, No. 24, 1912.

[3] *Ibid.*, No. 18, 1911.

to compete with the milling companies, whose elevators were virtually unaffected by the government expropriation proceedings.

Depending therefore for their revenue entirely on storage and handling charges, — for which the maximum rate fixed by the Grain Act allowed the narrowest of margins, — the government elevators could hope to be self-supporting only by handling grain to the extent of three or four times their capacity in the course of the year.[1] This condition signally failed of being realized.[2] The duplication of Commission elevators at local points was not in itself conducive to the realization of maximum business per unit, while the requirement of special binning facilities did not favor the maximum utilization of storage capacity. The potential patronage, moreover, was limited by the very conditions of operation. Since the Commission's elevators were intended to be operated on a special binning instead of a graded storage basis,[3] they were of little advantage to the growers with less than a carload to ship, except where two or more might agree to bin and ship their grain jointly. For wagonload sellers they were serviceable only where a local buyer had made arrangements to have his purchased grain stored therein.[4] Under monopoly conditions all street grain would necessarily have passed through the public elevators. Under the system of optional acquisition, however, most elevator companies which turned over their houses to the Commission ceased buying at such points. The farmer with less than a carload to market usually hauled his grain, therefore, to the unacquired houses of milling or line elevator companies. On the other hand, the large grower (unless he had a long distance to haul his wheat or heavy dockage to be cleaned out) generally preferred to save the elevator handling charge by shipping over the

[1] See evidence in this connection in Report of Saskatchewan Elevator Commission, 1910, pp. 42–53.

[2] During the year 1910–11 only 97 of the Commission's 174 elevators received grain, the total receipts aggregating only 5,051,922 bushels, an average of 29,068 bushels for each elevator owned, and 52,144 bushels for each elevator operated. *Manitoba Sessional Paper*, No. 24, 1912. The average capacity of country elevators in Manitoba was approximately 30,000 bushels.

[3] Manitoba Elevator Act, 1910, secs. 19, 20.

[4] *Ibid.*, sec. 18.

platform.[1] The Commission elevators were, therefore, patronized chiefly by farmers who wanted special binning or local cleaning, or who hoped to sell by sample.[2]

Where the government elevators effected no distinct advantage to the grain grower, the fact of his subscribing to the local petition for acquisition was found to be insufficient in itself to ensure his patronage. It was only in the case of applications for construction of new elevators that a patronage pledge was called for under the act, and even this was nugatory, since it was accompanied by no penalties.[3] Without either financial or legal responsibility in the matter, mere considerations of consistency were not adequate to sustain the patronage of Manitoba farmers, where no perceptible advantage accrued therefrom, and where their confidence in the system had been weakened through obvious political interference. With the volume of business thus restricted there was lacking the one condition on which depended the possibility of making the government elevators pay on a storing and shipping basis only.

III. Outcome of the Manitoba Elevator Experiment

Negotiations for Lease of Elevators to Grain Growers' Grain Company. — The government of Manitoba having found — or demonstrated, as its critics averred — after two years of experimental operation that public ownership of elevators meant a continuing public liability, now sought to transfer the responsibility for their future operation to the grain growers themselves. During the spring of 1912, therefore, negotiations were conducted with the Grain Growers' Grain Company, with a view to leasing the government elevators to the farmers' company. To these negotiations the latter was by no means a reluctant party, for to an in-

[1] From Sept. 30, 1911 to Jan. 31, 1912, 2,360 cars were loaded from government elevator points, while 5,279 carloads were shipped over loading platforms from the same points. Hon. R. Roblin in Manitoba Legislature, April 3, 1912.

[2] The Commission's sample room was little patronized, as most of the large milling companies had their own buying elevators, and exporters preferred to buy on government grade.

[3] Manitoba Elevator Act, sec. 21.

creasing extent its directors had been realizing the handicap it sustained in competing as a mere trading agency with the line elevator companies for the farmers' grain. These limitations had been explicitly indicated by President Crerar at the shareholders' annual meeting of the preceding year:

> I have before frequently pointed out that the possession of the country elevators gives the elevator companies a very strong lever in working against us. It is common knowledge that, in order to get the handling of a farmer's grain, country elevator operators, acting no doubt under instructions from their superiors, will offer every inducement possible. I might instance as chief of these the loading of grain through their elevators into cars free of charge, and the holding of it — often for considerable periods — free of storage. . . . It is quite possible for them to conduct their business at country points at a loss and still recoup themselves very handsomely from the profits at the terminal elevators. This they can do without in any way resorting to making profits by improper practices such as mixing of grades. A company operating country elevators and owning a terminal elevator — as they nearly all do — can buy a farmer's car in the country, apparently without profit, and ship it down to their terminal elevators for storage. The spread in price between the cash month in which they buy the grain, and, say, the May price, is usually from a cent to a cent and a quarter a month. The only charge they have against the spread at which they sell is the interest and insurance charge, which is low enough to give them a handsome profit on their turnover. This enables them to, at times, offer inducements at country points for carlots that apparently is difficult to understand; or at points where we are buying street grain to offer prices that we cannot pay unless we buy at a loss.[1]

Attitude of Grain Growers' Company. — During the first few years' operations of the company the resentment of the farmers against the monopolistic abuses of the elevator companies and the various attempts made by the grain interests to put the farmers' company out of business, had served to rally the grain growers in supporting and patronizing their own selling organization. As the elevator companies, under the competition of the farmers' company and commission dealers generally, and under the regulation of the amended Grain Act, began to offer inducements to secure the farmers' grain, growers showed an increasing tendency to bestow their patronage on strict calculations of relative advantage. The appeal to class loyalty, as Mr. Crerar emphasized in a contribution to the *Guide* at the end of 1911, was no longer sufficient in itself.

[1] G. G. G. Co., 1911.

The Company and the Grain Growers' Association [he declared] are at present perhaps passing through the most critical stage in their history. The old days of short weights and big spreads in prices have largely disappeared, at least in the general sense in which they were practised ten years ago. The farmer is no longer told that if he is not satisfied he can take his grain home. It was perhaps only to be expected that, once these striking abuses were in a large measure changed into better conditions, the consciousness of the need of continued united effort should wane.[1]

At the outset of its commercial career the goodwill of the Grain Growers' Company had consisted largely in the illwill of grain growers toward the elevator interests. While alert to capitalize this resentment,[2] the directors of the Grain Growers' Company had consistently sought to establish patronage on the basis of superior service, and to this end had developed the Claims and Sampling departments.[3] As a mere commission agency the company's serviceability, however, was virtually limited to the platform shipper or to local farmers' elevators. An arrangement had indeed been made in 1910 with the Manitoba Elevator Commission to buy and ship street grain through certain government elevators.[4] It was found, however, that independent street buying could not be profitably conducted in competition with the line elevator and milling companies with their integrated facilities. Without country elevators of its own, the company was not in a position to establish any extensive business relations with smaller-scale producers. Yet another consideration in the minds of the directors was that a line of country elevators might serve as nuclei for local organizations of shareholders, and as distributing centers for farmers' supplies which the company was now beginning to handle coöperatively. Such a double utilization of elevators, both as assembling and distributing centers, would not only afford greater serviec to patrons, but also contribute to greater efficiency in operation by making it possible to maintain a permanent staff of operators.[5]

[1] *G. G. Guide*, Dec. 6, 1911.

[2] Recall, for example, the appeals made through the columns of the *Guide* and circulars to shareholders at the time of the suspension of the commission rule by the Exchange. *Supra*, pp. 74, 75.

[3] See *supra*, pp. 68, 69.

[4] G. G. G. Co., 1912.

[5] *Ibid.*

On these various competitive, financial, and service considerations then, the Grain Growers' Company was quite disposed to negotiate with the Manitoba government in the matter of the leasing of the Commission's elevators. At the sixth annual meeting of the shareholders in July, 1912, the question was fully discussed. President Crerar, in reporting the negotiations that had taken place, represented that, if the provincial elevators were not taken over by the Grain Growers' Company, they would probably pass into other hands, and the old conditions surrounding the elevator business in Manitoba would be resumed. In accordance with a resolution of the shareholders, the directors signed an agreement on July 20 to lease the elevators of the Commission on a rental basis of six per cent of the capital investment of $1,160,000, taxes and repairs being assumed by the government.[1]

Results of Operating by Farmers' Company. — The first year's operation of the leased elevators by the company resulted in a loss of $30,000,[2] which, although $54,000 less than that incurred by the Commission in 1910–11, was far from encouraging to the lessees. The taking over at a single step of 174 highly capitalized elevators — of which it was found feasible to use only 135 — by a company without previous experience in elevator operation, with an unproved personnel, and with keenest competition to face,[3] was indeed an undertaking from which immediately successful results were scarcely to be expected. In the second year of operation, however, the deficit was converted into a small profit of $4,317.[4]

Although the Manitoba government had given notice of termination of the lease at the end of August 1914,[5] and although a higher rental was offered by outside firms (believed to be con-

[1] *G. G. Guide*, July 24, 1912, p. 4.

[2] G. G. G. Co., 1913. Despite this loss on its Manitoba elevators, the company's net earnings for the year amounted to $170,000, thanks to substantial profits on the commission and terminal operations.

[3] Competition was generally keener in Manitoba than in the newer provinces of Saskatchewan and Alberta where elevator companies found it difficult to keep pace with the rapidly expanding grain acreage. The buying competition of milling companies in Manitoba was particularly felt by the Grain Growers' Company in seasons of low yields. G. G. G. Co., 1915, p. 8.

[4] G. G. G. Co., 1914, p. 8.

[5] G. G. G. Co., 1913.

nected with Minneapolis grain interests), the provincial authorities finally decided that it was preferable that the elevators should remain in the hands of the Manitoba farmers. Accordingly the lease of the 135 elevators, which the company found it feasible to use, was renewed, on an annual basis, on somewhat more favorable terms to the Grain Growers' Company. The government rendered further assistance by depositing some $300,000 of provincial funds in the Home Bank, to facilitate the financing of street grain purchases at company elevator points.[1] In this year (1914–15), despite a less than average crop yield, the company's elevators showed a surplus of $7,391,[2] and in the following season, with over double the volume of grain passing through their bins, they yielded a profit of no less than $161,608 [3] — a striking illustration of the determining influence of volume of turnover upon the results of elevator operation. The company had commenced in 1913 construction or purchase of elevators of its own at selected points to supplement the government system. By 1916 fourteen of these had been added to the leased properties in Manitoba.[4]

Significance of the Settlement. — From the foregoing survey it will be seen that the entry of the Grain Growers' Company into the business of elevator operation represented an adjustment to circumstances rather than the deliberate execution of a preconceived policy. At the same time, the eagerness of an opportunist government to disembarrass itself of the elevator properties it had acquired as a concession to the demands of the Grain Growers' Association, coincided more or less with the growing realization on the part of the Grain Growers' Company of the desirability of a system of elevators under its own control, as a means of improving its competitive position and of rendering wider service to its farmer shareholders and patrons.

[1] G. G. G. Co., 1914. [2] On 6,540,923 bushels. G. G. G. Co., 1915.

[3] On 14,787,687 bushels. G. G. G. Co., 1916.

[4] G. G. G. Co., 1916. In the same year the rental of the leased elevators was appreciably reduced through a reappraisal of the property. In 1924 the United Grain Growers bought outright forty-three of the government elevators at a total cost of $365,000, and since then has purchased such of the remainder as it desired to retain, U. G. G., 1926, p. 14.

The government's emergency, moreover, presented an opportunity which the company was not excluded from considering on financial grounds. Its six years of successful operation as a commission agency, in which capital requirements were relatively slight, and earnings reasonably assured, served to provide both resources and experience on the basis of which the company might venture without undue risk into the more ambitious and exacting field of elevator operation. It proved able indeed to take over both country and terminal elevators in the same year without seeking loans either from the government or public investors. Beginning under leasing arrangements, it found it possible to meet the first year's deficit out of the profits of its strongly established commission business, and to finance its local buying operations, not merely through its credit relations with a bank in which it was an extensive shareholder, but also by means of its accumulated reserves. At the same time, its paid-up capital was being continually enlarged, as the number and holdings of its farmer shareholders increased. Beginning in this way, the company was able to undertake gradually the purchase or construction of elevators of its own to supplement the leased system.

Partridge had conceived the idea of a farmer-owned company and had been the leading protagonist of government-owned elevators. Both prospects came into being, but with very opposite results. The fiasco of the Manitoba government elevator enterprise provided the opportunity for the Grain Growers' Company to enlarge its participation and influence in the grain trade in the interests of grain producers. The organized Grain Growers had been disillusioned in regard to government ownership; they had been enlightened as to the possibilities of what might be done through their own commercial organization. The solution of the elevator problem in Manitoba, for the time being at least, was found, not in statutory monopoly, nor government ownership, nor in the divorce of the business of grain warehousing from that of grain merchandising, but in the competitive participation of the Grain Growers themselves in the operation of a farmers' line elevator system in accordance with the established methods of the trade.

CHAPTER VIII

ORIGIN OF THE SASKATCHEWAN CO-OPERATIVE ELEVATOR COMPANY

I. The Saskatchewan Elevator Commission, 1910

Appointment of Investigating Committee. — In Saskatchewan, as we have seen, the demand of the organized Grain Growers for government ownership of elevators, was no less insistent than in Manitoba.[1] The Saskatchewan government, however, followed an entirely different procedure from that of the Roblin administration in dealing with the situation, and adopted a solution without precedent in the history of governmental relations with agricultural producers.

Following the break-up of interprovincial negotiations for government ownership of elevators upon the rock of "constitutional difficulties," [2] the Saskatchewan Grain Growers' Association, concentrating its efforts upon its own government, presented a petition to the provincial legislature in the session of 1909, requesting the enactment of legislation "providing for the acquirement or creation of government-owned storage facilities by a commission." This petition had been referred to the House Committee on Agriculture, which, in reporting to the legislature, recommended that "a commission should be appointed by the government for the purpose of making searching inquiry into the proposals looking to the creation and operation of a system of elevators to effect the objects outlined by the Grain Growers' Association." [3] Premier Scott declared that such recommendation was acceptable to the government, and it was unanimously authorized by the legislature on December 14, 1909, just two days prior to the ministerial announcement at the convention of the Manitoba Grain Growers' Association of the "conversion" of the Roblin government to the principle of government ownership of

[1] See *supra*, p. 81. [2] See *supra*, pp. 83, 84.

[3] *Report of Saskatchewan Elevator Commission*, 1910, pp. 9, 10.

elevators. In the appointment of the Commission of Inquiry the Saskatchewan government selected as chairman a disinterested eastern party in the person of Dr. Robert Magill, Professor of Political Economy at Dalhousie University, Halifax. The other two commissioners were members of the executive of the Saskatchewan Grain Growers' Association: George Langley, M. L. A.,[1] and F. W. Green, secretary of the Association.

The report of the Commission was submitted in November, 1910.[2] It recognized that the integrated control and operation of both initial and terminal elevators by the large milling and line elevator companies gave them not only a dominating position in relation to the producers of grain, but also "overwhelming advantages" over other dealers on the Grain Exchange — commission men, track buyers, and exporters — who did not possess elevators of their own.[3] Such conditions permitted a potential, if not a formal monopoly on the part of interests centered outside the province. The problem for Saskatchewan grain growers was essentially, then, the discovery of the most effective method of control over the facilities for storage and shipping at initial points. In their report the commissioners reviewed and rejected in turn the various schemes for elevator control and operation presented to them in the course of their investigations.

Rejection of Grain Growers' Plan by Commission. — The memorandum which had been submitted to the Commission by the Saskatchewan Grain Growers' Association was in general correspondence with that which the Manitoba Grain Growers had shortly before presented to the Manitoba government.[4] In the responsibilities which it laid upon the provincial government the former, however, went even further than the latter. It called for an elevator commission nominated (as to majority at least) by the Grain Growers' Association, and responsible to the legislature,

[1] Who, it will be recalled, had been employed by the three Western premiers as their intermediary in replying to the representatives of the Interprovincial Council in 1908. See *supra*, p. 82 n.

[2] The report of the Saskatchewan Elevator Commission of 1910 constitutes one of the most instructive documents in the history of the grain trade of Western Canada.

[3] *Report of Saskatchewan Elevator Commission*, pp. 21, 22.

[4] See *supra*, pp. 85, 86.

a three-fifths vote of which would be necessary for removal of a commissioner. The government would be responsible, not only for providing the funds necessary to acquire and remodel the existing elevators, but also for meeting temporary deficits.[1] Initial guarantees of patronage by farmers were not favored, as tending to delay the inauguration of the system. Not only would the government elevators provide special binning and cleaning facilities, but the operators would also be Dominion samplers and weighmen, who would forward the samples for Winnipeg inspection, while preserving the identity of each farmer's grain in storage and shipment. Such a scheme, it was represented, would permit farmers to hold graded grain in interior instead of terminal storage, and to finance on warehouse certificates guaranteed as to grade and weight by the government.[2]

In reviewing the Grain Growers' plan, the commissioners pointed out the objections to a scheme in which the provincial government would assume all the financial responsibility while alienating the control; and in which farmers would be afforded special privileges without being directly liable for either financial or patronage guarantees. Leaving aside the question of the advisability of public ownership, they found the scheme objectionable by the inclusion of such collateral features as sampling by federal officials employed by a provincial authority; guarantee of grade and weight before shipment; government financing of grade certificates; and the substitution of initial for terminal main storage: all of which involved conflict between federal and provincial powers.

Findings of the Commission. — The plan embodied in the Manitoba Elevator Act was objected to on the grounds of its exposure both to political pressure in control, and political laxity in accounting, and of the inevitable financial risk arising from its failure to provide either a statutory monopoly or a separate system capable of competing with companies engaged in buying and

[1] "But we are willing that such temporary loss be charged to capital account, and repaid through the medium of the sinking fund, or met by a tax placed on the arable land of the province." *Report*, p. 34.

[2] *Report*, pp. 23–35.

selling grain, as well as in storing and shipping, for which services the regulated rates were already low.[1]

The proposal to furnish government loans to locally owned and controlled farmers' elevators, commended by its advocates as tending to develop the spirit of coöperation and community responsibility, was criticized as affording insufficient security to the province for its advances. The history of local farmers' elevators had shown many individual failures, due chiefly to poor management and competitive limitations.[2] Reluctance to pay adequate salaries, local favoritism or interference, and lack of expert supervision had generally been responsible for the former; while restriction to the mere storing or shipping of grain, or lack of centralized selling organization, made it difficult for farmers' elevators, even under capable management, to withstand the competition which line elevator companies not infrequently directed specifically against them.[3]

In the opinion of the commissioners, the scheme most likely to prove adequate was one in which government financial aid would be extended, not to independent local farmers' elevators, but to a farmers' line elevator company, in which local shareholding and patronage responsibility would be combined with centralized management. It was necessary to evolve a system of elevators which "would be protected alike from the influence of party politics, from the danger of a non-sympathetic government, and from the risks incidental to merely local management." [4] In conclusion, therefore, the commissioners expressed themselves as follows:

> The Commission are unanimous in holding that a solution of the elevator problem satisfactory to the farmers must give the farmers full control of the system. And they are unanimous in holding that no storing and handling elevator is likely to be a financial success unless a considerable number of the growers of grain have a direct personal interest in, and responsibility

---

[1] *Report*, pp. 38–40.

[2] Twenty-nine farmers' elevators were reported in operation in Saskatchewan in 1909–10, representing 3.5 per cent of all the licensed elevators in the provinces; 70 per cent of the farmers' elevators purchased as well as stored grain. *Ibid.*, pp. 115–117.

[3] *Ibid.*, pp. 85–88.

[4] *Ibid.*, p. 92.

for the elevator. The Commission therefore are unanimous in holding that the solution must be sought along the line of coöperation by the farmers themselves, assisted in the matter of finance by a provincial loan. The Commission consider that special legislation should be enacted providing for the creation of a coöperative organization of the farmers on the principle of:

1. The maximum amount of local control consistent with
2. Ownership by the whole body of shareholders and management through a central board of directors.

A basis of organization for such a provincial-wide coöperative elevator company was definitely outlined, and it was suggested that the executive of the Saskatchewan Grain Growers' Association should constitute its provisional directorate.[1]

II. The Saskatchewan Co-operative Elevator Act, 1911

A bill to incorporate the "Saskatchewan Co-operative Elevator Company" on the lines suggested by the Commission was promptly introduced by the Scott government at the next session of the legislature early in 1911. While the measure was being debated in the House, the Commission's report and the government's draft bill were being simultaneously and much more warmly discussed by the five hundred delegates of the Saskatchewan Grain Growers in convention at the capital city. In the end the report was unanimously approved by the convention, and the executive of the association entered into conference with the government, with suggestions for various amendments to the bill. The most important of those accepted by the government was one extending the powers of the company to enable it to "do all things incidental to the production, storing and marketing of grain," thereby enabling it to engage in the merchandising as well as in the warehousing of grain, and the operation of terminal as well as country elevators; while trading in farm supplies was also within its competence. The act incorporating the Saskatchewan Co-operative Elevator Company, which become law in March, 1911,[2] was thus the joint product of a Royal Commission (the majority of whose members were Grain Growers' officers), of the

[1] *Report*, pp. 96–98.

[2] Statutes of Saskatchewan, 1 Geo. v, c. 39, 1910–11. For text of act, see Appendix D.

provincial Parliament, and of the "Grain Growers' Parliament." It was therefore a much more carefully considered measure than the Manitoba Elevator Act of the preceding year, and one which the Grain Growers' Association not only unanimously endorsed, but also officially undertook to put into effect.

Features of the Act. — The distinctive features of the Saskatchewan Co-operative Elevator Act are found mainly in the relation which it established between the government and the company, and between the company and its shareholders' locals. The five members of the Grain Growers' executive named as provisional directors under the terms of incorporation were authorized to take subscriptions for shares of $50 from agriculturists only.[1] Any number of farmer shareholders might request the directors to establish a local at any railway shipping point in the province where it was desired to construct or acquire an elevator. Except, however, with the special consent of the Lieutenant-Governor in Council, the directors were not permitted to establish such locals, unless the amount of shares subscribed by the supporters of the proposed local was at least equal to the cost of the proposed elevator;[2] unless 15 per cent of the amount of such shares had been paid up; and unless the aggregate crop acreage of the shareholders concerned represented a proportion of not less than 2,000 acres for each 10,000 bushels of elevator capacity asked for.[3] The intent of this provision was of course to ensure adequate patronage for any elevator that the company might construct or acquire. No pledge of patronage was required, however, nor any penalty for diversion stipulated. Local financial participation, it was felt, constituted the best guarantee of support, and avoided the difficulty of having to enforce contracts that might become obnoxious. At the same time the risk of investment was lessened through the collective responsibility of the company for each of its local elevators.

[1] Saskatchewan Co-operative Elevator Act, 1911, secs. 2, 3, 6.

[2] A minimum of 180 shares ($9000 par value) was regarded as the approximate capital value of the company's standard 30,000 bushel elevators. Saskatchewan Co-operative Elevator Company, *Organization Pamphlet*, No. 1.

[3] Saskatchewan Co-operative Elevator Act, secs. 12, 13.

Relation between Government and Company. — When 15 per cent of the necessary stock subscribed by a local had been paid up, the government might loan to the company, for the purpose of constructing, acquiring, or remodelling the desired elevator, a sum equal to 85 per cent of the estimated cost.[1] So long as the above prerequisites were complied with, the government's loans did not involve any limitation of the company's liberty of action in regard to the location, purchase price, capacity, or equipment of elevators so financed. This was a feature of the act which had been strongly criticized by the leader of the Opposition in the legislature, as representing an abdication of governmental financial responsibility.[2] The government's security was provided for, however, by its control over the amount of the company's capital stock;[3] by the statutory conditions of the treasury loans which were made, not to the locals, but to the company, upon the joint liability of all the shareholders; and by the government's rights as first mortgagee upon the company's elevator properties,[4] as well as its claim upon uncalled capital stock.[5] The government's elevator loans were repayable in twenty equal annual instalments of principal and interest, the first payment becoming due on the second year of the loan.[6] By these provisions the government's advances were adequately protected without imposing duality of control in the company's operations.

Relation between Company and Locals. — The method of shareholders' control embodied in the act represented a compromise between corporation and coöperative practices, and between centralized management and local participation. No member might hold more than twenty shares,[7] and no assignment or transfer of shares was valid unless approved by the directors.[8] Shareholders, meetings were of two kinds, local and general. The members of

[1] Saskatchewan Co-operative Elevator Act, sec. 24.
[2] *Regina Leader*, Feb. 8, 1911.
[3] Saskatchewan Co-operative Elevator Act, sec. 3.
[4] *Ibid.*, sec. 25.
[5] *Ibid.*, sec. 25a, added by amendment, 1912.
[6] *Ibid.*, sec. 25.
[7] *Ibid.*, sec. 3, as amended in 1912. The limit was originally ten shares.
[8] *Ibid.*, sec. 3; By-law No. 9., Saskatchewan Co-operative Elevator Co.

each local were authorized to meet annually for the threefold purpose of discussing matters relating to the operation and management of the local elevator, of electing a local board of management of five members, and of choosing a delegate to represent the local at the general meeting of the company's shareholders.[1] In the local meetings, as provided by by-law, each shareholder present was entitled to one vote irrespective of his shareholdings, and no proxies were allowed.[2] At the annual general meetings, each shareholders' local was entitled to one delegate and one vote, regardless of the number of shares held by the members of any local.[3] The system of delegate representation and single voting at the annual meeting of the company was thus a reproduction of the method adopted in connection with the annual convention of the Grain Growers' Association. In order that there should be no financial impediment to full representation, it was subsequently provided by by-law that the transportation expenses and a daily allowance for all delegates should be chargeable to the current expenditures of the company.[4]

Shareholders' locals were thus given an equal voice in the election of the directors of the company,[5] and were enabled, through these delegates, to bring before the general meeting resolutions, recommendations, or complaints recorded in their local meetings. With regard to management, the local members might make suggestions concerning the type of elevator desired or representations regarding the local operator. The technical, financial, operating, and official responsibility for all elevators rested, however, with the central management, the functions of the local management being largely advisory and intermediary. While individual shareholders were most directly concerned with the operations of their local elevator, their equity and liability lay with the company as a whole, and the value of their shares did not depend merely on the results of local operation. By these methods it was sought to

[1] Saskatchewan Co-operative Elevator Act, sec. 14; By-laws 12 and 14.

[2] By-law no. 14, sec. 5. The act (sec. 15) originally stated that, unless otherwise provided by by-law, each shareholder at local meetings should have one vote for each share held, up to a maximum of five votes.

[3] Sec. 14; By-law no. 12, sec. 2.

[4] By-law no. 2, sec. 1.

[5] Nine in number, with three returned annually. Act, sec. 9.

combine the advantages of corporate strength and centralized efficiency with local interest and responsibility.

III. Initiation of Saskatchewan Co-operative Elevator Company, 1911

The act incorporating this unique type of farmer's elevator company stipulated that it should not begin business until at least twenty-five locals had been duly established.[1] The organization of these locals was the principal task of the provisional directorate, which circularized all the branches of the Saskatchewan Grain Growers' Association with a view to ascertaining the demand for elevator organization. Local requests were numerous enough, but the poor crop of the previous season made it exceedingly difficult for many farmers to pay up the necessary 15 per cent of the subscribed stock. A government grant of $7000 toward organization expenses afforded, however, a measure of assistance that had been denied the promoters of the Grain Growers' Grain Company, and by June 6, 1911, the requisite twenty-five locals had been organized. Before the arrival of the appointed date of the general meeting, July 6, twenty-one additional locals had been established. The first general meeting of the Saskatchewan Co-operative Company, held at Moose Jaw, was attended, therefore, by representatives of forty-six locals, representing a capitalization of $405,050. The 8,101 shares were distributed among 2,580 shareholders, the average holding being thus slightly over three shares. The nine directors elected at the Moose Jaw meeting selected as their executive, John A. Maharg, president, George Langley, vice-president, and Charles A. Dunning, secretary-treasurer. All three were likewise directors of both the association and the company, Mr. Maharg being president of both organizations. No such duality of office had existed between the Manitoba Grain Growers' Association and the Grain Growers' Grain Company, which had sprung up without the official sponsorship of the former, and whose shareholders and business had never been provincially limited. In Saskatchewan the interlock-

[1] Saskatchewan Co-operative Elevator Act, sec. 7.

ing arrangement ensured the closest relationship between the parent association and the Co-operative Elevator Company during the infancy of the latter.[1]

Construction Policy of Company. — In contrast with the procedure of the Manitoba Elevator Commission, the policy of the Saskatchewan Company was to build new elevators rather than to acquire existing ones.[2] The reasons for this were twofold: in the first place, the rapid expansion of grain production in Saskatchewan called for increased elevator facilities, whereas conditions in Manitoba had become relatively stable;[3] in the second place, the desire of Saskatchewan grain growers was for a type of elevator in which special binning facilities would be freely available. The adoption of the general policy of new construction also served to minimize the difficulties arising from the valuation, acquisition, and remodelling of old properties.

At the very outset the directors engaged their own engineer, on whose recommendation plans were selected for standard 30,000 and 40,000-bushel company elevators. In these liberal provision was made for special binning,[4] and all were equipped with standard cleaners and with 200-bushel hopper scales to permit accurate weighing out, thereby facilitating the collection of claims against railway companies in case of loss in transit.[5] Contracts for con-

[1] Subsequently this concentration of offices was to prove an occasion of dissent among Saskatchewan farmers.

[2] Of the first 46 elevators undertaken by the company, all but 6 represented new construction. C. A. Dunning, in *G. G. Guide*, Dec. 6, 1912.

[3] The relative situation at that time is strikingly indicated by the comparative statistics for the crop years 1908–09 and 1909–10.

	1908–09		1909–10	
	Man.	*Sask.*	*Man.*	*Sask.*
Crop area (million acres)	5.11	3.55	5.11	5.81
Grain production (million bus.)	112.48	67.08	128.94	181.52
Country elevators	689	615	696	834
Storage capacity (million bus.)	20.82	17.92	21.62	24.27

Canada Year Book, 1911. "*Report, Saskatchewan Elevator Commission*," 1910, p. 112.

[4] The 30,000-bushel standard elevators contained 14 carload bins, and two bins of 2-carload capacity, besides two large company bins for purchased grain. C. A. Dunning in *G. G. Guide*, Dec. 6, 1911, p. 28.

[5] See *supra*, p. 68.

struction of forty of these standard elevators were distributed among five firms during the summer of 1911. The special requirements of the company's houses and the difficulty of forwarding supplies on branch lines, in some cases still under construction, so extended the times of completion that only seventeen were in operation by the first of December, thus greatly limiting the quantity of grain which the company could handle during its first year of business. The unsatisfactory experience with elevator contractors and the rapid organization of new locals led the company, after the completion of these initial elevators, to establish its own construction department to undertake the erection, equipment, and upkeep of all its houses. This arrangement permitted the large-scale purchase of elevator building supplies, the rapid and uniform construction of the standard houses, the employment of a permanent and mobile staff, and the elimination of negotiations, disputes, and inspectional difficulties with outside contractors.

First Year's Operations. — During the very first year of operations, the plan was adopted of departmentalizing the company's business. In addition to the construction department, the directors established organization, operating, sales, and accounting departments, all under the superintendence of Mr. Dunning, who was appointed general manager. The organization department, under the direction of Mr. Langley, was charged with the organization of new locals, their early establishment being necessary in order to permit the completion of new elevators in time for the 1912 crop movement. The operating department, while taking into consideration the representations of local boards of management, was given full responsibility in the engagement and control of local operators, and in carrying out on a uniform and consistent basis the policy of the company in the storing, handling, and purchasing of grain. The sales department, under the personal direction of Mr. Dunning, handled all street grain purchases at the company's elevator points. During the first year an arrangement was made with the Grain Growers' Grain Company to act as selling agents on the Winnipeg Grain Exchange for the Saskatchewan organization. The older farmers' company thus received grain from the Saskatchewan Co-operative elevators before beginning to handle it through houses of its own.[1]

Despite the delay in the completion of its first forty elevators, the Saskatchewan Company handled 3,261,000 bushels of grain during its first year of operation. Of these deliveries more than half was specially binned for its patrons, the remainder being purchased by the company.[2] In storing and handling grain the company charged the statutory maximum rates, not desiring to prejudice the financial result of its first year's operations. The provision of special binning facilities was regarded as of greater benefit to the farmer than reduced storage charges. In purchasing street grain, its operators were given no stated margin on which to buy, but were instructed to pay prices above those offered by the line companies. This tended to reduce the spread between track and street prices at competitive points. At places where co-operative elevators were not established, line elevators, it was claimed, paid prices for street grain as much as five cents lower than those offered through the country by the Co-operative Company.[3]

The first annual meeting of the company's shareholders, held at Regina on August 21, 1912, showed a profit on the year's operations of $52,461. After distributing a dividend of 6 per cent[4] (on paid-up capital) the remaining surplus of $48,798 was appropriated in equal proportions to the "Elevator Reserve Account" for the purpose of financing grain purchases,[5] and to a "Trading Reserve" to finance prospective operations in coöperative supply.[6] The substantial surplus, averaging over $1,000 for each of the 46 elevators, most of which were in operation during only the latter portion of the grain-moving season, was regarded by most of the farmers as indicative of the large profits which the line

[1] Report of C. A. Dunning to S. G. G. A., *G. G. Guide*, Feb. 21, 1912.

[2] Saskatchewan Co-operative Elevator Company, 1912.

[3] G. Langley to S. G. G. A., *G. G. Guide*, Feb. 28, 1912.

[4] Six per cent was the maximum rate of dividend payable to shareholders under section 20 of the act of incorporation. This was raised to 10 per cent by amendment of 1913.

[5] Provision for such account was made under the act of incorporation, sec. 20, sub-sec. 4.

[6] Saskatchewan Co-operative Elevator Company, 1912.

elevators had been receiving from their monopolistic operations in the province.[1] The financial results of the first year's business stimulated materially the organization of new locals, which were more than quadrupled in number during 1912. If the Co-operative elevators could give superior service and at the same time yield handsome profits, the farmers wanted more of them.

Expansion of the Company. — So rapidly did the work of organization and construction proceed that the company had 137 elevators to handle the 1912 crop, compared with the 46 in operation during the initial year.[2] In the multiplication of its branches the directorate was actuated, not merely by the desire to meet the demands of Grain Growers' locals, but also by the expediency of widening its area of operations, so as to be less vulnerable to the concentrated competition of line elevator companies.[3] The rapidity of expansion aggravated the difficulty of securing reliable and efficient local operators. Experience of the exposure of managers of local farmers' elevators to interference from farmer shareholders had made many of the better type of operators reluctant at first to accept employment with the new Co-operative Elevator Company. The system of centralized responsibility and supervision adopted by the Saskatchewan Company, the financial support it enjoyed by the government, the superior type of its elevators, and the patronage which they commanded, all tended, however, to break down gradually such aloofness on the part of experienced operators, and the operating department began to build up a staff of efficient and loyal elevator managers, further recruited from seasonal assistants to whose training the department gave special attention. By the end of the second year 310 men were employed in the operating department alone.[4]

After the first year of business the Saskatchewan Company terminated its selling arrangement with the Grain Growers' Grain

[1] See *G. G. Guide*, Aug. 28, 1912.

[2] Saskatchewan Co-operative Elevator Company, 1913.

[3] "That was why endeavor had been made the second year to build a large number of elevators. . . . It was not difficult for a line company to squeeze a small farmers' elevator company out of existence at a given point; it was not impossible to do it at 46 points; but widen the area and it did become impossible." C. A. Dunning to S. G. G. A., *G. G. Guide*, Feb. 23, 1916.

[4] Saskatchewan Co-operative Elevator Company, 1913.

Company, acquiring its own seat on the Grain Exchange and opening up a commission department at Winnipeg, to handle consigned carloads and sell the company's purchased grain. To facilitate business, the Winnipeg office was connected by direct wire with the head office at Regina. Through the company's 137 elevators, 12,899,030 bushels of grain were handled during the 1912–13 season, representing the unusually high average of approximately 95,000 bushels per elevator. Of this quantity fully two thirds was special binned, a significant indication of the farmers' preference for this mode of grain marketing. The profits for the second year of operations (ending July 31, 1913) were over three times as great as in the first year, aggregating $167,927, from which an 8 per cent cash dividend and a 6 per cent stock dividend were distributed. At the date of the second annual meeting at Regina on November 10, 1913, the number of farmer shareholders had risen from the 2,508 reported at the first general meeting in July, 1911, to 13,156, grouped in 192 locals — more than a five-fold increase. The Saskatchewan Co-operative Elevator Company had undoubtedly taken root throughout the province.

The Manitoba Experiment and the Saskatchewan Plan. — The governments of both Manitoba and Saskatchewan had been simultaneously called on to meet virtually identical demands for government ownership of elevators from the provincial Grain Growers' Associations. Within the same week in December, 1909, both administrations had declared their readiness to create government commissions. The Manitoba Elevator Commission was to carry out an experiment in public ownership on lines laid down by the government. The Saskatchewan Elevator Commission, on the other hand, was to carry out an inquiry into the feasibility of provincial ownership of elevators. Both commissions included Grain Growers' officers in their personnel. But whereas the president of the Manitoba Grain Growers had been appointed to the responsibility of administering a system under ministerial control, the Grain Grower members of the Saskatchewan Commission were charged with the responsibility of collaborating in the drafting of a plan which would commend itself both to the government and to their association. In Manitoba the government enacted a scheme which the Grain Growers declared they could not support with confidence. In Saskatchewan the government gave legislative effect to a plan which Grain Grower commissioners had recommended, and which had obtained the unanimous endorsement of the Grain Growers' Parliament. In Manitoba the government had undertaken to establish and operate a public elevator system for farmers. In Saskatchewan the responsibility for organization, ownership, and operation was vested in the organized Grain Growers themselves. In Manitoba the government assumed the full financial responsibilities on both capital and current account. In Saskatchewan the government was merely lender and guarantor, with loans and commitments adequately secured.[1] The Manitoba Elevator Commission acquired within a few months a great number of elevators, generally at overcapitalized values, without guarantee of local patronage. The Saskatchewan Co-operative Company built most of its own elevators, each with its own minimum shareholding constituency and local board. The Manitoba government elevators were warehouses only. The Saskatchewan Co-operative elevators competed with the line companies in merchandising as well as in storing grain.

The Saskatchewan system was a year later than the Manitoba enterprise in coming into existence, but in 1912 the former was entering upon a programme of confident expansion, while the Manitoba government was seeking to disembarrass itself of its disastrous elevator enterprise. In both provinces the solution of the elevator crisis was found in the assumption of elevator operation by farmer-owned companies on a competitive basis. In Saskatchewan this solution was arrived at as the outcome of a thoroughgoing preliminary investigation. In Manitoba it came about as a sequel to the *débâcle* of an ill-considered government ownership experiment. In Saskatchewan the government assumed financial sponsorship of a statutory farmers' coöperative company. In Manitoba it was the Grain Growers' Company which came to the relief of the government in its embarrassment.

[1] By an amendment to the Co-operative Elevator Act (sec. 27a), in 1913, the Provincial Treasurer was authorized to guarantee, under appropriate securities, the repayment of approved bank loans made to the company for operating purposes.

CHAPTER IX

THE ALBERTA FARMERS' CO-OPERATIVE ELEVATOR COMPANY

I. The United Farmers of Alberta

In Alberta the demand for government ownership of elevators was less general and insistent than in Manitoba and Saskatchewan, although the Foothill Province had joined in the representations of the Interprovincial Council to the Western premiers in 1908. If Alberta farmers moved less aggressively in this matter than the Grain Growers' organizations in the other provinces, it was primarily because at that time wheat growing occupied a much less conspicuous place in Alberta's agricultural economy, and because the province did not then possess a united farmers' organization.

Wheat Growing in Alberta. — Until the opening of the twentieth century Alberta had been essentially a stock-raising country, with a growing tendency toward mixed farming in the park lands of the central and northern portions. The greater humidity and more broken topography of that region, with the relative frequency of early frosts, favored the production of oats rather than of wheat, especially before the evolution of the early maturing Marquis wheat.[1] With the setting in of the immigration tide at the turn of the century, and with the enclosure of much of the southern grazing lands into homestead holdings, the raising of winter wheat began to assume some importance, and Alberta Red Winter wheat had been added to the inspection grades of the Grain Inspection Act in 1906. It was not, however, until the Canadian Northern Railway penetrated central Alberta and the Marquis variety was introduced, that spring wheat growing attained ap-

[1] See Buller, *Essays on Wheat*, pp. 174–183. In the year 1900 the wheat production of that portion of the North-West Territories subsequently incorporated in the Province of Alberta amounted to only 797,839 bushels, while the oat yield aggregated 3,791,259 bushels.

preciable proportions in the westernmost prairie province.[1] In 1906, the year after the organization of the Province of Alberta, the area sown to wheat amounted to only 223,930 acres, compared with 2,721,079 acres in Manitoba and 2,117,484 acres in Saskatchewan.[2] Not until 1911 did the wheat crop of Alberta exceed 10,000,000 bushels.[3] Of Alberta's relatively limited grain production a considerable proportion was shipped in sacks to British Columbia and the Yukon.[4] The elevator problem was, therefore, a less significant issue with the farmers of Alberta at this time than with the Grain Growers' Associations in the other Prairie Provinces.

Farmers' Organizations in Alberta. — Not only was Alberta relatively backward as a wheat-producing province, but it also lacked as representative and as coherent a provincial farmers' organization as that of the Manitoba or Saskatchewan Grain Growers' Associations. A certain number of locals of the old Territorial Grain Growers' Association had been organized in the district of Alberta, and not a few Alberta farmers were included among the shareholders of the Grain Growers' Grain Company. Apart from local agricultural societies, however, no general farmers' organization developed within Alberta until just prior to the creation of the province, when a number of settlers who had recently migrated to the Edmonton district from Dakota and Nebraska, where they had been members of the American Society of Equity,[5] organized some branches of that society in their new home.

With the creation of the Province of Alberta in 1905, a movement was initiated with a view to bringing about a united and a

[1] Buller, *op. cit.*, pp. 157, 158.

[2] Census of North-West Provinces, 1906.

[3] In 1911, under exceptionally favorable crop conditions, Alberta produced 36,143,000 bushels of wheat, and 56,964,000 bushels of oats. *Canada Year Book*, 1911.

[4] See Elevator Report by Thos. Woolford to Alberta Farmers' Association. *Edmonton Bulletin*, January 15, 1909.

[5] This organization had originated in Indiana about 1902, obtaining its strongest hold in Wisconsin. Its central aim was "controlled marketing" through organization of producers and establishment of producers' warehouses. See B. H. Hibbard, *Marketing Agricultural Products*, chap. 20.

distinctly provincial farmers' organization. The lead in this agitation was taken by Rice Sheppard of the Strathcona local of the Territorial Grain Growers' Association, who pointed out that the organized influence of the farmers of Alberta was greatly limited through their division into branches of two organizations, one of which had its headquarters in Indiana, and the other of which was preparing to change its name to the Saskatchewan Grain Growers' Association. The Equity followers as a whole were loath, however, to relinquish their identity, and sought to remove the objection of American domination by forming the Canadian Society of Equity. The immediate result of this union movement was limited to the amalgamation in 1905 of the Strathcona local of the Territorial Association and the neighboring Clover Bar local of the Society of Equity, to form the Alberta Farmers' Association.[1]

During the next three years both organizations carried on active efforts to extend their membership and influence through the province. The Canadian Society of Equity entertained ambitious plans of farmer-owned flour and lumber mills, and so forth, and sold stock extensively in a coöperative company formed to develop a timber limit. The collapse of this concern in 1907 considerably weakened the prestige of the Society in the province.[2] The activities of the Alberta Farmers' Association were mainly of an educational, protective, and legislative character. They organized a provincial seed fair, secured the establishment of separate federal inspection grades for Alberta hard winter wheat,[3] and were instrumental in obtaining the appointment of a provincial pork commission to consider the establishment of a government pork-packing plant as a means of lessening the farmers' marketing dependence on the "packing monopoly." [4] In 1907, as previously recorded, the executive of the association had joined with the Saskatchewan and Manitoba Grain Growers to form the Interprovincial Council of Grain Growers' and Farmers' Associ-

[1] The use of the title "Farmers'" instead of "Grain Growers'" is significant of the more diversified character of Alberta's agriculture.

[2] Wood, *Farmers' Movements in Canada*, pp. 199–201.

[3] Amendments to Grain Inspection Act, 1908, sec. 17.

[4] *Canadian Annual Review*, 1908, p. 502.

ations, and had participated through the Council in the negotiations with the three Western premiers for government ownership of elevators.[1] In the 1908 convention of the association, however, the elevator question was not a subject of special discussion.

Formation of United Farmers of Alberta, 1909. — Despite a second unsuccessful attempt, in 1906, to amalgamate the Society of Equity and the Alberta Farmers' Association,[2] there was a growing realization among Alberta farmers of the obvious advantage of having a single inclusive organization to bring the farmers' needs and views before the government and to coöperate with the other provincial organizations, particularly in respect to the elevator and tariff issues. Moreover, the setback which the Society of Equity suffered from the failure of its timber enterprise made its leaders more disposed to negotiate with the Farmers' Association, whose constructive representations were receiving sympathetic consideration and action from the provincial government. Finally in September, 1908, representatives of the two organizations came together and drafted a basis of union, which, after consideration by the locals of the two bodies, was unanimously adopted by the two conventions meeting simultaneously in Edmonton in January, 1909. Much discussion had raged over the name of the new organization. A happy compromise was effected by adopting the designation of the "United Farmers of Alberta, Our Motto, Equity." Its principal objects were declared to be:

1. To further the interests of farmers and ranchers in all branches of agriculture; to promote the best methods of farm business; to seek to enlarge and increase our markets; to obtain by united effort profitable and equitable prices for farm produce; and to secure the best and cheapest transportation.
2. To study and teach the principles of coöperation and to promote the establishment of coöperative societies.
3. To watch and influence and promote legislation relative to the above objects and to take any political action necessary for this purpose.

[1] See *supra*, p. 82.

[2] The negotiations broke down mainly because the Society of Equity aimed at Dominion-wide organization, while the A. F. A. favored a distinctly provincial organization. Wood, *op. cit.*, p. 201.

4. To promote social intercourse and the study of economic and social questions bearing on our interest as farmers.[1]

Each organization at the time of amalgamation had approximately 2,500 members.[2] Under the constitution adopted, new local unions might be formed by a group of not less than ten qualified farmers in any locality subscribing to the constitution and duly reporting to the association. Each local was entitled to representation at the annual convention, on the basis of one delegate for each ten members in good standing. After considerable discussion the *Grain Growers' Guide* was adopted in preference to various Alberta farm journals as the official organ of the association. By this gesture the United Farmers of Alberta declared their solidarity with the Grain Growers' Movement.

II. The Alberta Co-operative Elevator Act, 1913

While the first U. F. A. convention placed on record its "approval of the movement made by the Interprovincial Council for government ownership of elevators," [3] no explicit instructions were given to the directors to press the matter with the Alberta government. The reply of the Western premiers to the representatives of the Interprovincial Council was made public a few days after the close of the U. F. A. convention.[4] When it became apparent toward the close of the year, that each province would have to work out its own elevator policy and plans,[5] the United Farmers of Alberta began to study more seriously and definitely their peculiar requirements in relation to grain storage and shipping. At the 1910 convention, an Elevator Committee under President Bower was appointed to formulate a detailed plan for a system of government elevators for submission to the legislature,[6] Premier Rutherford having given assurance that "if the farmers of Alberta present a request to the Alberta government, to consider a scheme for government ownership of elevators in this

[1] Constitution, United Farmers of Alberta, Art. 2.
[2] Convention Reports, *Edmonton Bulletin*, Jan. 14–16, 1909.
[3] U. F. A., 1909.
[4] See *supra*, p. 82.
[5] See *supra*, p. 84.
[6] U. F. A., 1910.

province, the request would be granted and any suggestion given full consideration." [1]

Nature of Alberta's Elevator Problem. — In rendering its report to the 1911 convention, the U. F. A. Elevator Committee emphasized the divergence between Alberta's grain-marketing problem and that of the other Prairie Provinces. The British Columbia interior market and the export route by Vancouver (from which much was expected through the prospective completion of the Panama Canal) offered the Alberta grain grower a more profitable and promising outlet for his product than the Winnipeg market, provided he had equal facilities for westward and eastward shipment.[2] The Manitoba Grain Act, however, had been formulated to meet the conditions of eastward movement solely, and of bulk sale by grade only. Elevator operators were allowed under the act to send forward farmers' grain in country storage to the lakehead terminals, upon mere notification to the owner. The farmer was not free, therefore, to take advantage of better prices that might be obtainable in British Columbia. Moreover, consigned cars could not be diverted westward from Calgary except at prohibitive cost, since that place was not a car-order point. Without an interior terminal elevator where the farmer might obtain government grade and weight, and store his grain for westward shipment, by carload, or in sacks, as generally required for British Columbia consumption, any advantages which the western market might offer accrued only to the elevator companies. The committee felt, therefore, that the establishment of Calgary as a car-order point, the construction there of an interior government terminal, and the amendment of the Grain and Inspection acts, were of greater concern to the Alberta grain grower than the government ownership of initial elevators. Before making definite recommendations in regard to the latter, the committee desired to observe the results of the elevator schemes under experiment in Manitoba and Saskatchewan.[3]

[1] *G. G. Guide*, Jan. 5, 1910.

[2] The distance from Calgary to Vancouver is 640 miles, whereas the distance from Calgary to Fort William is 1,250 miles, and to Montreal 2,250 miles, lake and rail.

[3] U. F. A., 1911; *G. G. Guide*, Jan. 25, 1911, p. 16.

During 1911–12 representatives of the U. F. A. pressed before the federal authorities the case for making Calgary a terminal point, as a means of securing to Alberta farmers the advantages of the western market. Declaration of such intention was made by the government in connection with the general overhauling of grain legislation through the enactment of the Canada Grain Act in 1912.[1] Meanwhile the problem of initial storage was becoming more urgent, as dry farming encroached further upon the former grazing lands of southern Alberta, and as the early maturing Marquis extended the wheat frontiers northward. Since Alberta shipping points were on the average between 1,000 and 1,200 miles from the head of the lakes, its growers not only had heavier freight charges to meet, but were also at a relative disadvantage in the securing of cars. Except when harvests were unusually early, cars were rarely able to make more than one or two return trips between Alberta points and the lake terminals before the close of navigation. After the first movement, therefore, the spread between track and street prices tended to be at a maximum at Alberta shipping stations, while opportunities for platform shipment were limited from the same cause.[2] Street sellers were disposed to blame the elevator companies for the extent of such spread, while carload shippers became increasingly insistent upon the necessity for special binning facilities. Thus the demand for a system of farmer-controlled elevators became steadily intensified in Alberta.

Elevator Policy of United Farmers of Alberta. — During 1911 the U. F. A. Elevator Committee investigated the Saskatchewan Co-operative Elevator plan, and recommended to the 1912 convention that the Alberta government be requested to introduce a similar act to incorporate the "Alberta Co-operative

[1] See *infra*, p. 218 n. With the completion of the federal government interior storage elevator at Calgary in 1915, Calgary was made a terminal inspection and car-order point. After the opening of the Panama Canal, a small transfer elevator was erected by the federal government at Vancouver, in 1916. The westward movement of Alberta grain did not attain any significant proportions, however, until after 1921, following enlargement of transfer facilities and freight-rate adjustments.

[2] See report of Thos. Woolford to U. F. A., *Edmonton Bulletin*, Jan. 18, 1909; also report of U. F. A. Elev. Comm., *G. G. Guide*, Jan. 29, 1913, p. 14.

Company." Premier Sifton, who had succeeded Hon. A. C. Rutherford in 1910, took the position, however, that the Saskatchewan system had not been in force long enough to demonstrate whether it would be suitable for the different conditions in Alberta.[1] By the time of the 1913 convention (January 21) the U. F. A. Elevator Committee had had an instructive opportunity of comparing the respective merits of the Manitoba and Saskatchewan systems, and of considering the details of adaptation of the latter to Alberta. They favored, however, even more complete control by the farmers than in the case of the Saskatchewan Company.[2] To this end they recommended that the government of Alberta should be asked merely to guarantee the bonds of a farmer-owned company for the erection of a line of elevators in the province. As considerable working capital and a strong selling organization on the Winnipeg Exchange would be needed, however, to operate such a system, it was contemplated that, while shareholders' locals should be established as in Saskatchewan, the operation of the elevators might be undertaken by the Grain Growers' Grain Company, with its strong resources and connections.[3] After a memorable debate, the report was adopted by the convention, and the directors were instructed to work out the scheme with the government, with power to vary the terms at their discretion.

The Alberta government, satisfied now as to the unanimity and definiteness of the farmers' demand, and impressed by the initial results of the Saskatchewan plan, was quite prepared to draft a bill in conference with the U. F. A. representatives. It was not willing, however, to guarantee the bonds of a company which contemplated turning over the operation of its elevators to another company with headquarters outside the province. It was

[1] *G. G. Guide*, Jan. 24, 1912.

[2] "The first requisite for a system of elevators in Alberta was the absolute control and management by the farmers themselves, with the very slightest possible chance for interference eliminated." *Report of U. F. A. Elev. Com.*, 1913.

[3] *Report of U. F. A. Elev. Com.*, 1913, *G. G. Guide*, Jan. 5, 1913. Address of E. J. Fream, U. F. A. Convention, 1913, *G. G. Guide*, Feb. 5, 1913. The G. G. G. Co. had opened a branch office at Calgary in August, 1909, to facilitate the handling of farmers' consignments from the rapidly expanding wheat-growing area of southern and central Alberta. G. G. G. Co., 1910.

prepared, on the other hand, to give the farmers complete control of the company's policy and operations; and as the bonds of the province could evidently be marketed on more advantageous terms than those of a farmers' company, carrying a provincial guarantee, it was agreed that the elevators should be financed by means of direct government loans to the company to the extent of 85 per cent of the cost of construction or acquisition, under provisions for security similar to those contained in the Saskatchewan plan.

Comparison of Alberta and Saskatchewan Elevator Acts. — The act incorporating the Alberta Farmers' Co-operative Elevator Company [1] reproduced the main features, and considerable of the text, of the Saskatchewan act. Certain significant modifications, however, may be noted. In the first place, under the Alberta act the powers of the incorporated farmers' company were more fully enumerated. In addition to being generally empowered "to construct, acquire by purchase, agreement, lease or otherwise, maintain and operate grain elevators, in the province of Alberta . . . and to buy and sell grain and generally do all things necessary to the production, storing and marketing of grain," the Alberta Company was specifically authorized "to act as commission or general agents for any person, company, or corporation in the purchase, sale, storing, and delivery of any and all goods and chattels required by farmers." [2] In this the intention of the Alberta Farmers' Company to engage in coöperative trading as well as in elevator operation is definitely implied.

In the second place, provision was made for possible operating arrangements, or even amalgamation with the Grain Growers' Grain Company, subject to the double proviso that no such "sale, lease, or agreement with any other company for the control or operation of the said elevators" would be valid unless previously submitted to all shareholders' locals, and approved by a majority of the whole number of shareholders voting; or enforceable until approved by the Lieutenant-Governor in Council.[3]

[1] Stat. of Alberta, 4 Geo. V, c. 13, 1913.

[2] *Ibid.*, sec. 5; compare Sask. Co-op. Elev. Act, sec. 2.

[3] *Ibid.*, secs. 5, 6.

The requirements of the Saskatchewan act as to local stock subscription equivalent to the estimated cost of elevator petitioned for, and as to minimum tributary crop area of 6,000 acres under subscribers' control, were reproduced in the Alberta measure.[1] In conformity, however, with the U. F. A. policy of retaining complete financial control in the hands of the farmers, the paid-up capital requirements were made more exacting in the case of Alberta stock subscribers. Shares were to be issued at $60 par value, of which 20 per cent was to be paid up prior to the erection or acquisition of local elevators, and the remaining 80 per cent in four annual instalments.[2] Since the government loan amounted to 85 per cent of the capital cost of elevators, a margin of 5 per cent was thus provided as working capital for the company.

With respect to the disposition of company revenues, provision was made for patronage distribution of profits, subject however, to the following priorities: (*a*) annual payments due the province, (*b*) all current liabilities, (*c*) such reserve appropriations as the directors should deem advisable.[3] No provision was made, as in the Saskatchewan act, for distribution in the form of stock dividends.[4] Some dissension had arisen among the directors over the failure to make patronage distribution compulsory. It was agreed by the majority, however, that adequate inducement must be offered to secure farmers' capital, and that a reserve would have to be accumulated for trading purposes before any dividend to patrons could be considered. The accounting difficulties involved in such distribution, where grain could be handled for patrons in half a dozen different ways, were also recognized.[5]

1 Alberta Co-op. Elev. Act, sec. 15; cf. Sask. Co-op. Elev. Act, sec. 13.

2 Alberta Co-op. Elev. Act, sec. 19. Since Saskatchewan Co-operative shareholders were required to pay up only 15 per cent on a $50 share, their initial payment was $7.50, while Alberta shareholders had to pay $12 per share. The latter had the option of paying up the remaining instalments by authorizing the company to deduct an extra one cent per bushel over and above the regular charge for handling their grain.

3 Alberta Co-op. Elev. Act, sec. 36.

4 Sask. Co-op. Elev. Act, sec. 20, sub-sec. 3(*e*).

5 Address of E. J. Fream, to U. F. A., *G. G. Guide*, Jan. 28, 1914.

Organization of Alberta Co-operative Elevator Company, 1913. — The Alberta Company was authorized to begin business when twenty locals should have been organized.[1] Following the Saskatchewan precedent, the officers of the United Farmers of Alberta were named as incorporators and authorized to act as provisional directors, the legislature making a grant of $5,000 for organizational expenses. The provisional board met on April 25 (1913), and chose as their provisional executives W. J. Tregillus, Calgary, president; E. Carswell, Red Deer, vice-president, and E. J. Fream, Calgary, secretary-treasurer.[2] So aggressively was the organization work prosecuted, and so ready were the farmers to participate in the enterprise, that the requisite initial twenty locals, each with a minimum of 134 shares, or $8,040 subscribed stock, were duly organized by July. As several others were in course of organization, it was decided to defer the first general meeting to permit larger representation. At the same time, in order to ensure that the new elevators would be in a position to handle the current crop, and thus avoid the embarrassments of the Saskatchewan Company during its initial season,[3] the provisional executive, feeling assured of the farmers' support, assumed the responsibility of ordering supplies, securing elevator sites from the railways, and initiating the construction of 22 elevators, in anticipation of the general meeting. It was decided from the first to avoid the unsatisfactory initial experience of the Saskatchewan Company in carrying on construction by contract. Accordingly, the provisional executive engaged its own company engineer, adopted a standard elevator type of 35,000 bushels average capacity, with 22 large carload bins, and employed extensively the labor of neighboring farmers at day rates.[4] When the general meeting of shareholders did assemble in Calgary, on August 19, instead of the statutory twenty locals, no less than

[1] Alta. Co-op. Elev. Act, sec. 9. Twenty-five initial locals had been required under the Saskatchewan act, sec. 7.

[2] These provisional officers were respectively, president, 4th vice-president, and honorary secretary-treasurer of the U. F. A.

[3] See *supra*, p. 108.

[4] Alberta Farmers' Co-operative Elevator Co., 1913; *Calgary Albertan*, Aug. 20, 1913.

forty-six, with 3,500 shareholders, were represented,[1] and the directors were able to report a subscribed capital of $360,000, with half the work of construction on 42 elevators completed.[2]

III. Operations of Alberta Farmers' Co-operative Elevator Coompany

With the provisional executive reappointed, the first year's operations of the Alberta Farmers' Co-operative Elevator Company were carried on through 52 elevators, 10 houses being purchased in addition to the 42 built by the company. Although all of these were not ready to receive grain when the movement began, nearly 4,000,000 bushels were handled.[3] While the Alberta Company had a seat on the Calgary Grain Exchange (a purely cash market), most of the grain purchased or shipped through its elevators was sold on the Winnipeg market through the Grain Growers' Grain Company, acting as its selling agency.[4]

Relations with Grain Growers' Company. — The Grain Growers' Grain Company stood indeed more or less in the relation of business guardian to the new-born farmers' company.[5] Not only did it handle the latter's grain on the Winnipeg Exchange, but it also loaned its capital and credit to assist the Alberta Company in financing purchases of street grain and advances to farmers on stored or consigned grain. The Grain Growers' Company thus undertook to do for the Alberta Co-operative what the Saskatchewan government had done for the farmers' elevator company in that province by guaranteeing its account with the bank. The

[1] By coincidence this was the same number of locals as were represented at the first general meeting of Saskatchewan Company. See *supra*, p. 106.

[2] A. F. C. E. Co., 1913.

[3] The amount of grain handled up to June 30, 1914, was 3,774,381 bushels. In the first year the Saskatchewan Co-op. handled 3,261,000 bushels through its 46 elevators. A. F. C. E. Co., 1914.

[4] The Grain Growers' Grain Co. registered one of its seats on the Winnipeg Exchange in the name of the manager of the Alberta Company, thereby entitling the latter to the commission rate chargeable to Exchange members. Statement of E. J. Fream to writer.

[5] The liaison between the two companies centered largely about the person of E. J. Fream, secretary-treasurer and manager of the Alberta Co-op., who had been Alberta director of the Grain Growers' Co., since 1911, continuing as such until 1916.

extent of the financial assistance rendered by the Winnipeg Company is indicated by the fact that at the end of the Alberta Company's first business year its current liability to the former stood at $328,000, nearly three times the amount of its total paid-up capital.[1] The financing of the 1914 crop was fraught with considerable difficulty, owing to the disturbance of credit following the outbreak of the war. Since the Alberta Company was not in a position to borrow on its own credit,[2] its operations were made possible only through the Grain Growers' Company ,whose liquid reserves made it less dependent on bank borrowings.[3] At the end of the second year the Alberta Company owed the latter $87,781, secured by stocks of grain and flour, and indirectly by unpaid calls on subscribed capital.[4]

Elevator Operations. — Owing to the much smaller volume of grain production in Alberta, the number of elevator locals, while steadily increasing, did not expand at as rapid a rate as in Saskatchewan. Both companies had commenced their first year's operations with 46 established locals. At the beginning of the fourth year's business, the Alberta Company had 103 local elevators, while the Saskatchewan Co-operative had owned 215 at the same stage.[5] In proportion to crop acreage, however, the density of coöperative elevators in Alberta was only slightly less than that in Saskatchewan at the relative dates.[6] Alberta farmers, being farther removed from the lakehead terminals, were disposed to make even greater use of special binning facilities than their Saskatchewan neighbors, no less than 60 per cent of the company's share of the great 1915 crop being so handled.[7] In

[1] A. F. C. E. Co. Balance Sheet, 1914.

[2] Since the company possessed no liquid assets, the banks refused to extend credit unless its account should be guaranteed by the provincial government or by some responsible grain firm. For five days in 1914 buying at company elevators had to be discontinued altogether. A. F. C. E. Co., 1915, pp. 27, 28.

[3] Credit requirements were considerably lessened by the low volume of the 1914 wheat crop — amounting in all to only 140,000,000 bushels.

[4] G. G. G. Co., 1915, p. 27.

[5] A. F. C. E. Co., Nov. 1916; Sask. Co-op. Nov., 1914.

[6] The area in wheat and coarse grains in Saskatchewan in 1914 was approximately 9,250,000 acres, while the corresponding crop area in Alberta in 1916 was about 5,250,000 acres. *Canada Year Book*, 1915, 1917.

[7] A. F. C. E. Co., 1916.

Alberta, as in Saskatchewan, the policy of the coöperative elevator companies of offering higher and at the same time uniform prices for street grain at all points taking the same freight rate, served to reduce the spread between street and track prices at competing points.[1] Thus the wagon-load seller, as well as the farmer desiring to have his grain specially binned, was benefited by the company's participation.

Collateral Coöperative Enterprises. — In contrast with the Saskatchewan Company, which concentrated its attention and resources on grain marketing exclusively, the Alberta Farmers' Company early availed itself of its wide powers of incorporation to diversify its operations. In the very first year of business a Livestock Department and a Co-operative Supply Department were initiated, as supplementary to the elevator operations. This policy of the Alberta Farmers' Company was in part a reflection of the more diversified character of Alberta's agriculture, and partly due no doubt to the influence of the Society of Equity strain in its origin, as well as to its close connection with the Grain Growers' Company, which had decided in 1912 to enter the field of coöperative supply. The new company, it was felt, should function as the general commercial coöperative agency of U. F. A. locals, and its elevator operators could be employed, not merely as local grain warehousemen, but also as livestock shipping and farm supply agents.[2]

For years the A. F. A. and the U. F. A. had endeavored to secure the establishment of a government pork-packing plant, but had failed to obtain the necessary patronage guarantee for hog deliveries requested by the government.[3] With the formation

[1] "The presence of the [Alberta] Company in the market has considerably reduced the spread between track and street prices. Whereas in former years a spread of six and seven cents was common, the highest spread this season has been four cents, and that on only two days." Address of E. J. Fream to U. F. A., 1914, *G. G. Guide*, Jan. 28, 1914.

"We have farmers who have drawn their grain twenty to thirty miles to our elevator rather than sell to those close at home." A. F. C. E. Co., 1914; *G. G. Guide*, Oct. 21, 1914.

[2] In 1915–16 the company undertook to pay its elevator agents a bonus based on the amount of co-operative supply and livestock business handled.

[3] See *supra*, p. 115; U. F. A. 1911, 1912, 1914. The provincial government had asked for minimum guaranteed delivery of 50,000 hogs a year.

of the Alberta Farmers' Co-operative Company it was felt that more immediate profits could be realized for livestock producers by establishing a farmer-owned marketing agency at the stockyards. Such activity was strongly favored by President Bower and Vice-President Carswell, both of whom had been officers of the Red Deer local of the A. F. A. which in 1909 had organized the first coöperative livestock marketing association in Canada.[1] Operating as a pioneer in its field, the Livestock Department of the Alberta Company found it necessary more than once to change its methods in response to producers' preferences and competitive conditions. Thus patronage considerations led to the abandonment of the Red Deer plan of prorating commission profits in the form of stock dividends, in favor of buying livestock at local shipping points for resale in the Calgary market. Insufficient working capital, and losses arising out of inexpert buying amid uncertain market conditions, compelled recourse in turn to the method of coöperative carload consignment to the company's Livestock Commission Department, buying being limited to stockers and feeders for farmers' orders. By 1916 the company was handling 20 per cent of all livestock shipments received at the Calgary yards, and had also established itself in the new Edmonton stockyards. But while its livestock operations were serviceable as a form of coöperative pioneering, they did not prove financially profitable to the company in these experimental years.[2]

In response to demands from numerous shareholders that the company should undertake the handling of the supplies the farmer had to buy, as well as of the grain and livestock he had to sell, the management made a beginning, in the spring of 1914, of supplying flour and feed through company elevators at points where locals requested such service. In the following year the range of commodities handled was extended to include coal, lumber, fenceposts, wire, binder twine, hay, fruit, salt, and so forth. The co-operative plan involved centralized buying or ordering from main sources of supply through the Co-operative Department, local distribution through company elevator operators, and the hand-

[1] "Red Deer U. F. A. Co-operative Association," *Agric. Gazette of Canada*, Nov. 1914.

[2] A. F. C. E. Co., 1914, 1915, 1916.

ling of individual orders and collections through secretaries of shareholders' locals. Owing to the company's limited trading capital, it was sought to handle supplies as far as possible on an order or commission basis, with the Co-operative Department acting merely as purchasing agency for locals. It was found, however, that in the case of such commodities as coal, flour, binder twine, and the like, buying could not be conducted on the most advantageous terms, nor effective competitive service rendered, unless the company carried stocks of its own and maintained local storage facilities. Accordingly coal-sheds and flour warehouses were erected at numerous points as adjuncts to company elevators, which thus served as distributing as well as assembling units.[1]

Financial Results. — While the Alberta Farmers' Co-operative Elevator Company was thus endeavoring to render the largest possible service to its shareholders, its initial financial returns were much less satisfactory than those of the Grain Growers' Company or the Saskatchewan Co-operative. While the profit and loss account at the end of the second year showed a credit balance of $36,240, no depreciation had been allowed on the company's elevators during the first year, and it was not until the exceptional crop of 1915 [2] resulted in a gross profit of $282,485 for the third year, that any dividend was paid by the company, and that on grounds of policy rather than of strict financial justification.[3] Considerable difficulty had been experienced in securing the payment of annual instalments on subscribed stock,[4] and the restricted working capital of the company imposed heavy expenditures on account of interest.[5] The financial difficulties of

[1] By 1917 the company had coal-sheds at 119 points. A. F. C. E. Co., 1917.

[2] The grain handled by the company in 1915–16 was equivalent to 222,075 bushels per elevator, compared with 82,050 bushels in 1913–14 and 66,300 in 1914–15. A. F. C. E. Co., Dec. 1916.

[3] "It was felt by your directors that, while possibly as a straight business proposition it might not be advisable to pay a dividend, still, from the point of view of policy it would without doubt well repay the company." A. F. C. E. Co., 1916.

[4] The paid-up capital of the company was actually less than 20 per cent of the subscribed stock at the end of the third year. A. F. C. E. Co., 1916.

[5] In 1914–15 the item of interest alone exceeded $75,000, equivalent to 38 per cent of operating expenses.

the company had been increased by premature entry into live-stock and farm-supply trading operations, which the Saskatchewan Company had avoided, and which the Grain Growers' Company had entered into only after building up large reserve funds. The Alberta Company's income was limited, moreover, by its inability to conduct its own selling operations on the Winnipeg Grain Exchange during the initial years. In its physical expansion and in its business services to its farmer shareholders the Alberta Company had made remarkable progress during its first three years. This had been largely made possible, however, only through the financial, commercial, and moral assistance of the Grain Growers' Grain Company, with which a closer identification was now being seriously considered.

CHAPTER X

THE GRAIN GROWERS AND THE TERMINALS

I. The Grain Growers' Demands

The campaign of the organized Grain Growers for provincial ownership of initial elevators had been coupled, it will be recalled, with the demand for federal ownership and operation of terminal elevators.[1] In aiming to remove the control of warehousing facilities from the hands of grain-trading interests the Grain Growers sought, consistently enough, to have elevators operated as public utilities, not only at local assembling points, but also at the strategic terminal points, where the entire exportable surplus was concentrated, and where grain in store commanded the basic prices from which country quotations were derived.

Although the railway companies had not found it feasible to undertake themselves the provision of grain storage facilities at initial shipping points, all terminal warehouses at Fort William and Port Arthur had been owned and operated by railway companies from 1883, when the C. P. R. built its first lakehead elevator, until 1904, when two public elevators were erected at Fort William by companies operating lines of country houses.[2] In 1906 the Canadian Northern Railway leased to grain companies the large terminal houses it had constructed at Port Arthur on completing its line to the head of the lakes in 1902. After 1904, therefore, the terminal storage facilities, which had hitherto been owned and operated exclusively by the railways, began to pass gradually under the control of grain companies, thus effecting an integration of country assembling systems and central storage.[3]

Grain might be received and held in privately owned public terminals under four different conditions of ownership. It might be (*a*) purchased grain belonging to the owners or lessees of the

[1] See *supra*, p. 89.

[2] The Ogilvie Milling Co., and the Empire Elevator Co.

[3] See *Report of Royal Grain Inquiry Commission*, 1925, pp. 76, 77.

terminal elevator; (*b*) grain bought by exporters, eastern millers, or other dealers, and held in store pending shipment; (*c*) grain shipped by farmers, over platform or through country elevators, for terminal storage pending sale; (*d*) grain delivered to country elevators by farmers on graded storage tickets, and shipped on to the terminal by the elevator company in order to clear its country bins.[1]

Complaints of Grain Growers against Terminal Elevators.— The operation of public terminal elevators by companies interested in the buying and selling of grain was regarded with suspicion and antagonism by the Grain Growers, for several reasons. It was believed, in the first place, that mixing of grades took place in public as well as private elevators, higher grades being diluted with admixtures of lower-grade grain, and lower grades being "promoted" by adding sufficient quantities of superior grain to enable the whole to meet the minimum requirements of the next higher grade. Thus, it was claimed, the average quality of grades exported from the terminals was lower than that on which the farmers' grain was sold. It was also generally believed that terminal elevator operators as a rule did not clean the grain to the full extent of the dockage set on the inspection certificate, thereby gaining on weights as well as lowering the quality of the inspected grain. Not only, it was inferred, did mixing and undercleaning of graded grain mean higher profits to dealers at the expense of growers, but it further reacted to the detriment of the latter by so affecting the reputation of Canadian grain on foreign markets as to lower the price its standard grades commanded abroad, which was in return reflected in lower prices received by producers on the Winnipeg market or at country points. In the third place, it was suspected that terminal operators not infrequently "loaned" quantities of farmers' grain held in terminal storage to lake shippers, to enable them to fill out cargoes. This meant, not only that the farmers concerned were paying storage charges on grain which elevator companies,

[1] Upon giving 48 hours notice to the owner, the operator of any country elevator might forward any grain stored in his elevator to any terminal elevator. Manitoba Grain Act, sec. 58.

although responsible for it, did not actually hold, but also that the involuntary release of such holdings served to defeat the very purpose for which it was being held off the market by the grower.[1] In the fourth place, the control of terminal facilities by line companies operating their own commission departments as well, was regarded by farmers as tending further to increase the power of such integrated interests to eliminate the competition of independent commission firms (such as the Grain Growers' Company), and thus strengthen their monopolistic position in the trade.[2]

Government acquisition of terminals had also been urged by Grain Growers' conventions as the necessary complement to the desired establishment of a sample market at Winnipeg.[3] Milling companies with their own country houses were able, while buying at grade prices, to select the cream of the grades brought to their elevators, offering perhaps slightly higher prices for specially desirable wagonloads at points where competition was active, or in seasons when the general average of the crop was low.[4] An organized sample market, it was felt, would enable the platform shipper or special bin shipper to realize a competitive premium on wheat believed to be above the average of the grade. It was recognized, however, that selling on sample implied the right of purchasers to mix grain so bought. To this the Grain Growers found no objection, so long as the mixed grain was not sold on straight government certificate. Their solution was to have grain bought on sample, or mixed in private houses,[5] specially binned in the government terminals, and shipped out under special certificates, instead of being binned with grain received into terminals on Winnipeg inspection.[6]

[1] Memorial of farmers' delegations to Sir Wilfrid Laurier, at Ottawa, Dec. 16, 1910; see *infra*, p. 138. [2] See *supra*, p. 93.

[3] M. G. G. A., 1908; S. G. G. A., 1908. This had also been involved in the Manitoba Grain Growers' provincial elevator scheme. See *supra*, p. 93.

[4] See *Report of Sask. Elev. Comm.*, 1910, pp. 71, 72.

[5] The first private mixing-house had appeared at the head of the lakes in 1907, and was followed by two others in 1909. Mixed grain from these houses was shipped into the public terminals and given official grade on being inspected. *Report of Royal Grain Commission*, 1925, p. 77.

[6] *G. G. Guide*, Feb. 7, 1912.

Existing Terminal Regulation. — The Royal Grain Commission of 1906–07 had given special attention to the operations of the terminals, and had carefully followed through the movement of grain, from initial elevators to the British market. While the commissioners did not find general evidence of mixing, their investigations showed that a good deal of grain reached eastern and overseas markets without being properly cleaned to grade.[1] They considered, however, that irregularities at the terminals could be controlled by extending the scope of government supervision, without resorting to government ownership and operation:

> To prevent the evils that are made possible by operation of the terminal elevators under the present system we do not think it wise to advise the government to go to the length of taking over the terminal elevators, or of prohibiting persons engaged in the grain trade being interested in such terminals. We believe it possible to obtain a good service from these elevators under present ownership by having a more thorough system of supervision and control.[2]

Provision for instituting "a more thorough system of supervision and control," in accordance with the commissioners' recommendations, was made through amendments to the Grain Inspection Act and the Manitoba Grain Act during the session of 1908. Under the former, the Inspection Department was given "full control of all grain in terminal elevators." Cleaning operations, the binning of all grain received, the transfer of grain from one bin to another, the shipping out of grain into vessels or cars — all were to be conducted under the supervision and control of

[1] "From evidence received in Ontario, and from samples taken directly by the commission from arrivals at Georgian Bay ports, it is quite clear that there is not a sufficient supervision or control of cleaning of grain at Fort William. There is a very general complaint throughout Ontario that they do not get the regular grade of Manitoba grain in as clean a condition as is called for by the Inspection Department. We also found from examination of arrivals in Great Britain, that grain as received there contains too great a percentage of foreign matter. It is quite evident to us that there should be complete supervision of cleaning operations at the terminals. . . . No serious complaints were received of grades being lowered by mixing, though in some cases samples were produced that would lead us to believe that there had been either manipulation or serious mistakes made somewhere." *Report of Royal Commission on Grain Trade*, Dom. Sess. Paper, No. 59, 1908, p. 18.

[2] *Ibid.*, Appendix E, p. 39.

inspectors.[1] As a further precaution against mixing, the Inspection Department was required to take stock during the closing month of each crop year (August) of each grade of grain in all public terminals, checking the same against the weekly returns furnished to the department by terminal operators.[2]

The commissioners found themselves unable to recommend the establishment of a sample market at Winnipeg, in view of the small proportion of the Western crop milled in the West, and of the delay in car movement involved in holding cars for sale by sample.[3] Since the bulk of the crop was exported or milled in the East, it was felt that the interests of growers could be best served by ensuring that grain shipments strictly conformed with the grade certificates they carried. To this end the Chief Inspector was authorized under the amendments of 1908 to make the necessary rules and regulations for satisfactorily identifying outward inspection certificates with the lake or railroad shipping bill and the parcel of grain covered by such certificate;[4] while all transfer elevators east of Port Arthur were brought under the scope of the Manitoba Inspection Division, "in so far as respects dealing with western grain."[5]

Such were the methods of "more thorough supervision and control" by which the government, on the recommendation of the commission, sought to prevent the terminal manipulations of which western farmers and eastern millers complained.[6] The Grain Growers placed little confidence, however, in the efficiency of mere government regulation, and continued to urge the actual taking over of the terminals by the government as the only certain means of eliminating the incentive to the malpractices com-

[1] Amendments to Grain Inspection Act, 1908, sec. 9.

[2] *Ibid.*

[3] *Report of Royal Grain Comm.*, 1906–07, pp. 12, 13.

[4] Grain Inspection Act, Amendments of 1908, sec. 10.

[5] Manitoba Grain Act, Amendments of 1908, sec. 5.

[6] Complaints were particularly numerous at this time from small eastern millers without elevator lines of their own in the West, that grain received on terminal warehouse receipts was frequently mixed, undercleaned, or above the average moisture content. *Report of Grain Comm.*, 1906–07, p. 18. The complaints have frequently been renewed. See *Report of Grain Inquiry Comm.*, 1923–25, p. 83.

plained of.[1] A deputation from the Interprovincial Council pressed the matter before Sir Richard Cartwright, the Minister of Trade and Commerce, in May, 1909, and was supported by the Dominion Millers' Association.[2] In presenting a second memorandum in the following January, the Grain Growers had the support, not merely of representatives of eastern millers, but also of a number of Winnipeg independent grain commission dealers.[3]

Irregularities at Terminals. — About this time evidence of an official nature appeared in substantiation of the Grain Growers' contentions. At the close of navigation in 1909, Warehouse Commissioner Castle, having discovered marked discrepancies between the reports of the Inspection Department and the returns made by certain terminal elevators, instituted an unannounced stock-taking of grain in store on the lake front. As a result of the investigation three terminal companies were prosecuted for making false returns under the Grain Act. The evidence proved that in the case of two of these, shipments and holdings of No. 1 Northern exceeded their recorded receipts by 1,035,786 bushels, while shortages of 832,806 bushels were found in Nos. 2, 3, and 4 Northern. Obviously there had been a general promotion of grades by mixing. The net surplus was presumably to be accounted for by cleaning below the dockage set. In the Winnipeg police court the two companies were fined $3,000 and $2,500 respectively, and threatened with loss of their licenses.[4] Although this incident might be taken as showing that such practices could not be carried on without detection under the existing system of regulation, the conclusion generally accepted by the Grain Growers and the public was that, in spite of the supervision of the numerous government checkers and inspectors, grain mixing was being extensively practised in the terminals. Was it not a waste, asked the Grain Growers, to employ men to

[1] "Just so long as these (terminal) elevators remain in private hands there will be the temptation of private gain. There is only one possible method by which the system of robbing the farmers' grain at the terminals can be abolished. That method is by federal government ownership." *G. G. Guide* (editorial) Dec. 28, 1909.

[2] *Canada Annual Review*, 1909, p. 486. [3] *G. G. Guide* (editorial), April 27, 1910.

[4] Report of C. C. Castle to Department of Trades and Commerce, April 22, 1910.

watch that elevator operators did not defraud the public, when the government employees might just as well operate the terminals themselves and eliminate both duplication of staff and suspicion of malpractice? [1]

In the meantime the Manitoba Grain Growers' Association had been conducting an investigation of its own. By arrangement with a Liverpool correspondent, samples were obtained from cargoes of Manitoba grain arriving in that port, and expressed, with notation of certificate carried, to Winnipeg, where they were inspected by a member of the Winnipeg Inspection staff. The results indicated in nearly every case that the grain had not been cleaned to the requirements of the grade, analysis of forty samples showing that all but four contained more than one per cent of dirt. Only eleven of the forty samples were found to be up to the average of the grade carried. The results of this investigation were transmitted by the secretary of the Manitoba Grain Growers to the Minister of Trade and Commerce.[2]

Grain Growers' Representations to Federal Government. — During the western tour of Sir Wilfrid Laurier in the summer of 1910, representatives of prairie farmers' organizations presented, whereever meetings were held, memorials urging government acquisition of terminal elevators and effective prevention of the mixing of wheat, together with demands for tariff reductions on the instruments of production and freer trade with Great Britain and the United States. Alberta farmers especially emphasized the need for an interior terminal elevator at Calgary and a transfer elevator at Vancouver, to facilitate the western movement of grain. Saskatchewan grain growers laid particular stress on government completion of the Hudson Bay Railway with a grain terminal at Port Nelson. While not committing himself to complete government ownership of terminals, the Premier declared that the government was prepared to provide additional terminal facilities where convinced of their necessity, and promised legislation to prevent the mixing of grain in terminal elevators.[3]

[1] *G. G. Guide* (editorial), Dec. 28, 1909. [2] *G. G. Guide*, April 27, 1910.

[3] See *Canadian Annual Review*, 1910, pp. 263–277.

In the course of his tour the Premier expressed his willingness to discuss the terminal elevator question with the Grain Growers, and following his return, a letter was addressed on October 28 to the provincial Grain Growers' Associations, intimating the government's readiness to receive their representations.[1] It was decided by the Grain Growers' executives, however, not to send a special deputation to discuss this matter, but to present their views on the terminals in conjunction with memorials on other important issues which the Canadian Council of Agriculture was preparing to lay before the government through a monster farmers' deputation in December.[2] In the promotion of this pilgrimage, the *Grain Growers' Guide* played an aggressive and influential part.

"The Siege of Ottawa" on December 15–16 (1910) by the delegations of some 500 Western Grain Growers and 300 Ontario Grangers, with smaller groups from Quebec and the Maritime Provinces, constituted the largest deputation that ever pressed its claims upon the federal parliament, and afforded an impressive demonstration of the solidarity of the farmers' movement. Following a joint conference of the provincial delegations on the 15th, the whole deputation marched the next morning to the House of Commons, and presented to the cabinet and members successive resolutions and memorials, requesting tariff reduction with increase of the British Preference, and reciprocity with the United States; federal acquisition and operation of terminal elevators; government construction and operation of the Hudson Bay Railway and terminals; federal establishment of a chilled-meat industry in the interests of livestock producers; federal

[1] *Canadian Annual Review*, 1910, p. 324.

[2] The Canadian Council of Agriculture represented a national affiliation between the members of the Interprovincial Council of Grain Growers' Associations and the Dominion Grange of Ontario. The project of a national farmers' organization had been discussed and a draft constitution evolved at the convention of the Dominion Grange at Toronto in November 1909, which E. A. Partridge, Roderick McKenzie and D. W. McCuaig had attended as western fraternal delegates. The draft constitution was ratified in turn by the Dominion Grange, the M. G. G. A., the U. F. A. and the S. G. G. A. At the convention of the latter at Prince Albert in Feb. 1910 the Council had been formally organized, with D. W. McCuaig as its first president. See L. A. Wood: *Farmers' Movements in Canada*, pp. 205, 206.

legislation for incorporation of coöperative societies; and various amendments to the Railway and Bank acts.[1]

The memorial on the terminals, after exhaustively reviewing the evidence of manipulation and false returns by the elevator companies, and expressing the conviction that "no amount of supervision or inspection can effectually prevent manipulation in our terminals so long as they are owned and operated by private interests which can be benefited thereby" proceeded to recommend:

> That the Dominion government take steps to acquire and operate as a public utility, under an independent commission, the terminal elevators at Fort William and Port Arthur, and immediately establish similar terminal facilities and conditions at the Pacific coast, and provide the same at Hudson Bay when necessary; also, such transfer and other elevators as are necessary to safeguard the quality of export grain.[2]

The farmers' memorial on the terminals was followed by supporting statements from representatives of the Dominion Millers' Association, the Toronto Board of Trade, and eastern and western exporters, in which the millers testified to the superior quality of grain received through the C. P. R. terminals, and contended that so long as terminal elevators were allowed to mix grain, Canadian millers would not be able to turn out the best quality of flour.[3] The farmers' voice, united as it was, did not speak alone.

II. The Government's Response

The Grain Bill of 1911. — The agrarian "Siege of Ottawa" was not without its appreciable results. The nation-wide declaration of Canadian farmers in favor of reciprocity with the United States had not a little to do in determining the course of the Canadian Ministers in the negotiation of the limited reciprocity pact at Washington during the following month, and in the presenta-

[1] The leaders of the western delegations were D. W. McCuaig, president of the Canadian Council of Agriculture; J. W. Scallion and Roderick McKenzie of Manitoba; F. W. Green and E. A. Partridge of Saskatchewan; and Jas. Bower, W. J. Tregillus and E. J. Fream of Alberta.

[2] Text of farmers' memorials. *Manitoba Free Press*, Dec. 17, 1910.

[3] See *The Siege of Ottawa* (pub. by *Grain Growers' Guide*, 1911); L. A. Wood, *op. cit.*, pp. 264–268.

tion of the agreement to the House on January 26 (1911). A little later, Sir Richard Cartwright, the veteran Minister of Trade and Commerce, introduced in the Senate a grain bill consolidating and overhauling the existing grain legislation, providing for a Board of Grain Commissioners with widely extended powers of supervision, prohibiting any person or corporation engaged in buying and selling grain from owning or operating a terminal elevator, and authorizing the Department of Trade and Commerce to construct or acquire terminal elevators.

Most of the discussion centered about section 123, prohibiting terminal elevator owners or operators from dealing in grain on their own account, and a special committee of the Senate was appointed to take evidence on the contentious clauses. The Grain Growers supported the provision as the most acceptable alternative to complete government ownership, believing that the enforcement of the section would result in the transfer to the government of some at least of the terminals controlled by line elevator interests. The latter, while repudiating mixing, opposed the clauses as an infringement of vested rights and as tending to prejudice the operation of their country elevators and divert Canadian grain to Duluth terminals. The majority of the Senate Committee reported in favor of striking out the contentious clauses. Sir Richard Cartwright, however, adhered to the principle of divorcement which, he declared, was the result of careful consideration by the government. A compromise was finally effected whereby exceptions were provided in the case of privately owned terminals leased to or operated by persons approved by the Board of Grain Commissioners. In this form the bill passed to the Commons. Here, however, sessional interest was focused about the Reciprocity agreement; and before the grain legislative process could be completed, the parliamentary obstruction of the Conservative Opposition to the trade pact with the United States brought about the dissolution of Parliament (July 29), to permit an appeal to the country on that burning issue.

The Canada Grain Act of 1912. — The course of the Reciprocity campaign, the part played in it by the farmers' organizations, and the causes of the defeat of the project, cannot be treated here. Suffice it to say that the agrarian disappointment over the failure to obtain freer entrance into the American market was considerably alleviated by the unconditional tariff reductions on agricultural products shortly afterwards effected through the Underwood Act passed by the Democratic Congress in 1913.[1] Meanwhile Mr. Borden, who had been called on to form a Conservative government after the defeat of the Laurier ministry in September, 1911, had promised to lose no time in enacting adequate grain legislation; and in December, 1911, Hon. George E. Foster, the new Minister of Trade and Commerce, introduced in the Commons a government grain bill of substantially the same form as that which had emerged from the Senate in the previous Parliament. "I am only the foster-father of the bill," declared Mr. Foster on the second reading, "but it represents the product of all those interested in the matter after successive years of examination and discussion." [2]

The Canada Grain Act, which became law on April 1, 1912,[3] represented a consolidation and general revision of the oft-amended Manitoba Grain Act and Grain Inspection Act; and its 248 sections, with their amplifying administrative regulations, constitute the most thoroughgoing system of national grain trade regulation to be found in any country.[4] The most significant feature of the new act was its creation of a Board of Grain Commissioners for Canada,[5] under the Department of Trade and Commerce, with supervision over the entire work of grain inspection and grain-trade regulation throughout the Dominion.[6] The new

[1] See H. S. Patton, "Canadian-American Reciprocity," in *Quarterly Journal of Economics*, Aug., 1921.

[2] *Commons Debates*, Jan. 30, 1912.

[3] Stat. of Canada, 2 Geo. V, c. 27, 1912.

[4] Following the report of the Royal Grain Inquiry Commission appointed in 1923, the Canada Grain Act was reënacted in 1925 with substantial amendments, 15–16 Geo. V, c. 33.

[5] Consisting of three members appointed by the Governor in Council, to hold office during good behavior for ten years (sec. 3). All appointments under the Board were to be made by the Minister of Trade and Commerce on the recommendation of the Commissioners (sec. 8).

[6] For inspectional purposes, the Dominion was divided into the Eastern Inspection Division (all Canada east of Port Arthur), and the Western Inspection Division—as the Manitoba Inspection Division was now more properly styled (sec. 21).

Board thus not only superseded the functions of the Warehouse Commissioner created under the Manitoba Grain Act, but also exercised jurisdiction over the work of the Chief Inspector's and Chief Weighmaster's departments. Considerable discretionary power was entrusted to the Board by authorizing the Commissioners to issue rules and regulations "necessary to the proper carrying out of the act, subject, however, to the approval of the Governor-in-Council."[1]

With respect to the contentious problem of the terminals, the government, while declining to undertake the complete nationalization of existing terminal elevators, introduced certain important provisions in the new Grain Act which it was hoped would effectually eliminate the abuses complained of by grain growers and eastern millers. These had to do with (*a*) the ownership of licensed public terminals; (*b*) the supervision of terminal operations; (*c*) the regulation of mixing; (*d*) the supplementary operation of government-owned elevators.

(*a*) Licensing of Public Terminals. — The principle of prohibiting the operation of public terminal elevators by those interested in the buying and selling of grain, which had been so keenly debated in Sir Richard Cartwright's bill of the previous year, was now reaffirmed in the following form: "No person owning, managing, operating, or otherwise interested in any terminal elevator shall buy or sell grain at any point in the Eastern or Western Inspection Division" (sec. 123). In the succeeding subsection, however, it was stipulated that the above prohibition should not apply to any person owning, operating or interested in any terminal elevator, "which, with the approval of the Governor-in-Council, has been leased to the Board for operation, or has been leased to any person for operation with the approval of the Board, or is managed and operated by persons approved by the Board" (sec. 123, sub-sec. 2 [*a*]).

The comprehensive exemptions thus sanctioned obviously

[1] Canada Grain Act, sec. 20. The latter provision was strongly objected to during the discussion of the bill by the Grain Growers' representatives, who demanded a completely independent commission. The government insisted, however, upon that principle of financial responsibility and ultimate ministerial control. See *G. G. Guide*, Feb. 7, 1912.

made the prohibition enunciated in the preceding sub-section virtually nugatory, even if it could have been made effective against the circumventions of subsidiary incorporation and community of stockholding. The real intent of the section was to give the Board discretionary authority in determining who should be allowed to operate public terminals. The potential safeguard lay in the proviso, "with the approval of the Board." Thus it was sought, through discretionary licensing control to guard against the possible abuses of concentrated ownership, without outlawing the potential economies of integrated operation of initial and terminal grain handling facilities.

(*b*) Supervision of Terminal Operations. — Under section 95 even more elaborate provision was made for supervision of the cleaning, binning and shipping of grain in terminals than that introduced under the legislation of 1908. The Inspection Department was to keep records of each carload received, the number of the bin in which it was stored or transferred, and particulars of each parcel shipped out.[1] In practice the Board [2] found such detailed supervision and individual bin records impracticable, and in its first year of operation substituted for this unduly complicated system the simpler and more effective method of compulsory registration with the Board of all warehouse receipts issued by terminal elevators,[3] and compulsory cancellation of the same when surrendered for outward shipment of grain. A comparison of each elevator's outstanding certificates with Inspection Department records and with stocks of each grade shown by the annual weighings, afforded a direct check on the operations of each warehouse.[4] Where shortages were revealed in any grade,

[1] Sec. 95, sub-sec. 2.

[2] The first chairman of the Board of Grain Commissioners was Dr. Robert Magill whose work as chairman of the Saskatchewan Elevator Commission had gained for him the confidence both of the Grain Growers and of the grain trade. In 1918 Dr. Magill resigned the chairmanship of the Board, to become secretary of the Winnipeg Grain Exchange.

[3] Registration of terminal warehouse receipts carries with it the guarantee of the government as to both grade and weight. Only registered warehouse receipts, are deliverable in fulfilment of Grain Exchange contracts.

[4] See memorandum of Dr. Magill to Royal Grain Inquiry Commission, 1924, *Report*, p. 41.

the terminal operator concerned was required to make up the deficiency by purchase on the open market.[1]

(*c*) Regulations regarding Mixing. — Although the mixing of grain of different grades in store in public terminal elevators was explicitly prohibited,[2] the act contained two provisions which made mixing permissible under certain conditions. In the first place, it was provided that sample markets might be established at Winnipeg, Fort William, and Calgary, "and the mixing of grain permitted in connection therewith, under such rules and regulations as are recommended by the Board and approved by the Governor-in-Council."[3] This provision did not meet, however, with the approval of the Manitoba Grain Growers' Association, which wanted a sample market only on condition that grain sold thereon was special binned in government terminals, and shipped out on a special form of certificate differentiating such parcel from grain stored in public bins on straight grade.[4] Being unwilling, therefore to have mixing legalized, apart from government operation of terminals, the Grain Growers ceased after this time to press officially for sample markets. In the second place, the way was indirectly opened to mixing by provision made in the new act for licensing of "hospital elevators" for the treatment of tough, damp, rejected[5] or otherwise damaged grain.[6] It was recognized that such facilities were necessary for the drying, cleaning, and reconditioning of otherwise unmarketable grain, which in adverse seasons might constitute a considerable proportion of the crop. Since grain so treated might be inspected into public terminals,[7] it was quite

[1] *Report of Board of Grain Commission*, Dom. Sess. Paper, No. 10d, 1912–13.

[2] Canada Grain Act, sec. 126, sub-sec. 8.

[3] *Ibid.*, sec. 57, sub-sec. 2. This sub-section was to come into force only upon proclamation made by the Governor-in-Council, when satisfied that the proper conditions existed therefor (sub-sec. 4).

[4] Resolution, M. G. G. A., 1912; *G. G. Guide* (ed.) Feb. 28, 1912; see *supra*, p. 132.

[5] "Rejected" grain is defined under the act (sec. 115 [3]), as "all grain that is unsound, musty, dirty, smutty or sprouted, or that contains a large admixture of other kinds of grain, seeds, or wild oats, or that from any other causes is unfit to be classed under any of the recognized grades."

[6] Canada Grain Act, sec. 124, sub-secs. 1, 2.

[7] *Ibid.*, sec. 124, sub-sec. 3.

possible for the owners of such houses to carry on mixing as well as hospital operations, and ship their grain into terminals under official grades.[1] "Private terminal elevators" were not recognized as such under the act. They were able, however, to obtain licenses as "hospital elevators," and their number increased markedly after the passing of the act. On recommendation of the Board, an order-in-council was passed, in 1917, prescribing rules and regulations for the establishment of sample markets and the operation of private terminal elevators in connection therewith. The effect of these was to authorize the Board to issue private terminal licenses, and to inspect grain outward from private terminals on the same basis as grain from public terminals. Although the sample markets so established failed to function, mixing thus became legalized in private houses, and the owner of mixed grain became entitled to undifferentiated government grade certificates. The safeguard against abuse depended on the vigilance and consistency of the Inspection Department in maintaining uniformity of grade requirements as between grain inspected out of private and public terminals.[2] While the government thus sought, through the Canada Grain Act and the Board of Grain Commissioners, to eliminate mixing of stored grain in public terminals, it opened the way, through the provisions relating to sample markets and hospital elevators, for the legalized and regulated mixing of purchased grain in private elevators.

(*d*) Provision for Government Terminals. — While the government's policy was thus to bring privately owned terminals

[1] As a safeguard against mixing manipulations in hospital elevators, they were made subject to the stipulation that if grain shipped from them was "being systematically reduced in quality below the general average quality of grain of similar grades in the bins of terminal elevators, the Chief Inspector may allow no such grain to pass inspection except on a lower grade" (sec. 99).

[2] The steps leading to the legalization of mixing in private terminal elevators, and the successive regulations imposed are reviewed in detail in *Report of Royal Grain Inquiry Commission*, 1925, pp. 75–85. Prior to the passing of the Canada Grain Act only three private elevators were in operation at the head of the lakes. Four more were built in 1912. At the present time 25 of the 35 elevators at Fort William and Port Arthur are licensed as private terminals. *Ibid.* The subject of mixing in relation to the farmers' elevator companies is discussed below, pp. 149, 150.

under more effective regulation, instead of nationalizing them, it compromised with the Grain Growers' demands for public ownership to the extent of making provision for the experimental establishment of government elevators as an alternative for shippers dissatisfied with the privately owned houses. "We propose," said Mr. Foster in introducing the bill, "to apply the principle of public ownership and to undertake the experiment to see whether or not the claim on behalf of that peculiar type of operation is well founded. We do not intend to undertake the financial or experimental responsibility of taking the whole terminal elevator system under government operation for the present, but we wish to give to the people of the West a choice between the terminal elevators that are run by corporations or individuals and those that are run by the government either as owners or lessees."[1] The act therefore authorized the government to construct, lease, or acquire any terminal elevator where funds were provided for such purpose by Parliament, and to place such elevator under the Board of Grain Commissioners for operation and management.[2]

In considering the best method of carrying out the government's pledge of experimental operation of terminal facilities, the Board experienced a general refusal on the part of grain companies owning their own terminals to lease them, on the ground that such alienation would dislocate their whole system and make their country elevators unprofitable. Under the circumstances the Board found it inadvisable to recommend purchase or expropriation, and in view of the inadequacy of lake-head storage capacity,[3] it advised that the government should itself build a large terminal elevator equipped for cleaning and drying, as well as for storing grain. In accordance with this recommendation the government constructed an elevator of 3,250,000

[1] *Commons Debates*, Dec. 28, 1912. [2] Canada Grain Act, sec. 13.

[3] In 1911 the total storage capacity at the head of the lakes amounted to 25,711,400 bushels, which had to be supplemented by arranging for American vessels to winter in Thunder Bay as floating elevators. During 1912–13 the terminal accommodation was increased by 11,120,000 bushels, of which the government elevator supplied over one quarter. *Report of Board of Grain Commissioners*, 1912–13.

bushels capacity at Port Arthur, which was taken over for operation by the Board in October, over 7,000,000 bushels being handled during the first four months.[1] It had been anticipated by the Commissioners that in operating a modern terminal of their own they would gain a direct, working knowledge of operation problems that would prove highly serviceable in their regulation of the privately owned terminals.[2] While this arrangement doubtless made both for greater reasonableness and for greater vigilance in supervision, it involved the distinctly anomalous situation of making a semi-judicial body, vested with the responsibility of licensing, regulating, inspecting, and hearing complaints against terminal elevator companies, itself the operator of a competing unit in the system it supervised.[3] The Board was thus charged with the somewhat conflicting duties of making a favorable showing for the government elevator, and at the same time making rules and authorizing tariffs designed to limit the opportunities for more than "public utility margins" in terminal operations.[4]

Significance of New Legislation. — A comparison of the contents of the Canada Grain Act of 1912 with the Grain Inspection Act of 1899 and the Manitoba Grain Act of 1900 affords a significant commentary on the expanded scope and elaborated intensiveness of federal government regulation of the grain trade of Western Canada during the first dozen years of the century.

[1] *Report of Board of Grain Commissioners.* Dom. Sess. Paper, No. 10d, 1914.

[2] *Report of Board of Grain Commissioners*, 1912–13, p. 141.

[3] On the recommendation of the Board, the government also undertook in 1913–14 the construction of interior terminal storage elevators at Saskatoon, Moose Jaw, and Calgary, with a view to providing final inspection and terminal storage nearer the grain fields of Saskatchewan and Alberta, and affording concentration and car-order points for grain moving north-eastward by the prospective Hudson Bay route, southward to the American interior market, and westward by the Pacific route. These elevators were also operated by the Board of Grain Commissioners. R. Magill, *Grain Inspection in Western Canada*, pp. 56–58; *Report of Royal Grain Inquiry Commission*, 1925, p. 42.

[4] The Grain Inquiry Commission of 1923–24 recommended that all publicly owned elevators in the Western Inspection Division should be placed for operation under a separate body, subject, under the same conditions as privately owned elevators, to the jurisdiction of the Board of Grain Commissioners, whose functions should thus be made purely regulative. *Report*, pp. 151–154.

While the complexity of the system was a reflection of the rapidly increasing proportions and rapidly changing organization of the Canadian grain trade itself during this period, the nature and content of the regulations had been to a very considerable extent determined by the studied representations of the organized Grain Growers themselves. The supervision exercised by the Board of Grain Commissioners under the chairmanship of Dr. Magill, acting under the powers of the new Grain Act, commanded an increasing measure of confidence among grain growers as a whole. While individual complaints and demands for particular changes in the grain legislation continued to be frequent, the common feeling of grievance and suspicion against the elevator monopoly perceptibly diminished after 1912, under the double influence of more efficient regulation, and of the alternatives offered by farmer-owned and government-owned agencies.

III. Terminal Operations of the Grain Growers' Company

Although the Grain Growers' agitation for government monopolization of terminal facilities had failed to accomplish its specific object, it had been effective in leading the government to intensify its control and to enter into operation itself to such extent as to prevent any private monopolization. In recommending the construction of an experimental government elevator at Port Arthur, the Grain Commissioners had at the same time expressed their approval of the leasing of one of the C. P. R. terminals to the Grain Growers' Grain Company, as a means of affording shippers yet another alternative to dependence on terminal facilities controlled by the regular companies.[1]

Entry of Grain Growers' Grain Co. into Terminal Operation. — The expression of the federal government's policy in regard to the terminals, through the provisions of the Canada Grain Act, coincided, it will be observed, with the negotiations of the Manitoba government for the leasing of its country elevators to the Grain Growers' Company. In default of a general nationalization of

[1] *Report of Board of Grain Commissioners*, Dom. Sess. Paper, No. 10d, 1913, p. 14.

terminal facilities, the company's directors realized the desirability of acquiring their own elevator at the head of the lakes, with the twofold object of permitting competition on more even terms with line companies controlling their own terminals, and of enabling them to handle the farmers' grain from the point of production to the point of lake shipment through houses operated by themselves. This policy had been unanimously endorsed by the shareholders' meeting in July, 1912, and the directors had been authorized to conclude leasing arrangements with the C. P. R., which owned three large terminals at the head of the lakes.[1] Before the 1912 crop movement set in, the Grain Growers' Company was in duly licensed occupation of C. P. R. terminal B at Fort William, with storage capacity of 2,300,000 bushels.[2]

In addition to obtaining a federal charter for the Grain Growers' Grain Company in 1911,[3] the directors had secured incorporation, under federal letters patent, of the Grain Growers' Export Company, Limited, with extensive powers to deal in agricultural products of every kind, and carry on the business of exporting, shipping, warehousing, etc.[4] The initial paid-up stock of $50,000 in the new subsidiary was held entirely by the Grain Growers' Grain Company, whose directors also constituted the directorate of the Export Company.[5] In the handling of the 1912 crop, therefore, the Grain Growers' Company operated as a fully integrated grain business. Grain bought on street or track through its leased country elevators, or farmers' grain consigned to its commission department, might be sold to the Grain Growers' Export Company, which held its own seat on the Winnipeg Grain Exchange.[6] In the leased public terminal at Fort William, the parent company stored grain for farmers, for other dealers, and for its own Export Company. The elasticity of the much-debated section 123 of the Canada Grain Act was here found to

[1] *G. G. Guide*, July 24, 1912.

[2] The lease was on a rental basis of $6\frac{1}{2}$ per cent of the construction cost, equivalent to approximately $70,000 per annum. G. G. G. Co., 1915, p. 10.

[3] See *infra*, pp. 154–56.

[4] *G. G. Guide*, Jan. 3, 1912, p. 21.

[5] G. G. G. Co., 1912, 1914.

[6] See evidence of J. R. Murray, (U. G. G.) before Grain Inquiry Commission, Winnipeg, March 10, 1924.

be of distinct advantage to the farmers' company. It enabled it, with the approval of the Grain Commissioners, to centralize and pool the operations of country buying and warehousing, Grain Exchange trading, terminal storage, and exporting. After 1912 the Grain Growers' demand for the divorcement of terminal operation from the business of grain dealing ceased to be articulate. Integration was found to possess its economic merits, so long as it was not associated with irresponsible monopoly.

Mixing Operations of Farmers' Company.—The terminal operations of the farmers' company were carried still further along the lines of integrated trade practice, when in the same season a "hospital" elevator license was taken out, and a small "inland" house,[1] elevator H, was acquired at Fort William, for the cleaning and reconditioning of tough and "off grade" grain purchased by the company, for the mixing of treated and lower grade grain, and for the sacking of seed and feed grain for Ontario farmers.[2] This private elevator was leased to the Export Company for operation.[3] When it was destroyed by fire, in March, 1916, the directors, finding a hospital and mixing elevator indispensable in their competitive operations, decided to rebuild on a more extensive scale. In so doing a water-front site was secured at Port Arthur, so as to permit direct shipment to vessels, and a 300,000-bushel private terminal elevator erected thereon.[4] When in the following year mixing was "regularized," under the rules issued by the Grain Commissioners in connection with the proclamation establishing sample markets, the capacity of the Grain Growers' private terminal was doubled, to take advantage of the new opportunities afforded thereby.

The action of the directors in expanding the equipment for large-scale mixing operations did not fail to elicit criticism from farmer shareholders as well as non-shareholders. The directorate justified the operation of such a type of elevator, however, as

[1] That is, one not located on the waterfront. Treated, mixed or sacked grain was loaded from such houses into cars, either for direct rail shipment to the east, or for inspection into public terminals.

[2] G. G. G. Co., 1913, 14.

[3] Evidence of J. R. Murray, *loc. cit.*

[4] G. G. G. Co., 1916.

tending to improve the market for lower grades and rejected grades, and thus reducing the spread between these and the contract grades. It was claimed that during the season of 1915–16 the company had paid throughout, on all grain going into their private terminal, a premium of half a cent a bushel over the price the same grade would have commanded if delivered to public terminals. They further maintained that the insistence by the Inspection Department, as required by regulations of the Grain Commissioners, that all grain inspected out of private terminals should conform to the average, and not to the minimum, of the grade inspected out of the public terminal, ensured that the export grades were not lowered in quality, and prices thereby depressed.[1] Thus, as the experience of the farmers' company on the Grain Exchange had caused it on a former occasion to justify the commission rule to its shareholders and patrons, so now experience at the terminals made its directors apologists for the practice of commercial mixing.

Terminal Policy of Company. — In the operation of the company's public terminal, on which the fixed charges for rent, taxes and upkeep amounted to some $90,000 annually,[2] it was found that the revenues from handling and storage charges, at the maximum rates authorized by the Grain Commissioners,[3] yielded a profit only in seasons when the volume of grain handled was relatively large. The main profits from terminal operation, it was discovered, were derived from the accrual of surpluses or overages in the turnover of stocks. Such surpluses might arise, quite legitimately, from the recleaning of screenings, which public terminals were allowed to retain where the dockage set by the inspector did not exceed 3 per cent.[4] Surpluses might also arise, more questionably, from cleaning grain slightly under the dockage set. The prevalence of this practice had been urged by the

[1] G. G. G. Co., 1916, pp. 12, 13.

[2] G. G. G. Co., 1915.

[3] Namely, $\frac{3}{4}$ cent per bushel for receiving, cleaning, binning, and shipping out grain, with 15 days storage. Beyond 15 days, storage charges were at the rate of $\frac{1}{30}$ cent per day. Rising costs of operation during the war period led to a somewhat belated authorization of $1\frac{1}{4}$ cent maximum handling charge in 1919.

[4] In such case no charge was made for cleaning. See Piper, *Principles of Grain Trade*, pp. 116–120

Grain Growers' Associations as one of the patent justifications for nationalization of the terminals. It is not without significance that at an annual meeting of the Grain Growers' Grain Company we find the "shading" of dockage removal justified by the directors as more or less necessary in view of the responsibility of public terminals to the Grain Commissioners for all shortages.[1] Once again it was apparent that the Grain Growers in business regarded the established practices of the grain trade in a somewhat different light from the Grain Growers in convention.

Significance of Events of 1912. — It will be realized from the foregoing chapters that the year 1912 was a pivotal point in the history both of the Grain Growers' Movement and of the Canadian grain trade. It marked the end of the organized agitation for provincial ownership both of initial elevators and of nationalization of terminal elevators. It witnessed the termination of Manitoba's experiment in government ownership of elevators, and the beginning of country elevator operation by the Grain Growers' Grain Company. It found in Saskatchewan a government-aided but farmer-controlled provincial elevator company completing its initial year under reassuring circumstances. It found Alberta farmers conferring with their government for the organization of a coöperative elevator company on similar lines. It was a year, moreover, which marked the consolidation and general revision of Canadian grain legislation through the Canada Grain Act, and the establishment of the Board of Grain Commissioners as an effective agency of regulation. It witnessed the intensification of government control of the terminals, and the initiation of the policy of establishing supplementary government terminal elevators under the operation of the Grain Commissioners. It marked, too, the entry of the Grain Growers' Company into the field of terminal operation, and its emergence as a fully integrated grain corporation, competing on a basis of equality with concerns hitherto referred to as the "elevator monopoly."

In the first decade of their organized existence the Grain Growers, in pursuing their united efforts along the parallel paths of legislative regulation and business coöperation, had accom-

[1] U. G. G., 1918, pp. 14–18; see *supra*, pp. 142, 143.

plished much toward lessening their economic dependence upon the private interests which had enjoyed strategic control of the physical facilities and organization of grain marketing. Legislation and government action had indeed fallen short of the demands of the Interprovincial Council, but public control, public assistance, and public investigation had been carried far in the direction of remedying the grievances behind these demands. At the same time "the organized farmers in business" were showing a surprising adaptability to the established practices of the system which, as mere growers, they had regarded with suspicion and hostility.

CHAPTER XI

AMALGAMATION: THE UNITED GRAIN GROWERS LTD.

I. Parallel Development of the Coöperative Companies

While the year 1913 found three farmers' centralized coöperative grain companies functioning in the Prairie Provinces, the basis of organization and the course of development were by no means identical. The Saskatchewan and Alberta Co-operative Elevator Companies had become incorporated by special act of their respective legislatures. Their capital undertakings, while fully subscribed by farmer shareholders, had been largely financed through treasury loans, and were consequently provincially limited. The Grain Growers' Grain Company, on the other hand, had been initiated and developed without any government assistance whatever, and its stockholders and operations were distributed interprovincially. The shareholders of the Saskatchewan and Alberta Co-operatives were organized in "locals," with delegate voting at annual meetings. The Grain Growers' Company, on the other hand, had been incorporated under the Manitoba Joint Stock Companies Act. Although the two provincial companies operated country elevators, owned and for the most part built, by themselves, while the pioneer company did not operate even leased elevators until its sixth year, the latter had the advantage of a strongly established position on the Winnipeg Grain Exchange, as well as operating both public and private terminal elevators. The "Co-operatives" in the new provinces were thus more solidly established at initial shipping points, while the strength of the original company lay rather in its position on the central market and at the terminals. While the fixed assets of the former were relatively greater, — thanks to low-margined government capital loans, — the latter was self-financing, and had most of its capital in circulating form. As between the

Alberta Co-operative and the Grain Growers' Company, these respective advantages had been brought into more or less complementary relation through the inter-company coöperative arrangement, by which the latter acted as the selling and financial agent of the former. In Saskatchewan, as we have noticed, the intimate financial relations of government and "Co-operative" and the policy of capitalizing earnings, had enabled the farmers' elevator company in that province, after its initial year, to function quite independently of the pioneer concern.[1]

In another respect the policy of the Saskatchewan Co-operative differed from that of the other farmers' companies. Its resources and its efforts were advisedly confined to elevator construction and operation and grain marketing. The Alberta Company, on the other hand, had inaugurated Livestock and Co-operative Supply departments, as supplementary to its elevator operations, in its first year of business. Although the directors of the Grain Growers' Grain Company had concentrated their efforts during the initial years in establishing its position on the Grain Exchange and in building up farmer patronage for its commission business, the policy of applying the company's resources and organization to enterprises designed to reduce the farmer's cost of production, as well as improve his marketing returns, was given serious consideration, once the company's commercial and financial position became reasonably assured.[2]

Federal Incorporation of G. G. G. Co., 1911. — With a view to widening both the functional and the territorial scope of the company's operations, the directors renewed in 1911 the efforts to obtain a federal charter, which, it will be recalled, had been refused on technical grounds when originally applied for in 1906.[3] As no coöperative associations act was to be found at this time on the federal statute books,[4] and as it was desired to obtain powers broad enough to enable the company to function as a

[1] See *supra*, pp. 110, 111.

[2] G. G. G. Co., 1911, 1912.

[3] See *supra*, pp. 47, 48.

[4] A general act for incorporation of coöperative organizations was one of the demands contained in the memorial of the Canadian Council of Agriculture, presented at Ottawa in December, 1910; see *supra*, pp. 137, 138.

general business and financial organization for Western farmers on a coöperative, or quasi-coöperative basis, the new charter was sought by special act of Parliament instead of by letters patent under the federal Companies Act. In the bill which emerged from the Private Bills Committee of the Senate, the coöperative features were found in the sections which limited the eligibility of stockholders to farmers or farm-owners (and their wives); which restricted individual stockholdings to a maximum of forty shares (of $25 par value); which allowed each shareholder but one vote; and which permitted conditional distribution of profits to shareholders on other than a share basis, when earnings should exceed 8 per cent on capital, plus appropriations to reserve made by the directors.[1] The authorized objects of the company were declared to be:

> To produce, manufacture, export, import, buy, sell, deal in and deal with all cereals . . . and all products or by-products of the farm, and all machinery, implements, goods, wares, and merchandise which may be used in the production and manufacture of the products of the farm, and all articles, substances, and things which may be utilized in the said product or in the maintenance, cultivation, improvement, and development of farms.[2]

For the furtherance of the above objects the company was empowered to engage in manufacturing as well as in merchandizing; to develop timber lands, coal mines, and waterpowers; to build or operate ships, and development works as well as elevators and warehouses; to hold shares (not exceeding one quarter of the capital stock) in any bank; and so forth. In the Commons the spacious character of the powers granted to the company elicited considerable opposition from certain members, notably from Mr. Gervais of Montreal, who had piloted through the House the bill incorporating the Retail Merchants' Association, and had been largely instrumental in securing the defeat of the coöperative associations bill in the previous session. A company seeking such all-inclusive powers should be incorporated, he protested, as "The General Schemers and Promoters Company."[3] Friends of the bill, including the Premier, maintained that it conferred no

[1] Stat. of Canada (Local and Private Acts), 1–2 Geo. V, c. 80, secs. 4, 5, 6, 8, 17.
[2] Ibid., sec. 12.
[3] *Commons Debates*, May 1, 1911.

wider powers than were obtainable under the Companies Act; and with an amendment explicitly debarring the company from engaging in the business of banking, insurance, or public railway operation,[1] the measure was passed (May, 1911).

The transfer of the franchises and assets of the Manitoba Company to the federally incorporated Grain Growers' Grain Company was effected by a par exchange of stock certificates, the paid-up capital of the company (as of June 30, 1911) amounting to $492,062, out of a subscribed capital of $615,050. Although no stock bonus was issued in connection with the reorganization, it was decided at this time that the assets of the company warranted the placing of a premium of 20 per cent on its shares, the treasury price of its stock being $30 thereafter.[2]

Subsidiary Enterprises. — Acting under the enlarged powers of its new charter, and actuated by the policy of developing the company as a farmers' general coöperative corporation,[3] the Grain Growers' Grain Company rapidly extended the scope of its operations, with a view to lessening the farmers' dependence, not only on the vested elevator interests in the marketing of his grain, but also on manufacturers' and dealers' combines in the purchasing of his farm supplies. Thus toward the end of 1911, when incorporation of the subsidiary Grain Growers' Export Company was obtained,[4] a controlling interest was also secured in a British Columbia timber limit.[5] In 1912 the Manitoba government elevators and C. P. R. terminal B had been taken over on lease, followed by the purchase of its hospital elevator at Fort William in 1913. In the same year a 30,000-bushel elevator was acquired at New Westminster, B. C., with an immediate view of supplying sacked grain and feed from Alberta to the Fraser Valley market, and with a prospective view to being in an established position to take advantage of the westward movement of

[1] Stat. of Canada, 1911, c. 80, sec. 19.

[2] G. G. G. Co., 1911, 1912.

[3] "One thing is absolutely certain, we have got to ultimately extend coöperative principles into every department of our business." Pres. Crerar to G. G. G. Co., July, 1912.

[4] See *supra*, p. 148.

[5] G. G. G. Co., 1912.

Alberta grain, which it was anticipated would follow the completion of the Panama Canal.[1] In the field of coöperative supply, the company took the step in 1913 of leasing the Rapid City Flour Mill, and supplying flour and feed in carload lots to Grain Growers' locals.[2] In the following year an investment was made in the Western Farmers' Lumber Company, and lumber, fencing material, coal, and binder-twine were added to the commodities handled by the Co-operative Department.[3] A beginning was also made in the supplying of farm machinery on a commission basis,[4] leading in 1915 to the establishment of supply warehouses at Winnipeg, Regina, and Calgary.[5] In March, 1916, a Livestock Department was inaugurated, the company entering the stockyards at St. Boniface (East Winnipeg) and buying cattle from and for farmers, in addition to handling consigned carloads of livestock on commission. Most of these subsidiary enterprises were initiated in a small way, but developed rapidly. In all cases they were financed by the paid-up capital and reserves of the parent company, without resort to bond issues or government loans. At the same time the company was assisting in financing extensively the operations of the Alberta Farmers' Company.

While the Grain Growers' Company was thus developing each year new enterprises and services in the interests of its farmer shareholders, its principal and most remunerative business continued to be the handling of grain. Up to 1916 its country elevator operations remained virtually stationary, since it did not enjoy the government financial assistance available to the Saskatchewan and Alberta Co-operative Elevator Companies, and since new grain shipping points were not arising in Manitoba as in the newer provinces. Up to the end of the 1915 crop year, the company had added but fourteen elevators, by purchase or construction, to the leased Manitoba government elevators.

[1] The Pacific enterprise was conducted under the name of the Grain Growers' B. C. Agency, in which the G. G. G. Co. held the controlling stock interest, the remaining shares being owned chiefly by B. C. farmers. G. G. G. Co., 1913, 1914.

[2] G. G. G. Co., 1913. [3] G. G. G. Co., 1914, pp. 13, 34.

[4] G. G. G. Co., 1914., p. 15.

[5] G. G. G. Co., 1916, p. 14. The enterprises of the company in coöperative supply are separately discussed in Chapter XVII.

The large profits realized in the handling of the phenomenal crop of 1915 [1] permitted, however, the assumption of a considerable building programme, which it was decided to extend into Saskatchewan, at points not served by the Saskatchewan Co-operative. By the end of the next crop year the Grain Growers' Company possessed sixty elevators of its own, about equally divided between Manitoba and Saskatchewan.[2] During these years it also continued to handle all the grain of the Alberta Farmers' Company on the Winnipeg Exchange.

Operations of Grain Growers' Export Companies. — The first year's operations of the Grain Growers' Export Company, which had been incorporated as a separate subsidiary in 1911, were decidedly inauspicious, resulting in losses exceeding $200,000.[3] The farmers' company was learning in the costly school of experience the hazards and complications of the grain-export trade, a business which even under favorable conditions is conducted upon the narrowest of competitive margins. The losses were temporarily taken care of by drawing on the reserve funds of the parent company, whose investment of $50,000 in the Export Company was thus maintained intact.[4] A new manager of extensive experience was secured, in the person of Mr. Stemper, whose direct interest in the enterprise was assured by his investment in Export Company stock, and by his election to its board as managing director. The reorganized export subsidiary was henceforth required to stand entirely on its own feet, without financial guarantee from the parent company.[5]

The outbreak of the war in the following year soon served to

[1] In 1915–16, the G. G. G. Co. handled 48,375,000 bushels of grain, compared with 18,821,402 bushels during the previous crop year.

[2] G. G. G. Co., 1917, p. 9.

[3] The losses were attributed partly to a large quantity of grain going out of condition in ocean transit, partly to overchartering of tonnage, and partly to the shipment (as a means of utilizing the excess chartered space) of grain for which a market — that proved to be a falling one — had to be found on arrival in Great Britain. G. G. G. Co., 1913; *Manitoba Free Press*, Nov. 12, 1913.

[4] G. G. G. Co., 1914, p. 11.

[5] Ibid. One half of the capital in the reorganized export company was furnished by English importing interests whose shares were subsequently repurchased by the parent company. T. A. Crerar to author.

rehabilitate the fortunes of the Export Company. The Canadian crop of 1914 was exceptionally light, and the exportable surplus had been practically shipped out by the close of navigation. At the suggestion of Mr. Stemper, it was decided by the board of the Export Company to establish a temporary agency in New York, to take advantage of the export activity in American grain under conditions of European war demand. The New York office was opened by Mr. Stemper in January, 1915, and a satisfactory line of credit arranged with a New York bank. The venture proved exceptionally opportune. Whereas scarcely more than 6,000,000 bushels of Canadian grain had been shipped by the Export Company during the season, nearly 40,000,000 bushels of American grain were handled through the Grain Growers' New York office. The total export business yielded a profit of $531,000,[1] thus doubly restoring the impairment of the parent company's reserves arising from the export losses in 1912–13.

It was decided by the directorate of the Export Company to retain Mr. Stemper at New York, as it was found that even the Canadian export business could be more effectively managed from New York than Winnipeg, since the former location permitted closer contact with ocean shipping and foreign exchange conditions.[2] Following Mr. Stemper's sudden death in June, 1916, it was decided to place the New York business on a permanent basis, and in 1917 a new subsidiary, the Grain Growers' Export Company, Inc. (N. Y.) was incorporated under New York State laws.[3] The American company, however, enjoyed only a few months of profit-making operation. With the entry of the United States into the war, the export grain trade of the country became concentrated in the hands of the United States Grain Corporation, and the Wheat Export Company, buying for

[1] Of this amount $180,000 was subsequently paid over to the Dominion government as excess profits tax; $250,000 was added to the paid-up capital of the Export Company. G. G. G. Co., 1915, 1917.

[2] G. G. G. Co. 1915, p. 22. Most exporters of Canadian grain, operating from Montreal or New York, do their buying from or through "lake shippers" operating on the Winnipeg market. See U. S. Dept. of Commerce, *Trade Information Bulletin, No. 281*, "Marketing Canadian Wheat," p. 99.

[3] G. G. G. Co., 1917.

the Allies. Under these conditions the Grain Growers' New York Company, was asked to undertake, for the British and Allied governments, the purchasing and shipping of all their oat requirements in the United States, and partially in Canada as well. For this purpose the Grain Growers' Company turned over its New York office *in toto* to the Wheat Export Company, receiving in compensation its actual expenses only, but preserving thereby its American organization intact.[1] During the crop season 1917–1918, the Grain Growers' New York subsidiary purchased and shipped 120,000,000 bushels of oats on account of the Allies [2] — a spacious responsibility for a farmers' company which but a decade before had fought for trading privileges on the Winnipeg Exchange.

Ten Years' Progress. — By 1913 the Grain Growers' Grain Company, in handling grain of the value of more than $60,000,000, could claim to be the largest grain company doing business in Canada.[3] The high prices and augmented production of grain during the war years still further promoted the material expansion of the company, while its impressive record of earnings and its readiness to employ its resources in any form of coöperative enterprise deemed likely to improve the economic position of Western farmers generally, steadily strengthened its prestige among the grain growers. The development of the farmers' company during the first decade of its existence may be briefly indicated by a statistical comparison of its position at the end of its first and its tenth years of operation.[4]

	Year ending June 30, 1907	Year ending August 31, 1916
Number shareholders	1,540	18,163
Shares allotted	1,853	57,605
Capital subscribed	$46,325	$1,440,160
Capital paid-up	$11,795	$1,073,180
Grain handled	2,340,000 bush.	48,375,420 bush.
Profits	$790	$572,804

During the decade the company had handled over 205,000,000 bushels of farmers' grain, equivalent to 10.7 per cent of the total

[1] G. G. G. Co., 1916, pp. 11, 12.
[2] G. G. G. Co., 1918, pp. 23, 24.
[3] G. G. G. Co., 1913.
[4] G. G. G. Co., 1916, pp. 54, 55.

amount inspected in the Prairie Provinces during that period.[1] The total profits earned in the ten years' business amounted to $1,488,141, of which $550,000 had been distributed in dividends to farmer shareholders. At the same time the effective capital of the company had been augmented to the extent of more than $700,000 through the accumulation of reserves and undivided profits.

Growth of the Saskatchewan Co-operative. — In contrast with the multiple enterprises of the Grain Growers' Company and the diversified operations of the Alberta Farmers' Company, the Saskatchewan Co-operative Elevator Company had concentrated its efforts and its resources entirely on elevator construction and grain marketing. The accelerated extension of the grain growing acreage of the central prairie province during this period [2] offered an opportunity for physical expansion of which the substantial and sustained financial assistance of the Saskatchewan government made it possible for the company to take large advantage. The 46 elevators through which the first season's operations had been carried on in 1911–12, had been increased to 258 at the end of the fifth year (July 31, 1916). During the same time the number of shareholders had grown from the 2,580 at the time the company legally began business, to 18,077 persons holding an aggregate of 47,178 shares.[3] Even at this rate of expansion the work of organization and construction failed to keep pace with the demands of Saskatchewan grain growers for coöperative elevators. Thus during 1915–16 formal petitions were received by the organization department from 200 shipping points, at which it was found possible to establish not more than 30 new elevator locals.[4]

The rapid increase in the company's shareholders was no doubt accelerated by the smallness of the cash payment required from stock subscribers,[5] and by the company's policy of distributing

[1] Estimated from reports of G. G. G. Co. and Dominion Bureau of Statistics.

[2] When the Sask. Co-op. began operations in 1911, the grain area of Saskatchewan was 4,704,660 acres; in 1916 it had expanded to 9,032,109 acres.

[3] Sask. Co-op. Elev. Co., 1916.

[4] Sask. Co-op. Elev. Co., 1916.

[5] Amounting to $7.50 per share of $50 par value, compared with initial payments of $12 in the case of stock in the Alberta Company; see *infra*, p. 172 n.

stock dividends from the very first year of business,[1] instead of calling on subscribers for annual instalments, as in the case of the Alberta Company. Saskatchewan shareholders thus found the paid-up value of their shares increasing automatically, while the company enjoyed the use of the capitalized earnings. With the provincial government guaranteeing the company's current account with the banks, as well as advancing 85 per cent of the capital cost of elevator construction, repayable on extended terms,[2] it was possible for the company to expand its equipment and operations with a minimum of paid-up capital and a maximum of shareholder patrons.

Probably the best statistical index of the rising patronage enjoyed by the coöperative elevators in Saskatchewan is to be found in the annual percentage of the marketed grain crop in that province handled by the farmers' company. The ratio was as follows during the first five years of operation:[3]

1911 crop	3.16 per cent.
1912 "	9.78 " "
1913 "	12.39 " "
1914 "	15.41 " "
1915 "	16.00 " "

The statutory requirements as to local stock subscriptions, and the policy of the company in providing maximum special binning accommodation and in reducing and equalizing margins on street grain purchases,[4] were thus shown to be effective in ensuring local support, despite the absence of patronage guarantees or contracts, and despite the inducements offered by line companies in cutting elevator charges at competing points from the legal maximum of 1¾ cents to 1¼ cents a bushel. As in the case of the Grain Growers' Company at the time of the suspension of the commission rule by the Grain Exchange, the directors of the

[1] Stock dividends of $3 per share were paid in 1912, 1913, and 1914, $2 in 1915, and $6 in 1916. Sask. Co-op., 1916.

[2] The first of the 20 annual instalments in which the government's loan were repayable did not become due until August 31 in the year following that in which the loan was granted. Sask. Co-op. Elev. Act, sec. 25.

[3] C. A. Dunning to S. G. G. A., Feb., 1916; Sask. Co-op., 1916.

[4] See *supra*, p. 109.

Saskatchewan Co-operative laid the situation fully and frankly before the shareholders and continued to charge the regular rate.[1]

The first four years of the company's operations were fully absorbed in endeavoring to meet the demand for new elevator locals in the province, and in consolidating its position against opposition interests. By 1915, however, the question of entering into terminal operations began to be seriously discussed, and at the annual meeting in November of that year, the directors were instructed to consider carefully the advisability of erecting a company terminal elevator at the head of the lakes. The capital requirements for such an undertaking were formidable. The Saskatchewan Co-operative Elevator Act did not provide for government loans for the purpose of erecting elevators outside the province; and while the company had accumulated reserves exceeding $320,000 by the end of the fourth year, these funds were mostly required to finance the expanding country business and Grain Exchange operations of the company. There was, therefore, some disposition on the part of the directors to consider proposals which were being made at this time for a federation of the three Western grain growers' companies, involving the joint establishment of a farmer-owned terminal elevator.

II. The Movement for Federation

Although the Saskatchewan and Alberta Co-operative Elevator companies had not been organized as competitors of the Grain Growers' Grain Company, but had been evolved as provincial organizations out of the Grain Growers' united campaign for public ownership of elevators, the possible dangers of overlapping and rivalry, and the potential advantages of coördination and consolidation began to suggest themselves as the three companies pursued their parallel but independent development. The Canadian Council of Agriculture, as the agrarian counterpart of the Canadian Manufacturers' Association, and the Dominion

[1] Sask. Co-op., 1915; Report of C. A. Dunning, *G. G. Guide*, Feb. 23, 1916, p. 31. It was pointed out that the line companies did not provide special binning service, and claimed that the discriminating reductions in elevator charges were recouped at the expense of street sellers at points where Co-operative elevators were not established.

Trades and Labor Council, had already demonstrated the advantages of a permanent interprovincial organization, to represent the farmers' common interests and claims before the government and the public. The possibilities of a central commercial organization to coördinate the operations of the different grain growers' companies and to combine the great selling and buying power of western farmers now began to receive the attention of certain of their leaders.

The Case for Federation of Farmers' Companies. — It was quite in the nature of things that the first suggestions for federation should emanate from the Grain Growers' Company as the pioneer farmers' business organization in the West. Its operations had never been provincially limited, it had shown itself the readiest to undertake subsidiary coöperative enterprises, and it had subsidized the *Grain Growers' Guide* as the organ of the Western farmers' movement. While it handled the grain of the Alberta Company on the Winnipeg Exchange, its selling organization was in virtual competition with that of the Saskatchewan Company on the central market. Many of the original shareholders of the Grain Growers' Company had been Saskatchewan farmers, and both companies solicited the consignment of farmers' cars from Saskatchewan shipping points. Moreover, the organization in 1914 of a Co-operative Trading Department by the Saskatchewan Grain Growers' Association raised jurisdictional questions in connection with the coöperative supply business of the older company in Saskatchewan territory.[1]

The desirability of a central farmers' business organization as a means of eliminating overlapping and friction had been stressed by President Crerar in his address at the annual meeting of the Grain Growers' Company in 1914:

> With the development of the Saskatchewan Co-operative Elevator Company, and now of the Alberta Co-operative Elevator Company, we must not ignore the possibility of misunderstanding, jealousy, and difference of opinion arising. I say it boldly, that it is the business of the men connected more closely with the guiding of the destinies of these concerns, to build and mould them on harmonious lines. The interests of the farmers of Western Canada, individually or otherwise, are in all essentials the same. They must

[1] See *infra*, pp. 293–297.

be brought more closely together and must not be permitted to drift apart. It is not too much to conceive of one great central organization purchasing the supplies required by tens of thousands of our farmers, and of the creation of the proper agencies and the means for distributing these, down to the individual unit. The same applies to the sale of produce. Such an organization, welded together for a common purpose, could not help but have a powerful influence on the moulding of public opinion that will find its reflection in the character of our laws.[1]

Attitude of the G. G. G. Co. — While no formal expression of opinion on the subject of federation was registered or sought at this meeting, the question began to command increasing attention on the part of the directors of the Grain Growers' Company. The development of the Saskatchewan and Alberta Co-operative Elevator Companies meant that a considerable number of shareholders of the pioneer company resident in those provinces became shareholders of the new provincial companies as well. In such cases it was natural that they should market their grain through their local coöperative elevator instead of sending it to the Grain Growers' Company. Owing to the nature of its origin, the shareholders of the latter had not been built up around local elevator units, and despite the remarkable growth of the company's capitalization and business, the directors had not infrequently expressed their concern over the number of shareholders who were content to draw dividends without contributing their patronage to the company, and to receive notices of annual meetings without ever attempting to attend them. The Saskatchewan and Alberta system of shareholders' locals, of local boards of management, and of delegate representation at annual meetings, appeared to demonstrate the possibilities of calling forth greater interest in, and support of, the company, by shareholders so organized. Closely related, therefore, to the question of federation, the assimilation of the internal organization of the Grain Growers' Company to the more distinctly coöperative form represented by the newer farmers' companies was a matter that seriously occupied the attention of the directors of the older organization at this time. Said President Crerar at the 1915 meeting of the Grain Growers' Grain Company:

[1] G. G. G. Co., 1914, pp. 22, 23.

It seems necessary in some way to bring about a change that will bring the individual shareholder much closer to the company, cement his interest in it, and increase in him the sense of individual responsibility, since personal interest and a sense of individual responsibility are the only foundations upon which a permanent structure can be built. It is unquestionably a weakness of our farmers in Western Canada that they do not feel the importance of devoting attention and thought to the business of building up their own institutions.[1]

In the minds of those who shared Mr. Crerar's views, the consolidation of the Western farmers' commercial organizations did not mean the absorption of the newer by the older, or of the smaller by the larger, but a combination of effort, and a general reproduction of the soundest coöperative features of the constituent organizations. In reviewing the position of the Grain Growers' Company at the 1915 meeting, he pointed out clearly to the shareholders that the future of their company was bound up very largely with the future of the other farmers' organizations in Western Canada, and that "some step must be taken to draw them more closely together in such a way and by such means as will tend steadily to weave into the very fibre of their organizations the elements that will lead to increase stability as their various enterprises and activities expand and develop."

The bringing about of some form of federation among the farmers' companies was freely discussed at this meeting of the shareholders, resulting in the unanimous adoption of the following resolution:

Whereas it is desirable to federate as closely as possible the farmers' business organizations of Western Canada in order that they may carry on their work with the highest degree of efficiency and avoid the development of possible rivalries and jealousies that could not fail to be injurious to the work of the organized farmers of Canada.

Therefore be it resolved that the shareholders of this company hereby express their approval of the principle of federating the various organizations referred to, and urge the directors to take such steps as they think advisable to promote and carry out such a plan.

Position of the Alberta Company. — In Alberta, whose Coöperative Elevator Company was in a somewhat less independent position than the two older organizations, the possibility of sub-

[1] G. G. G. Co., 1915, pp. 32, 33.

sequent amalgamation with the Grain Growers' Company had been anticipated in the very act of incorporation which empowered it — subject to the approval of a referendum of shareholders' locals, and to the consent of the Lieutenant-Governor in Council — to sell or lease its elevators to any company.[1] While the financial accommodation extended to the Alberta Co-operative by the Grain Growers' Company does not appear to have been employed by the latter as a means of applying pressure to bring about amalgamation, it was well realized by the Alberta shareholders that the fuller expansion of their coöperative enterprises could be earlier realized and more advantageously accomplished by closer federation than by independent action. Accordingly, at the annual meeting at Calgary in November, 1915, a resolution in favor of federation was passed in terms almost identical with those embodied in the resolution adopted the previous week at the meeting of the Grain Growers' Grain Company in Winnipeg.[2]

Attitude of the Saskatchewan Company. — In Saskatchewan the sentiment in favor of federation was less pronounced. The Saskatchewan Co-operative Elevator Company, with its steadily accumulating reserves, and with the financial aid of the provincial government in the operation as well as in the construction of its elevators, was less concerned than the Alberta Company with amalgamation on considerations of finance. With Saskatchewan producing as much wheat as Manitoba and Alberta combined, and with requests for new elevators ever keeping ahead of the organization and construction departments, the company was, moreover, not particularly affected by considerations of competitive overlapping. If it was not the only farmers' grain company operating in Saskatchewan, it was not at any rate losing any business to the Grain Growers' Grain Company. While federation did not thus offer any special inducement to the Saskatchewan Company in respect to its country elevator business, the contemplated extension of its operation into the terminal and export fields did, however, call for a consideration of the relative

[1] See *supra*, p. 121.
[2] A. F. C. E. Co., 1915; *G. G. Guide*, Nov. 24, 1915.

advantages of taking such a step independently, or jointly with the other farmers' companies. On the whole, the Saskatchewan directors were disposed to favor the general principle of federation in the interests of solidarity and of centralized marketing and purchasing, provided that the autonomy, policy, and prospective earning power of their company was not likely to be prejudiced thereby. At the annual meeting at Regina in November, 1915, the shareholders expressed themselves reservedly upon the subject as follows:

> That this meeting hereby expresses its approval of the principles of federating the various organizations referred to, and urges the directors to look thoroughly into the matter, but to take no definite action without first submitting the scheme to a general meeting of this company.[1]

Proposed Basis of Federation. — In pursuance of the above resolution a meeting was held early in 1916 in the offices of the Saskatchewan Co-operative Elevator Company, attended by representatives of the three farmers' companies and the three provincial farmers' associations. The plan of federation there discussed involved the formation of a central company owned and controlled jointly by the provincial farmers' companies, in a relationship similar to that borne by the English and Scottish Wholesale Coöperative Societies to their constituent local coöperative societies. In the Grain Growers' case, however, it was contemplated that the central organization would function both as a marketing and as a supply agency. It would not only operate farmers' terminal elevators and centralise the selling and export of farmers' grain, but would also undertake the purchase or manufacture of farmers' staple supplies and equipment, as well as conducting such common enterprises as the *Grain Growers' Guide*. The provincial companies would retain their identity and organization, each looking after the assembling and warehousing of grain or other farm products, and the distribution of collectively purchased or manufactured supplies, through their respective shareholders' locals. Since the federal charter of the Grain Growers' Grain Company contained virtually all the powers requisite for such a central, it was proposed to use it for the

[1] Sask. Co-op. Elev. Co., Nov. 17, 1915.

purpose.[1] The plan thus involved the conversion of the Grain Growers' Grain Company into a central agency, and the organization of its Manitoba shareholders into a provincial company with constituent locals, after the model of the Saskatchewan and Alberta companies.

Dissent of Saskatchewan Representatives. — Upon the main lines of the scheme there appeared to be general agreement among the conferring representatives. In the discussion of functional and organizational details, however, a distinct divergence of opinion developed between the Saskatchewan representatives and those of the other bodies concerned, in respect to the method to be followed in the selling of grain. While agreeable to the plan of a common terminal and export agency, the officials of the Saskatchewan Co-operative contended that each provincial company should retain the right to operate its own selling ageny on the Winnipeg Exchange, or elsewhere if necessary, with the liberty of disposing in these markets of the grain it controlled or handled. Controlling as it did a large volume of grain in the principal producing province, the Saskatchewan Company was in fact reluctant to relinquish its profitable and well-established commission and sales business, for participation in the earnings of a central company, in the determination of whose policy and methods it would have only a partial voice. Objection was made also to the policy of the same company being both grain commission agency and exporter of grain, and thus in practice frequently selling to itself the grain consigned to it. These views were fully shared by the Saskatchewan Grain Growers' Association,[2] whose directorate was closely interlocked with that of the Elevator Company. The representatives of the other four farmers' organizations all felt, however, that only through a common sales agency could selling competition between the different coöperative companies be eliminated, and the flow of farmers' grain upon the market so controlled as to exercise any influence upon price movements. Federation on a basis

[1] *President's Report on Negotiations for Amalgamation of Farmers' Companies*, G. G. G. Co., 1916, pp. 34–36.

[2] S. G. G. A. Executive report, 1917, in *G. G. Guide*, Feb. 21, 1917.

which left it to the provincial companies to choose what proportion of their grain they would turn over to the central company would largely defeat its own object, and afford very little departure, in actual practice, from the existing situation, under which the Grain Growers' Company operated a terminal elevator and an export company with which the other farmers' companies might do business at any time.

While a continuation committee was appointed at the Regina conference to explore a scheme of federation acceptable to all concerned, subsequent conferences during 1916 showed the divergence of views between the Saskatchewan representatives and those of the other farmers' organizations to be irreconcilable.[1] The essence of the matter would seem to be that the Saskatchewan Company, with its advantageous territory, its assured patronage and its strong financial position, had less to gain from federation than the other companies concerned. The close identification between the company, the provincial government, and the Saskatchewan Grain Growers' Association had engendered, moreover, a strong provincial solidarity in the coöperative enterprise, and a reluctance to compromise the preservation of its identity.[2]

III. Formation of the United Grain Growers Ltd.

Negotiations for Limited Union. — While the Saskatchewan representatives thus dissented from the proposed plan of federation, the Alberta Company, with its less independent position, was eager for its consummation. At a joint meeting in July, 1916, of the directorate of the Alberta Co-operative Elevator Company and the executive of the United Farmers of Alberta, it was decided that the unwillingness of the Saskatchewan organization to proceed with federation should not be allowed to interfere with the continuation of negotiations among the interests who favored it, the way being left open for Saskatchewan to enter, if

[1] *President's Report on Negotiations*, etc., G. G. G. Co., 1916, p. 37; S. G. G. A., 1917.

[2] From interviews of the writer with persons concerned in the negotiations, it would appear also that the distribution of offices in the projected reorganization was by no means an irrelevant factor in the *impasse*.

it should subsequently choose to do so. A resolution to this effect was forwarded to the directorate of the Grain Growers' Grain Company, who acted on it by authorizing Mr. Crerar to collaborate with Mr. Rice-Jones, president of the Alberta Company, in working out a detailed plan for submission to their respective boards.[1] Approval by the latter of the recommendations presented by these negotiations was followed by a joint meeting, in the fall of 1916, of the directorates of the two companies, with representatives of the United Farmers of Alberta and the Manitoba Grain Growers' Association. Here it was agreed that, so far as the two companies were concerned, complete amalgamation was preferable to the joint establishment of a central company. At first it was proposed to procure a charter for an entirely new company, to be known as the United Grain Growers Limited, which should absorb the two existing companies. As the charter of the Grain Growers' Grain Company was broad enough however, to cover all the purposes for which it was desired to amalgamate, it was decided that it would be simpler to secure amendments to such charter, changing the name of the company to the United Grain Growers Limited, and assimilating its form of internal government to that of the Alberta Company. A joint committee, including in its personnel the presidents of the two companies and of the two provincial farmers' associations concerned, was appointed to draft amendments to the Grain Growers' charter in accordance with the resolutions adopted; to draw up by-laws for the new company; and to obtain a complete valuation of the assets of the amalgamating concerns. The report of this committee was laid before the annual meetings of the two companies toward the close of 1916.

Basis of Amalgamation. — While in the matter of financial resources, business turnover, and commercial prestige, the Grain Growers' Company was the stronger party to the amalgamation, it was the internal organization and coöperative features of the Alberta Company that were reproduced in the proposed constitution of the amalgamated concern. The shareholders of the former company residing in Manitoba and Saskatchewan were as

[1] *President's Report on Amalgamation*, etc., pp. 38, 39.

far as possible to be organized into locals, with boards of management, each local to have a minimum of 40 shareholders, and $8,000 of subscribed stock. At the annual meetings of the United Grain Growers, which were to be held alternately in Manitoba and Alberta, individual and proxy voting were to be replaced by delegate representation and voting on the Saskatchewan and Alberta plan.[1] It was recommended that the Alberta government should be requested to continue in favor of the new company the advances for elevator construction within that province, as provided by the Alberta Co-operative Elevator Act. While being invited to merge their identity with that of the pioneer company, the shareholders of the Alberta Company were not asked, therefore, to compromise their polity or policy. On the contrary, the directors of the Grain Growers' Grain Company recommended to their shareholders that the charter amendments in regard to organization and voting should be secured, whether or not amalgamation were affected. Such changes, it was felt, were necessary, if closer interest were to be developed between shareholders and management, and concentration of control prevented.[2]

The valuation made of the assets of the two companies revealed that those of the Alberta Company were equivalent to approximately $69 per outstanding share (par value $60), and that those of the Grain Growers' Grain Company were in the neighborhood of $71 for each two paid-up shares (treasury value $30 each). In view of the relatively slight disparity between the asset value of corresponding shares in the two companies, Mr. Crerar had proposed, on behalf of his directorate, that the difference should be disregarded in the issue of stock in the United Grain Growers Limited.[3] As shares in the latter were to be

[1] Each local was entitled to "one delegate for each 125 shareholders or less, or major portion thereof for the second delegate," the expenses of each delegate to be paid by the company.

[2] "At the present time, out of 18,000 shareholders not more than 300 attend the meetings in person, and not more than 2,000 of the remainder are represented by proxy. This unquestionably leaves the way open for a group of designing shareholders to secure control of an annual meeting." G. G. G. Co., 1916, p. 44. A resolution instructing the directors to take steps to have the company's charter amended so as to eliminate proxy voting had been passed at the 1914 meeting of the G. G. G. Co. G. G. G. Co., 1916, p. 44.

[3] Statement of E. J. Fream to writer.

issued at $30 (par value $25) the basis of amalgamation was, therefore, one share of Grain Growers' Grain Company stock and one half-share of Alberta Co-operative stock in exchange for each share of stock in the United Company. The maximum number of shares which any individual might hold was placed at 80.[1] Subscribed shares were to be paid up in 20 per cent annual instalments.

Formation of United Grain Growers Limited. — At the annual meeting of the Alberta Farmers' Co-operative Elevator Company in November, 1916, the plan of amalgamation was unanimously adopted, and the directors were instructed to secure the necessary legislative amendments, and to submit the plan of amalgamation to the 103 shareholders' locals, as required by the act of incorporation. The merger was fully endorsed by this referendum, as it was by one voted on concurrently by the U. F. A. locals. With a view to providing for continuation of the Alberta government's financial assistance under the new organization, an amendment to the act of incorporation was secured in the provincial legislature during the session of 1917, authorizing the company "to amalgamate with any other company having objects altogether or in part similar to the [Alberta] company — provided that no such sale, amalgamation, or other disposition of the assets shall take place until the terms thereof are approved by the Lieutenant-Governor in Council." [2]

At the 1916 meeting of the Grain Growers' Grain Company, the basis of amalgamation was overwhelmingly endorsed, although certain shareholders who were also stockholders in the Saskatchewan Co-operative spoke against the plan. The only change made in the *seriatim* discussion of the terms was the raising of the maximum number of shares that might be held by one shareholder in the united company from 80 to 100 ($2,500 par), while preserving the principle of one man one vote.[3]

[1] In the Grain Growers' Company the maximum had been 40 shares, and in the Alberta Company 20 shares.

[2] Stat. of Alberta, 7 Geo. V, c. 29, 1917, sec. 1.

[3] G. G. G. Co., 1916, pp. 47, 48. This change was made partly in view of the considerable number of Alberta farmers who held stock in both companies, and partly, no doubt, with a view to facilitating the expansion of the company's capital.

During the 1917 session of the federal Parliament, charter amendments were secured, authorizing the Grain Growers' Grain Company to change its name to the United Grain Growers Limited; increasing its authorized capital from two million to five million dollars; and enabling the shareholders, through by-laws adopted by a two-thirds vote, to substitute delegate voting for individual and proxy voting, to group its shareholders into local bodies, and delegate powers to the same.[1] Under this statutory authority the shareholders of the Grain Growers' Company were called together in special meeting in August, 1917, to ratify formally the agreement with the Alberta Co-operative and to pass the relevant by-laws. Concurrently, by an order-in-council the amalgamation was approved by the government of Alberta, in consideration of the formal undertaking by the United Grain Growers to assume and discharge all the liabilities and obligations of the Alberta Farmers' Co-operative Elevator Company.[2] With the close of the financial year (August 31), the separate existence of the eleven-years-old Grain Growers' Grain Company, and the four-year-old Alberta Co-operative Elevator Company came to a voluntary end, and on September 1, 1917, the United Grain Growers Limited officially began its commercial career.

Resources and Enterprises of the United Grain Growers. — The United Grain Growers represented a merger of considerable magnitude. The subscribed capital of the amalgamated companies exceeded $2,750,000 (of which approximately two thirds was paid up), held by over 30,000 farmer shareholders.[3] The policy of retaining earnings in the business, followed by both companies, had resulted in the accumulation of reserves which came not far short of the aggregate paid-up capital. The combined assets were valued at $6,180,526, of which the pioneer company contributed 60 per cent.[4] The Alberta Company, with its

[1] Stat. of Canada, 7–8 Geo. V, c. 79, 1917.

[2] An act formally winding up the Alberta Company, as of August 15, 1917, was passed in the session of 1919 (chap. 23).

[3] Not allowing for the considerable number of cases in which the same farmer held stock in both companies.

[4] The financial position of the constituent companies and of the United Grain

extensive investments in elevator buildings and supply warehouses, had a larger proportion of its assets in the form of fixed capital than the Grain Growers' Company, with its large commission and export business and with its policy of leasing elevators. The strong liquid position of the united company, however, was reflected in the fact that more than half of its total assets were classed as current, its cash funds and War Loan investments alone aggregating $872,000. Seats on Winnipeg, Calgary, Fort William, and Vancouver grain exchanges, and stock holdings, chiefly in the Home Bank and subsidiary companies, represented other current assets valued at $641,632. Of the combined capital assets amounting to slightly under $3,000,000, elevator buildings, warehouses and equipment accounted for $2,282,000. At the end of its first year's business the United Company owned or controlled 343 country elevators,[1] in conjunction with which it operated 231 flour warehouses and 181 coal warehouses.[2] At the head of the lakes the company owned its new private terminal of 600,000 bushels capacity, besides leasing the C. P. R. public terminal of 2,500,000 bushels. Supply and machinery warehouses were maintained at Winnipeg, Calgary, Regina, and Saskatoon; livestock offices were operated at Winnipeg, Calgary, and Edmonton; and a supply elevator was owned at New Westminster, B. C. In central British Columbia

Growers Limited is shown by the following statement taken from the balance sheets of the three companies, as of Aug. 31, 1917. G. G. G. Co., 1917, pp. 24–31.

	G. G. G. Co.	A. F. C. E. Co.	U G. G.
Current Assets	$1,982,099	$1,230,796	$3,212,895
Capital Assets	1,649,347	1,318,282	2,967,629
	3,631,446	2,549,078	6,180,524
Current Liabilities	1,066,712	754,476	1,821,188
Capital Liabilities	89,000	785,679	874,679
Capital Stock sub'd.	1,705,771	1,076,350	2,782,121
Capital Stock paid-up	1,357,382	467,918	1,825,300
Net Surplus	1,118,351	541,004	1,659,355

[1] Of these 343 elevators, the company owned 146 in Alberta, 40 in Saskatchewan and 20 in Manitoba, besides 137 houses which the company continued to lease from the Manitoba government. U. G. G., 1918, p. 40.

[2] One hundred and forty-five of these flour warehouses and 122 of the coal warehouses were taken over from the Alberta Co-op. Elev. Co. U. G. G., 1918, p. 41.

over $260,000 had been invested in acquiring and developing the Grain Growers' 300,000,000-feet timber limit. Subsidiaries included the Grain Growers' Canadian and New York Export Companies, and the Public Press Limited, publishing the *Grain Growers' Guide* with a circulation of over 35,000.[1]

Nature of Merger. — While the amalgamation of the oldest and youngest farmers' companies made the United Grain Growers the largest grain company doing business in Western Canada, the merger was free from the usual objections raised against business combinations. It did not establish anything in the nature of a monopoly. The negotiations and discussions leading to it had been publicly conducted, and the basis approved by the Canadian Council of Agriculture, and conventions and referenda of the provincial farmers' associations, as well as by the shareholders of the companies concerned. It was formally authorized by special legislation of the Dominion and the Alberta legislatures. There was no watered stock issued to the shareholders, the total assets of the united company being considerably more than three times as great as its liability to shareholders. With stock ownership restricted to farmers and members of their families, with individual holdings limited to $2,500, and with shares transferable only through the company's offices, opportunities for speculative trading in the company's stock were excluded. Moreover, with share and proxy voting eliminated in favor of delegate voting, and with delegates' expenses at annual meetings paid by the company, group manipulation and minority control were made distinctly difficult. The United Grain Growers merger was in fact unique, in that the creation of this particular business combination was conditioned by the adoption of a democratic form of internal government that made it distinctly coöperative in character.

Organization of United Company. — The newly constituted board of directors of the United Grain Growers elected T. A. Crerar as president, with C. Rice-Jones as first vice-president and general manager, thus associating as chief executives of the new concern the two leaders who had principally worked out the

[1] G. G. G. Co., 1917, p. 21.

plan of amalgamation.[1] The broad territorial scope of the united company's enterprises led in the first year to the organization for administrative purposes of an Eastern and a Western division. Under the former were placed the country elevators in Manitoba and Saskatchewan, the supervision of the supply warehouses at Regina and Saskatoon, the lakehead terminals, the Grain Growers' Export Company, with its Winnipeg and New York offices, and the Public Press, with the business of the *Grain Growers' Guide*. The Western Division, with its administrative headquarters at Calgary, supervised the country elevators in Alberta, and the business of the two subsidiaries in British Columbia, namely the United Grain Growers (B. C.) Limited (engaged chiefly in conducting a farmers' feed and supply business on the Pacific Coast), and the U. G. G. Sawmills, Limited, operating the large lumber mill erected on the company's timber limit on the line of the Grand Trunk Pacific, at Hutton, B. C.

The infant company which Partridge had brought into being as a means of giving the Western farmers direct participation in the organized grain trade, had thus attained, within a dozen years, the full stature of Big Business.

[1] In the fall of 1917, Mr. Crerar was appointed Minister of Agriculture in Sir Robert Borden's Union Ministry. While continuing in the presidency of the United Grain Crowers, Mr. Crerar had necessarily to leave the executive direction of the company's affairs largely to Mr. Rice-Jones.

CHAPTER XII

INDEPENDENT EXPANSION OF THE SASKATCHEWAN CO-OPERATIVE

The reluctance of the Saskatchewan Co-operative Elevator Company to compromise its autonomy by participating in a strongly centralized scheme of federation had led, as we have seen, to the substitution of limited amalgamation for inclusive federation. Henceforth the farmer-controlled grain marketing organization in Western Canada consisted of two highly centralized, but democratically constituted companies: one interprovincial in the distribution of its shareholders' locals and operating units, the other provincially constituted and provincially controlled; one operating mainly on its own capital, the other receiving far-reaching government financial assistance; one diversifying its enterprises in the field of supply as well as of marketing, the other concentrating its resources and efforts on the warehousing and merchandising of grain.

The resources and business of the amalgamated company and the independent Saskatchewan Co-operative showed a striking correspondence. The subscribed capital of the former at the date of amalgamation amounted to $2,782,121; that of the Saskatchewan Company at the same date, $2,778,450. The total assets of the United Grain Growers on September 1, 1917, stood at $6,180,524; those of the Saskatchewan Co-operative on July 31, 1917, amounted to $5,935,615. Each company controlled approximately 300 country elevators. For the crop year 1917–18 the United Grain Growers handled slightly under 30,000,000 bushels of grain, while a little over 27,000,000 bushels passed through the hands of the Saskatchewan concern.[1] While the two companies operated along different lines and pursued distinctive policies, their financial strength and commercial importance were thus fairly evenly balanced.

[1] G. G. G. Co., 1917, U. G. G., 1918; Sask. Co-op., 1917, 1918.

Entry into Terminal Operations. — The dissent of the Saskatchewan Company from the federation proposals involved the abandonment of the idea of an interprovincially controlled farmers' terminal elevator. The directors of the company, to whom the question of terminal policy had been referred by the annual meeting of 1915,[1] decided alternatively, that the time had come for the Saskatchewan Company to erect a terminal of its own at the head of the lakes. Although government financial aid was not available for such an extra-provincial undertaking, the record earnings made in the handling of the great 1915 crop permitted a substantial addition to the company's available capital.[2] In pursuance of its decision the directorate selected a spacious terminal site at Port Arthur, and engaged C. D. Howe, chief engineer for the Board of Grain Commissioners, as consulting, designing, and supervising engineer for a modern terminal with initial capacity of 2,500,000 bushels, at an estimated cost of $1,225,000.[3] Construction operations were begun on July 3, 1916, but progressed slowly, under war-time labor and supply conditions; so that it proved impossible to fulfil the expectation of receiving the 1917 crop before the close of navigation. Not until January, 1918, was the company able to receive grain into this, the first public terminal elevator to be built by organized farmers. A few months later a contract was let for the construction of a private hospital elevator of 600,000 bushels capacity. With the completion of this latter in February, 1919, the company thus became fully established in the terminal business, with the advantage over the United Grain Growers of being the owner instead of the lessee of its public terminal, and of possessing a much more modern equipment.

In its first full year of operation the Saskatchewan Co-operative public terminal took in 11,500,000 bushels, being approximately 50 per cent of all the grain handled by the company. In fact, a much larger quantity of grain was available for storage than

[1] See *supra*, p. 168.

[2] The company's profits for the year 1915–16 amounted to $757,275, which, after deducting excess profits tax of $200,000 and paying an 8 per cent cash dividend, left a disposable surplus of over half a million. Sask. Co-op., 1916.

[3] Sask. Co-op., 1916.

the elevator could take care of. Under these conditions it was considered desirable by the directors to increase the company's terminal capacity at once by 2,000,000 bushels, despite the inflated costs of war-time construction.[1] As the company's own reserves did not permit complete internal financing, negotiations were entered into with an Eastern Canadian bond house, which found it necessary to look to the New York market for the necessary capital. The heavy premium prevailing on American exchange at that time (1919–20) made financing from that quarter decidedly costly, however, and it was suggested[2] that the Saskatchewan government might aid the company in financing its terminal as well as its country elevator construction, although the act of incorporation did not provide for government assistance for extra-provincial undertakings. It was, perhaps, fortunate for the company that the office of provincial treasurer was filled at this time by Hon. C. A. Dunning, its former general manager.[3] This circumstance assured for the Saskatchewan Company in its financial relations with the provincial government the sympathetic and intelligent consideration of a minister who at the same time appears to have been fully mindful of his responsibilities as political custodian of the provincial funds. Largely through the influence of Mr. Dunning and Mr. Langley there was passed in the session of 1919–20 an amendment to the act of incorporation authorizing

> the Lieutenant-Governor in Council from time to time, and on such terms and conditions as may be agreed upon with the company, to lend to the company for the purpose of aiding in the construction or extension or remodelling of terminal elevators at points outside the province, or towards reimbursing to the company moneys already expended for that purpose, a sum not to exceed fifty per cent of cost or estimated cost of such elevator,

---

[1] Sask. Co-op., 1919. Subsequent extensions have increased the capacity of the Sask. Co-op. terminal to 7,650,000 bushels, while in 1923 the Canadian Northern Elevator at Port Arthur was also leased, giving an additional 7,500,000 bushels of controlled terminal storage. Sask. Co-op., 1924.

[2] By Hon. George Langley, Minister of Municipal Affairs in the Saskatchewan government, as well as director of the Co-operative Company.

[3] Mr. Dunning had resigned the general managership of the company on being called to the Saskatchewan cabinet as provincial treasurer in 1916. He was succeeded as general manager by F. W. Riddell.

or of extension or remodelling thereof, as may be considered advisable or necessary.[1]

This advancing of public moneys to assist a joint-stock company in the financing of its enterprises in another province represented an unusual degree of government assistance that might indeed be questioned on strictly constitutional, if not on fiscal, grounds. The policy of the Saskatchewan government appears to have been, however, to regard the Co-operative Elevator Company as a semi-public institution whose prosperity was of direct or indirect interest to a very considerable portion of the productive population of the province. The terminal operations of the company were considered as an essential complement of the coöperative local elevators. Moreover, the record of the company in meeting its financial obligations to the treasury in the past, and the ample security taken for the government's advances,[2] were deemed to justify fully this further extension of the government financial aid to the farmers' company.

Saskatchewan Co-operative Export Subsidiaries. — In order to comply the better with certain provisions of the Canadian Bank Act and the Canada Grain Act,[3] it was considered expedient to conduct the company's public terminal business through a separate corporation. It has been noted that in the case of the Grain Growers' Grain Company a subsidiary export company had been incorporated under federal charter in 1911, and that the parent company had turned over its private terminal to this subsidiary, while operating under its own name the public terminal leased

[1] Stat. of Sask., 9–10 Geo. V, c. 58, 1919–20, sec. 1.

[2] See act to confirm agreement between Government and Sask. Co-op. Elev. Co. Stat. of Sask., 3 Geo. V, c. 42, 1912–13.

[3] Under the interpretation section of the Bank Act, a "warehouse receipt means any receipt given by any person for any goods, wares or merchandise in his actual, visible and continued possession as bailee thereof in good faith, and not as his own property." (Sec. 2). In accepting warehouse receipts as security for loans, the banks, therefore, generally followed the practice of insisting that such receipts should be made out in the name of persons or corporations other than those issuing the documents.

It has already been noted that under sec. 123 of the Canada Grain Act owners or operators of public terminals were not permitted to buy or sell grain on their own account, except in cases specially approved by the Board of Grain Commissioners. See *supra*, p. 141.

from the C. P. R.[1] The Saskatchewan Company followed a different procedure. The Saskatchewan Co-operative Export Company was incorporated, not by federal charter, but under the Saskatchewan Companies Act.[2] While this subsidiary company operated the Saskatchewan public terminal, the hospital elevator remained under the parent company, thus reversing the arrangement of the Grain Growers' Company. Furthermore, the stock of the Saskatchewan Co-operative Export Company was, from the first, held entirely by the parent company,[3] and its by-laws provided that directors of the latter should constitute the directorate of the subsidiary as well, each director holding one share of subsidiary stock in trust for the parent corporation.[4]

Inasmuch as the Saskatchewan Co-operative Export Company was strictly a public warehousing concern, and as it was organized at a time when the Canadian wheat crop was handled in its entirety by the Canadian Wheat Board, the name of the company was somewhat misleading. With the discontinuance in the latter part of 1920 of that Board (of which Mr. James Stewart of Winnipeg, and Mr. F. W. Riddell, general manager of the Saskatchewan company had been chairman and vice-chairman respectively),[5] it was decided to organize a separate export company. Mr. Stewart, enjoying considerable prestige as a result of the satisfactory operations of the Canadian Wheat Board, agreed to continue his association with Mr. Riddell by undertaking the management of the export business of the Saskatchewan Company, on the understanding that his name would be incorporated in the designation of the export subsidiary. In accordance with this arrangement, which was regarded as highly advantageous to the company, the James Stewart Company Limited, was incorporated under Dominion charter, in February, 1921, with an authorized capitalization of $500,000. In the meantime, the name of the Saskatchewan Co-operative Export Company had been changed to the Saskatchewan Co-operative Terminals Limited,

[1] See *supra*, pp. 148, 149.
[2] Under date of July 29, 1920, with authorized capitalization of $100,000.
[3] Compare procedure, G. G. G. Co., p. 158 n.
[4] Sask. Co-op., 1920.
[5] See *infra*, p. 196 n.

and its capital increased to half a million.[1] The latter now invested $250,000 of its own capital and reserves in the stock of the James Stewart Company, which thus became a subsidiary of the senior subsidiary, with Mr. Stewart holding a qualifying share as director.[2]

Hitherto the Saskatchewan Co-operative had not conducted mixing operations in its private terminal, which had functioned merely as a hospital elevator. With the discontinuance of government grain marketing, however, and with the organization of the James Stewart Company, it was decided by a majority of the directors that the company was justified on competitive considerations in carrying on mixing operations under the conditions recognized by the Board of Grain Commissioners.[3] Accordingly, in July, 1922, the company's private terminal at Port Arthur was leased by the parent corporation to the James Stewart Company, and operated in connection with the latter's export business.[4] The first year's export operations of the new subsidiary were distinctly satisfactory, yielding a dividend of 8 per cent to the parent organization, and permitting a substantial balance to be carried to reserve account. The next year, 1922–23, was, however, unfavorable to export operations generally, owing to the dislocation of European buying, and the James Stewart Company suffered losses which reduced its surplus to $28,000.

An export company operating merely in Winnipeg and at the head of the lakes comes in direct contact with European buyers to only a limited extent. The latter deal chiefly with export agencies on the Eastern seaboard, particularly in New York, Winnipeg "exporters" being for the most part intermediaries between western elevator companies and eastern shippers, who are in direct touch with European tonnage, cables, and exchange.[5] In 1922, therefore, the directors of the Saskatchewan Co-operative decided to follow the precedent of the United Grain Growers,

[1] *Saskatchewan Co-operative News*, Feb., 1921, p. 11.

[2] Sask. Co-op., 1921; *Co-operative News*, March, 1924, p. 9.

[3] *Co-operative News*, Feb., 1924, p. 7; Evidence of George Langley before Royal Grain Inquiry Commission, April 10, 1924.

[4] *Co-operative News*, March, 1924, p. 9.

[5] See *supra*, p. 159 n.

and establish their own New York agency. This took the form of a third subsidiary, incorporated under New York state laws, as the James Stewart Grain Corporation of New York, with an authorized capitalization of $200,000. The paid-up capital of $100,000 was provided in full by the James Stewart Company of Winnipeg, which was itself two removes from the parent company.[1] The Saskatchewan farmers' company had thus found it expedient, from legal and trade considerations, to follow the familiar devices of large-scale business in operating under a diversity of designations, while retaining unity of control through corporate stock ownership and interlocking or identical directorates.

Consolidation of Export Subsidiaries. — As all the stock of the three subsidiaries was held indirectly by the farmer shareholders of the Saskatchewan Co-operative Elevator Company, it was now necessary to present four different reports and financial statements at the annual shareholders' meeting. Considerable difficulty was experienced by the directors in making clear to some of the new delegates the method of subsidiary organization and financial relationship, and the legal expediency of such an apparently complex system. In the minds of some shareholders there was a certain incompatibility in the formal association of a coöperative company with a corporation bearing the name of a prominent Winnipeg grain dealer. Losses sustained in the export operations of both the Winnipeg and New York James Stewart companies during the unfavorable grain-trade year of 1922–23 did not tend to reassure members who found difficulty in appreciating the method of organization adopted by the directors.

At the annual meeting of the company in November, 1923, the advisability of consolidating the various subsidiaries with the parent company was discussed at some length. Despite efforts to set forth the *raison d'être* of the subsidiary corporations through the medium of the *Co-operative News*[2] and local meetings, it was

[1] *Co-operative News*, April, 1924, p. 9.

[2] See issues of Feb., March, and April, 1924. The *Co-operative News* had been established in April, 1918, as a company organ. It was sent monthly to all share-

felt by the directors that under the delegate system of shareholder representation there would always be difficulty in conveying to new delegates an intelligent understanding of the formal and financial relationship of the various organizations. Furthermore, in actual administration certain inconveniences were experienced in referring closely related matters to separate meetings of the same directors in their appropriate formal capacity. It was further pointed out that the United Grain Growers had always operated their leased terminal elevator under the direct control of the parent company, to the evident satisfaction of both the banks and the Board of Grain Commissioners. Consultations with the banks by the Saskatchewan management elicited the assurance from all except one that terminal warehouse receipts issued by the company for deliveries of its own grain would be acceptable as bank loan security, inasmuch as such receipts were required to be registered with the Board of Grain Commissioners.[1] On these considerations the directors decided to consolidate the four organizations, and in August, 1924, the assets of the three subsidiaries were formally transferred to the parent company.[2] The New York office was henceforth operated directly by the Saskatchewan Company under a state license.

The Saskatchewan Co-operative, after a brief experiment, had thus found the method of intercorporate organization and personal affiliation incompatible with its coöperative character. In reverting, however, to the simpler form of a single corporation, the company did not in any way contract the range of its operations.

Later Terminal Expansion. — On the contrary, the expansion of its export business accompanying the growth of its country elevator feeder system[3] led the company to undertake extensive new commitments by way of facilitating its contact with world

holders, as a means of keeping them in touch with matters affecting the company's interests and development, and as a medium through which complaints and criticisms against the company could be answered.

[1] Canada Grain Act, sec. 12.

[2] *Co-operative News*, Sept., 1924.

[3] By the end of 1924 the company's elevator locals numbered 435.

markets. Additions to its Port Arthur terminal, and the leasing of the Canadian Northern public elevator, gave the Saskatchewan company control, by the end of 1923, of 15,000,000 bushels terminal storage, equivalent to over 25 per cent of the total capacity on Thunder Bay.[1] As export freight-rate adjustments began to cause grain from Western Saskatchewan to move westward to Pacific ports, the company opened an export office at Vancouver early in 1924, while in the following year a European sales office was established at London, England.[2] In 1924 it was decided to construct a 1,100,000 bushel transfer elevator at Buffalo, New York, which began handling grain at the close of 1925.[3] The latter decision was based upon the strategic importance of Buffalo as a transfer point and milling centre.[4] Grain rushed to Buffalo in deep-draught lake carriers before the close of inland navigation is in ideal position to be moved out during the winter to New York and other North Atlantic ports, or to be supplied to eastern American mills.[5]

In the financing of these later extra-provincial undertakings, the company did not find it necessary to have recourse either to the provincial treasury or to bond underwriters, but was able to provide for its new capital commitments entirely out of reinvested earnings, its reserve at the end of the 1924–25 financial year being close to $2,500,000.[6] In extending its operations from provincial to interprovincial and international proportions, the Saskatchewan Co-operative Elevator Company, like the Grain Growers' Company, had self-financed its expansion.

[1] *Report of Board of Grain Commissioners*, 1923–24.

[2] *Co-operative News*, Jan., 1926.

[3] In the following year the capacity of the Buffalo transfer elevator was enlarged to 2,000,000 bushels. *Co-operative News*, March, 1926.

[4] For the three crop years 1920–23, 47.5 per cent of all grain shipped by lake from Thunder Bay ports was delivered at Buffalo. See U. S. Dept. of Commerce, *Trade Information Bulletin, No. 251*, "Marketing Canadian Wheat," pp. 76, 77.

[5] Since the passing of the Fordney-McCumber Tariff Act the milling of Canadian wheat in bond for export has reached large proportions at Buffalo. *Report of Royal Grain Inquiry Commission*, 1925, p. 145.

[6] Sask. Co-op. Balance Sheet, Aug. 31, 1925.

PART III

THE MOVEMENT FOR COLLECTIVE MARKETING, 1919–27

CHAPTER XIII

THE WHEAT BOARD MOVEMENT, 1919–23

I. STATUS OF FARMERS' ELEVATOR COMPANIES AT CLOSE OF THE WORLD WAR

Achievements of the Farmers' Companies. — By the end of the World War the two great farmers' companies had attained a position of competitive ascendancy in the Western grain trade. In 1919 the two organizations, with their 57,000 farmer shareholders, operated between them 649 coöperative elevators, which meant that their competition was effective at 45 per cent of the country elevator points in the Prairie Provinces.[1] During the crop year 1918–19 the two farmers' companies together handled one-fourth of all grain inspected in the Western Division.[2] The earning record of both companies had been impressive. After its initial year the Grain Growers' Company had never failed to pay less than 10 per cent to its shareholders, while the Saskatchewan Co-operative, in addition to a regular 8 per cent cash dividend, had generally declared substantial stock dividends. At the same time both companies had built up reserves of significant proportions.[3]

The benefits which the farmers' companies had brought to Western grain growers had been of a fourfold character. First, they had reduced, in all three provinces, the dependence of producers upon private middleman agencies by providing them with grain-handling facilities of their own, entering local, primary, terminal, and export markets. Second, and probably of chief importance, their extended and centralized competition had been effective to a very large degree, in improving marketing services,

[1] In 1919, there were 1438 country elevator stations in the Prairie Provinces. *Canada Year Book*, 1920.

[2] The U. G. G. handled 22,200,000 bushels and the Sask. Co-op. 21,800,000 bushels out of grain inspections amounting in all to 175,000,000 bushels.

[3] The financial records of the farmers' companies are discussed in Chapter xviii.

in lessening marketing discriminations, and in increasing marketing returns to growers generally.[1] Third, the profits realized through their participation in the grain trade had been returned to Western farmers, either directly in the form of cash or stock dividends distributed among approximately one quarter of prairie grain growers, or indirectly in the form of extended facilities or services. Fourth, the annual grants made by the companies to the provincial and interprovincial farmers' associations had been largely instrumental in strengthening the effective influence of the latter in obtaining provincial and federal legislation advantageous to agrarian interests.[2] At the close of the war, the Canadian Council of Agriculture had become an organization whose representations could not be disregarded by the Union government, which had deemed it expedient to include the president of the United Grain Growers as its Minister of Agriculture.

Farmer Criticisms of Coöperative Companies.—The very achievements of the grain growers' companies, it was now found, were having the effect of relaxing the loyalty of some of their farmer supporters, and of engendering certain criticisms within the ranks of farmers themselves. The companies had been launched at a time of rapidly expanding grain production in Western Canada, and of acute and widespread dissatisfaction among growers over the inadequate facilities, the independent attitude, and monopolistic practices of private grain-handling agencies. Under these conditions Western farmers in general had welcomed the services, competition, and marketing participation offered by the Grain Growers' Company and the two provincial coöperative elevator companies. The very opposition, open or covert, which these had received at the outset from the established trade served only to rally farmers more solidly behind their own marketing organizations. When, however, the "regulars," reconciling themselves to the participation of the farmers' companies, sought to offer

[1] "The Grain Growers' Grain Company has the record of cleaning up many cloudy phases of the trade, and enabling all shippers of grain to receive more for their produce than would otherwise have been possible." Letter of H. C. Wells, *G. G. Guide*, Aug. 18, 1915.

[2] The coöperative accomplishments of the farmers' companies are more fully discussed in Chapter xix.

inducements to growers at competing points, in the form of higher street prices, better grades or extra services, not a few farmer shareholders, being bound to their own organization neither by contracts nor by expectation of patronage dividends, were disposed to deliver their grain to whichever agency offered the greatest direct advantage. Whereas the three farmers' elevator companies had together handled approximately one third of all grain inspected in the crop years 1915–16 and 1916–17, the combined share of the United Grain Growers and the Saskatchewan Co-operative in succeeding years ranged between one quarter and one fifth of the total annual marketings.[1]

In various quarters and at various times, uncertain loyalty passed into open criticism by farmers of the policies and practices of their own companies. The very facility and success with which the latter had adapted their operations to the competitive conditions of the grain trade were regarded by some as a compromise of growers' interests and of true coöperative principles with the profit-seeking incentive and the corporation outlook.[2] It has been pointed out on more than one occasion in preceding chapters that the farmers in business were disposed to regard trading practices in a somewhat different light from the farmers in convention.[3] Thus the Grain Growers' Grain Company had identified itself with other commission firms in denouncing the suspension of the commission rule of the Exchange. In 1920 both farmers' companies joined in an application made to the Board of Grain Commissioners by the Northwest Grain Dealers Association for an increase in elevator handling tariffs.[4] They made use of the futures market in the same manner as regular companies, and in 1911 the very survival of the Grain Growers' Company had been prejudiced by the speculative operations of

[1] See table, p. 325.

[2] See, for example, letter of John Campbell, in which he complains of "the capitalist structure which confines the trading enterprises of the farmers of the West." *G. G. Guide*, April 14, 1915. Also letter of Frank Mason to *Courier* of Unity, Sask., condemning both companies as being concerned chiefly in piling up profits, "like the big interests the *Guide* condemns." Cited in *G. G. Guide*, Jan. 17, 1917.

[3] See *supra*, pp. 76, 151.

[4] U. G. G., 1920, p. 50.

the company's manager in oat futures.[1] In handling street grain and in carrying on mixing and export operations they dealt, not as the farmers' agent, but as principals. As such they were interested primarily in making gains for farmers as shareholders, not as the actual contributors of the grain on which the trading profits were realized. The Grain Growers' New York export subsidiary had made huge war-time profits in the handling of American grain.[2] At annual meetings the directors repeatedly found themselves called upon to justify the company's participation in mixing operations, and its profits from terminal "overages" and screenings.[3]

The Question of Patronage Distribution. — Probably the criticism most frequently directed against the farmers' companies was of their failure to distribute patronage dividends while paying high cash dividends to their stockholders and accumulating large surpluses.[4] In the organization of all three companies, distribution of earnings on a patronage basis had been contemplated. It was the circularized announcement of the intention of the Grain Growers' Grain Company to rebate commission profits among farmer shippers in proportion to their consignments that had been given as the reason for the suspension of the parvenu farmers' company by the Grain Exchange in 1906–07.[5] In securing federal incorporation in 1911, the company had obtained the inclusion in its charter of a provision whereby, on adoption at any annual meeting of a resolution of which due notice had been given, the company might order that any surplus remaining after providing for dividend on paid-up capital and such sums as the directors might set apart as reserve, should be "dis-

[1] G. G. G. Co., 1911. See also Moorhouse, *op. cit.*, chap. 16.

[2] See *supra*, p. 159.

[3] G. G. G. Co., 1916, pp. 12, 13 (*re* mixing); U. G. G., 1918, pp. 15–18; 1920, pp. 61–64 (*re* terminal overages and screenings). See also U. G. G., 1921, pp. 67–89, "Charges Against the Company."

[4] "Their whole and sole concern is to pay dividends to their shareholders and pile up comfortable surpluses." *Saskatchewan Farmer* (ed.), Aug., 1923. "The Saskatchewan Co-op. is masquerading under the name of 'Co-operative' in the proper and better sense of the word, when it is in reality to-day simply a joint-stock company." B. T. George in *The Progressive*, Sept. 11, 1924.

[5] See *supra*, pp. 50, 51.

tributed among the shareholders and customers of the company upon such basis and in such proportions as may be set out in such resolution."[1] The acts incorporating both the Saskatchewan and Alberta Co-operative Elevator Companies also provided for alternative distribution of 50 per cent of the surplus, either among individual patrons, or among shareholders' locals according to the volume of business contributed.[2]

Whenever the application of these powers was seriously considered by the directors, however, they had found themselves confronted by accounting difficulties and financial considerations which appeared to make any payment of patronage dividends impracticable.[3] The very diversity of methods of handling the farmers' grain made the determination of equitable patronage dividends a matter of well-nigh baffling complexity. A farmer might "patronize" his company merely by consigning to its commission department grain which he had loaded over platform, or he might store it to grade, or special bin it in one of the company's elevators, from which he might have it forwarded through the commission department for immediate sale after inspection at Winnipeg, or for terminal storage pending selling instructions. Or he might sell his grain outright on street to the company's elevator agent. The separate determination of profits from each of these methods of handling and the prorating of them to each class of patron presented obvious difficulties. These were further complicated by the integrated operations of the companies in terminal warehousing, mixing, and exporting. Grain was received into the companies' terminals which did not originate at their own country elevator points; while in their mixing and export operations they also purchased grain on the open markets, sometimes outside of Canada altogether, as through their New York subsidiaries. Further difficulties were to be found in deciding whether patronage dividends should be paid to non-share-

[1] Act of Incorporation, 1911, sec. 17, sub-sec. 2.

[2] Sask. Co-op. Elev. Act, sec. 20, sub-sec. 3; Alberta Co-op. Elev. Act, sec. 36 (*e*).

[3] G. G. G. Co., 1915; U. G. G., 1918; *Co-operative News*, May 1921, Dec. 1923.

holder patrons, and if so, whether on the same basis as to shareholders.[1]

The second set of considerations which deterred the companies from making patronage distributions were of a financial nature. The rebate to patrons of earnings in excess of a fixed maximum return on share capital was realized to be incompatible with the financing of additional facilities and extended services through the reinvestment of earnings. Minute individual patronage disbursements — even if a satisfactory method of distribution could be worked out — were felt to be of less advantage to grain growers as a whole than the enlargement of the resources and serviceableness of the farmers' companies.[2]

While the presentation of such considerations served to satisfy shareholders as a whole of the impracticability and inexpediency of any immediate application of the patronage distribution system in relation to grain handling, an increasing number of voices were to be heard challenging the coöperative character of the farmers' companies, and charging them with becoming capitalistic in outlook. In various quarters, too, an interest began to be evidenced in the non-stock, non-profit type of commodity pooling whose development in California appeared to offer a purer form of agricultural coöperation.

The pooling idea was brought home to every grain grower in Western Canada — howbeit on a compulsory basis — during the operation of the Canadian Wheat Board in 1919–20. This experience in collective marketing, and the collapse of wheat prices following disestablishment of the Board and the restoration of speculative trading, — coming as they did at a time when the more radically minded farmers were evincing an openly critical attitude towards their own "coöperative" companies, — combined to introduce a new phase in the history of grain growers' coöperation in Western Canada. Henceforth the pooling method, first on a compulsory and then on a voluntary contract basis, became the objective of the majority of Prairie farmers.

[1] The nature and complexity of the accounting problems involved in patronage distribution are discussed at length by W. A. Mackintosh, *Agricultural Coöperation in Western Canada*, pp. 92–101.

[2] These considerations are further discussed below, pp. 489–494.

II. The Canadian Wheat Board, 1919–20

War-time Control of Grain Marketing in Canada. — Although functioning during a single crop year only, the Canadian Wheat Board established a precedent and a performance which led grain growers during four successive years of depressed prices to agitate for its reëstablishment. During the last two years of the war the crops of 1917 and 1918 had been marketed in Canada under the control of a Board of Grain Supervisors.[1] This body was authorized to fix a government guaranteed price at which grain should be sold, whether for export or domestic consumption.[2] Unlike the United States Grain Corporation, which was established contemporaneously, the Canadian Board was not a buying corporation, ready to enter the market to maintain the minimum guaranteed price.[3] It regulated, however, the movement and distribution of the crop between domestic millers and the Wheat Export Company, which purchased North American wheat for the Royal Commission on Wheat Supplies, acting jointly for the United Kingdom, France, and Italy.[4]

Although the inter-Allied food-purchasing organization was temporarily relaxed after the Armistice, the Supreme Economic Council at Paris took steps in the summer of 1919 to reconstitute the Royal Commission on Wheat Supplies as the joint purchasing agency for the United Kingdom, France, and Italy, while government control of wheat imports was retained by European neutrals. This consideration, combined with the continued government control of ocean tonnage, the decision of the Washington administration to extend the operations of the Grain Corporation for another year, and the exceptionally low yield of the 1919

[1] The appointment of this body followed the voluntary action of the Winnipeg Grain Exchange in suspending future trading after an investigation into speculative price aberrations in May 1917. — President's address, *Ninth Annual Report*, Winnipeg Grain Exchange, Sept., 1917.

[2] The Board's first order (July 20, 1917) fixed the price at $2.40, basis No. 1 Northern, in store at Fort William. Later (by order of Sept. 12, 1917) the basic price was fixed at $2.21, to correspond with the minimum price established in the United States.

[3] See W. Eldred, "Wheat and Flour Trade under Food Administration Control," *Quart. Journ. of Econ.*, Nov., 1918.

[4] *Report of Canadian Wheat Board*, Dom. Sess. Paper No. 54 (1921), p. 3.

crop in Western Canada, — carrying with it the prospect of speculative manipulations under private marketing, — led the Canadian government, after a series of consultative conferences with representatives of the Council of Agriculture and the grain trade, to decide, in the interests of both producers and domestic consumers, to create the Canadian Wheat Board, with exclusive power to handle the entire 1919 crop.

Operations of Canadian Wheat Board, 1919–20. — The Wheat Board, established by order-in-council of July 31, which reproduced almost identically the plan submitted by the Council of Agriculture,[1] differed from the preceding Board of Grain Supervisors in being a marketing instead of a merely regulating and price-fixing body. It differed, further, from the United States Grain Corporation in being vested with a statutory monopoly in the selling of the entire crop for both domestic and export consumption.[2] While analogous in the latter respect to the Australian Wheat Board, it did not, like that body, function in coördination with state or provincial wheat boards.[3] The plan adopted involved the establishment of a compulsory national pool, with the Board as sole selling agency. No open trading took place on the Winnipeg Grain Exchange, existing grain-handling agencies merely receiving and forwarding wheat at fixed margins to the Board's account. Producers received on delivery an initial payment of $2.15 per bushel (basis No. 1 Northern, in store Fort William) and a participation certificate. Fixed "spreads" between street and track wheat, and between the different grades, were maintained by the Board throughout the period of control.[4]

[1] *Record of U. G. G. on Question of Pool Marketing* (Nov., 1925), p. 2. The chairman of the Board was Mr. James Stewart, president of the Wheat Export Co., and the vice-chairman, Mr. F. W. Riddell, general manager of the Saskatchewan Co-op., both of whom had been members of the Board of Grain Supervisors. Of the remaining ten members of the Canadian Wheat Board, two represented the organized farmers, three, the flour-milling interests, four, grain-trading interests, and one, organized labor. *Report of Canadian Wheat Board*, p. 4.

[2] The Board also controlled the export trade in flour, and until April 8, 1920, the domestic price of flour as well. *Ibid.*, p. 4.

[3] See report on Australian Wheat Pools, by Trade Commissioner D. H. Ross in *Commercial Intelligence Journal* (Ottawa), Oct. 28, 1922.

[4] "The 'spreads' were never before so narrow in the history of the trade." *Report of Canadian Wheat Board*, p. 12.

At the outset many farmers were not favorably disposed toward the Board and its method of operation. It was regarded by some as being established in the interests of consumers rather than of producers. Many growers, observing the extent to which current cash prices on American markets exceeded the minimum guaranteed by the United States government,[1] would have preferred to sell on an open market, instead of receiving an initial payment of 11 cents less than the United States guaranteed price, and a participation certificate of deferred and speculative value. A considerable number of farmers, anxious for ready cash, and doubtful as to the redemption date and worth of certificates with whose use they were unfamiliar, traded them at wide speculative discounts.[2] With a view to deterring growers from disposing of their certificates below their prospective worth, the Board announced on May 5 that the redemption value of participation certificates would not be less than 40 cents, and it solicited the coöperation of the press and the grain trade in dissuading farmers from parting with their scrip. As a means of relieving their borrowing necessities, the Board began in July an interim payment aggregating $38,000,000. The final distribution, announced on October 20, represented a net pooled return of $2.63 (basis No. 1 Northern, Fort William). The full redemption value of certificates thus amounted to 48 cents. The total costs of administration and liquidation of participation certificates were equivalent to one half-cent per bushel of the wheat handled.[3]

Grain Growers' Opposition to Disestablishment of Board. — The substantial returns realized on participation certificates, the maintenance of fixed spreads, the elimination of future speculation, and the general efficiency of the Wheat Board's adminis-

[1] The average of high and low prices of No. 1 Dark Northern at Chicago on each Saturday of the 1919–20 crop year ranged from $2.40 in August and September to $3.28 in December, 1919, and $3.32 in May, 1920. The U. S. guaranteed price was $2.26. W. Eldred, "The Grain Corporation and the Guaranteed Wheat Price," *Quart. Journ. of Econ.*, August, 1920, p. 709.

[2] *Report of Canadian Wheat Board*, p. 11. Speech of Sir Geo. Foster, *Commons Debates*, June 24, 1920.

[3] *Report of Canadian Wheat Board*, pp. 11, 14.

tration, were effective in creating a sentiment among the majority of grain growers in favor of a continuation of its operation. On the other hand, the grain trade, the milling interests, and eastern consumers generally, were strongly opposed to any renewal of compulsory government marketing monopoly or price guarantee. It was argued in press and Parliament that no justification existed for extending control over the 1920 crop, in view of the relaxation of government purchasing and control in European countries,[1] and of the refusal of the United States Congress to renew the Wheat Guarantee Act or the powers of the Grain Corporation upon their expiration on June 1, 1920.

Although the government, through an enabling act passed in the closing days of the 1920 session, had obtained authority to continue or reconstitute the Canadian Wheat Board by proclamation, if it should subsequently be found expedient to do so in connection with the handling of the 1920 crop,[2] it was announced by the Minister of Trade and Commerce on July 16 — the day following the resumption of future trading on American grain exchanges — that since the factors which had influenced the government in creating the Wheat Board no longer existed, it had been decided to take no steps at present to proclaim the enabling act, "which means that the present Wheat Board will not function in so far as the crop of 1920 is concerned, and that the marketing of this crop will revert to the normal methods of pre-war times." [3] Control was terminated at the close of the Canadian crop year, and future trading was resumed on the Winnipeg Grain Exchange on August 18, after being suspended since May, 1917 (with the exception of one week in July, 1919).

[1] See speeches of H. H. Stevens, J. A. Robb, and others, *Commons Debates*, June 24, 27, 1920. The attitude of eastern consumers was thus expressed by the *Toronto Globe* (Sept. 22, 1920): "The conditions which made government price-fixing or guarantees in respect of wheat justifiable no longer exist. The market should be left to find its natural level. To raise the price of wheat artificially in these days of dear food would be class legislation and bad economics."

[2] Canadian Wheat Board Act, Stat. of Canada, 10–11 Geo. V, c. 40, 1920.

[3] Cited in *Canadian Annual Review*, 1920, p. 105.

III. The Movement for Wheat Board Reëstablishment

The Aftermath of Wheat Decontrol. — The drastic and continued decline in the price of wheat during the ensuing months [1] produced widespread and intense agitation among Western grain growers for a revival of the Wheat Board, whose operations were associated with the highest seasonal price returns in their experience. In the Saskatchewan legislature, Hon. George Langley, president of the Co-operative Elevator Company, carried through a resolution declaring that the Wheat Board had marketed the 1919 crop to the great satisfaction of farmers, claiming that the reopening of the grain exchanges at home and abroad was primarily responsible for the abrupt decline of 75 cents in the price of wheat, and urging the federal government to reappoint the Wheat Board under Messrs. Stewart and Riddell, to market the balance of the 1920 crop.[2] H. W. Wood, president of the Canadian Council of Agriculture and a member of the late Wheat Board, declared at a Saskatchewan Grain Growers' meeting that the price of wheat could undoubtedly have been kept up to at least $2.50 had the Board been continued.[3]

While the decline in wheat prices was fundamentally a reflection of such complex international factors as the release of supplies from Southern Hemisphere countries under open shipping conditions, the revival of European agricultural production, the discontinuance of credits by the governments of the United States and Canada, the relaxation of government purchasing in Europe, and the dislocation of the foreign exchanges, there is reason to believe that a continuation of Wheat Board marketing would have enabled Western wheat growers to realize a somewhat higher average return than that received under competitive, individual selling.[4] In any case, however, the results would

[1] The average monthly cash price for No. 1 Northern on the Winnipeg Exchange fell from $2.78½ in Sept., 1920, to $2.32 in Oct., $2.05 in Nov., $1.93½ in Dec., and $1.76½ in April, 1921. Dom. Bureau of Statistics.

[2] *Regina Leader*, Nov. 17, 1920.

[3] Speech at Wynyard, Sask., *Regina Leader*. Oct. 24, 1920.

[4] "It is perfectly obvious that under a system of control, where only one seller exists and buyers are numerous, the advantage is with the seller." Report of Messrs.

have been disappointing and distressing to producers. A guaranteed price was not a part of the Canadian Wheat Board system, and the initial payment which a revived Board could have made without compromising the Treasury, would necessarily have been very much lower than that paid in 1919–20, while the returns from participation certificates would have been disappointingly small as well as deferred. A government which was primarily concerned with the interests of Western grain producers might have undertaken to pool the crop with the least possible loss upon a falling world market. It was not at all strange, however, that a federal government which had to look mainly to the East for its support in an election that was being insistently called for, should be reluctant to assume the responsibility for perpetuating a compulsory marketing board which producers were likely to blame for not obtaining higher returns, which consumers were sure to criticize for keeping prices above the competitive market level, which grain-trading and business interests generally were openly opposed to as an unwarrantable measure of government interference, and which taxpayers as a whole viewed with distrust as a possible source of Treasury loss.

C. C. A. Voluntary Contract Pool Plan. — The Canadian Council of Agriculture, of which the two farmers' companies were organic units, and which had now assumed the organization of the National Progressive Party under the leadership of Mr. Crerar,[1] had passed a resolution at a meeting in Winnipeg on October 22, 1920, strongly urging the reappointment of the Canadian Wheat Board. It was recognized, however, that the Ottawa administration was not likely to take such action, and that compulsory marketing through a government board, even if restored, was justifiable only as a temporary emergency measure. Accordingly the Council appointed a Wheat Markets Com-

Stewart and Riddell to Premier Martin of Saskatchewan. *Co-operative News*, June, 1921. In reply to a question by the Agricultural Committee of the Commons as to whether a wheat board marketing the 1921 crop could have prevented the disastrous drop in prices, Mr. Stewart stated that the decline would undoubtedly have been less severe if the Board had been in operation. *Manitoba Free Press*, April 30, 1922.

[1] See L. A. Wood, *Farmers' Movements in Canada*, pp. 351, 352.

mittee to consider the feasibility of organizing a coöperative wheat pool on a voluntary contract basis.[1] A tentative form of wheat marketing agreement was drawn up by the committee and presented to a meeting of the Council in December, as a result of which the executives of the various provincial farmers' associations and of the two farmers' companies were asked to study the proposed basis, and to appoint representatives to an enlarged Wheat Pool Committee which should take steps to organize a workable pool. The Council's plan proposed the establishment of a United Farmers' Grain Corporation, to sell the pooled wheat of farmers in all three provinces on a five-year-contract basis. The farmers' elevator companies, it was contemplated, would handle wheat for the coöperative pool, on the same basis on which they had operated under the Canadian Wheat Board.[2]

Throughout 1921 — a year agitated by a prolonged federal election campaign and by the political activities of the Progressive Party — the new marketing project was carefully studied by the Wheat Pool Committee of the Council of Agriculture. It was considered that a voluntary pool which did not command at least 60 per cent of the Western wheat crop acreage would not be capable of exercising any effective influence over market movements or market prices. The chief difficulties anticipated were the securing of the necessary number of long-term growers' contracts, and the general unwillingness of elevator companies, other than those owned by farmers (which controlled but 20 per cent of the total number of licensed elevators) to handle pool wheat on satisfactory terms. At a meeting of the Wheat Pool Committee in November, 1921, it was decided that the scheme of a large-scale, voluntary contract pool was impracticable for the following reasons:

1. That under existing financial conditions it would not be possible to secure contracts from farmers assuring delivery to the pool for five years of all their wheat, covering 60 per cent of the crop area.

---

[1] The committee was composed of Messrs. H. W. Wood, president of the United Farmers of Alberta, F. W. Riddell, general manager of the Sask. Co-op., and J. R. Murray, assistant general manager of U. G. G. *G. G. Guide*, Oct. 30, 1920.

[2] "Wheat Marketing Agreement," *G. G. Guide*, Dec. 15, 1920.

2. That if a sufficient number of farmers could be induced to sign such contracts, many of them, owing to financial pressure would find it difficult, if not impossible, to fulfil their obligations, and that it would be impracticable, if not legally impossible, to enforce such contracts.
3. That without the subscription of a considerable amount of working capital and the assurance of a large percentage of contracts, no progress could be made in negotiating financial arrangements with the banks, or handling arrangements with private elevator companies.[1]

Renewed Demand for Government Wheat Board, 1922. — The fundamental difficulty implied here would seem to be the necessity of a prolonged and costly campaign of coöperative education and organization as the essential preliminary to establishing a voluntary pool on an effective commercial basis. Several members took the view that, while such an organization was the ultimate objective, the present plight of Western grain growers demanded the reëstablishment of a compulsory government marketing board as an emergency measure. This position was strongly held by the representatives of the Saskatchewan Grain Growers and the Saskatchewan Co-operative Elevator Company,[2] and as that province supplied approximately 60 per cent of the Western wheat crop, no inclusive coöperative pool could be realized without the unreserved participation of its representatives.[3] The grain growers' demand for a revived Wheat Board was intensified by the further disastrous decline in wheat prices following the harvesting of the 1921 crop,[4] aggravated as it was by the restriction of the American market under the 35 cent duty imposed by the Fordney Emergency Tariff in May, 1921.

[1] U. G. G., 1921, pp. 93, 94.

[2] At the annual meeting of the company, on Nov. 23, 1921, a resolution favoring "the reinstatement of the Canadian Wheat Board under the old management" had been carried with only two dissentients. *Co-operative News*, Dec. 1921.

[3] Wheat Board sentiment in Saskatchewan had been influenced considerably by the report submitted in May, 1921, at the request of Premier Martin of Saskatchewan, by Messrs. Stewart and Riddell, in which the former chiefs of the Canadian Wheat Board expressed the opinion that a voluntary wheat pool could not be so effective under existing conditions as a government agency with compulsory powers. Stewart-Riddell Report on Wheat Marketing, *Regina*, 1921.

[4] The average monthly price for No. 1 Northern at Winnipeg fell from \$1.80 for Aug. to \$1.48 for Sept., \$1.15½ for Oct. and \$1.11 for Nov., 1921. Dom. Bureau of Statistics.

In the course of the general election campaign of 1921, Premier Meighen, while expressing his opposition to any renewal of government marketing monopoly, had declared that he was prepared to establish a government board to market the farmers' wheat on a voluntary pooling basis.[1] The overwhelming defeat of the Conservative administration in an election in which 38 out of the 42 seats in the Prairie Provinces were carried by the Progressive Party, left the question of government wheat board policy to be decided by the new Liberal Ministry, whose exiguous majority did not permit it to be indifferent to the Progressive vote in the House.[2]

Wheat Board Legislation of 1922. — In the new Parliament the Wheat Board issue was considered by the House Committee on Agriculture. At its suggestion the constitutional aspects of the question were referred to the law officers of the Crown. In the report submitted by the Deputy Minister of Justice the opinion was rendered that as the federal government no longer possessed the extraordinary powers conferred upon it under the War Measures Act, the reëstablishment of the Canadian Wheat Board on the compulsory basis of 1919–20, would involve a constitutional encroachment upon the freedom of contract, capacity to buy and sell, and the exercise of proprietary rights which exist under the provincial laws.[3] In view of this finding, the Agricultural Committee unanimously recommended the immediate legislative creation of a national wheat-marketing agency to handle the 1922 wheat crop with all the powers enjoyed by the Wheat Board of 1919–20 (except as to flour and mill products), "such act to become effective by proclamation as soon as two or more of the provinces have conferred upon this agency such powers possessed by the Board of 1919 as come within provincial jurisdiction." [4] A bill based upon the committee's report was

[1] *Can. Annual Review*, 1921, p. 450. Mr. Meighen's plan was similar to that adopted by the State of West Australia, after the discontinuance in 1921 of the compulsory Australian Wheat Boards. See *Commercial Intelligence Journal* (Dept. of Trade and Commerce, Ottawa), Oct. 28, 1922.

[2] The election resulted in the return of 117 Liberals, 65 Progressives, and 50 Conservatives.

[3] Cited in *Can. Annual Review*, 1922, p. 241. [4] *Ibid.*

introduced by the government in June and July, and duly passed by the House, despite Mr. Meighen's counter proposal of a voluntary federal government pool which might exercise compulsory powers in any province passing the appropriate legislation. As the act was passed primarily in the interests of the Prairie Provinces, and as their concurrent legislation was necessary to make it effective, it was stipulated that the federal government should assume no responsibility for any deficits that might arise in the Board's operations, while any surplus should be divided among the concurring provinces on a pro rata basis.[1] The powers conferred upon the Board were limited to August 15, 1923, unless the operation of the act should be extended for an additional year by order-in-council prior to July 1, 1923.[2]

Special sessions of the Saskatchewan and Alberta legislatures were called in July, and legislation giving the Board compulsory control over all wheat offered for sale in those provinces passed with a minimum of dissent. In accordance with the request of the federal government to nominate men suitable for appointment as chairman and vice-chairman of the Board, the premiers of the concurring provinces invited Messrs. Stewart and Riddell to act. The former chiefs of the Canadian Wheat Board were not willing, however, to assume the responsibility of administering a board under the restricted powers conferred by the act, and under the changed conditions of the grain trade.[3] Upon the refusal of other persons approached to accept the post,[4] Premiers Dunning and Greenfield issued the following statement:

> We have canvassed the field fully for suitable men and have to state that men having the necessary ability and experience are unwilling to assume the great responsibility involved. One of our greatest difficulties lay in the fact that most of the men best qualified for these positions belong to the

---

[1] Stat. of Canada, 12–13 Geo. V, c. 14, 1922, sec. 16.

[2] Ibid., sec. 17.

[3] In a statement to the shareholders of the Sask. Co-op. on Nov. 22, 1922, Mr. Riddell claimed that satisfactory results could not be obtained under legislation which excluded the sale and export of flour, and the control of the transportation of wheat, from the powers of the Board, and which did not include all the Western provinces under its jurisdiction. *Co-operative News*, Dec., 1922.

[4] Including J. R. Murray, asst. general manager of the U. G. G. Letter of refusal published in *The U. F. A.* (Calgary), Aug. 18, 1922.

ordinary grain trade, and there is no doubt that the great majority of the men in the grain trade are opposed to the Wheat Board idea. Those who believe the Board to be a necessity this year declined to take the positions because of the opposition in the grain trade in general. In this connection they repeatedly pointed out to us that the use of facilities controlled by the various branches of the trade was absolutely necessary.[1]

It had thus been found easier to overcome the constitutional difficulties and obtain the enabling legislation, than to secure the services of those whose managerial ability could command confidence, and the coöperation of those who controlled the necessary handling facilities.

The Dunning Plan. — Toward the close of 1922 Premier Dunning of Saskatchewan, in a speech at Saskatoon, proposed an alternative solution through the formation of a Canadian Farmers' Export Company by amalgamating the export subsidiaries of the Saskatchewan Co-operative Elevator Company and the United Grain Growers. Under this plan the joint farmer-owned export company would make initial payments and issue participation certificates, on a pooling basis, for wheat delivered to its account through the elevators of the two parent companies, or other companies that might agree to coöperate. Surplus receipts remaining after the payment of a 10 per cent dividend on the paid-up capital invested in the export corporation by the farmers' companies, and the setting aside of 20 per cent of the remander for reserve, would be distributed to participation receipt holders after the manner of the Canadian Wheat Board.[2] The Dunning plan thus involved the substitution of a voluntary coöperative pool for the compulsory government board sought by the grain growers. It differed, however, from the plan considered by the Wheat Pool Committee of the Canadian Council of Agriculture in 1920–21, in being on an optional instead of a contract basis. The proposal possessed several commendable features. It offered a permanent instead of a merely emergency solution. It involved the coördinated utilization of the country, Grain Exchange, terminal and export facilities and connections already owned and developed by the farmers' companies. It

[1] Cited in *Can. Annual Review*, 1922, p. 243.

[2] *Manitoba Free Press*, Dec. 16, 1922; *Can. Annual Review*, 1922, pp. 793, 794.

represented a combination of the plan of federation considered by the farmers' companies in 1916,[1] with a system of coöperative pooling on an interprovincial scale. It involved the minimum of financial difficulty, resting as it did upon the combined resources of the two great farmers' companies. It was neither dependent on government support, nor subject to government interference. It was likely to meet the minimum of antagonism from the regular grain trade, and it offered a basis for estimating the relative merits of pool marketing and individual, competitive selling.

Although emanating from the Premier of Saskatchewan and the former manager of the Saskatchewan Coöperative, the Dunning plan was received more favorably by Mr. Crerar and Mr. Rice-Jones of the United Grain Growers [2] than by the directors of the Saskatchewan Company. Mr. Langley, president of the latter, criticized the Premier's proposal as a substitute for the Wheat Board, on the ground of the uncertainty of deliveries under a voluntary pool, and of the limited market influence to be expected from the operations of a farmers' export company which could not hope to handle even 25 per cent of the marketable crop, and which would be subject to the concentrated competition of the regular grain trade.[3]

The shareholders and directors of the Saskatchewan Company were unwilling indeed to consider any less inclusive plan so long as there remained any prospect of reëstablishing the Wheat Board. Winnipeg wheat prices had fallen below the dollar mark with the initial marketing of the 1922 crop, and an emergency solution was still sought. At the company's annual meeting in November, unanimous support had been given to a resolution calling on the Council of Agriculture "to solicit the support of the three prairie provincial government in an endeavor to secure from the federal government such amendments to the Wheat Board Act of 1922 as in its opinion will make full success of the Board possible." [4] For a second time, federation between the two companies had been mooted without result. And for a second time, the plan of a voluntary coöperative wheat pool had

[1] See *supra*, p. 168.

[2] *Manitoba Free Press*, Dec. 18, 1922.

[3] *Ibid.*

[4] *Co-operative News*, Dec., 1922.

been discarded by the Council of Agriculture, mainly under Saskatchewan influence, in favor of a reconstituted Wheat Board.

Attitude of Manitoba. — It was hoped by those who looked to a compulsory Wheat Board as the most effective form of market relief for grain growers, that by obtaining wider federal powers for the Board, and by securing the legislative concurrence of Manitoba as well as of Saskatchewan and Alberta, suitable administrators could be found to undertake Wheat Board marketing of the 1923 crop. While the federal government was not willing to extend the powers of the Board to include flour or shipping control, or to make it a non-corporate body exempt from legal suit,[1] it announced its willingness to extend by order-in-council the operation of the Wheat Board legislation passed in the previous session. The sentiment in favor of the Wheat Board revival had been less pronounced in Manitoba than in Saskatchewan and Alberta. Its wheat acreage represented only 15 per cent of that of the Prairie Provinces. The greater proportionate urban population of Manitoba, and the concentrated influence of the grain-trading and milling interests at Winnipeg, further served to neutralize Wheat Board sentiment in that province. The United Farmers of Manitoba had triumphed, however, in the provincial elections in the preceding summer, and it was anticipated that a sympathetic attitude would be shown by the new farmers' government. In addressing the convention of the U. F. M. at Brandon in January, 1923, Premier-elect Bracken announced that he would recommend to his party in the legislature that supplementary legislation similar to that enacted in Saskatchewan and Alberta should be passed at Winnipeg. He made it clear, however, that he spoke only as an individual, and that he would recommend Wheat Board legislation for one year only, and on the distinct condition that the farmers' organizations and the governments of the Prairie Provinces should first

[1] Section 4 of the Wheat Board Act of 1922 had declared that the members of the Board should be a corporation. It had been pointed out at the annual meeting of the Sask. Co-op. that this made the Board liable to have suit entered against it by grain interests opposed to its functioning. See Speech of Premier Dunning, *Saskatoon Star*, Dec. 22, 1922.

express their intention of developing a purely coöperative, non-profit, non-compulsory marketing organization to handle subsequent crops.[1] Premier Greenfield, addressing the convention of the United Farmers of Alberta, and Premier Dunning, on appearing before the Saskatchewan Grain Growers' convention in the same month, both declared that they were prepared to support a Wheat Board only as a temporary emergency expedient, and that the permanent solution must be found in some voluntary co-operative plan.[2] In the Manitoba legislature in April, the Wheat Board bill was introduced by Premier Bracken as a non-party measure, and was finally rejected by a narrow majority, three ministers voting against it.

Abandonment of Efforts for Wheat Board Reëstablishment.— The refusal of the Manitoba legislature to coöperate with the other Prairie Provinces meant the continuation of open trading on the Winnipeg Grain Exchange, and the persistence of the same conditions which had made it impossible in the preceding year to secure the expert services necessary for the functioning of a compulsory Wheat Board. Failing in their negotiations with private individuals, Premiers Dunning and Greenfield turned to the farmers' grain companies, and requested them to appoint representatives to assist the premiers in securing the necessary expert personnel and to act as members of a Wheat Board when formed. Both companies appointed advisory members, and gave assurance of their willingness to release any experts on their respective staffs, while stipulating that such persons would have to be approached as individuals by those acting for the Wheat Board.[3] The action of the directorates of the farmers' companies was thus largely passive. None of the staff of the latter approached on behalf of the Board being found willing to assume the posts of chief responsibility, the premiers made a public announcement on June 22, stating that they had "found it impossible to secure a Board combining all necessary elements

[1] *Manitoba Free Press*, Jan. 13, 1923.

[2] *Can. Annual Review*, 1923, pp. 678, 679.

[3] Statement of Messrs. Greenfield and Dunning, *Manitoba Free Press*, June 23, 1923.

of experience, ability and public confidence." For the fourth successive crop year the efforts to secure the reëstablishment of a compulsory Wheat Board had failed. The *Grain Growers' Guide* which had supported the movement, although not with the same intensity as it had formerly championed the cause of public ownership of elevators, observed editorially: [1]

> In view of the efforts of the past two years to secure a Wheat Board, and the complete failure that has been the result of these efforts, it may reasonably be assumed now that the Wheat Board idea is dead. There seems no likelihood of any conditions arising more favorable to the establishment of a Wheat Board than have prevailed during the past two years.

---

[1] *G. G. Guide*, June 27, 1923.

CHAPTER XIV

INCEPTION OF THE WESTERN WHEAT POOLS, 1923–24

I. The First Wheat Pool Campaign, 1923

As the failure of the interprovincial campaign for public ownership of elevators at an earlier period had led the organized Grain Growers to undertake the coöperative ownership and operation of elevators, so in 1923, when the futility of the campaign for a reëstablishment of government marketing became conclusive, the Western farmers' organizations turned their efforts from the direction of government compulsion and monopoly to voluntary and coöperative action. In the years preceding the war, their aim had been to participate competitively, through their own warehousing and marketing institutions, in the organized grain trade, under a system of government regulation whose form they had been largely influential in determining. In the post-war years, their object has been to create a new method of producer-controlled collective marketing, designed to supplant the competitive speculative system.

Revival of Coöperative Wheat Pool Plan. — The earlier proposal for a voluntary wheat pool considered by the Council of Agriculture in 1920–21 had been abandoned because the overwhelming sentiment of grain growers was in favor of emergency relief through a revived government Wheat Board, and because of the formidable organizational and financial difficulties and the extended educational preparation involved in developing a coöperative pool on an interprovincial basis. The coöperative policy had at that time been strongly supported by the directorate of the United Grain Growers and by the *Grain Growers' Guide.* The former had conveyed to the Council of Agriculture its readiness to advance $50,000 toward the initial expenses of organization.[1] The *Guide* sent a staff representative to investigate farmers' co-

[1] Memorandum of U. G. G. to C. C. A., in *G. G. Guide*, Aug. 1, 1923.

operative marketing organizations in California and elsewhere, and during 1920 and 1921 published an extended series of articles designed to inform its readers regarding the methods and achievements of non-profit commodity pool organizations — a form of coöperation with which Western grain growers were as a whole unfamiliar.[1] Owing, however, to the insistent demand of the great majority of farmers for immediate concentration upon the restoration of the Wheat Board, the coöperative plan remained in abeyance until the latter part of 1923. While the shareholders of the United Grain Growers were scarcely less strongly in favor of the Wheat Board than those of the Saskatchewan Coöperative, the directors of the former had shown much less faith in the efficacy of that expedient [2] than had the directorate of the Saskatchewan Company. Little could be done, however, by those who favored coöperative effort, so long as the grain growers as a whole rested their hopes on the application of governmental compulsion.

With the definite abandonment of the Wheat Board movement implied in the Greenfield-Dunning statement of June 22, 1923, the U. G. G. directorate took the initiative in the direction of coöperative action by asking for a meeting of the Western Section of the Council of Agriculture to consider what steps should be taken in view of the premiers' announcement. At the same time the *Guide* expressed the editorial opinion that "farmers in the Prairie Provinces will be wise now to turn their efforts toward the establishment of a voluntary pooling system under their own control." [3] At the meeting of the Council of Agriculture in Winnipeg on July 4, the United Grain Growers' representatives submitted a memorandum offering an alternative to the abandoned Wheat Board plan. This proposed that the Western Section of the Council of Agriculture should take the initiative in organizing a voluntary interprovincial wheat pool, operating on perpetual con-

[1] See articles by R. D. Colquette, in *G. G. Guide*, April, 1920, to Feb., 1921.

[2] See report of U. G. G., 1922 meeting, in *G. G. Guide*, Nov. 29, 1922. In addressing the U. F. M. convention at Brandon on Jan. 10, 1923, President Crerar had declared that he had no faith in government boards for the marketing of wheat, and that nothing could be done by government boards which could not be achieved by coöperation. *G. G. Guide*, Jan. 17, 1923.

[3] *G. G. Guide*, June 27, 1923.

tracts with growers, terminable upon fair notice, and making initial advances and participation distribution as in the case of the Canadian Wheat Board. The two farmers' companies, it was further suggested, might advance the funds for the first year's operations, and should place their elevator facilities and handling organization at the disposal of the pool, on a basis similar to the arrangements with the Wheat Board in 1919–20.[1] These proposals, it will be observed, differed from those made in the previous year by Premier Dunning, in suggesting that the farmers' companies should assist a pool organized by the provincial associations, instead of assuming the responsibility of jointly initiating and operating one of their own. The reasons for proposing that the pool organization should be kept distinct from the farmers' companies appeared to be threefold. In the first place, it was felt that, owing to the experimental character of a voluntary wheat pool, the commercial stability of the farmers' companies might be compromised if they assumed direct responsibility for its operation.[2] Secondly, it was recognized that grain growers would be more disposed to support a pool in which they exercised direct and complete control, rather than one organized for them, albeit by farmer-owned companies. Thirdly, the Saskatchewan Co-operative had already expressed its opposition to the Dunning plan, and had not evidenced in the past any disposition to operate jointly with the United Grain Growers. Under these circumstances, Mr. Crerar offered the fullest assistance and coöperation of the United Grain Growers, and bespoke the same from the sister company, in the formation of a common pool by the provincial associations. He intimated further that, if the pool became successfully established, it might subsequently take over the grain-handling facilities of the two companies on a basis equitable to the shareholders. In this way there might be developed a single "coöperative, non-profit-making organization controlled by the farmers interested in it." [3]

[1] Text of memorandum, in *G. G. Guide*, Aug. 1, 1923.

[2] "If the two companies became responsible for the pool's administration, and it failed to give satisfaction, this would be bound to have a prejudicial effect upon their future business." *Ibid.*

[3] *Ibid.*

Movement for Organization of Provincial Pools. — No action was taken at this meeting on the U. G. G. proposal for a single interprovincial pool, the decision being to leave the matter of wheat pool organization to the separate provincial associations, whose representatives should meet again on July 23. The sentiment in favor of provincial initiative was most pronounced in Alberta, where, on the day preceding the Council meeting (July 3), the directorate of the U. F. A. had appointed a Wheat Pool Committee to take immediate steps, in consultation with the marketing committee of the provincial cabinet,[1] toward the organization of an Alberta wheat pool on a five-year contract basis. Although the proximity of harvest made it doubtful if organization could be completed in time to handle the crop as a whole, it was felt that the sentiment of Alberta farmers warranted the inauguration of an immediate campaign to secure the signature of contracts.[2] In this effort the highly developed organization of U. F. A. locals throughout the province afforded an admirable medium of contact between the Wheat Pool Committee and the individual growers.

In Saskatchewan action was less united and clear-cut than in the Foothill Province. The situation in the former was distinctly complicated by the existence and activities of the newly established Farmers' Union of Canada, which had been initially organized at Saskatoon at the end of 1921 by some of the more radically minded farmers of the province. The new movement had its roots in the post-war agricultural depression and in a growing reaction against the alleged domination of the conventions and policies of the Saskatchewan Grain Growers' Association by a group who also variously shared offices in the Saskatchewan Co-operative Elevator Company and the Saskatchewan government.[3] While drawing its membership mainly from Saskatch-

[1] Since 1921 the provincial administration had been in the hands of the United Farmers of Alberta. Following the abandonment of the Wheat Board negotiations, a marketing committee of three cabinet ministers had been appointed to confer with the U. F. A. directorate on alternative policies. Two of the ministers visited coöperative organizations in the Pacific states during the summer.

[2] *The U. F. A.*, July 16, 1923.

[3] There had always been considerable interlocking between the directorates of the two Saskatchewan farmers' organizations (see *supra*, p. 106). For several

ewan, the Farmers' Union was organized upon a national basis, with local lodges, instructed voting, and closed-door conventions.[1] It brought pressure to bear upon the Saskatchewan government to declare a moratorium in favor of farmer debtors, and in common with the Farmers' Union in the United States, upon which it was modeled,[2] its declared aim was "to organize farmers so that they may be enabled to fix their own price above cost of production."[3] To this end, it was primarily interested in promoting commodity pool marketing. At its second annual convention at Saskatoon (July 2–4, 1923), the Farmers' Union passed resolutions in favor of the immediate inauguration of a provincial wheat pool, and invited the coöperation of the Saskatoon Board of Trade, the provincial government, the Saskatchewan Grain Growers' Association and the Canadian Council of Agriculture.[4] It was also decided to extend an invitation to Aaron Sapiro, the California coöperative marketing expert, to visit Saskatchewan in the interests of wheat pool organization.

Meanwhile the directors of the Saskatchewan Grain Growers' Association, meeting on July 17–18, had decided to proceed at once with the organization of "a provincial wheat pool for the marketing of this year's crop, looking towards the fullest measure of interprovincial corporation." Thus in Saskatchewan the two rival farmers' associations were taking the initiative independently in the organization of wheat pools. In Manitoba, the U. F. M. executive, while expressing itself in favor of moving toward a coöperative wheat-marketing organization along with

years J. A. Maharg was president of both bodies, besides being variously a member of the federal Parliament and of the Saskatchewan legislature. G. A. Langley had enjoyed a similar distribution of presidential and vice-presidential offices and provincial cabinet preferment. J. B. Musselman, secretary of the S. G. G. A. continuously from 1915 to 1922, had been throughout a director of the Elevator Company, becoming managing director upon relinquishing the secretarial post in the association.

[1] Farmers' Union of Canada, Constitution and By-Laws. In July, 1923, the Union claimed over 50 lodges, some of which were located in Alberta and Manitoba. See *G. G. Guide*, July 18, 1923, p. 4.

[2] The organization and aims of the Farmers' Union in the United States are discussed in Hibbard, *Marketing Agricultural Products*, chap. 21.

[3] Farmers' Union of Canada, Preamble to Constitution.

[4] *G. G. Guide*, July 18, 1923.

the other provinces, decided to defer definite action pending the interprovincial meeting arranged for July 23 at Regina. At this conference (which was attended unofficially by representatives of the Farmers' Union) it was decided that each association should be responsible for the organization of a wheat pool within its province, but that there should be one interprovincial selling agency. A committee of three representing each organization was appointed to draft a uniform contract and formulate plans for a central sales agency.[1] Henceforth the Council of Agriculture as such ceased to be either the promoting or the coördinating medium in relation to wheat-pool organization.

Sectionalism Averted. — Despite the appointment of the coördinating committee and the reciprocal expressions in favor of "the fullest possible interprovincial coöperation," development during 1923 took place along distinctly provincial lines. The driving force lay in the provincial associations, with their cellular locals, and conditions differed considerably in the three provinces. Alberta enjoyed the advantages of general unanimity, of close working relations between the farmers' association and the farmers' government, and of an earlier start in the work of organization. In Saskatchewan the initiative had been taken by a minority organization, which had arranged to bring in Mr. Sapiro. The S. G. G. A. Wheat Pool Committee announced on August 1 that, in view of the short time available for organization before harvest, it would operate a voluntary, non-contract pool for handling the 1923 crop. For the organization of such pool the directors of the Co-operative Elevator Company voted a grant of $14,000. In Manitoba, where wheat pool sentiment was less pronounced, the executive of the U. F. M. was disposed to await developments in Alberta and Saskatchewan. In all three provinces doubts were expressed as to the possibility of completing organization in time for the pooling of the current crop.

Amid this atmosphere of hesitancy and threatened sectionalism,[2] Mr. Sapiro's visit early in August proved both timely and

[1] *Canadian Wheat Pool Year Book*, 1925, p. 16.

[2] The *Guide* had at this time (Aug. 8) sounded a note of warning that "unless there is the closest coöperation between the various committees in charge of these pools, it may become a case of too many pools and too little pooling."

salutary. Of perhaps even greater assistance for the pool movement than the stimulating effect of his mass meetings in Calgary, Edmonton, Saskatoon, and Regina,[1] was the unifying influence which, as an outsider of established prestige, he was able to bring to bear in conference, not only upon the different farmers' organizations, but also upon different classes of the community. In Alberta his meetings were followed by the immediate organization of an enlarged Wheat Pool Committee of seventeen, comprising, in addition to ten farmer members, representatives of the provincial government, the grain trade, and of banking, commercial and journalistic interests.[2] In Saskatchewan Mr. Sapiro emphasized the necessity of a single contract pool for the province. As a direct result of his visit, the Saskatchewan Grain Growers and the Farmers' Union came together. The former agreed to drop their non-contract pool, and a representative provincial committee similar to that created in Alberta, was formed to organize a contract pool that should be neither a Grain Growers' Association nor a Farmers' Union pool, but simply a Saskatchewan farmers' pool.[3] Even as the organized farmers of Saskatchewan and Alberta had previously been united in their demands for Wheat Board action by the federal government, they were now united in working out their own coöperative solution. In the latter movement, moreover, they enjoyed the general support of the press and business interests, which for the most part had not been favorable to the Wheat Board agitation.

Limitation of 1923 Pool to Alberta. — In both provinces an objective was set of securing growers' contracts covering at least 50 per cent of the wheat crop acreage. In Saskatchewan the contracts stipulated that, unless the desired quota were obtained by September 12, the contracts would be null and void. An enthusiastic and intensive campaign was carried on in the midst of the harvest season. The time was too short, however, and the area to

[1] Through the instrumentality of the *Calgary Herald* and the *Edmonton Journal*, Mr. Sapiro had been invited to address meetings in Alberta prior to his appearance in Saskatchewan under Farmer's Union auspices.

[2] *G. G. Guide*, Aug. 8, 1923. E. S. McRory, manager of Western Division of U. G. G., served as a member of this committee.

[3] *G. G. Guide*, Aug. 15, 1923.

be canvassed too great, to realize much more than two thirds of the objective of 6,000,000 acres under contract before the stipulated date. While this precluded pool handling of the 1923 crop, the trustees decided, in view of the interest manifested, to continue the campaign, contract signers being asked to subscribe to a waiver extending the time limit to a "date to be fixed by resolution of the directors."[1] In Manitoba, where the harvest was earlier and the wheat crop much below the average, the Wheat Pool Committee of the U. F. M. had already decided to abandon the project of a pool for the current crop, while proceeding with the thorough organization of one for the following season.

In Alberta contracts had been offered on a somewhat more elastic basis than in Saskatchewan. Instead of making contracts void if the objective were not realized by the stipulated date, contract signers were given the option of withdrawing from the pool, if 50 per cent of wheat crop acreage were not signed up by September 5. At the end of the fortnight's campaign, over 25,000 contracts had been signed, covering 45 per cent of the previous year's acreage. In view of this strong response and of the unprecedented volume of the season's crop,[2] it was decided by the pool trustees to proceed with the work of organization and operation, while permitting contract holders to exercise their option of withdrawal up to September 22. When that date arrived, it was announced that the withdrawals amounted to less than the additional acreage signed up. Before the pool could proceed to take delivery of the farmers' wheat, however, three things were necessary: financial arrangements with the banks, handling arrangements with the elevator companies, and the establishment of a sales organization. The patronage assured by the contracts which continued to be received, the assistance of the United Grain Growers, and the support of the provincial government, did much to reduce the difficulties in these negotiations. The Canadian Bankers' Association agreed to provide $15,000,000 at 6½ per

[1] Address by A. J. McPhail on "History and Accomplishments of the Canadian Wheat Pool." *Proceedings of Third National Coöperative Marketing Conference* (Washington, 1925), pp. 29–31.

[2] The Alberta wheat crop of 1923 exceeded 166,000,000 bushels, being twice the volume of the largest crop in any preceding year.

cent, to permit an initial payment of 75 cents per bushel (basis No. 1 Northern, Fort William) on condition of a guarantee by the Alberta government for the maintenance of a 15 per cent margin between such advance and the market price.[1] The United Grain Growers and, shortly afterwards, the Alberta Pacific Elevator Company, controlling together 40 per cent of the elevators in the province, offered the use of their elevators to the pool on terms similar to those made with the Canadian Wheat Board in 1919–20, and the example of these companies was subsequently followed by most of the other elevator firms operating in Alberta.[2] In the important business of selling the pooled crop on the central market, the United Grain Growers assisted the Alberta Pool — as the old Grain Growers' Grain Company had done ten years previously when the Alberta Co-operative Company had been launched. In addition to making a loan of $10,000 to the pool for the acquisition of a seat on the Winnipeg Grain Exchange, and other expenses, and assisting it in the organization of its accounting system, the United Grain Growers released two of their experienced officials, C. M. Elliott (of their Calgary office) and D. L. Smith (manager of the Grain Growers' Export Co.) to act as Alberta Pool manager and Winnipeg sales manager respectively.[3]

Although it was not until October 29 — when a considerable portion of the record 1923 crop had been already marketed — that the Alberta Co-operative Wheat Producers Limited[4] was in a position to take delivery of its members' wheat, more than 34,000,000 bushels were handled by this pioneer wheat pool in Canada in its initial season. This was equivalent to 26 per cent of the 1923 wheat crop marketed in Alberta, or 40 per cent of the amount shipped during the 8½ months of pool operations. At the close of the pool year (July 15, 1924) it was announced by the trustees that the average price realized on its handlings amounted to slightly over $1.02 per bushel (basis No. 1, Northern, Fort

[1] *The U. F. A.*, Nov. 1, 1923. [2] *Ibid.*, Oct. 1, Nov. 15, 1925.

[3] *Record of U. G. G.. re Pool Marketing*, pp. 7, 8. The company had also offered to guarantee the credit of the Alberta Pool with the banks, to the extent of $250,000, before it was known that the government's guarantee would be available.

[4] The pool had been registered under this name in August, 1923, with provi-

William). The total costs of administration averaged 0.4 cents per bushel, leaving $1.016 to the credit of pool members, of which $1.01 was actually distributed, the remainder being retained as a commercial reserve.[1] Although the Alberta Pool began operations in the year in which wheat prices reached their lowest annual average since 1914, the results to pool members were generally regarded as satisfactory.[2]

II. The Canadian Co-operative Wheat Producers Limited, 1924

Organization of Saskatchewan and Manitoba Pools. — Although the precise financial benefit accruing to Alberta Pool members as a whole was debatable, the results shown by a single hastily organized provincial pool, unable to receive deliveries until nearly two months after harvest, and handling but a quarter of the province's crop, were sufficiently reassuring to attract a large accession of Alberta contracts, and to stimulate wheat pool organization in the other Prairie Provinces. In Saskatchewan the pool campaign had been carried on throughout the winter. The much larger acreage to be secured, the necessity of having to obtain time waivers to original contracts as well as new signatures, and the lack of harmony between the Farmers' Union and the Saskatchewan Grain Growers, made the task a more formidable one than in Alberta.

sional trustees in accordance with the Alberta Coöperative Associations Act. During the 1924 season a special act was passed by the Alberta legislature (chap. 7) retroactively validating the incorporation of the Alberta Co-operative Wheat Producers Limited, and setting forth in particularity its powers and the commitments of the provincial government in respect to it.

[1] Report of Alberta Co-operative Wheat Producers. *The U. F. A.*, Aug. 15, 1924.

[2] The average spot price of No. 1 Northern from Sept. 1, 1923, to July 31, 1924, was 103.7 cents, and for the eight full months in which the Alberta Pool was in operation (Nov. 1 to June 30) it was equivalent to 100.2 cents. *Report on Grain Trade of Canada*, 1924, p. 141. Analysis of 1923–24 wheat prices and deliveries by a Winnipeg grain expert showed that of the 90,500,000 bushels marketed in Alberta during the period of pool operations, approximately 79 per cent was delivered when the cash price was 98 cents or less. *The U. F. A.*, Aug. 15, 1924. While deliveries are not identical with sales, they afford a fair index of the periodic volume of sales.

The work of organization was substantially assisted, however, by grants of $15,000 from the Saskatchewan Co-operative Elevator Company and of $5,000 from the United Grain Growers,[1] and by advances aggregating $45,000 from the Saskatchewan government.[2] By June 26, 1924, the 50 per cent objective had been exceeded, with 46,509 contracts covering 6,433,788 acres.[3] Arrangements were made with the Saskatchewan Co-operative and other elevator companies for handling pool wheat. At a meeting on July 25 of the new pool directors, representing each of the sixteen pool districts into which the province had been divided, A. J. McPhail, secretary of the Grain Growers' Association, and L. C. Brouillette of the Farmers' Union executive, were elected president and vice-president respectively of the Saskatchewan Co-operative Wheat Producers Limited. In accordance with the new attitude in Saskatchewan toward multiple office-holding, both officers resigned their positions on the executives of their respective associations.

In Manitoba, which had not attempted to organize a pool for the 1923 crop, the annual convention of the U. F. M., meeting at the beginning of 1924, formally endorsed the formation of a provincial wheat pool, in accordance with the plans presented by the executive's Wheat Pool Committee, which had previously submitted a draft contract for study by the farmers of the province. In the same month the Manitoba Co-operative Wheat Producers Limited was incorporated, and C. H. Burnell, president of the U. F. M. was chosen as provisional president of the pool.[4] With the aid of an organization loan of $10,000 from the United Grain Growers, a "sign-up" campaign was conducted during March, with an objective of 40 per cent of the 1922 wheat acreage. Although only three fifths of the 1,000,000 acres aimed at had been signed up by April 1, withdrawals were negligible, and the campaign was renewed, with the result that the Manitoba Pool began

[1] These grants were regarded as loans by the Saskatchewan Pool, and subsequently repaid to the companies.

[2] *Wheat Pool Year Book*, 1925, pp. 29–31; *Record of U. G. G.*, etc., p. 9.

[3] Sask. Co-op. Wheat Producers Handbook No. 2, p. 3.

[4] On his formal election to the pool chairmanship following the delegate meeting in July, Mr. Burnell resigned the presidency of the U. F. M.

operations with a little over one third of the wheat acreage of the province under contract.[1]

Establishment of Central Sales Agency. — With the three provincial pools thus organized to handle the 1924 wheat crop, the policy of establishing a central sales agency, which had been anticipated by the appointment of the coördinating committee at the interprovincial meeting in Regina in July 1923,[2] was now given practical effort. Federal incorporation was obtained for the Canadian Co-operative Wheat Producers Limited, with a capitalization of $150,000, equally distributed among the three provincial pools.[3] Although the pool acreage in Saskatchewan was more than double that of Alberta, and over seven times as great as that of Manitoba, the coöperative principle of equal representation and voting power was recognized in the allotment of three representatives to each province in the composition of the directorate of the interprovincial agency. Following a meeting of this board in August at which organization was completed,[4] it was announced that the eight principal chartered banks operating in the West had collectively authorized a credit of $25,000,000 to the Central Sales Agency, without requiring any government guarantee as to margin maintenance.[5] It was also announced that the initial payment on 1924 crop deliveries in all provinces would be on the basis of $1 No. 1 Northern, Fort William, this being 25 cents higher than that made by the Alberta Pool in the preceding year.[6]

[1] *Wheat Pool Year Book*, 1925, pp. 37, 38. [2] See *supra*, p. 215.

[3] Under the articles of agreement, each provincial pool subscribed to 497 shares (per value $10) with one additional share held by each of its three representatives. See Appendix F.

[4] The following officers were elected: President, A. J. McPhail; Vice-president, H. W. Wood; Secretary, C. H. Burnell, these being the chairmen of the wheat pool boards of Saskatchewan, Alberta, and Manitoba respectively. Hon. J. G. Brownlee, Attorney-General of Alberta, was named general counsel. Messrs. D. L. Smith and C. N. Elliott, the two U. G. G. officials released to the Alberta pool in 1923, were appointed Eastern and Western sales managers respectively. *The U. F. A.*, Sept. 2, 1924.

[5] The credit of the C. S. A. with the banks is jointly guaranteed by the provincial pools in proportion to the number of bushels delivered to it by each. Sask. Co-op. Wheat Producers Handbook No. 2, p. 14.

[6] Winnipeg cash wheat prices, which had remained below $1.00 until May, 1924,

Handling Arrangements with Elevator Companies. — The real asset of the pools lay in their contracts as evidence of the goodwill and long-term patronage of over 91,000 growers,[1] representing fully half the wheat acreage of the Prairie Provinces.[2] Although possessing no facilities of their own for handling and storing the wheat so controlled, the magnitude of their contractual patronage and the ready coöperation of the two great farmers' companies, controlling as they did elevators at one half of the grain-shipping points in the West, made it possible for the pools to secure satisfactory handling contracts upon a uniform basis from practically all the Western elevator companies. Under these arrangements the companies undertook, as under the Canadian Wheat Board, to perform all services in connection with the handling of pool wheat except the actual selling of it.

They agreed to handle pool members' wheat in any of the four methods recognized by the Canada Grain Act, namely: as street wheat, special binned, stored to grade, or stored subject to inspector's grade.[3] They made initial payments out of their own funds on street deliveries, upon the basis of pool price-lists, and advances on stored grain as required by the owner. They issued grower's participation certificates to pool patrons, sending copies to the central pool offices. They forwarded daily returns showing wheat held to pool account, and guaranteed grades as well as weights in the case of street wheat or wheat stored to grade. They shipped wheat to terminals or Western mills on behalf of the pool, and attended to all checking and documentation. Upon the delivery of terminal warehouse receipts or bills of lading to the pools, they received payment for carrying charges on street wheat, and repayment of all cash advances made to pool members.[4]

averaged $1.43½ in August. The short crop in Western Canada was an important factor in this advance.

[1] Contracts in all three provinces ran to the end of the 1927 crop year.

[2] The total wheat acreage in the three provinces in 1924 was officially reported as 21,067,221 acres. Wheat pool contracts covered 10,744,346 acres.

[3] See *Wheat Pool Lectures*, No. 6, issued by Alberta Co-op. Wheat Producers, 1927.

[4] In the case of wheat other than street, the elevator companies were authorized to deduct the regular 1½ cents handling charge, plus a service charge of three fourths of a cent a bushel, covering the services (other than actual selling) ordinarily per-

The pools thus operated under three sets of contractual agreements. First with the grower, calling for the delivery of his entire marketable wheat crop to pool account, under penalty of liquidated damages for diversion, at the rate of 25 cents a bushel. Second, with the elevator companies for the storing, forwarding, and initial financing of pool deliveries. Third, with the Central Sales Agency, covering the merchandising of all pool wheat and the distribution of payments.

Results of Pool Operations, 1924-25. — Conditions in the world's wheat trade were distinctly favorable to the Canadian wheat pools in their first year of joint operation. The year 1924 marked the turning point in world wheat prices following the drastic post-war decline, which reached its lowest level in 1923. For the crop year 1924-25 the world's wheat production as a whole was 385,000,000 bushels below that of the preceding year. In Western Canada the crop amounted to only 262,000,000 bushels compared with an average yield of 360,000,000 for the four years, 1920-23.[1] These supply conditions served to carry Canadian spring wheat to a substantial premium in world markets, accompanied as they were by the improvement in European purchasing power reflected in the approach of sterling to parity and the stabilization of continental exchanges generally.

The total pool handlings aggregated 81,670,305 bushels, equivalent to 38 per cent of total wheat inspections in the Western Division.[2] With the declaration of the fourth and final payment in September 1, 1925, the total price realized by the Canadian Co-operative Wheat Producers amounted to $1.66 (basis No. 1 Northern, Fort William), the administrative costs having averaged

formed by commission departments, namely, checking government inspection, paying freight, inspection, and weighing charges, handling railway claims, and delivering terminal warehouse receipts. In the case of street wheat, where the companies assumed the risk of grade losses and had to secure cars, as well as to absorb the weighing and inspection fees, they received a flat handling charge of 5 cents for contract grades (Nos. 1, 2 and 3) and 6 cents on all other grades, plus a carrying charge of one thirtieth of a cent per day. The pools agreed to maintain at all times a margin of 10 cents a bushel between the initial payment made by elevators on street deliveries and the current spot price. See Appendix G.

[1] *Report on Grain Trade of Canada*, 1925.

[2] These amounted to 214,400,000 bushels for the crop year 1924-25.

$\frac{1}{3}$ cent per bushel. It was claimed by the Saskatchewan Pool that its payments were considerably above those received on the average by non-pool farmers.[1] This was challenged by the Northwest Grain Dealers' Association, which pointed out that the average cash closing price for the year on the Winnipeg Exchange was \$1.71$\frac{1}{8}$.

However debatable the precise financial advantage as between pool and non-pool farmers,[2] the rise in wheat prices accompanying the first year's operations of the associated pools served to enhance their prestige among growers. This was markedly reflected in the accession of new contracts. Whereas the three pools had received deliveries of the 1924 crop from 91,195 members representing 10,744,346 acres, they were able to command patronage in the marketing of the 1925 crop from 122,385 growers controlling 14,080,154 acres.[3]

Establishment of Coarse Grains Pools. — In Saskatchewan and Manitoba the results of the first year's operations led to the decision to organize pools for handling coarse grains (oats, rye, barley, flax, mixed grains) as well as wheat during the 1925–26 season.[4] Although these grains (apart from flax) are largely consumed as feed on western farms, and thus have much less significance than wheat as cash crops, their combined marketing volume

[1] Circular, Sask. Co-op. Wheat Producers, July 14, 1925.

[2] The relation between pool payments and market prices is discussed below, pp. 465–468.

[3] See Table II, p. 253.

[4] Coarse grains in Western Canada are generally grown less by way of rotation with wheat than as pioneer crops in newly cleared or frontier lands, and as substitutes for wheat in sections where rust has become prevalent, as in the older settled parts of Manitoba. See J. A. Bracken, *Crop Production in Western Canada.*

In 1925 the harvested grain acreage of the Prairie Provinces was distributed as follows:

	Manitoba	Saskatchewan (*thousands of acres*)	Alberta
Wheat	2,200	13,002	5,720
Oats	1,922	5,071	2,397
Barley	1,874	1,065	553
Rye	328	270	134
Flax	156	954	5

— *Report on Grain Trade of Canada,* 1925

is considerable.[1] Moreover, they pass through country elevators, government inspection, and terminals, and are traded in on the exchange in exactly the same way as wheat. To no small degree the decision of the Saskatchewan and Manitoba Pools to extend the pooling method to the marketing of coarse grains was influenced by their action at this time in creating pool elevator subsidiaries, in which the handling of coarse grains must necessarily be associated with that of wheat.

Since the acts incorporating the provincial wheat pools empowered them to handle all "grain" produced by their members, no separate organization was required in the establishment of coarse grains pools. On the other hand, it was necessary to present separate "coarse grains contracts" to growers for such purpose. In Saskatchewan the principle was adopted that farmers signing the latter must also be signers of wheat pool contracts, but that wheat pool members should not be required to sign coarse grains contracts. In Manitoba, where wheat acreage was relatively less important, growers might sign either contract without obligation in respect to the other.[2] The coarse grains contract closely followed the form of the wheat pool contracts, except that in Saskatchewan the deductions authorized on account of elevator reserve, as well as the scale of "liquidated damages," varied with the different grains according to their relative value.[3] Contracts with elevator companies for 1925–26 likewise made provision for the handling of coarse grains as well as wheat, with variable handling charges for each of the former.[4]

[1] The extent to which coarse grain crops reach central markets in Western Canada is indicated by the following figures covering the 1925 crop:

	Total Production Prairie Provinces	Inspections	Per Cent Inspected
	(thousands of bushels)		
Oats	332,254	53,774	16
Barley	94,141	42,075	45
Rye	11,545	5,480	48
Flax	9,138	5,892	65

[2] *Wheat Pool Year Book*, 1925, pp. 32, 38.

[3] Text of Saskatchewan and Manitoba coarse grains contracts in *Wheat Pool Year Book*, 1925, App. A. Maximum deductions for elevator reserve were set in the former at 3 cents in case of flax, 1½ cents for barley and rye, and 1 cent for oats.

[4] Elevator companies were allowed handling charges on street deliveries at the rate of 4½ cents per bushel on oats, 5½ cent on barley and rye, and 10 cents on flax. Mem. of Agreement, *Wheat Pool Year Book*, App. B.

In Saskatchewan contractual objectives were stipulated of 50 per cent rye and flax acreages and 33⅓ per cent of oats and barley acreages. In Manitoba, on the other hand, a minimum objective of 5,000 signatures was defined.[1] Relatively, the results of the coarse grains campaigns were more important in the latter province. At the end of 1925 the Saskatchewan Pool had secured coarse grains contracts from 34,781 growers covering about 2,500,000 of the 9,000,000 acres sown to these grains in that province. Although failing to reach the quota aimed at, the Saskatchewan trustees decided to operate a coarse-grains pool for the current year. In Manitoba the objective was nearly doubled, the coarse grains acreage under contract substantially exceeding the pool wheat acreage.[2] Thus, although Saskatchewan and Manitoba were a year later than Alberta in getting their wheat pools under way, they offered in their second year pooling facilities for all kinds of Western grains.

[1] Saskatchewan coarse grains contract (sec. 24); Manitoba coarse grains contract (sec. 23).

[2] Nine thousand nine hundred and fifty-seven contracts were secured by the end of 1925, covering 1,326,575 acres, compared with 1,058,182 acres under wheat pool contract, *Wheat Pool Year Book*, 1925, p. 31.

CHAPTER XV

THE POOLS AND THE CO-OPERATIVE ELEVATOR COMPANIES

I. Relations between Old and New Grain Growers' Institutions

Status of Grain Growers' Marketing Organizations in 1924.—In the handling of the 1924 wheat crop in Western Canada, it has been seen, there were functioning six different farmer-owned marketing organizations, representing two systems of coöperation. On the one hand, the Alberta, the Saskatchewan, and the Manitoba Co-operative Wheat Producers, respectively, with their jointly controlled, Canadian Co-operative Wheat Producers Limited — all organized under the auspices of the various provincial farmers' associations — represented the non-stock, non-profit pooling system, with their assets mainly in the form of some 91,000 growers' contracts. On the other hand stood the two co-operative elevator companies, with some 63,000 farmer shareholders, owning and operating elevators at approximately one half of the grain-shipping stations in the Prairie Provinces, and controlling nearly one third of the terminal elevator capacity at the head of the lakes. A majority of the shareholders of these companies were also members of the provincial pools, with a consequently divided financial interest in the two types of farmers' coöperative marketing organizations. As contract signers, they were interested in having the greatest possible amount of wheat brought under pool control. As elevator shareholders they were financially interested in the purchases of non-pool wheat by their companies, as well as in having the maxium volume of both pool and non-pool grain handled through their own houses. The pools controlled an increasing proportion of the farmers' wheat. The farmers' companies controlled a large proportion of the facilities necessary for its reception and movement into selling position. The former depended for its finances mainly upon the "deduction" method. The latter possessed large paid-up capital and reserves, accumulated through many years of successful operation. The interdependence of the two sets of farmers' marketing organizations was obvious. The problem was whether the two could coöperate with each other, while maintaining separate existences, or whether they should be assimilated into one system.

Although the organized Grain Growers had rejected both the Dunning plan for a central selling pool, to be formed by amalgamation of the export subsidiaries of the two farmers' companies, and the Crerar plan for an interprovincial pool under the auspices of the Council of Agriculture, with the financial and handling resources of the companies at its disposal[1]; and although the pools which did emerge had been organized entirely upon the initiative and responsibility of the provincial associations, nevertheless, the actual functioning of these pools had been greatly facilitated by the organization grants and loans of the coöperative companies. Moreover, it was largely owing to their readiness in placing their elevator facilities at the disposal of the pools, that the latter were able to make satisfactory handling contracts with the line companies, without which their operation would have been virtually impossible.

Reasons for Demand for Pool Elevators. — While the Canadian Wheat Board had been able to function effectively, with the existing elevator companies handling its wheat on a basis similar to that provided in the above contracts, the pools, not possessing any compulsory monopoly in the marketing of the farmers' grain, soon found that their operations were handicapped by not being able to take delivery of their members' wheat through country houses of their own. They also found themselves at a disadvantage in not having permanent representatives at local shipping stations, which constitute the only point where the grower actually appears in the marketing of his grain. However conscientiously the agents of the coöperative or other elevator companies might carry out the terms of the contract governing the handling of pool wheat, their primary responsibility was to secure grain for their own principals, and to forward it as promptly as possible to

[1] See *supra*, pp. 205–206, 211–212.

terminal position. Even if not unfriendly to the pool, they were hardly likely to be interested in promoting the smooth running and the extension of the pooling method in their locality. Under contract relations the pools could not send instructions to them directly, or deal on the spot with questions and difficulties arising among pool shippers unfamiliar as yet with the intricacies of the new system. Particularly in the case of street wheat it was felt that the grower was less likely to be undergraded or overdocked by a pool elevator operator than by the agent of the contracting elevator company which must carry grade and weight risks.[1]

Among pool officials and members generally it was also believed that the returns to growers could be appreciably increased through ownership of their own elevator facilities. Not only could lower handling deductions be made than those provided for in contracts with elevator companies, but surpluses might also be expected to accrue to growers through the larger volume of turnover which could be anticipated at pool elevators, as well as through overages and gains in grades.[2] Furthermore, the acquisition of country elevators was desired as an accompaniment to the terminal business of the pools. Mixing operations and satisfactory export shipment necessitated the possession of private terminal elevators, and at the very beginning of its operations the Central Sales Agency had leased two small terminals at Fort William, followed in 1925 by the purchase of the 1,500,000-bushel Davidson and Smith house at Port Arthur.[3] Under both the Canada Grain Act and their contracts with the pools, line elevator companies were free to ship customers' grain to any public terminal elevator,[4] and were naturally disposed to forward it to such as

[1] "The agent of a pool elevator would be as unpopular with the members, also the management, if he produced a large overage in weights or gain in grades, as an agent for a line elevator company would be with his management, if he produced a shortage in weights or a loss in grades." — Alberta Co-operative Wheat Producers, *Wheat Pool Lectures*, p. 12.

[2] "Earnings made by line elevator companies out of pool grain mean money lost to pool members." Sask. Co-op. Wheat Producers Handbook No. 2, p. 18. See also, *Western Producer* (ed.), March 31, 1927.

[3] *Wheat Pool Year Book*, p. 46. The purchase was financed through loans from the elevator reserve funds of the provincial pools.

[4] See Appendix G., sec. 15.

they owned or possessed an interest in, so that they might earn the additional handling and storage charges, with possible profits from overages and screenings as well. If the pools desired to have any of their wheat directed to their own terminals or to western mills, they were required to pay a "diversion" charge to the elevator company.[1] It was also claimed that the companies tended to give preference to their own grain in forwarding the contents of their elevators to lakehead to take advantage of cash premiums.[2] Without a country elevator system of their own, the pools were obviously restricted in their terminal and mixing operations and in their participation in the attendant earnings.

The growers' contracts used by all three pools contained authorization for pool trustees to make deductions up to two cents a bushel from each grower's returns, to be applied to the acquisition of subsidiary grain elevators. Early in 1925 the Saskatchewan Pool board, in response to numerous local demands, announced the adoption of a general policy of acquiring elevators at points where the "sign-up" warranted it, and where no farmer-owned elevator existed.[3] In accordance with this declaration of policy, provincial incorporation was obtained on February 13 of the Saskatchewan Pool Elevators Limited, as a subsidiary of the Saskatchewan Co-operative Wheat Producers,[4] and steps were taken to purchase or build elevators at several points not served by either the Saskatchewan Co-operative or the United Grain Growers.

Proposals for Coöperation between Pools and Companies. — While many pool members, especially those identified with the Farmers' Union, urged that the pools should immediately seek to acquire the elevator facilities of the two farmers' companies, the more responsible pool leaders were disposed to explore first the possibility of having their needs at country points met through special arrangements with the coöperative companies which maintained elevators at some 515 of the 883 stations in Saskatchewan. At the same time the officers of the latter were naturally anxious

[1] Sask. Co-op. Wheat Growers Handbook No. 2, p. 19. The premium on diversion to mills was 1 cent, and to pool terminals ½ cent per bushel.

[2] See complaint of Manitoba Pool in this regard. U. G. G., 1926, p. 22.

[3] *Western Producer*, Jan. 29, 1925.

[4] *Ibid.*, Feb. 19, 1925.

to avert overlapping or competition between pool elevator systems and their own.

With this mutual end in view, a series of conferences was held during the early part of 1925, between representatives of the three pools and the two farmers' companies, At the first of these (February 2), a joint committee was named under the following resolution:

> Having regard to the fact that the pools and the Saskatchewan Co-operative Elevator Company and the United Grain Growers are all farmers' marketing organizations, owned and controlled by farmers in Western Canada, with a mutuality and identity of interest, the committee shall inquire into and report upon:
>
> (*a*) How can the pools and the companies coöperate in the handling of grain to further and protect the interest of both pool members and shareholders?
>
> (*b*) Upon what basis can fair and equitable arrangements be made for the use of the companies' elevators by the pools? [1]

In the discussions of this committee the pool representatives maintained that the existing arrangements with the farmers' companies were unsatisfactory, inasmuch as they did not afford a means of direct contact between pool headquarters and pool members. Furthermore, such gains in grades and overages as might result from handling pool wheat through company elevators accrued to company shareholders, not to pool patrons. To meet these objections a memorandum was drawn up by the committee at the suggestion of the Saskatchewan "Co-op" representatives, containing the following compromise arrangements:

1. Elevator agents of farmers' companies to act also as agents for the pools, receiving instructions over pool signature and through the companies' regular operating machinery.
2. Appointment of a standing joint advisory committee with representatives of each provincial pool and the two farmers' companies, to make recommendations on matters of policy and operation affecting business between pools and companies.
3. Ascertainment of actual cost of handling wheat through company elevators, and return to pools of profits so shown, on the basis of the proportion of pool wheat to total handlings.
4. Concentration of pool wheat through companies' terminals and handling of same at cost.[2]

---

[1] "Review of Negotiations," *Co-operative News*, Jan., 1926; U. G. G., 1925, pp. 21, 22.

[2] U. G. G. 1925, pp. 23, 24.

Breakdown of Negotiations. — In the consideration of these proposals by the respective pool boards, it became evident that they were unacceptable, for different reasons. In Alberta and Manitoba, where the U. G. G. did not cover the same proportion of elevator points that the two companies together did in Saskatchewan, it was felt that preferential arrangements of this nature with the U. G. G. would create difficulties in the arrangement of terms between the pools and other elevator companies. Both the Manitoba and Alberta Pools accordingly withdrew from the conferences. The fundamental obstacle to further negotiations was revealed, however, in the communicated declaration of the Manitoba Pool board that,

> Owing to the fact that the pools represent one system of marketing and the farmers' companies another, it does not appear to be possible to bring about any substantially closer relationship than that under existing elevator arrangements until such time as the shareholders of the farmers' companies indicate their readiness to accept the pool system of marketing.[1]

This pronouncement was followed by the incorporation of the Manitoba Pool Elevators Limited.[2]

While discussions and correspondence were continued between the Saskatchewan Pool and the two companies, a deadlock developed through the pool's demand that the companies should limit their elevator operations to the handling of pool grain and "stored" grain,[3] and through the companies' insistence that they could not accept any proposal "which would deny the use of the company's facilities for either warehousing or marketing to those of its shareholders and patrons who had not seen fit to become pool members." [4] Reconciliation between the two coöperative systems had been found impossible.

II. Absorption of Saskatchewan Co-operative Elevator Company

Throughout the period of these negotiations the directorate of the Saskatchewan "Co-op" was exposed to both overt and covert

[1] *The Scoop Shovel*, March, 1925, Nov., 1925.

[2] Stat. of Manitoba, 15 Geo. V, c. 113, 1925.

[3] This would of course have prevented the companies from buying street grain on their own account.

[4] *Co-operative News*, Jan., 1926, p. 9; U. G. G., 1925, p. 26.

attacks from Farmers' Union members of the Saskatchewan Pool, who regarded the company's policy and methods as incompatible with the progress of the pool, and who sought by a process of "boring from within" to influence local shareholders to elect delegates who favored the turning over of its assets as well as its patronage to the pool.[1] With a view to countering such propaganda, and maintaining its shareholders' patronage,[2] the company had established a Field Service Department, whose activities were the subject of an acrimonious debate and investigation by a special shareholders' committee at the annual meeting in December, 1924.[3]

Proposals by the Saskatchewan Pool for the leasing in whole or part of the company's elevator system were declared by the "Co-op" to be unacceptable, in view of its "established policy of maintaining its facilities intact as a system under the complete control of the company." [4] Meanwhile the pool was proceeding with its own programme of elevator construction and purchase, 89 houses being so acquired during 1925. In the selection of locations for these, the pool had diverged from its originally declared intention of building or buying elevators only at points not served by either of the farmers' companies. In their first annual report, the pool directors stated that they had acquired elevators at 14

[1] See "Farmers' Union" page and "Open Forum" page in issues of the *Progressive*, Sept.–Dec., 1924, and the *Western Producer* (continuing the same) during 1925. The following extract from the letter of a pool member (who was also a "Co-op." shareholder) is indicative of the attitude of a vocal section of Saskatchewan farmers at this period: "The Co-operative Elevator Company is not what it was intended to be — a coöperative elevator system — but a 'big interest' as big interests are known in Canada to-day. They are not so much concerned about the coöperative part as they are about the dividends they pay to the shareholders. — You should see to it that the delegate you send to the annual meeting be instructed to pass a resolution calling for the resignation of any or all directors who are not in favor of turning the "Co-op" system over to the wheat pool." Letter of E. Miltimore, *Western Producer*, Oct. 8, 1925.

[2] "Probably never before in its history has so much misrepresentation and falsehood been spread abroad regarding the business and policies of the company as during the past year, in an effort to arouse suspicion and prejudice in the minds of shareholders, so as to weaken the essential unity of the company." Directors' report, Sask. Co-op., 1924.

[3] *Co-operative News*, Jan., 1925.

[4] *Ibid.*, Jan., 1926, p. 8.

points served by the "Co-op," although they had insisted on a minimum of 30,000 tributary acres under contract as a condition of entry at such places.[1] Such action was regarded by the "Co-op" management as designed to lessen the value of the company's assets and to force them to sell them to the pool.[2]

Overtures for Purchase of "Co-op" by Saskatchewan Pool. — At the annual meeting of Saskatchewan Pool delegates on October 21–22, 1925, the possibility of consolidating all farmer-owned grain marketing facilities within the province was vigorously discussed and the directors were authorized to make a formal offer to purchare the entire country elevator system of the company at a price to be determined by arbitration, and to lease its terminal elevators. While finally signing on October 27th a contract offered by the "Co-op" for handling pool grain on a cost basis,[3] the pool directors promptly followed such action by submitting an offer to purchase the company's system. The "Co-op" directors replied that it was not within their sphere to consider such a proposal without a mandate from the shareholders.[4]

When the annual meeting of the "Co-op" shareholders took place in the following month, it became evident that the majority of the delegates had come prepared to bring about the merger of the farmers' rival marketing organizations. A resolution was carried, instructing the directors to give full consideration to the pool's offer, and to call a special meeting of the company at an early date for the purpose of taking definite action upon it, the shareholders to be furnished in the interval with "full details of the matters involved." [5]

As the Saskatchewan Co-operative Elevator Company had been created by special act of the legislature, and as the government

[1] Elsewhere a minimum pool acreage of only 10,000 acres was required. *Western Producer*, Oct. 27, 1925.

[2] *Co-operative News*, Jan., 1926, p. 9.

[3] The cost basis applied to the handling of pool grain through the company's country elevators, commission department and terminals. Text of Agreement in *Wheat Pool Year Book*, App. C. As in the previous year, the company charged one cent a bushel less for handling pool street wheat than that provided for in contracts with other companies.

[4] *Co-operative News*, Jan., 1926, p. 11.

[5] *Ibid.*, p. 17.

stood in the relation of a mortgagee to the company,[1] it was necessary to obtain legislative authority for entering into terms of sale, as in the case of the Alberta Co-operative Elevator Company ten years previously.[2] Such enabling legislation, in the form of an amendment to the company's act of incorporation, was passed in January, 1926, the interests of the province being safeguarded through authority granted to the Lieutenant-Governor in Council to withhold approval of sale until satisfied that the mortgages held by the treasury would be either prepaid or adequately secured. The interests of the shareholders were protected by a provision inserted at the directors' request, that the sale must be approved by a three-fourths majority of the voting delegates at a special meeting.[3]

Consummation of the Sale and its Significance. — After considerable negotiation, an offer to purchase was received on March 8, which was referred to shareholders by the directors for consideration by locals pending the special meeting called for April 9. The offer was made in the name, not of the pool itself, but of its subsidiary, the Saskatchewan Pool Elevators, and proposed purchase of the company's terminals, as well as its country elevator system, at a price to be determined by a board of three arbitrators whose appraisal should be on a basis of replacement value less depreciation, without allowance for goodwill or earning capacity as a going concern. A deposit of $500,000 accompanied the execution of the offer, with provision for payment of $1,500,000 on August 1, 1926 and the balance in annual instalments of $1,000,000 payable each August first, with interest at 6 per cent. For the purpose of ensuring payments due the government, the pool covenanted to invest sufficient sums in the capital stock of the Saskatchewan Pool Elevators, from elevator reserve deductions, to cover such obligations during the three remaining years of the pool contract. Although the directors' statement accompanying the submission of the offer to the shareholders criticized it in re-

[1] Mortgage and trust agreements ratified in the past by the legislature had contained provisions designed to prevent sale of any part of the system without due protection to the claims of the Crown.

[2] See *supra*, p. 173.

[3] Stat. of Sask., 16 Geo. V, c. 2, 1926.

spect to the limited liability assumed by the pool itself, the inadequacy of the instalment payments and the restricted basis of arbitration,[1] most of the shareholders came prepared to endorse the deal, the vote showing 366 in favor of acceptance and only 77 opposed.[2] The situation was unique. Approximately two thirds of the "Co-op" shareholders and a considerably larger proportion of the delegates, were pool members, so that in effect most of them were voting to change the control of facilities in which they possessed both a purchaser's and a vendor's interest. The decision represented a change in coöperative policy rather than in farmer ownership.

Toward the end of July, 1926, the board of arbitrators handed down its award.[3] The majority report placed a valuation of $11,059,310 upon the transferred assets of the company,[4] against which the government held mortgages to the amount of slightly over $2,300,000.[5] With the payment on August 1 by the pool of its contractual instalment of $1,500,000, the ownership of the great elevator system which had been built up by the Saskatchewan Co-operative since 1911, passed into the hands of the Saskatchewan Pool Elevators Limited, which, with 451 country elevators added to its own line, now operated over 575 houses within the province. In taking over the "Co-op's" two terminals at Port Arthur, and assuming the company's leasehold of the 7,500,000 bushel C. N. R. terminal, it acquired practically one quarter of the terminal elevator capacity on Thunder Bay, in addition to the new 2,000,000-bushel transfer elevator at Buffalo.[6] Thus in

[1] Text of offer, and "Co-op." directors' comment thereon, *Co-operative News*, April, 1926, pp. 4–7; Pool comments, *Western Producer*, March 25, 1926.

[2] Report of debate, *Co-operative News*, May, 1926.

[3] The "Co-op." had named C. D. Howe, elevator engineer, as its arbitrator, and the pool, W. G. Styles of the National Trust Co. The two had chosen as chairman Mr. Justice W. F. A. Turgeon, late chairman of the Royal Grain Inquiry Commission of 1923–25.

[4] This represented a compromise between the vendor's valuation of $12,424,331 and the purchaser's valuation of $10,308,822. Mr. Styles dissented from the majority of the arbitrators in respect to the basis of depreciation of country elevators adopted by them. Certain real estate and grain exchange seats belonging to the company were not included in the transfer. *Western Producer*, Aug. 8, 1926.

[5] For distribution of the shareholders' equity, see *infra*, pp. 462, 463.

[6] See *supra*, p. 186.

the second year of its existence Saskatchewan Pool Elevators Limited had become the largest integrated elevator system in Canada, if not in the world.

The final meeting of the "Co-op" shareholders was held at Regina, March 2–4, 1927, concurrently with the enactment by the Saskatchewan Parliament of special legislation validating the terms of sale [1] and winding up the company.[2] At this meeting a suggestion was received from the Saskatchewan Pool for the payment at the next instalment date, August 1, 1927, of the entire balance of the sum due the shareholders, approximately $7,000,000, provided a discount of 10 per cent should be allowed on the prepayment.[3] A motion approving this proposal was passed by the shareholders' meeting as a recommendation to the liquidators.[4] At a special meeting of pool delegates in June, at which the financial position of the pool was disclosed, the directors were authorized to submit such offer of prepayment on August 1, 1927 to the liquidators.[5] The latter did not feel justified, however, in acting upon such offer without a more inclusive expression of the wishes of individual shareholders. A postal ballot submitted to the latter during August-September 1927, accompanied by the recommendation of the liquidators against acceptance, indicated that the majority of "Co-op" shareholders prefer to retain their 6 per cent liquidation certificates rather than discount them on such terms. While the Saskatchewan Pool's offer of prepayment has not therefore been accepted, its very capacity to make such a proposal is a significant commentary on the effectiveness of the "deduction" method of finance, as applied by the Canadian wheat pools.

[1] Stat. of Sask., 17 Geo. V, c. 71, 1927. The act recites the securities given by the Saskatchewan Pool Elevators and the liability assumed by the Saskatchewan Coöperative Wheat Producers in respect to the claims of "Co-op." shareholders and of the provincial government.

[2] Stat. of Sask., 1927, c. 72. The provisions regarding distribution of shareholders' equities, and sale of shares are discussed below, pp. 462, 463.

[3] As $1,000,000 was due on principal at the above date, the discounted prepayment of the balance of $5,967,745 would have amounted to $5,370,471.

[4] *Western Producer*, March 10, 1927.

[5] *Ibid.*, June 16, 1927.

III. Pool Policy of United Grain Growers

The United Grain Growers had been a party to the series of conferences held during the first half of 1925, first between the three pools and the two farmers' companies, and afterwards, between the latter and the Saskatchewan Pool, with a view to working out a *modus operandi* consistent with the coöperative policies and distinctive existence of each.[1] While, as has been seen, no plan acceptable to all parties proved capable of attainment, the position of the United Grain Growers was somewhat different from that of the Saskatchewan Company. In the first place, being an interprovincial organization and having only some 65 elevators in Saskatchewan, the U. G. G. was less directly exposed to the criticisms and absorption campaign of the Farmers' Union section of the Saskatchewan Pool than was the provincially instituted and owned Co-operative Elevator Company. In the second place, the U. G. G. was not exclusively an elevator and grain-marketing corporation, but a composite organization carrying on farm supply, livestock marketing, publishing, insurance, and other subsidiary enterprises. On the other hand the directors of the U. G. G. had to deal with three different pools, whereas the Saskatchewan "Co-op" was concerned with only one, howbeit the largest and most aggressive. The far-reaching assistance rendered by the U. G. G. to the Alberta Pool in its initial operations has been previously noted.[2] It had been the first elevator company to offer its facilities to the pool, and its handling contract served as a basis for those entered into by the other companies. When interprovincial pool operation became assured, in the summer of 1924, the U. G. G. signed a three-years handling contract with each of the provincial pools. The terms of this, however, were no more favorable to the latter than those contained in the contracts executed by the line companies. Following the breakdown of the conferences between the pools and the farmers' companies with a view to the coördination of the two systems, the U. G. G. entered into separate arrangements with each of the pools.[3]

[1] U. G. G., 1925, pp. 21–33.

[2] See *supra*, p. 218.

[3] At its annual meeting in 1925, the U. G. G. passed a resolution asserting the

Elevator Negotiations with Alberta Pool. — In Alberta where no deduction for elevator reserve had been made in the first year of pool operation, and where relations between pool and company had continued on a fairly harmonious basis, a resolution was passed nevertheless at the annual meeting in August, 1925, recommending "the incoming pool board to make every endeavor to erect elevators along railway lines where the pool sign-up would warrant the same." [1] Pursuing a cautious policy, the Alberta Pool Elevators Limited, which was soon afterwards incorporated, proceeded to build three elevators at points not served by the U. G. G.[2] Desirous of averting future competition or duplication by this newest pool elevator subsidiary, the U. G. G. executive arranged a meeting with the Alberta Pool board on October 19, at which it was agreed that, before any new elevator construction should be undertaken by either party, the other party should be notified of the points at which construction was contemplated, and that the elevator committees of the two concerns should thereupon meet and "endeavor to amicably agree which should build at such point." Provision was also made for a joint committee to confer on a permanent policy as to elevator ownership and operation in Alberta.[3]

Out of this coördinating committee a plan emerged for the operation of the elevators of the two interests by a jointly owned company which should handle both pool and non-pool grain. This proposal was approved at a special meeting of Alberta Pool delegates, and negotiations were carried to the point of agreement on the detailed terms of the arrangement. Consummation was prevented, however, by failure to agree upon the appointment of manager for the joint operating company, the U. G. G. being reluctant to entrust the management of its extensive elevator properties in Alberta to an outside official, as desired by the pool, whose directors felt that their members' interests would not be

inadvisability of "any arrangement or consolidation of facilities upon any basis that would deny to any shareholder or patron the advantages of U. G. G. country elevators in the disposal of their grain by shipping, selling by wagonload, or otherwise, which they now enjoy."

[1] *The U. F. A.*, Aug. 15, 1925, p. 7.
[2] *The U. F. A.*, Oct. 1, 1925, p. 5.
[3] U. G. G., 1925, p. 31.

best served under a U. G. G. manager.[1] Although the proposed unification between the Alberta Pool Elevators and the U. G. G. elevators in Alberta had proved to be less realizable than amalgamation between the Alberta Farmers' Co-operative Elevator Company and the Grain Growers' Grain Company ten years previously, the U. G. G. undertook to handle pool wheat for the 1926 crop year through its Alberta elevators and lakehead terminals ona cost basis, as contemplated in the abandoned joint arrangement.[2] In September, following the annual meeting of Alberta Pool delegates, the U. G. G. was approached by a committee with a view to the sale of its Alberta elevators to the pool.

Relations withSaskatchewan andManitoba Pools.—In Saskatchewan the U. G. G. entered into arrangements for handling pool grain upon the same basis as the Saskatchewan "Co-op," that is, to charge one cent less on pool wheat and one half-cent less on pool oats, barley, and rye than the contract rates with line companies,[3] and likewise to return to the Saskatchewan Pool any surplus realized on the handling of its grain through the company's country elevators, or on the diversion of pool grain to the U. G. G. terminals.[4]

In Manitoba, whose pool board had announced in March, 1925, a policy of building or acquiring elevators at points where local pool organizations would pledge a minimum acreage to their support, pool elevators were acquired during the summer at four points served by the U. G. G.[5] A proposal made by the latter for a joint elevator operating company as contemplated in Alberta, was rejected by the Manitoba Pool board on the reaffirmed grounds that, inasmuch as the pool and the U. G. G. represented

[1] Joint press statement of U. G. G. and Alberta Pool, July 12, 1926.

[2] "Cost" was to include depreciation and rental at 6 per cent of appraised value of country elevators; and prorating of terminal profits was conditioned on eastward concentration of pool grain through U. G. G. terminals. *The U. F. A.*, Aug. 16, 1926, p. 4.

[3] In effect, this meant that line companies had to meet the farmers' companies' rates at competing points.

[4] A return of $1\frac{1}{4}$ cents a bushel was made to the Saskatchewan Pool on pool grain directed to U. G. G. terminals in this year. U. G. G., 1926, p. 22.

[5] *The Scoop Shovel*, March 1925; U. G. G., 1925, p. 30.

two fundamentally different systems of grain marketing, the proposed "amalgamation" was not practicable.[1] This was followed by an offer from the pool to purchase or lease U. G. G. elevators in Manitoba at points where local members made application for pool elevators.

Decision of U. G. G. Shareholders to Retain Elevators. — During 1926 the U. G. G. had thus been approached independently by the three pools, with a view to the sale or lease of its country elevators. A week preceding the annual meeting of the U. G. G. shareholder delegates on December 1, a letter was received from the Canadian Co-operative Wheat Producers, on behalf of the three provincial pools, intimating their readiness to enter into negotiations for the purchase of the entire elevator system of the U. G. G., with a view to handling the 1927 crop.[2]

A resolution recommending such sale was introduced into the shareholders' meeting, and in a debate notable for its representative range, good feeling, and the thoughtfulness of the speeches,[3] opponents of the motion drew attention to the fact that 52 per cent of the grain handled through the company's elevators during the last crop year had been non-pool grain, and that the alienation of the company's elevator system would mean that those farmers who had not seen fit to sign pool contracts, would have no alternative but to sell their grain to the line companies. The pools were approaching the end of their first contract period, and it would be undesirable to have the U. G. G. as well as the Saskatchewan "Co-op" go out of business before the permanence of the pools was assured. In the meantime the company was handling pool grain at cost through its country and terminal elevators. When the vote was taken it was found that more than four-fifths of the delegates were opposed to the sale, — almost exactly the same proportion as that which had endorsed the transfer of the Saskatchewan "Co-op" system to the Saskatchewan Pool eight months previously.

[1] *The Scoop Shovel*, Aug. 1926.

[2] U. G. G., 1926, p. 25.

[3] The matter had been previously discussed by a large number of shareholders' locals, 41 of which had sent in resolutions regarding it to the general meeting.

While the principle of preserving the company's independent existence was thus decisively upheld, a policy of meeting the pool's needs at local points was endorsed, by the adoption of the following resolution submitted by the directorate:

That the board of directors be authorized to lease or sell such of the company's elevators as may be necessary to avoid undesirable duplication of country elevators between the company and the three provincial pools.[1]

In accordance with this compromise policy of local accommodation the U. G. G. has sold twenty-seven of its elevators to the Alberta Pool, and leased nineteen to the Saskatchewan Pool. One only has been leased to the Manitoba Pool which has generally been unwilling to buy existing elevators except on a wrecking basis valuation. Although thus turning over to the pools a considerable number of its country houses at points where the pool "sign-up" represents a high proportion of the tributary acreage, and where there is not normally sufficient business for two farmer-owned elevators, the U. G. G. has continued to add to its own system by construction on new railway branch lines, twenty-one additional elevators being thus built in Alberta alone during 1927. Meanwhile the provincial pools have been actively prosecuting their own construction programmes, so that by the end of 1927 there were no less than 118 points where both pool and U. G. G. elevators were in operation.[2] While this has involved a certain amount of undesirable duplication in Manitoba, the coexistence of the two occurs for the most part at points where there appears to be adequate patronage for both.[3] In such cases non-pool growers may still market their grain through a farmer-owned elevator which is also available for handling on a cost basis contract grain which the local pool elevator may be unable to receive.

The renewed expansion of grain growing in Saskatchewan and Alberta in response to the higher prices that have prevailed since

[1] Minutes of U. G. G. annual meeting, Dec. 1–3, 1927.

[2] Of these points, 75 were in Alberta, 27 in Saskatchewan, and 16 in Manitoba

[3] In his presidential report at the U. G. G. annual meeting in 1927 Mr. Crerar stated in this connection: "Practically without exception the farmers at these points are desirous of having both pool and U. G. G. elevators, rather than only one of these organizations and another elevator owned by a line company."

1924,[1] has in fact permitted the U. G. G. to extend its facilities and business despite the operation of the pools, and the transfer to them of a number of its local houses. At the end of 1927 the company owned 401 country elevators, of which it operated in that year 368. In the terminal field it has enlarged its undertakings both east and west. At the head of the lakes it has just completed the construction of one of the largest and best equipped terminal elevators on the continent, with a capacity of 5,500,000 bushels. On the Pacific coast it has leased since 1925 from the Vancouver Harbor Commission the Burrard elevator, recently enlarged to 1,500,000 bushels capacity.[2] A large part of the grain received through the company's Alberta houses now passes through this western outlet.

Thus the oldest of the Western farmers' grain companies has not merely preserved its identity under the competition of the pools as well as of the regular trade, but also finds itself in its twenty-first anniversary year in the strongest position in its history. Thanks to the conciliatory and patient policy of its leaders, the relations of the U. G. G. with the pools are becoming increasingly harmonious, the two systems offering alternative methods of coöperative grain marketing, both under producer control.

[1] Between 1921 and 1926 the field crop acreage of the Prairie Provinces increased from 30,200,000 acres to 35,000,000 acres . While this increase is in part due to the northerly extension of the grain growing frontier through the construction of new railway branch lines and the development of earlier maturing varieties of wheat, it is mainly attributable to an enlargement of the average field crop acreage per farm from 126 acres in 1921 to 141 acres in 1926. Census of Prairie Provinces, 1926.

[2] U. G. G., 1927.

CHAPTER XVI

POOL POLICIES AND OPERATIONS

I. Internal Economy of the Pools

The Pool Structure. — The Canadian wheat pool structure is notable both for its democratic organization and its commercial centralization. While rooted in hundreds of local units, and while recognizing full provincial autonomy, it is coördinated as a single marketing institution. The six provincially incorporated institutions, the Alberta, the Saskatchewan, and the Manitoba Co-operative Wheat Producers Limited, and the Alberta, the Saskatchewan, and the Manitoba Pool Elevators Limited, respectively, are adaptations to the realities of territorial and functional division, while the Canadian Co-operative Wheat Producers Limited serves as the channel through which commodity deliveries from each, and monetary returns to each, are concentrated and pooled.

While the binding medium of the whole structure lies in the contract between the individual grower and the provincial pool, and the agreement between the latter and the central selling agency, the organic cell of the system is to be found in the pool "locals," of which there are 260 in Alberta, 1050 in Saskatchewan, and 90 in Manitoba (where there are also "shipping committees.") The organization and function of these differ somewhat in the three provinces according to territorial conditions. In Alberta the area of the pool local corresponds to that of the fostering U. F. A. locals. Each is organized, with a chairman and secretary, and any number of directors up to five. Their chief function is to serve as a medium of contact between pool headquarters and pool members, arranging meetings, distribution of pool literature, securing new contracts, and communicating questions, complaints or recommendations to pool headquarters. For purposes of democratic representation and control, the province is divided into seven main districts, each of which is again divided into ten sub-districts. From each of the seventy sub-districts are chosen delegates to the annual (or special) provincial pool meetings,[1] while the ten delegates of each district foregather to elect one of their number as the district representative on the board of seven pool directors, who in turn elect their executive.

In Saskatchewan efforts have been made to form two or more "pool committees," centering about "convenient rallying places" — shipping points or country school houses — within each rural municipality. In view of the greater extent of its grain-growing area, the province is divided into sixteen pool districts, each with ten sub-districts comprising blocks of municipalities. Thus the annual meetings of the Saskatchewan Wheat Pool are attended by 160 delegates, — nominated and elected as in Alberta, — and its affairs are governed by a board of sixteen directors.[2] In Manitoba, where agricultural population is more concentrated and railway trackage is of greater density, "sub-districts" are eliminated, while the areas of the 90 pool locals are coextensive with those of the rural municipalities. The Manitoba Pool locals perform a double function. They elect delegates (proportional to their membership) directly to the annual general pool meeting, at which delegates from each of the seven districts choose a director to represent them on the pool board. In the second place, they appoint "shipping committees" of three members for each shipping point within the municipality where the pool membership justifies it, these committees functioning in much the same manner as the local pool organizations in the other provinces.[3] The expenses of pool locals are provided for out of the general organization funds of the pools.[4]

Under the Manitoba pool elevator plan the various coöperative

[1] Any pool member may secure the nomination of his choice for delegate by obtaining signatures of ten members on a nomination paper. The names of all duly nominated candidates are then mailed to each contract signer in the sub-district, who marks his ballot by the preferential system, and must return it by post to the pool secretary by July 31. Alberta Co-op. Wheat Producers, *Wheat Pool Lectures*, No. 3.

[2] Sask. Co-op. Wheat Producers, Handbook No. 2, pp. 7, 8.

[3] *Wheat Pool Year Book*, pp. 38–41.

[4] See By-laws for Pool Locals, *Western Producer*, Oct. 21, 1926.

elevator associations constitute a new and significant form of grain growers' local organization.[1] In Saskatchewan the old shareholders' locals of the Saskatchewan "Co-op" have of course been dissolved with the winding up of the company. While no distinct local coöperative elevator organization has taken the place of these as yet, pool elevators, where they exist, serve as tangible centers for members' locals, whose value the pools have not been slow to recognize. They stand as the physical symbol of the pool to contract-holders, who have a patronage as well as an investment interest in them, while the pool elevator operator serves as a resident liaison agent between pool members and pool headquarters. Contact is further maintained through field service staffs (with one man usually for each district) which seek to remove local difficulties and misunderstandings and to promote expansion and contract observance.

Management and Control. — In the management of the pools the general policy has been to offer inducements to secure the best available talent, regardless of the individual's former connection. While the general sales manager of the Central Sales Agency is the former manager of the United Grain Growers' Export Company,[2] and the manager of the Saskatchewan Pool is the former chief superintendent of the Saskatchewan Co-operative Elevator Company,[3] on the other hand, the western sales manager of the C. S. A.,[4] the Alberta Pool Elevators' manager,[5] and the manager of the Manitoba Pool,[6] were all secured from line companies, while the manager of the Alberta Pool was taken from a bank.[7] Repeated efforts were made to secure the services of the former Attorney-General and present Premier of Alberta, as general pool manager.[8] The pools in fact have not hesitated to apply Aaron Sapiro's dictum: "Don't demand a fair price for your product, and deny a fair price to brains."

[1] See *infra*, pp. 254, 255.

[2] Mr. D. L. Smith, see *supra*, p. 218.

[3] Mr. D. R. MacRae.

[4] Mr. George McIvor, former general manager, James Richardson Grain Company.

[5] Mr. C. M. Hall, former general manager, Alberta Pacific Grain Co.

[6] Mr. R. M. Mahoney, formerly of Home Grain Company.

[7] Mr. R. D. Purdy, former assistant manager, Bank of Montreal, Edmonton.

[8] Hon. A. J. Brownlee.

While expert management has thus been selected from the trade at large, every provision has been made to ensure democratic control by the growers themselves. In Alberta and Saskatchewan, as has been seen, the nomination and election of pool delegates is conducted by mail, as an alternative to selection through unrepresentative or "managed" meetings. Directors are elected by districts instead of at large,[1] and hold office for one year only, although eligible for reëlection. In Alberta both delegates and directors are subject to "recall." In Saskatchewan and Manitoba the principle of single office-holding has been insisted upon, in deference to which President McPhail of the Saskatchewan Pool and President Burnell of the Manitoba Pool, upon election, resigned the secretaryship of the S. G. G. A. and the presidency of the U. F. M., respectively.[2] In this there is to be seen a reaction, finding its most uncompromising expression in the Farmers' Union, against the recurring directorships in the farmers' companies and the interlocking of offices in grain growers' associations and commercial organizations, not infrequently combined with parliamentary incumbency.[3] In the interests of coördination and trusteeship, however, the organization of the pool structure makes the directorates of the provincial pools and of their respective pool elevator subsidiaries identical, and provides that the board of the Canadian Co-operative Wheat Producers shall be composed of three directors from each of the three provincial pool boards. Thus Mr. McPhail, as president of the largest provincial pool, is also president of the Canadian Pool.

Nature and Value of the Pool Contract. — The real nexus and the primary asset of the pools lie in their grower's contracts. In the drafting of these the California model and the counsel of Aaron Sapiro have been essentially followed, with certain adaptations to prairie conditions and Canadian Wheat Board experience. Although the Saskatchewan and Manitoba Wheat Pools

[1] This principle has long been applied in the election of directors in the provincial farmers' associations.

[2] While farmer sentiment in Alberta has insisted upon Mr. H. W. Wood retaining the presidency of the U. F. A. as well as of the Alberta Wheat Pool, Mr. Wood since 1924 has not drawn any salary from the former organization.

[3] See *supra*, pp. 213, 214.

were established a year later than the Alberta Pool, the contracts of all three are virtually identical in form.[1] The contract signer covenants to deliver to the pool or its order, and to no other party, all the wheat produced or acquired by him during the lifetime of the contract except registered seed wheat,[2] and such wheat as he may require for his own seed and feed.[3] If the grower wishes to sell wheat directly to other farmers for seed or feed purposes, he must obtain a permit for such sale from the pool.[4] In the case of land rented on a crop-share basis the wheat produced thereon is subject to separate contracts by tenant and landowner. If a farmer moves to another location during the contract period, or buys additional land, he is bound, to deliver all his wheat, regardless of his location or the number of his holdings within the province, the principle being that "the contract follows the wheat not the land." [5]

In signing a pool contract, the grower agrees to four separate payments or deductions: (*a*) the sum of one dollar as price of one share in the stock of the pool association[6]; (*b*) two dollars for purposes of organization, field service, and educational work of the pool; (*c*) a deduction for elevator reserve, not exceeding two cents a bushel (in the case of wheat, with varying amounts in the case of the different coarse grains); (*d*) a further deduction, not exceeding one per cent, of gross sales for purposes of commercial

[1] In the case of the Alberta and Saskatchewan Pools, all current contracts, regardless of the date of signature, expire with the end of the 1927 crop year. Since 1926, however, all farmers joining these pools have been required to sign contracts for the 1928–32 period, as well as for the remainder of the present term. In Manitoba all contracts have a five-years currency, thus ensuring continuously overlapping membership. An objection to the latter plan is that changes which it may be desirable to insert in new contracts do not apply to the whole membership.

[2] Registered seed produced by members of the Canadian Seed Growers' Association is tested, labelled and largely marketed, in behalf of the growers, by the Seed Branches of the Dominion and provincial Departments of Agriculture. See H. G. L. Strange, "The Canadian Seed Growers' Association," in *G. G. Guide*, Sept. 15, 1927.

[3] See Appendix E, secs. 4, 8, 9.

[4] Such permits are generally issued through pool locals. In the case of coarse grains which are sold extensively for farm feed, off the market, peımits are issued in blank.

[5] Sask. Pool, Handbook No. 2, p. 12; Sask. Co-op. Wheat Producers, Handbook No. 2.

This concession to the joint-stock principle was necessary in order to comply with the provincial coöperative associations acts.

reserve.[1] The first item does not apply in the case of a wheat pool member signing a coarse-grains contract, or in the renewal of contracts for a further pool period. It is in effect an initiation fee paid once for all. The two reserve times are in the nature of contractual investments, to provide fixed and circulating capital, interest being paid to members on elevator reserve deductions.[2]

The contracts which they hold are of indispensable value to the pools. They afford an assurance both of a calculable volume of business and of continuity of operation. It is the legal control over members' grain which they give to the pool as the growers' "agent, factor and attorney in fact," and the minimization of risk involved in the system of deferred payment which they authorize, that place the Central Sales Agency in a preferred credit position in relation to the banks.[3] But for the continuity of existence assured by long-term contracts, the pools would scarcely have been able to secure the services of men of superior qualifications in the established grain trade.[4] It was the assured revenues from successive elevator reserve deductions that made it possible for the Saskatchewan Pool to submit an offer for the purchase of the Co-operative Elevator Company system that could be accepted by the shareholders and sanctioned by the provincial government. And it is the long-term contractual control of the grain produced by its army of growers that enables the Canadian Wheat Pool to make contracts for future delivery without the necessity of "hedging" on such commitments, and which justifies it in building up a far-reaching system of overseas selling agencies.

[1] See Appendix E, secs. 13, 14, 6 (*f*), 6 (*d*).

[2] The matter of pool deductions is further discussed below, pp. 468–474.

[3] In the first year's operations of the Alberta Pool the banks had insisted on a guarantee as to margin maintenance from the provincial government. Since the establishment of the Central Sales Agency, no government guarantees have been asked for. In August, 1924, the banks, in view of the pools' possession of 85,000 contracts, agreed to reduce the rate of interest on loans to the C. S. A. from the customary 7 to 6 per cent, conditional on maintenance of a 15 per cent margin between initial payments and the future price, jointly guaranteed by the provincial pools.— Official information.

[4] It will be recalled that it was largely owing to the temporary existence contemplated for the reëstablished Wheat Board in 1922–23, that it proved impossible to secure the services of the executives sought. See *supra*, pp. 208, 209.

The combination of coarse grains pooling with wheat pooling, while calling for separate contracts, has not involved separate organization. On the other hand, it permits manifest economies. The cost and effort of sign-up campaigns are distributed over two sets of contracts. The volume of turnover in pool elevators is substantially increased, with consequent savings in unit handling costs. At the same time, the overhead and selling expenses of the Central Sales Agency are distributed over a greater volume of grain.

Effectiveness of Pool Contracts. — While the possession of these uniform, long-term contracts is thus of far-reaching value to the pools, their effectiveness is of course dependent upon the extent to which they are carried out by pool members. A comparison of the proportion of total crop acreage under contract, and of the proportion which pool marketings bear to total wheat inspections, reveals a considerable disparity. Thus pool records showed at the end of 1925 an aggregate of 122,385 contracts, covering 14,080,154 acres under wheat in the three provinces, representing 67 per cent of the officially reported total wheat crop acreage in Western Canada for 1925. The total wheat deliveries marketed by the Central Sales Agency during the 1925–26 crop year amounted to 187,247,886 bushels, equivalent to 53 per cent of the total wheat inspections in that year. Various causes are given by pool officials to account for this discrepancy: contracts received after the grower had already marketed his 1925 crop in whole or in part; over-estimates or duplications of pool crop acreage (for example, between landowner and tenant); natural shrinkage through death, retirement or removal of pool members[1]; failure of members properly to notify elevator agents that they were delivering pool wheat; delivery of crop shares to non-pool landlords or farm vendors; crop-payments to mortgage companies and banks, crop-lien executions, and the like.[2] With all due allowance for such factors, it would appear that a by no means negligible amount of "bootlegging" exists on the part of members, who may sell a wagonload or so to elevator companies when hard pressed for ready cash, or

[1] See Table I, p. 252.

[2] Sask. Wheat Pool, Handbook No. 2, p. 15. Personal information. Sask. Co-op. Wheat Producers, Handbook No. 2.

when the current market price seems specially favorable. Opportunities for evasion are, of course, greater at points where no pool elevator exists, and in this is to be found one of the reasons for the eagerness to extend the pool elevator system.

The Canadian wheat pool contract — in conformity with Sapiro principles — contains provisions under which the grower obligates himself to pay "liquidated damages" at the rate of 25 cents a bushel for any wheat "sold, delivered or withheld by him otherwise than in accordance with the terms of the contract"; and in which he recognizes the right of the pool to take out injunction to restrain any further breach.[1] During the first year's operations of the Saskatchewan Pool, legal action was taken in respect to two established cases of contract violation. One of these was settled out of court.[2] The other, after a decision unfavorable to the pool, was carried as a test case to the Saskatchewan Court of Appeals. The latter, by a majority judgment, reversed the finding of the trial judge, and found the defendant liable for the full damages claimed by the pool, the court maintaining that the contract was not in restraint of trade, but "reasonable and consistent with the public interest."[3] In Saskatchewan and Manitoba, the Co-operative Marketing Associations Acts, passed in 1925, give specific legal recognition to the liquidated damages and injunction provisions of coöperative marketing contracts.[4]

While the legality of the pool contract has thus been recognized and its enforceability upheld, pool officials have been loath to exercise this right except in extreme cases. Non-deliveries reported by members, local committees, or pool elevator operators are checked up by field service men, who have reported that in the majority of cases misunderstanding of the terms of the contract rather than deliberate evasion has existed.[5] Pool leaders in general realize that in goodwill and understanding lie the best

[1] Appendix E, secs. 21, 22.

[2] Statement of A. J. McPhail, *Western Producer*, Sept. 3, 1925.

[3] Sask. Co-op. Wheat Producers *v.* Zurowski, 3 (1926) W. W. R. 604.

[4] Stat. of Sask. c. 37, 1925–26; Stat. of Man. c. 8, sec. 26, 1925.

[5] Eighty-one complaints of non-delivery were investigated by the Alberta Pool in 1925–26. Evidence was regarded as justifying suit in only seven cases, in three of which judgment was secured by the Pool. *The U. F. A.*, Aug. 16, 1926.

guarantees of contract observance, and that reliance must be placed upon the rendering of superior service rather than upon the serving of writs.[1] The pool's stability is not assured by the mere securing of contract signatures. Hence pool policy has been persistently directed to the development of local responsibility through the organization of pool committees, and to the continuous dissemination of information and coöperative education.

Growth of the Pools.—The aggressiveness of the pools' organizational and educational activities, and the extent to which their

TABLE I. GROWTH OF POOL MEMBERSHIP, 1923–27

Year	Alta.	Sask.	Man.	Total
	Wheat Pool Contracts			
1923 crop	25,601			
1924 "	30,711	51,268	9,216	91,195
1925 "	35,997	72,016	14,372	122,385
1926 "	38,460	80,418	17,234	136,112
1927 "	39,300	83,500	19,000 *	141,800
Nov. 1, 1927	40,000 (app.)	85,059	19,200	144,259
	Coarse Grains Contracts			
1925 crop		34,781	7,082	41,863
1926 "		37,312	10,656	47,968
1927 "		38,700	13,188	51,888
Nov. 1927		38,972	13,583	52,555

* At the annual meeting of the Manitoba Pool in July, 1927, the membership figures reported an allowance for a loss of 1005 members since the inauguration of the pool, due to death or removal from farm. A proportionate allowance for such natural shrinkage should probably be made to show the actual number of effective contracts in the other provinces.

methods and performances have commended themselves to the grain growers of Western Canada, are reflected in the growth of pool membership and contract acreage since the anxious initiation of the Alberta Pool in the late fall of 1923.

[1] "Your board is of opinion that the real solution of this problem lies in the education of the members rather than in compulsion." *Ibid.*

TABLE II. ACREAGE UNDER POOL CONTRACT, DEC. 31, 1926 †

	Wheat			Coarse Grains		
	Pool Acreage	Provincial crop acreage	Per cent under contract	Pool Acreage	Provincial crop acreage	Per cent under contract
Alberta	3,651,000	6,114,000	60	....	....	..
Saskatchewan ..	10,675,000	13,496,000	79	2,679,000	5,631,000	48
Manitoba	1,215,000	2,286,000	53	1,646,000	4,368,000	38
Total	15,541,000	21,896,000	70	4,325,000	9,999,000	43

† Compiled from provincial pool reports and *Report on Grain Trade of Canada.*

Extension to Other Provinces. — The scope of the marketing control of the Canadian Co-operative Wheat Producers has recently spread beyond the confines of the Prairie Provinces, both westward and eastward. Although wheat is grown to too limited an extent in British Columbia to justify the organization of a separate pool in that province,[1] some scores of farmers in the valleys of the Pacific Province have signed contracts with the Alberta Wheat Pool, which operates terminal elevators both at Vancouver and at Prince Rupert.

In Ontario the example of the Western grain growers has led to the recent organization of a grain pool by the Ontario farmers' Co-operative Company, the commercial auxiliary of the United Farmers of Ontario. At the end of July, 1927, over 8,000 contracts had been signed, covering wheat, oats, and barley jointly.[2] Under arrangements with the Canadian Co-operative Wheat Producers, Ontario grain pool deliveries will be marketed through the Toronto office of the Central Selling Agency. Inasmuch as only an insignificant portion of Ontario grain is exported, the sales made by the pool will be mainly to domestic millers, cereal manufacturers, and grain merchants. While a grain pool has much less

[1] In 1925 the total wheat production of British Columbia was only a little over one million bushels. With the recent completion of a government terminal elevator at Prince Rupert (operated by the Alberta Pool), and the development of the Oriental market, wheat-growing is attaining some importance in the Bulkley Valley section of the Grand Trunk Pacific.

[2] *Manitoba Free Press*, July 28, 1927.

economic significance for the more intensively operating, mixed farmers of Ontario than for large-scale prairie grain growers, and while the resulting addition to the volume marketed by the Central Selling Agency will be relatively slight, the Ontario development not only affords a further demonstration of farmer faith in the pooling system, but also constitutes a definite coöperative affiliation between the farmers of Western and Eastern Canada.

II. Pool Elevator Policies

In the preceding chapter the considerations leading to the establishment of elevator subsidiaries by the three pools, and the acquisition of the Saskatchewan "Co-op" elevator system by the Saskatchewan Pool were discussed. In order to ensure adequate patronage for their elevators, the general policy followed by the pools has been to acquire or build elevators only at points where such a request has been definitely made by local pool organizations, and where a minimum acreage — usually 10,000 acres — has been signed up.

The Manitoba Pool Elevator Plan. — In Manitoba a distinctive plan has been evolved with a view to ensuring local responsibility. A petition, carrying with it a pledge to support a local pool elevator, from growers representing a minimum of 7,000 tributary crop acres, is prerequisite to action by the Manitoba Pool Elevators toward the establishment of a local unit.[1] If the plan as presented by headquarters officials at a special meeting of those interested is approved, the petitioners are then formed into a local co-operative elevator association, chartered under the Manitoba Co-operative Associations Act, and its members are required to sign individual agreements for the exclusive delivery of all their grain to such elevator during the lifetime of their wheat and coarse grains contracts with the Manitoba Pool.[2] The acquisition or construction of the elevator, as well as its operation, is handled by the Manitoba Pool Elevators, which "leases" it to the local

[1] In the case of a leased elevator a minimum of 4,500 acres may be accepted if the rental is sufficiently low to warrant it. *The Scoop Shovel*, Jan., 1927, p. 7.

[2] Each member of the local elevator association must have signed both wheat and coarse-grain contracts covering the new (1928–1932) as well as the current contract period. *Ibid.*, Feb., 1926, p. 5.

association for an annual sum equivalent to 10 per cent "depreciation," plus an annual rental equal to 7 per cent of investment cost, less the amount deducted each year on account of "depreciation."[1] The 10 per cent annual "depreciation" payment is in effect a purchase instalment, the intention being that the elevator should become the property of the local association at the end of ten years. The 7 per cent rental permits the Manitoba Pool Elevators, which is the operating company, to pay the interest to which pool members are entitled on account of elevator reserve deductions. The Manitoba pool elevator plan thus provides for centralized management, with local incorporation and elevator patronage contract. By the end of 1927 fifty-eight local co-operative elevator associations had been so established in the province where the ill-fated experiment in government elevator operation had been initiated seventeen years previously.

In Alberta and Saskatchewan new elevators have been built chiefly at new shipping points, or where pool officials have not been able to purchase existing houses at satisfactory prices. In Manitoba peculiar conditions prevail. Most of the country elevators in that province are of old construction and inadequately equipped with cleaning machinery.[2] As the Manitoba Pool has been unwilling to purchase obsolescent elevators at prices acceptable to the owners, and as local associations have demanded houses with improved binning and cleaning facilities, the result is that most of the Manitoba pool elevators represent new construction or reconstruction. This applies indeed to twenty points served by U. G. G. elevators which the pool was prepared to buy at scrap prices only. In the operation of these improved houses, the return of screenings to the grower, the saving of freight on dockage otherwise shipped to terminals, and improvement of

[1] The text of the Manitoba Co-operative Elevator agreement is given in Appendix H. Elevators which the pool acquires by lease are re-leased to local associations concerned, which assume the rental agreed upon. *Wheat Pool Year Book*, pp. 42, 43.

[2] Owing to the high proportion of dockage which Manitoba grain generally shows, and owing to the large local demand for screenings for stock-feeding purposes, it is more economical to have grain cleaned at country elevators in Manitoba than at terminal elevators where the lower dockage grain from Saskatchewan and Alberta is generally separated. See on this point, *Report of Royal Grain Inquiry Commission*, 1925, pp. 67–74.

grades through use of Carter disc cleaners, are claimed as "invisible gains" to pool elevator patrons.[1]

Growth of the Pool Elevator System. — During the crop year 1925–26 the Saskatchewan Pool, through its subsidiary, operated 89 elevators, the Manitoba Pool 8, and the Alberta Pool 16 (mostly acquired late in the season). On August 1, 1926 the 451 country elevators and the four terminals of the Saskatchewan "Co-op" passed into the hands of the Saskatchewan Pool Elevators. With mounting elevator reserve funds and with urgent requests from locals not hitherto served, for the more general establishment of pool elevators, very considerable expansion was undertaken in all three provinces during 1927. The growth and distribution of the pool country elevator system is indicated by the following table:

TABLE III. GROWTH OF POOL COUNTRY ELEVATOR SYSTEM

Year	Alberta	Sask'n.	Manitoba	Total
1925	3	89	8	100
1926	42	586	30	658
1927	157	731	58	946

With some 950 country elevators the pools are now physically established at more than half the elevator stations in the Prairie Provinces.[2] At the Saskatchewan Pool convention in November, 1927, resolutions were passed instructing the directors to provide as far as practicable during 1928 pool-owned shipping facilities at every shipping point in the province, and that at the heavier shipping points a second pool elevator should be established where warranted by the volume of pool deliveries.[3] In Alberta and Manitoba, where the U. G. G. still retains some 300 country houses, the prospect of pool elevator establishment at each shipping point is much more remote.

Besides their country elevator systems the pools individually or collectively control, by ownership or lease, approximately 30 per

[1] *The Scoop Shovel*, Dec. 1926, p. 6.

[2] For the crop year 1926–27 the 4427 country elevators were located at 1769 points distributed as follows: Manitoba, 380; Saskatchewan, 929; Alberta, 460. *Report of Board of Grain Commissioners*, 1926–27.

[3] *Western Producer*, Nov. 24, 1927, p. 1.

cent of the total terminal storage capacity at the head of the lakes, and at British Columbia ports. The distribution of the pool terminals is shown in the following table:

TABLE IV. POOL TERMINAL ELEVATORS, 1927

Canadian Co-operative Wheat Producers:	bushels
Pool Elevator No. 1 (Owned) Port Arthur	1,500,000
Pool Elevator No. 2 (Leased) Fort William	600,000
Pool Elevator No. 3 (Leased) Fort William	250,000
Total, Central Selling Agency	2,350,000
Saskatchewan Pool Elevators Ltd.:	
Pool Elevator No. 4 (Owned) Port Arthur	6,425,000
Pool Elevator No. 5 (Owned) Port Arthur	1,150,000
Pool Elevator No. 6 (Leased) Port Arthur	7,500,000
Eastern Transfer Elevator (Owned) Buffalo	2,000,000
Total, Saskatchewan Pool Elevators	17,075,000
Alberta Pool Elevators Ltd.:	
Canadian Government Elevator (Leased) Pr. Rupert	1,250,000
Harbor Commission Terminal No. 2 (Leased) Vancouver	1,650,000
Total, Alberta Pool Elevators	2,900,000
Grand total, Pool terminals	*22,325,000

* The Alberta Pool has at present under construction a 2,400,000 bushel terminal elevator at Vancouver, which is expected to be available for the 1928 crop.

Financing of Pool Elevators. — The financing of this huge programme of elevator acquisition within less than three years has been accomplished by the coöperative device of deducting two cents a bushel as elevator revenue from each grower's returns. In the aggregate these petty individual contributions reach impressive proportions, where the volume of grain handled is as great as in the case of the Canadian Wheat Pool. For the three years in which such deductions have been made, the following elevator revenues have been accumulated:

TABLE V. POOL ELEVATOR RESERVE FUNDS, 1925–27

	Alberta	Saskatchewan	Manitoba
Deductions, 1925	$442,191	$941,000	$159,579
Deductions, 1926	903,193	2,751,262	379,265
Deductions, 1927	885,748	2,513,637	488,319
Elevator Reserve at end of 1927	$2,231,132	$6,205,899	$1,027,163

As funds are required for elevator purchase or construction, they are invested by the pools in the stock of their respective elevator subsidiaries. Except for the qualifying shares allotted to the directors, this stock is held entirely by the pools, instead of being issued to members. The latter, however, receive each year statements showing the amount of elevator reserve deductions to their credit, upon which interest is allowed at 6 per cent.[1] Although no definite arrangement has yet been made for the redemption of these outstanding elevator reserve certificates, it is anticipated that when the programme of elevator acquisition has been substantially completed, future deductions will be applied, on a revolving plan, to the retirement of certificates covering deductions made in the earlier years.[2]

All pool elevators have been purchased or built upon a purely cash basis, the extent of each year's performance being governed by the size of the pool's actual or anticipated elevator reserve funds. At the annual meeting of the Manitoba Pool in July, 1927, however, the directors were authorized to issue bonds up to $1,000,000 if deemed advisable, for purposes of additional elevator acquisition.[3] If such authorization is availed of, it will constitute the only case, so far, of public capital borrowing by the pools.

Pool Elevator Operating Policies. — At the outset it was contemplated that pool elevators would handle only the grain of contract holders. Their right to do so exclusively has indeed been authorized in the revision of the Canada Grain Act in 1925 following the report of the Turgeon Grain Inquiry Commission. The amendment in question provides that any association of grain producers owning or operating country elevators which it is desired to use exclusively for the handling of its members' grain, may obtain a license from the Board of Grain Commissioners to

[1] In the Alberta and Manitoba Pools each member receives interest payments annually on his elevator reserve deduction certificate. In Saskatchewan interest is credited each year, but becomes payable only at the end of the contract period, when interest-bearing certificates covering each member's total deductions will be issued. Sask. Co-op. Wheat Producers, Handbook No. 2, p. 23.

[2] A recommendation upon this basis was made by the directors of the Saskatchewan Pool in their report for 1926–27, and approved by the delegates at the annual convention. *Western Producer*, Nov. 24, 1927, pp. 2, 8.

[3] *Manitoba Free Press*, July 29, 1927.

operate these as private country elevators, which shall not be obliged to store grain for any person other than the members of such association.[1] In view, however, of the economic desirability of having the largest possible volume of grain pass through their houses as a means of reducing unit operating costs, the pool elevator companies have not seen fit to avail themselves of this statutory right, all their houses being licensed at present as public country elevators. Non-pool grain is handled purely on a storage basis, being billed by the pool elevator to the order of the selling agent designated by the owners.[2] Although not purchasing non-pool street grain, the pool elevators have sought the patronage of wagonload sellers by taking in their grain on a graded storage basis, and shipping it out with pool grain of the same grade in divided-account carload lots.[3]

The organization of coarse-grains pools was largely an outcome of the establishment of pool elevators. Otherwise a wheat pool member who wanted to sell any of his coarse grains for cash would find it necessary to deal with a non-pool elevator. In Alberta, where a coarse-grains pool has not been operated as yet, pool elevators undertake to purchase such grain as a service to members. Thus, considerations of economic elevator operation have led to a compromise with orthodox pooling practice in this regard.

Distribution of Pool Elevator Earnings. — In the endeavor to carry out their "non-profit" policy in relation to elevator operation the pools have encountered certain difficulties. The strict application of the principle would mean charging patrons the actual costs as ascertained at the end of the annual operating period. This would involve, however, not only manifest accounting difficulties, but also variations in charges from year to year according to the volume handled and gains in grades. Conse-

[1] Canada Grain Act (1925), sec. 143(2). At points where there is no other elevator than that owned by such an association, the Board may grant only a license to operate as a public country elevator.

[2] It will be recalled that it was the insistence by the pools that the Sask. Co-op. and U. G. G. elevators should not continue to buy grain on their own account, that deadlocked the negotiations for affiliation of the two systems. See *supra*, p. 232.

[3] During the 1926–27 crop year, 7.92 per cent of the grain handled through Saskatchewan Pool elevators was non-pool grain, while in Manitoba during the same period the proportion was about 5 per cent. — Official information.

quently, it has been found expedient to charge a regular tariff, somewhat below the contract rates with line companies.[1] In the disposal of surpluses realized from these charges and from participation in pool terminal earnings, various plans have been experimented with.

In the case of the Saskatchewan Pool Elevators "surplus" earnings are arrived at after providing for operating costs, operating reserve, depreciation at 5 per cent, and interest due to the liquidators of the Saskatchewan Co-op., to the Saskatchewan government, and to the pool on account of elevator reserve advances. Out of profits earned during the 1925–26 pool year, together with share of surplus realised from pool terminals operated by the Central Selling Agency, the Saskatchewan Pool Elevators made a patronage payment aggregating $474,614. This was distributed in the form of a return of 2 cents a bushel on wheat and 1 cent on coarse grains delivered through pool elevators, and of 1½ cents on wheat and ½ cent on coarse grains shipped over platform to pool terminals.[2] This was done admittedly as an experiment and as an inducement to patronize pool elevators.[3] The policy was sharply criticized, however, by a considerable number of pool members, who claimed that it discriminated against contract holders who were inaccessible to pool elevators, or whose grain could not be taken in, owing to insufficient capacity. It was

[1] "It was not the intention, when incorporating the subsidiary company for the purpose of operating elevators for the pool, to modify in any way the non-profit principle upon which the pool was organized. Owing to the necessity of operating on a fixed tariff in order to maintain a basis for cost comparison and control, surpluses in the form of excess charges are inavoidable. This also obtains in the operation of the Canadian Co-operative terminals." Sask. Co-op. Wheat Producers, Oct., 1926.

In Saskatchewan pool elevators charge 1¾c. a bushel on "stored to grade" wheat, plus a service charge of ½c. a bushel. On street wheat (less than carload lots) a charge of 4c. (formerly 5c) is now made. A similar tariff is charged by Alberta Pool Elevators. In Manitoba a uniform initial charge of 2½c. is made, both wagonload and carload lots being handled on a graded storage basis. The contract rates with line companies for handling street wheat is 5c. on contract grades, and 6c. on lower grades. The corresponding contract charges by U. G. G. elevators on pool wheat are 4c. and 5c. — Official information.

[2] Sask. Co-op. Wheat Producers, Oct. 1926.

[3] See "Problems of Distribution of Elevator Earnings," in *Western Producer*, Feb. 10, 1927.

also pointed out that pool elevator acquisition had been made possible by deductions from all members, whereas under such distribution only a limited number of favored members participated in surplus earnings of these elevators.[1] As a result, it was decided at the annual meeting of Saskatchewan Pool delegates in October, 1926, that any elevator surplus realized during the following year should be retained for the purpose of extending the elevator facilities of the pool. Patrons were to be credited, however, with their share of such surplus, with interest at 6 per cent, as in the case of elevator reserve deductions.

At the end of the 1926–27 pool year the net surplus realised by the Saskatchewan Pool Elevators (including terminals) reached the impressive figure of $1,372,538. In view of the wide extension of the pool elevator system within that year, and in view of the non-acceptance by the liquidators of the Saskatchewan Co-op. of the pool's offer to prepay the balance of the purchase price,[2] the delegates to the Saskatchewan Pool convention in November, 1927, carried a resolution authorising the distribution of the surplus elevator earnings to patrons on the basis of a return of 1¾ cents a bushel on all grain handled through pool country elevators, and of one cent a bushel on grain shipped to Saskatchewan Pool terminals over platform or diverted from line elevators.[3] The action of the Saskatchewan Pool has thus followed pragmatic lines, representing a compromise between the orthodox pool principle of non-profit operation, and the policy of reinvesting surplus earnings as practised by the farmers' elevators companies.

In Alberta no attempt has been made to credit or distribute elevator surplus to individual members on a patronage basis. Instead, the profits of Alberta Pool Elevators and the province's share of the surplus earnings of pool lakehead terminals are taken into general pool revenue and applied against pool operating expenses.[4] This plan possesses the merit of simplicity in accounting, and of distribution for common benefit.

[1] A number of such criticisms, which appeared in the "Open Forum" page of the *Western Producer*, are reproduced in *Facts on Grain Marketing*, pp. 20–22, issued by the Northwest Grain Dealers' Association.

[2] See *supra*, p. 237.

[3] *Western Producer*, Nov. 24, 1927, pp. 2, 8.

[4] Official information.

In Manitoba a unique plan of non-profit operation has been adopted in connection with that province's system of local co-operative elevator associations and patronage contracts. So far as possible the grain of all members using pool elevators is handled on a graded storage basis — whether delivered in wagonload or carload lots, street spreads thus being eliminated. For such services patrons are charged a flat rate of $2\frac{1}{2}$ cents a bushel. If the revenue at this rate should prove insufficient to cover all the "costs" for which the local association is liable under its leasing arrangement with the Manitoba Pool Elevators,[1] the deficit is to be made up by the necessary proportional deductions from the local member-patrons' final pool payment. If, on the other hand, a local surplus is realised, it is credited to members in proportion to their individual patronage. This amount, together with half the annual 10 per cent "depreciation" charge, stands to the credit of members of the local association as a reserve fund bearing interest at 7 per cent. Such sums (which are available for the redemption of Manitoba Pool Elevators stock invested by the pool from elevator reserve deductions) represent the equity of the association members in the local elevator. In this way surplus elevator earnings are applied to the liquidation of capital cost, being converted into what is equivalent to patrons' stock dividends. At the end of the first year's operations of the Manitoba Pool Elevators, revenues from its eight houses (including premiums allowed on shipments to pool terminals) yielded a net surplus of $28,878 (after providing for physical depreciation at 5 per cent and interest at 7 per cent on capital investment of $97,079). This represented a realised equity by the associations of nearly 30 per cent in a single year.[2] While distinctly complicated in its working, the Manitoba Pool Elevator scheme represents an ingenious attempt to apply the coöperative, non-profit principle to elevator acquisition and operation.

[1] See Appendix H, sec. 5.

[2] Directors report, Manitoba Wheat Pool, 1926; *The Scoop Shovel*, Aug. 1926. During 1926–27 the pool elevator at Sperling, Manitoba (of 60,000 bushels capacity) showed a turnover of 400,000 bushels. Revenues from handling, storage and cleaning charges, grade gains and overages, sale of screenings and premiums, yielded a net surplus to members equivalent to the entire cost of the elevator. This represents, of course, an exceptional showing. *Western Producer*, Nov. 24, 1927, p. 47.

Pool Terminal Policy. — The possession of their own terminal elevators is of great value to the pools. In recent years terminal operations have tended to become the most profitable branch of the elevator business. This has come about largely owing to various orders-in-council and rules of the Board of Grain Commissioners since 1917,[1] which have had the effect of making it legal for licensed private terminal elevators to combine the operations of mixing houses, hospital elevators, and public terminal warehouses.[2] Thus profits are derived from storage charges, overages, sale of screenings, and gains in grade through reconditioning and mixing.[3] As a result, most terminal elevators now operate under private in preference to public licenses,[4] and country lines have come to be valued more largely as feeders to terminals than as sources of local profit. Among country elevator operators the practice has developed of forwarding farmers' street grain, as well as company purchased grain, to terminals which their companies own or in which they have an investment interest. In cases where such relationship does not exist, competition has led to the payment of premiums to country elevators for shipment or diversion to private terminals of grain which they control.

When the pools, through their Central Selling Agency, entered the terminal field in 1924–25, they found themselves handicapped by not being able to control the movement of pool wheat into their own terminals. Under their handling contracts with elevator companies, the latter were free to forward pool grain to terminals of their own selection,[5] which were naturally those in which they were financially interested. Delivery into pool terminals, where obtained, usually involved the payment of a special diversion

[1] See *supra*, pp. 143, 144.

[2] The nature and effect of these regulations are discussed at length in *Report of Royal Grain Inquiry Commission*, 1925, pp. 75–82.

[3] See *supra*, pp. 150, 151.

[4] In 1926 all but 7 of the 26 terminal elevators on the Thunder Bay waterfront were licensed as private terminals. *Can. Grain Trade Year Book*, 1925–26. Although receipts issued by private terminals are registered by the Board of Grain Commissioners as to quantity only, those of "private regular" houses are registered by the Winnipeg Grain Exchange as to grade as well as quantity, and are guaranteed by it in settlement of future contracts. *Report of Grain Inquiry Commission*, 1925, p. 81.

[5] See Appendix G, secs. 14, 15.

premium.[1] This situation led to a twofold development. In the first place, it was an important consideration — as previously noted — in bringing about the decision of the pools to acquire country elevators of their own, through which their grain could be shipped to pool terminals.[2] In the second place, it led to the demand by the pools and Western farmers generally for an amendment to the Grain Act which would definitely recognize the right, to which the farmer, it was contended, had always been entitled under the Act (prior to amendment in 1925) of having his street grain delivered to such terminal elevator as he might designate himself.[3] In the past the grower had not usually been interested in exercising this right. If he delivered his grain to a Saskatchewan "Co-op" or U. G. G. elevator, it would naturally be shipped to the terminals of these farmers' companies. If he patronized a line elevator, it was a matter of relative indifference to which terminal it was shipped, since all were subject to supervision by the Board of Grain Commissioners. Thus, in practice, the selection of the terminal generally lay with the elevator operator. With the pools operating their own terminals, however, the destination of pool deliveries became a matter of direct concern to contract holders. In the meantime, the legal right of terminal designation had been lost to the farmer under the amendment of 1925.

A bill to make the farmers' former right effective was introduced in Parliament in 1926. The intervention of a general election, however, left it in suspense, and it was reintroduced as a government measure in the new House. Although the bill was strongly opposed by grain trade interests in the hearings of the Banking and Commerce Committee of the Senate in both ses-

[1] Annual Report, Sask. Wheat Pool, Oct., 1926. [2] See *supra*, pp. 229, 230.

[3] Section 159 (2), covering the billing of grain to terminals, provided that grain in carload lots might be forwarded, if *either* owner or elevator company so desired, to any terminal elevator in the Western Inspection Division. In the general revision of the Grain Act in 1925, following the Report of the Turgeon Commission, this section was amended — contrary to the Turgeon recommendation — to read that the *owner* might specify the terminal *point* (not the terminal elevator) to which his grain should be billed. The change was strongly supported by Mr. Crerar, on the ground that the privilege of terminal disposal made it possible for country elevators to take narrower spreads on street grain and give better grades.

sions, its enactment was secured in April, 1927. By virtue of this Campbell amendment, as it is known, elevator companies are now bound to deliver the farmers' stored grain in such terminal as he designates, while still being responsible for the grade and weight as shown on his storage ticket.[1] Thus, with rapidly expanding country elevator systems of their own, and with their members able to have their grain — even if delivered through non-pool elevators — concentrated in the extensive terminal facilities which they now control, the pools are in a position to realize for themselves the full gains arising from terminal handling and mixing operations.[2]

While the possession of their own elevator facilities is thus proving of distinct advantage to the pools, the effects of their activities in this field are being seriously felt by the established elevator companies. The taking over of the Saskatchewan "Co-op" system by the provincial pool, it is true, involved merely a change in farmer ownership of elevators whose competition had previously existed. At other points selected for pool elevators, however, the existing companies generally find themselves confronted by the alternatives of selling their houses at the pool's price, or meeting the competition of new elevators to which they are likely to lose the handling not only of most pool grain, but also of a certain amount of non-pool grain, owing to the superior facilities offered by the more modern pool elevators. The effect is probably most marked at pool points in Manitoba where patronage contracts are insisted upon, and where many of the existing elevators show a high degree of obsolescence. The operations of the pools also mean a very marked contraction in the volume of grain offered for sale on street, from which country elevators have been accustomed to derive most of their profits. Under the operation of the Campbell amendment, the opportunities of supplementing country earnings by terminal profits and premiums promise to be appreciably restricted.[3] It was predicted, indeed,

[1] Stat. of Canada, 17–18 Geo. V, c. 41, 1927.

[2] The significance of the Campbell amendment from the pool view point is discussed in *Western Producer*, June 10, 1926, and April 7, 1927, and in *The U. F. A.* July 15, 1926.

[3] See *Financial Post*, April 15, 1927.

at the time of its enactment that the line companies would decide to close down their country houses and leave them to be operated by the government. In any case, reduced earnings are to be expected for elevator companies under existing conditions, and a number of the older or unprofitable houses are likely to be closed down. It may, indeed, become necessary to authorize increased maximum handling tariffs for country elevators, to ensure maintenance of adequate service at less remunerative points. In the meantime, the pool elevators appear to be demonstrating the possibility of realizing substantial surpluses from elevator operation at rates below the standard country charges, under conditions of large volume handling and terminal affiliation. In view of all this, amalgamation among line companies may be expected as the answer of the trade to the aggressive competition of the pools.

III. Marketing Policies of the Canadian Wheat Pool

In concentrating the marketing of their grain through the Central Selling Agency the provincial pools have sought, not merely to eliminate competition among themselves, but also to carry out their declared policy of "orderly wheat marketing," "eliminating speculation," "stabilizing the wheat market," and "reducing the margin between producer and consumer."[1] As a marketing institution the Central Selling Agency possesses at least three substantial advantages. (*a*) It enjoys assured long-term control over more than one half of the wheat deliveries and about a third of the coarse-grain marketings in Western Canada. (*b*) It operates under the minimum of risk and of marketing cost, since it does not buy grain from the farmer, but acts merely as his unrestricted selling agent, making an initial advance on delivery, and having no purchase price to cover, or selling price to guarantee. Thus hedging costs are eliminated and borrowing costs substantially reduced. (*c*) Having command over its own extensive terminal facilities, it can control its shipments eastward or westward, and carry on mixing operations based on a wide delivery of grades. It is instructive to examine how far the Canadian Co-

[1] See Preamble to Wheat Pool Contract, Appendix E; also *Wheat Pool Lectures*, No. 8.

operative Wheat Producers, possessing the above advantages, have found it possible or practicable to carry out the marketing aims and policies proclaimed by pool leaders and organizations.

"Orderly Marketing." — During the pool sign-up campaigns, few claims were more frequently made than that prices to farmers under the competitive, speculative system were invariably depressed through the dumping of grain during the fall months, and that under the pooling system sales could be more evenly distributed throughout the year. In its more naïve statement, the principle of "orderly marketing" was represented as the selling of approximately uniform quantities each month in accordance with the periodic uniformity of consumption.

Observers and critics of pool operations have called attention to the statistics of grain deliveries at terminals before and since the advent of the pools, as evidence that their participation and policy have not brought about any more even movement.[1] For the four years preceding the establishment of the Central Selling Agency, 70.3 per cent of the total grain shipments from country points were made during the three months of September, October, and November. During the corresponding months of 1924 when the three pools were in operation, deliveries amounted to 68.5 per cent of the total for the 1924–25 crop year. During the second pool year the proportion for these months was 70.1 per cent. In the export of wheat from Canada for the four-year period 1920–24, an average of 58.3 per cent of the total shipments moved out during the four months September–December (the average being considerably affected by the early and relatively small crop of 1922). For the crop year 1924–25, the proportion of total wheat exports during the above months was 55.4 per cent, and for 1925–26 it amounted to 54.3 per cent.[2] In the light of these figures it has been asserted that "there is no evidence that pool policy has done anything to modify the early rush of wheat out of Canada or to hold back any bigger proportion to the end of the season." [3]

[1] See *Facts on Grain Marketing*, issued by Northwest Grain Dealers' Association, pp. 16, 18, 19.

[2] *Canadian Grain Trade Year Books* for years cited.

[3] Address of W. Sanford Evans before Grain Dealers' National Association at Buffalo, Oct. 19, 1926.

Grain shipments in Canada, however, do not afford any direct measure of grain sales. The forwarding of grain from country stations, through inspection points, to terminals represents a movement from congested country storage to selling and shipping position before the close of inland navigation. Grain in store at terminals is grain which has been officially graded and cleaned of dockage, and which is in position to command spot prices and be tendered in fulfilment of future contracts. Particularly in seasons when weather conditions cause a large proportion of the crop to be "tough," damp, or frosted, the initial movement represents to such extent the transfer of "off-grade" grain to terminal drying plants or hospital elevators where it can be reconditioned. So far as street grain enters into the movement, corresponding hedging sales will be made by elevator companies on the futures market; and in so far as such grain is promptly resold, and as carload shippers give instructions to commission houses or departments to sell on arrival, the cash market trading will reflect such deliveries. The movement of pool grain, however, — whether street, stored, or platform, — does not involve either hedging sales or cash consignment sales by individual shippers. It represents rather a physical concentration of pool deliveries at strategic points.[1] Thus, while the Pool's participation has not involved any change in the initial movement of grain, it does mean that the sales during this period of the grain so delivered by pool members are determined by one, instead of by some 140,000 individual sellers.

Misleading conclusions may be drawn from the statistics of Canadian wheat exports. Wheat rushed out of lakehead terminals before the close of navigation, and stored at Buffalo or other American lower lake ports for seaboard export or delivery to eastern mills during the winter months, appears as an export from Canada in customs returns.[2] Thus heavy fall shipments of pool wheat to the pool transfer elevator at Buffalo, in order to take

[1] "The impression that farmers who held their wheat back were helping the pool is wrong. Wheat should be moved to selling position in the fall as rapidly as it can be got out." A. J. McPhail, in *Western Producer*, Nov. 11, 1926.

[2] Of lake shipments from Fort William–Port Arthur, aggregating 249,000,000 bushels of wheat in 1925–26, — a representative year, — 132,600,000 bushels were delivered at American lake ports. *Grain Trade Year Book*, 1925–26.

advantage of cheaper freight rates by water, would be recorded as Canadian exports at such times, but would represent movement into advanced selling position rather than delivery of sales, and as such would constitute the essence of orderly and economical marketing.

Figures of terminal deliveries or export shipments cannot be taken, therefore, as an index of the distribution of actual sales by the Pool. Even Grain Exchange members can only guess at the day-to-day marketings of the Central Selling Agency, since three quarters of its sales in 1925–26 were made directly to foreign millers or importers,[1] and some of the transactions which it does make on the trading floor are executed through cash brokers. Until recently the nearest public indication given by a pool official as to the distribution of its marketing was to be found in the statement made at the International Wheat Pool conference in Kansas City in May, 1927, by D. L. Smith, General Sales Manager of the C. S. A., that in the handling of 187,000,000 bushels of the 1925 crop, the Canadian Pool did not sell more than 20,000,000 bushels in any one month of the year.[2] He added, however: "We did not adopt any definite policy as to the quantity to be sold in any

[1] Statement by D. L. Smith at Kansas City, May 7, 1927.

[2] In the report of the Central Selling Agency for 1926–27 figures showing monthly deliveries and sales of pool wheat were published for the first time. These were as follows:

		Deliveries	Sales
Carryover 1926		10,319,764	
15/20	Sept. 1926	28,484,500	10,417,555
	Oct.	26,434,164	14,814,308
	Nov.	43,131,886	20,481,982
	Dec.	23,245,397	20,123,190
	Jan. 1927	17,154,266	17,319,700
	Feb.	9,695,512	13,714,785
	March	8,966,533	14,552,133
	April	7,386,050	15,662,517
	May	14,610,541	21,774,818
	June	5,322,172	14,290,607
	July	13,623,951	7,349,960
	Aug.	1,103,340	17,131,482
	Sept.	23,402	14,449,470
Carryover 1927		....	7,418,971
		209,501,478	209,501,478

month, our selling being governed entirely by demand, prices obtainable, and general world conditions." At the same gathering, President Wood of the Alberta Pool made the following declaration:

> "Orderly marketing" is a dangerous phrase. Too frequently it is taken to mean the systematic placing of wheat on the market in equal portions, day by day or month by month. This may be "orderly dumping," but it is not marketing in any sense of the word. The selling of wheat is a purely business proposition, and the Pool must decide when it is best to sell or hold, just as the buyers have to decide when to buy or not to buy.

It has been admitted by officials of the Pool that in the marketing of the 1924 crop somewhat too large a proportion was held back, which had to be sold at a lower price than might have been realized if sold before the prospects of a largely increased wheat production in 1925 had exercised their influence upon the market.[1] In a speech in November, 1926, President McPhail of the Canadian Co-operative Wheat Producers declared:

> There is a bigger demand for Canadian wheat in the fall months than at any other season, and a much larger quantity can be disposed of now than in other months. You have to sell when the demand exists or you will find yourself holding the bag in your hands. We have already had that experience to some extent.[2]

In such statements there is to be perceived an accommodation of pool marketing policy to the realities of the world's wheat trade, and a recognition that orderly marketing does not involve any appreciable change in the established movement of Canadian wheat into export markets. The latter, indeed, goes on in a much more even and orderly manner than the actual distribution of farmers' deliveries and terminal shipments would suggest. In 1923–24, when the Alberta Pool alone was in operation, and — that belatedly, — there was shipped from Canadian and United States ocean ports in the first quarter of the shipping year, September–November, 24.4 per cent of the total overseas exports of Canadian wheat, in the second quarter 26.8 per cent, in the third quarter 27.2 per cent, and in the last quarter 21.6 per cent; or, in the first half year 51.2 per cent, and in the second half 48.8 per

[1] Personal information. [2] *Western Producer*, Nov. 11, 1926.

cent.[1] Under the individual competitive system, however, the relatively even export sales are made mostly by dealers who have bought their wheat from elevator companies, who in turn have purchased it from farmers whose marketings show a high degree of seasonal concentration, reflected normally in lower seasonal cash prices, especially for street wheat. In other words, it is through the middleman that the irregularity of the primary movement and selling is converted into the relatively even flow of export distribution, from which service the middleman derives his profit. Under the pool system, the Central Selling Agency performs this function, but with this significant difference, that while deliveries by farmers remain much the same as before, individual selling by pool farmers is eliminated. The day-to-day sales made by the Pool on behalf of its members are based, not on deliveries, but on current international demand; and it is the averaged returns realized from such final sales that the pool member receives. The "orderliness" of pool marketing, in short, lies not in any more measured movement of wheat from farm to consuming market, but in unified selling on the basis of the available knowledge of world supply and demand conditions.

Direct Selling. — Closely related to the idea of "orderly marketing" as an objective of the pooling system has been that of "direct selling" and "elimination of speculative trading." Under ordinary conditions it is possible for the farmer's street wheat to pass through half a dozen middleman hands before it reaches European millers. The elevator company which buys at country points may sell to a "lake shipper" — not infrequently through the medium of cash grain brokers. Shippers generally buy as correspondents of eastern exporters located chiefly in New York or Montreal, who take delivery at lower lake ports (principally Buffalo), Montreal, or Atlantic ports.[2] The seaboard exporters in turn largely sell to European importers, or traders who resell to millers. At every exchange, purchases or sales will be hedged on future markets. Marketing will be more direct, of course,

[1] Cited by W. Sanford Evans, *loc. cit.*

[2] See T. D. Hammatt, "Marketing Canadian Wheat," U. S. Department of Commerce, *Trade Information Bulletin, No. 251,* pp. 99–102. There are about forty firms in Winnipeg operating as "lake shippers."

where elevator companies operate export departments or subsidiaries, or where Winnipeg buyers are themselves exporting houses.[1]

In the first year's operations of the Alberta Pool, all its wheat was sold on the Grain Exchange. In the first year's operation of the Central Selling Agency, also, about 60 per cent of its wheat was sold on the open market. Efforts were early made, however, to establish overseas connections, and in 1925–26 about 75 per cent of the wheat which it handled was exported directly. For 1926–27, the proportion of direct sales to importers and millers was about the same.[2]

In addition to its main office at Winnipeg, the Central Selling Agency maintains a western sales office at Calgary through which most of the Alberta Pool deliveries are handled.[3] A Toronto office has charge of sales to eastern millers, and will handle grain for the affiliated grain pool recently organized by the United Farmers of Ontario. At Fort William, Port Arthur, Vancouver, Montreal, and New York, offices are maintained to look after the chartering of shipping space and the loading and insurance of export shipments. Special connections have been established with some of the larger British milling and importing firms, and in France its sales are concentrated through its Paris agency, 80 per cent of all Canadian wheat shipped to France in 1925–26 being purchased directly from the Pool. Altogether 28 agencies have

[1] "There are probably not more than four or five strictly Canadian firms that sell any considerable quantity of wheat directly to foreign countries." *Ibid.*, p. 99.

[2] For 1926–27 the sales of the Central Selling Agency were distributed as follows:

Wheat			Coarse Grains		
Domestic	77,947,199	bus.	Local	17,353,226	bus.
Exports:			Eastern	4,334,587	"
Via Eastern Canada	107,802,000	"	Export	1,489,492	"
Via Western Canada	16,333,308	"			
Total	202,082,507	"		23,177,305	"

— Directors Report, Can. Co-op. Wheat Producers, 1926–27.

[3] During 1926 pool officials visited Japan and China, with a view to the development of Oriental markets and connections. A large part of Canadian wheat exports to the Orient from Vancouver, and all those from Prince Rupert, are pool shipments.

been established in fifteen importing countries.[1] In addition to the British Isles and France, these include Germany, Holland, Belgium, Sweden, Denmark, Switzerland, Italy, Greece, Portugal, Mexico, Brazil, and China. With a view to maintaining more direct contact with its Continental agencies, and keeping the Central more intimately informed concerning European conditions, an office was opened in London at the end of 1927, in charge of Mr. D. L. Smith, formerly Export Sales Manager.[2]

It will thus be seen that within the three years of its existence the Canadian Wheat Pool has largely realized its aim of direct selling. It has not initiated integration in grain marketing, but it has realized it more completely and applied it on a much larger scale than any competing agency. To the extent that it is able to reduce the number of separate middleman transactions, to eliminate the costs of hedging, to secure shipping space on more favorable terms, owing to the greater volume and regularity of its shipments, and to the extent that it has been able to handle increased deliveries without a proportionate increase in selling expenses, it is in a position to reduce the margin between pool producers and world consumers. In such a highly organized and competitive business as the grain trade, however, the potential economies are much more limited than in the case of less staple agricultural products. Whether or not the net returns of pool farmers have been increased as a result of the Pool's selling policy will not be examined at this point.[3] The significant thing is that, instead of selling his wheat at a speculatively discounted world price, the grower, through the Pool, is receiving the actual price in world markets less the specific costs of getting his product there.

Effect of Pool Selling Policy on Canadian Milling Industry. — The direct selling policy of the Canadian Wheat Pool has recently elicited protests from Canadian millers as being discriminatory to their industry. At a meeting of the Canadian National Millers' Association in Toronto in May, 1927, the following resolution was adopted:

[1] Canadian Co-operative Wheat Producers, Department of Publicity.

[2] "Structure and Functions of Central Selling Agency," *Western Producer*, Nov. 24, 1927.

[3] This matter is considered below, pp. 464–474.

Whereas it has repeatedly been reported that the Pool has sold wheat abroad to foreign millers at prices less than those offered at the same time to Canadian millers — and as this method has reached such an extent as to actually imperil the existence of the milling industry in Canada, therefore be it

Resolved, that the executives of the Canadian National Millers' Association, representing over 75 per cent of the milling industry in Canada, do protest in the strongest terms the continuance of the practice, and do strongly urge the directors of the Canadian Co-operative Wheat Producers, Ltd., to stand behind the Canadian industry by at once putting into effect some such rigid plan or rules as will prevent sales being made abroad at less than the equivalent prices given to Canadian buyers.[1]

There would appear to be little doubt that the operations of the Canadian Wheat Pool have tended to reduce the profits of Canadian millers. In the case of milling companies operating their own lines of country elevators, the presence of the pools and of pool elevators means that there is a much more restricted quantity and range of farmers' wheat available for purchase at country points than in the days when mill elevators could select the cream of the grades hauled to local shipping stations.[2] In the case of mills buying wheat on the Winnipeg Grain Exchange, the policy of the Pool in selling as much as possible of its wheat directly, means that a smaller volume is offered upon the cash market, and that premiums may have to be paid at times to secure the grade and quantity desired. In other words, there is a tendency at such times for Winnipeg cash prices to be a reflection of domestic demand rather than of world demand. Thus, in respect both to country purchasing and buying on the grain exchange, Canadian millers are finding it necessary to bid somewhat higher for their wheat, while on the other hand, the Pool, through its advantages in large volume handling, in chartering tonnage, and in direct selling, may find it possible to quote or accept a somewhat closer price from overseas millers than competing exporters can afford to do. Exports of Canadian flour to the United Kingdom have indeed fallen off within recent years, the figures for the last six fiscal years being as follows:[3]

[1] Quoted in *Northwestern Miller*, May 25, 1927.

[2] *Report of Sask. Elev. Comm.*, 1910, pp. 71, 72.

[3] *Canada Year Books.*

1921–22	4,737,020 bbls.	1924–25	3,274,976 bbls.
1922–23	4,723,527 "	1925–26	2,791,646 "
1923–24	4,234,084 "	1926–27	3,589,007 "

While the falling off in flour exports and milling profits, in comparison with the war-time and post-armistice years, is mainly attributable to such external causes as discontinuance of government purchases, embargoes and greatly increased flour import duties, combined with government blending regulations in European countries, reduced Atlantic freight rates on wheat unaccompanied by corresponding reductions on flour cargoes, and the milling in bond of Canadian wheat at Buffalo, it would seem that the export policy of the Canadian Wheat Pool is not a negligible factor at the present time.[1]

The present attitude of pool officials is that they are concerned with getting the best possible price for the producers' wheat, irrespective of its destination, and that they are not interested in showing preferential consideration to the Canadian milling industry on national or sentimental grounds. They point out that British millers are blenders of world wheat, and are willing to pay a premium on hard Canadian spring wheat for blending purposes, and that the mass of British consumers demand bread from a cheaper flour than Canadian patent flour. British farmers, moreover, being livestock feeders rather than wheat growers, are interested in an abundant supply of mill screenings from imported wheat. Flour exports of Canadian millers should not be dependent upon the securing of domestic wheat below its full world value.[2] On similar grounds the pools have strongly opposed any proposal to impose any export duty on Canadian wheat entering the United States,[3] as suggested for government consideration by the Turgeon Grain Inquiry Commission.[4]

The most equitable arrangement would appear to be for the Pool to sell wheat directly to Canadian as well as foreign millers. Such sales are, indeed, made to eastern Canadian mills through the Pool's Toronto Sales Office. As the outcome of a conference

[1] See *Financial Post*, July 15, 1927.

[2] Statements made to writer. See letter of D. L. Smith to *Northwestern Miller*, May 18, 1927.

[3] See *The U. F. A.*, March 11, April 1, 1926.

[4] *Report*, p. 145.

held in Winnipeg on January 12, 1926, between directors of the Canadian National Millers' Association and the Canadian Co-operative Wheat Producers, the latter agreed to a tentative plan of giving limits on cash wheat to the mills, good until close of market the following day.[1] It was claimed by the Millers' Association, however, that the limits so given were unduly above the closing prices. Pool officials, on the other hand, declared that millers bought on the Exchange instead of from the Pool, whenever there appeared to be any advantage in so doing. The arrangement was accordingly abandoned.

While the operations of the Pool involve a certain readjustment in the Canadian milling industry, the former is not in a position to exercise a monopoly advantage. It will not intentionally sell wheat abroad for any lower net price than it can realize at home. Nor can it afford to allow the bulk of wheat sales to the domestic milling industry to fall to non-pool sellers. It is possible indeed for the Pool to overreach itself by concentrating upon overseas sales. The British wheat market is a more highly competitive one than the domestic market, and unduly large forward sales or consignments abroad may mean at times the realization of a smaller return than could have been obtained from larger sales in Canadian markets.[2] The Pool cannot afford to injure the Canadian milling industry, or give grounds for complaint of discrimination against domestic flour consumers. Moreover, it is in the long-run interest of Western Canadian agriculture that a well-established milling industry should develop in the Prairies Provinces, not merely as a means of realizing local premiums on preferred milling grades, but, even more significantly, as a home source of mill feeds through which the exhaustible plant food elements can be more largely returned to the soil. On the other hand, the Canadian milling industry must accommodate itself to conditions in which the positions of wheat producer and mill buyer are more evenly balanced than in former years. Accommodation will probably be realized through the negotiation of new direct selling arrangements between pool and millers, and through the functioning of

[1] *Northwestern Miller*, May 25, 1927.

[2] See article by A. H. Bailey, *Northwestern Miller*, May 4, 1927.

an organized Winnipeg sample market, which has been discussed by every royal grain commission, and provided for in the Canada Grain Act, but which has not as yet been established on a commercial basis.[1]

Elimination of Speculation. — While the virtue of the pooling method as a means of eliminating speculation has been much emphasized by pool propagandists, the Canadian Wheat Pool has found it expedient to make certain use of the future market. Although under no need of making hedging sales against its members' deliveries, it does not eliminate the necessity for hedging on the part of those to whom it sells cash grain. In selling cash wheat to millers on the Winnipeg Exchange, it is the practice of the Central Selling Agency to take their hedging options in exchange, so that the immediate sale of these may not have a depressing effect upon the market. These options are disposed of by the Pool as it finds most advantageous.[2]

Although selling the greater part of its grain off the floor of the Exchange, the Pool also makes sales for future delivery "when prices look attractive."[3] This, however, is merely a forward disposal of grain which the Pool already controls. As an exporter the Pool has no interest in temporarily depressing Winnipeg prices through short selling on the future market, with a view to buying wheat for shipment at the widest possible margin below the overseas selling prices.[4] It is interested rather in maintaining consistently high prices on the Winnipeg market, since it is only exceptionally anything but a seller upon it.[5] To the extent that it

[1] See *supra*, pp. 143, 144; *Report of Royal Grain Inquiry Commission*, 1925, pp. 106–108.

[2] Alberta Co-op. Wheat Producers, *Wheat Pool Lectures*, p. 22.

[3] Evidence of C. M. Elliott before Royal Grain Inquiry Commission, *Report*, p. 131.

[4] In an address before the American Institute of Coöperation at Chicago, on June 23, 1927, President Burnell of the Manitoba Pool made the assertion that one of the biggest accomplishments of the Canadian Pool was in taking away the control of the price of wheat on the Winnipeg option market from the three big exporting companies, which entirely controlled that market from the time the Canadian Wheat Board was discontinued in 1920, until the Canadian Pool began to operate its Selling Agency in 1924.

[5] Open market purchases have been made at times by the Central Selling Agency to complete shipments of particular grades. In 1926–27 these amounted to 2,691,472

succeeds, it incidentally benefits farmers selling independently of the Pool. During the speculative reaction on the Winnipeg market in the spring of 1925, following the sensational advances of the preceding winter, the Pool entered the futures market on occasions as a buyer, with a view to exercising a stabilizing influence upon prices which were known to be lower than the real market conditions warranted.[1] During the latter part of the crop year, when the greater portion of the existing Canadian wheat surplus is controlled by the Pool, it is able to exercise very considerable influence on the Winnipeg market. Under these conditions, its interest, of course, is in keeping prices there as close as possible to those in world markets.[2]

In the broad sense of assuming the risk of future price fluctuations, speculation cannot be eliminated by any pool. The pooling system merely shifts the carrying of such risks from specialized middlemen to producer-members as a whole. With a single seller, as in the case of the Canadian Wheat Board, the futures market may be dispensed with. But so long as the Canadian Wheat Pool is merely the largest of a number of sellers, future trading will continue. So far as the Pool's influence is effective, however, it is in the direction of stabilization at world-price levels.

bushels of wheat and 1,300,962 bushels of coarse grains. — Can. Co-op. Wheat Producers, 1926–27.

[1] Official information.

[2] In addressing the International Wheat Pool Conference at Kansas City, May 5, 1927, Mr. D. L. Smith made the following statement: "With a very large proportion of non-pool grain marketed before the end of the year, we are in a position after January of being practically in control of the entire Canadian wheat surplus. This, of course, gives us a wonderful advantage, as our policy of securing as high a price as general world conditions warrant meets no interference by the selling of individual traders."

PART IV

RESULTS AND TENDENCIES IN THE GRAIN GROWERS' COÖPERATIVE MOVEMENT

CHAPTER XVII

EXPERIENCES IN COÖPERATIVE SUPPLY

I. Initial Enterprises in Collective Purchasing

While the organized activities of the Western Grain Growers have been mainly directed toward securing for producers a larger share of the world market price of wheat through reduction and redistribution of marketing margins, the possibilities of applying collective action with a view to reducing costs of farm production have also been pursued. Efforts in the latter direction have taken two principal forms. In the first place, the farmers' organizations, acting jointly through the Canadian Council of Agriculture, have exerted collective representation and political pressure toward bringing about reduction of tariff duties on commodities entering into farm production and consumption. In the second place, collective purchasing has been undertaken with a view to narrowing the spread between the manufacturing or importing costs and the prices paid by growers for farm supplies. Enterprises in the latter field have been prosecuted, on the one hand, by the United Grain Growers, continuing the earlier efforts of its constituent farmers' elevator companies, and on the other hand, by the Saskatchewan Grain Growers' Association. The policies and methods pursued, the relations involved, and the results realized, constitute an instructive chapter in the history and technique of Grain Growers' coöperation in Western Canada. The tariff policies of the organized farmers belong rather to the history of the political activities of the Grain Growers, and will be considered here only incidentally.

Early Undertakings by Grain Growers' Grain Company. — The possibilities of utilizing the Grain Growers' Grain Company as a farmers' purchasing as well as selling agency were considered at an early stage of the company's existence. The grain grower was at scarcely less disadvantage in buying singly than in selling individually. While selling on a wholesale market, he ordinarily purchased his producer's goods as well as his consumer's goods at retail. As the operation of the farmer-owned marketing agency made him less dependent on "the elevator combine," so the establishment of facilities for collective purchasing through the farmers' company would tend, it was felt, to make him less dependent on manufacturers' and dealers' selling combinations, and permit realization of the economies of bulk distribution. It was, indeed, primarily with a view to entering the field of coöperative supply that the Grain Growers' Grain Company had sought the extensive powers enumerated in the federal charter obtained in 1911,[1] authorizing the company "to produce, manufacture, import, buy, sell, and deal in all machinery, implements, goods, wares, and merchandise which may be utilized in the production of the products of the farm, or in the maintenance, cultivation, improvement, and development of the farm."[2] The effective exercise of such powers involved, however, a distinctly different relationship between the company and its farmer patrons than in the case of grain marketing. As the selling agent of the carload shipper, the company dealt individually with the grain grower. But while many farmers were individual carload-sellers, few were individual carload-purchasers. If the potential economies of bulk distribution were to be realized, the company as a supply agency must deal with its patrons as local groups. Coöperative supply implies not merely centralized buying, but also local trading organization.

Problem of Local Distribution. — The history of consumers' coöperation in Europe and elsewhere shows that the initiative has usually been taken by local associations which have subsequently united for the purpose of larger-scale centralized purchasing. In the Grain Growers' Grain Company the farmers of Western Canada owned a business organization which possessed both the legal powers and the financial resources to undertake wholesale trading. There was lacking, however, the requisite medium of local coöperative distribution. Grain Growers' Association locals, it is true, were to be found actively functioning in most rural districts. They had been organized for other than commercial purposes, however, and they had no organic connection with the

[1] See *supra*, pp. 154, 155. [2] Stat. of Canada, 1 Geo. V, c. 80, 1911, sec. 12.

Grain Growers' Company. Nor were the shareholders of the latter, at the time it secured its federal charter, organized into locals.

The decision of the Grain Growers' Company to lease the deficit-yielding Manitoba government elevators had been considerably influenced, it may be recalled, by the prospect of making the distribution of supplies through these local warehouses during the spring and summer months complementary to the main business of grain storage during the major part of the year, and incidentally permitting the retention of a more permanent staff of elevator agents.[1] The possibility of making these newly acquired elevators local coöperative centres had been emphasized by President Crerar at the annual meeting of the shareholders in 1912:

> We must develop the local unit. . . . There is no doubt whatever that the Company, if it wished, could from its position financially buy such staples as coal, lumber, and flour in bulk, a great deal cheaper than the average farmer can buy individually, and once having bought, could through its organizations in the country, by virtue of its operation of the elevators, distribute much more cheaply than can the average firm handling these commodities.[2]

He proposed that the farmer shareholders tributary to each elevator might elect local committees which could prepare in the spring estimates of the requirements of their members, forward them to the company's headquarters, attend to the local distribution of the supplies so ordered, and act in an advisory capacity to the company's head office. Such business would have to be conducted as far as possible on a cash basis, with provision for credit extension only where approved by the local committee and where secured by the farmer's agreement to have the unpaid amount deducted from the proceeds of his grain when sold through the company's Commission Department.[3] Grain Growers' Association locals might also make collective purchases from the company for distribution to their members.

Nature of Supply Business of Grain Growers' Grain Company. — The first steps in coöperative supply followed closely upon the leasing of the Manitoba government elevators in 1912. Quite

[1] See *supra*, p. 94. [2] G. G. G. Co., 1912. [3] G. G. G. Co., 1912.

naturally the first commodities to be handled were feed and seed grain. Grain below the standard and commercial grades (classed as "feed") and screenings from "cleaners" entered the bins of the elevators in the ordinary course of operations, while farmers who had surplus seed grain to sell were invited to dispose of it through the Grain Growers' Company. This modest beginning provided a convenient but limited means of exchange between the straight grain grower and the general or dairy farmer whose numbers were increasing in Manitoba. The private elevator purchased at Fort William shortly after the leasing of the C. P. R. terminal was first used as a sacking and cleaning establishment, with a view primarily to supplying Ontario farmers with western feed.[1] Similarly, the acquisition about the same time of the 30,000-bushel elevator at New Westminster, B. C., provided facilities for supplying sacked Alberta feed grain to the dairymen and poultrymen of the Pacific coast.[2]

Western farmers entertained a special grievance in the wide spread existing between the price they received for their wheat and the price they had to pay for flour ground from it by western mills.[3] With a view to narrowing this margin, the Grain Growers' Grain Company took over, in the fall of 1913, the Rapid City Flour Mill, with a capacity of 150 barrels a day. The output of this mill was shipped in carload lots to local Grain Growers' associations at a price of $2.60 per bag, after one of the milling companies had quoted the company a price at the mill of $2.80.[4] It was claimed that the 130 carloads of flour supplied by the company during the first season involved an average saving of 50 cents a hundredweight to its customers. A more far-reaching effect was to be found in the action of milling companies in meeting the Grain Growers' competition by undertaking to supply flour to farmers' locals direct from the mill at wholesale prices.[5]

[1] See *supra*, p. 149. [2] See *supra*, pp. 156, 157.

[3] It was claimed that western flour sold in some of the towns in Saskatchewan and Alberta at $3.75 per bag, at a time when the same flour was being retailed in Great Britain at $2.50 per bag. The farm price of No. 1 Northern at this date averaged about 70 cents a bushel, or $1.58 for the wheat equivalent of a 100-pound bag of flour. *G. G. Guide*, Jan. 29, 1913.

[4] G. G. G. Co., 1913. [5] *Farmers in Business, 1906–1916*, p. 12.

During 1913 a separate Co-operative Supply Department was organized at Winnipeg by the Grain Growers' Company, and the handling of coal and apples undertaken, in addition to flour and feed. The coal consumed in the Prairie Provinces is supplied mainly by the bituminous and lignite mines of Alberta, supplemented by westward shipments of Ohio and Pennsylvania coal, brought to the head of the lakes as return cargoes by grain- and ore-carriers. Arrangements were made accordingly with Alberta mine operators and lakehead importers to supply carload shipments to Grain Growers' locals, or to company elevator points where the distribution might be handled by the company's elevator operator. As in the case of coal, the apple supply of the Prairie Provinces, where orchards are unknown, moves both eastward and westward, from British Columbia on the one hand, and Ontario on the other. Frequent suggestions had been made at farmers' conventions attended by fraternal delegates from other provinces, and at meetings of the Canadian Council of Agriculture, of the possibilities of exchanging the products of eastern and western farmers. As the Grain Growers' Company had undertaken to supply western feed to eastern farmers through its Fort William sacking plant, so it now made arrangements with the Ontario Fruit Growers' Association to sell carload lots of apples to western farmers on a commission of 10 cents a barrel. Similar arrangements were later made with British Columbia growers, the company's buyers making seasonal contracts on the basis of advance orders secured through Grain Growers' locals or company elevator agents. In the first year in which coal and apples were handled (1913–14), the company distributed 8926 tons of coal and 5336 barrels of apples.[1]

The rapid transformation of a vast prairie region into improved farms creates a demand of large aggregate proportions for building and fencing materials. The log cabin and "snake" fence of the pioneer settler of Eastern Canada find few reproductions in the Prairie Provinces, except in the more northerly or extreme western portions of the Grain Belt. The enclosing of one half the perimeter of the homesteader's quarter section as one of the statutory

[1] G. G. G. Co., 1914.

"improvements" has called for fence-posts on a large scale, and as the homesteader's sod cabin or tar-paper shack is replaced by the shingled farmhouse and enlarged barns and stables of the permanent farmer, the demand for lumber assumes increasing dimensions. With the exception of small quantities produced by local sawmills in the wooded northern margin of the prairies and in the Rainy River district at the eastern limit, most of the lumber consumed in the Grain Belt is shipped from British Columbia mills. A few big lumber companies maintain retail yards at a large number of country points. Against these concerns, as against elevator and farm machinery "line" companies, the grain grower has been disposed to raise charges of combination, price agreement, and exploitation of the farmer.

The eagerness of Western farmers to lessen their dependence upon these line lumber companies had led the Grain Growers' Company, as far back as 1911, to acquire a controlling interest in a timber limit in Central British Columbia, estimated to contain over 300,000,000 feet of lumber, chiefly spruce, fir, and cedar. While the purchase price was not large, the development of the property had to await the completion of the Grand Trunk Pacific Railway construction through the area in which it was located. Pending the production of lumber from its own timber limit, the company took steps toward providing an immediate lumber supply service for its patrons by purchasing stock in the newly formed Western Farmers' Lumber Company.[1] The Grain Growers' Cooperative Department began handling lumber and fence-posts in March, 1914, 150 carloads being shipped to Grain Growers' locals and individual farmers during that year. As the business grew, a separate Lumber and Builders' Supplies Department was organized, which handled not merely dressed lumber, but also such supplies as shingles, lath, sash and doors, plaster and cement, galvanized roofing, and so forth. This department also undertook to prepare estimates and specifications of assorted lumber and materials required for farmers' individual plans, and to make complete shipments of the same on acceptance of such estimates.[2]

The supply operations of the company's Co-operative Depart-

[1] G. G. G. Co., 1913.

[2] G. G. G. Co., 1914, p. 14.

ment were further extended during 1914 to include wire fencing, binder twine, and farm implements. Under the conditions of large-scale grain growing and harvesting in Western Canada the outlay for binder twine constitutes a very significant item in the farmer's seasonal costs of production. Although binder twine had been free-listed under the Canadian tariff in 1897, the farmer generally purchased it on a retail basis from local stores. The Grain Growers' Company now made arrangements with an Ontario cordage concern to manufacture its own "G. G. G." brand, which it supplied in bulk to local purchasing groups, nearly 2,500,000 pounds being handled during the first season, and 6,750,000 pounds during the second. From replies received to questionnaires addressed to patrons, it was estimated that the company's participation in this line had meant a direct saving to users of $2\frac{1}{4}$ cents per pound on the quantity handled, irrespective of the indirect benefit to other farmers through the company's competition.[1]

Coöperative Handling of Farm Machinery. — There are few grievances which the Western grain grower has been more disposed to magnify than the conditions under which he buys his farm implements and machinery. Operating normally a large acreage, and specializing in cereal crops which make relatively brief but highly concentrated seasonal demands on his labor, he finds a considerable equipment in tillage implements and harvesting machinery indispensable. The danger of crop deterioration through early frosts, and the risk of having to take lower prices if delivery of his grain to the head of the lakes cannot be assured before close of navigation, often make it expedient for the large grain grower to own more than one binder, or to employ tractors to expedite harvesting. The representative Western farmer is thus potentially a purchaser of agricultural machinery up to the limit of his resources or credit.

Owing to geographical and historical circumstances the manufacture of agricultural implements in Canada is highly concentrated in southern Ontario, over a thousand miles from the eastern limits of the western grain belt; whereas in the United States the

[1] G. G. G. Co., 1914, p. 14.

same industry is localized principally in the Mississippi Valley, in the heart of the richest agricultural regions. The heavy freight charges on Canadian implements shipped from Ontario factories to the Western prairies, the necessity of importing at various rates of duty most of the steel bars, rods and plates required in their manufacture, and the more limited opportunities for large-scale production which the Canadian market affords,[1] combine to place the Canadian implement manufacturers at more or less of a disadvantage in supplying the Western farmer in open competition with the great American harvester companies of the Middle West. Canadian manufacturers of agricultural machinery, therefore, had always strongly insisted on their need of tariff protection. Such protective duties were even more strongly resented by Western farmers, to whom the tariff could bring no relief in upholding the prices of their own export products. Their demands became still more insistent after the complete free-listing of agricultural implements in the United States by the Underwood Tariff of 1913. It is true that under persistent agrarian pressure the duties on agricultural implements under the Canadian tariff had been substantially reduced from the high levels established when the National Policy Tariff had been enacted in 1879.[2] In 1914, however, when the Grain Growers' Company commenced to handle farm machinery, the duties on reapers, binders, and mowers stood at 12½ per cent.

The resentment of the Western grain growers was directed, not merely against the moderate tariff protection afforded implement manufacturers, but also against the concentration and combination prevailing in that industry. Most of the general farm-machinery business in Western Canada was in the hands of three

[1] This disadvantage is to no small extent mitigated by the extensive export market in Europe, Australia, and the Argentine, which certain of the older Canadian implement companies had built up. Furthermore, since 1907 a drawback of 99 per cent had been allowed on customs duties paid on certain materials entering into the manufacture of agricultural implements for domestic consumption, as well as for export. Loss of interest on such deferred refunds constituted, however, an appreciable addition to real cost.

[2] Under the Canadian tariff of 1883 the duties on reapers, binders, and mowers had been placed at 35 per cent. In 1894 they were reduced to 20 per cent, in 1906 to 17½ per cent, and in 1914 to 12½ per cent.

or four eastern line companies,[1] who maintained western branch warehouses, and distributed their implements through their own local agents exclusively. The farmer's attitude of suspicion toward these large-scale concerns was very similar to that which he had entertained toward the line elevator companies, and he firmly believed in the existence of price agreements amongst ostensible competitors in the field of implement-selling as of grain buying. He complained particularly of the prices charged for repair parts, for which he was wholly dependent on the maker of the machine. Further grievance was found in the high rate of interest charged on implement notes,[2] and in the frequent action of company agents in pressing farmers to liquidate the same by selling their crops immediately after threshing, with depressing effect on the market.

In investigating the possibilities of handling farm machinery, the Grain Growers' management found that the large line companies were not willing to prejudice their own distributing organization by supplying their standard lines to the farmer company for competitive distribution.[3] As it was out of the question to negotiate with smaller Canadian concerns which were not capable of turning out complete lines of farm machinery, and whose permanent ability to supply repair parts was not assured, the

[1] Of which the largest were the Massey-Harris Company of Toronto, and the International Harvester Company of Canada at Hamilton, Ontario. The latter had been established to develop the parent company's patents and processes within the Canadian tariff.

[2] The rates charged ranged generally between 8 and 10 per cent. Evidence of Massey-Harris Company before Special House Committee on Agricultural Conditions, Ottawa, May 2, 1923.

[3] The attitude of the line companies is clearly expressed in the evidence given by Mr. Thomas Bradshaw, General Manager of the Massey-Harris Co. before the special parliamentary Committee on Agriculture, on May 2, 1923. "The Massey-Harris Co. has built up, over a period of 74 years, an agency organization. It has in Canada approximately 2500 agents; it markets its product direct from the factory to the consumer through its own agents, not through middlemen concerns. If we sold to the United Grain Growers or any other middle concern, it would be impossible for us to control the prices of our goods to the farmer, as it would mean that the U. G. G. and other concerns could charge any price they like to the farmer for our goods. It would spoil the whole of our agency organization and their agents would be in competition with ours. Those are the reasons why we cannot sell to the United Grain Growers or any other concern in Canada."

Grain Growers' Company decided, after considerable inquiry and negotiation, to establish importing connections with independent implement companies in the American Middle West. Accordingly, arrangements were made with the La Crosse Plow Company of La Crosse, Wisconsin, for the farmers' company to act as Canadian distributors for plows and tillage tools of all descriptions, and with the Abingdon Wagon Company of Abingdon, Illinois, to handle wagons and trucks. Contracts were also closed with other American and Canadian concerns for supplying special lines, such as gas engines, tractors, grain grinders, fanning mills, and so forth.[1]

At the outset the company conducted its farm-machinery operations mainly on a commission basis, carrying small stocks on consignment, and forwarding carlot orders to the respective factories for direct shipment.[2] The limitations of such a method were soon demonstrated. Numerous complaints were received from farmers who were inconvenienced by the delay involved in having their orders transmitted to American factories for execution and shipment, with frequent further complications arising out of customs clearance and freight transshipment. An even more serious limitation of the commission method arose out of the difficulty of promptly supplying spare parts, and making repairs to machinery so distributed. In the case of implements supplied through the regular line companies, a farmer is always able to call on the local agent when anything goes wrong with his machine, while complete stocks of repairs are maintained in district warehouses. The disadvantages of a mail-order system in this regard had not been unanticipated by the Grain Growers' directors. It was pointed out, however, that the agent's service was always figured in the cost of the implement to the farmer, and that by acting as far as possible as his own mechanic in using Grain Growers' machinery, he could save appreciably in his implement bills.[3] Experience soon demonstrated, however, that the farmer's patronage could be neither extended nor maintained unless the company was prepared to compete in service as well as in prices with the

[1] G. G. G. Co., 1916, pp. 64–68.
[2] G. G. G. Co., 1916, pp. 14, 15.
[3] G. G. G. Co., 1914, p. 15.

line companies. If it was to continue in the machinery business, it must maintain stocks within closer reach of the consumer, even if the attendant warehousing, carrying, and insurance costs meant charging a higher price for its implements. Such considerations, combined with the expanding range of the company's supply business, led to the establishment, in 1916–17, of warehouses at Winnipeg, Calgary, and Regina, as provincial bases for farm supplies and machinery. By the time, therefore, when the amalgamation of the farmers' companies was being discussed, the Grain Growers' Company, in its supply business, had definitely passed from the status of a farmers' purchasing agency to that of a wholesale distributor, with considerable capital invested in this subsidiary enterprise.

Coöperative Supply Operations of Alberta Farmers' Company. — As noted elsewhere, the handling of farm supplies was undertaken by the Alberta Farmers' Company in its first year of operation.[1] Here the establishment of shareholders' locals in connection with the company's coöperative elevators provided from the outset the local distributive organization and facilities which President Crerar had declared to be essential to an effective coöperative supply service by the Grain Growers' Company. It was, in fact, mainly due to the existence of such local machinery, and to the combination of local cash trading with centralized purchasing on commission or short-time basis, that the company was able to conduct, on its exiguous trading capital, a volume of coöperative business which for the year 1915–16 (13 months) amounted to approximately one thousand carloads of farm supplies, representing a turnover of $749,668. Coal accounted for more than a third of the carlots handled, with posts, flour and feed, and twine next in order of bulk. This business was distributed among 86 elevator locals, with some 80 carloads shipped to U. F. A. locals.[2]

Although the Grain Growers' Company carried on a supply as well as a grain-handling business through its Calgary office, coöperation between the two farmers' companies had obtained in the former as well as in the latter operations.[3] A considerable amount

[1] See *supra*, pp. 127, 128.

[2] A. F. C. E. Co., 1915, p. 25; 1916, pp. 25–27.

[3] See *supra*, pp. 124, 125.

of the purchasing of the Alberta Company's Co-operative Department was done through the Grain Growers' Company, and it depended entirely on the latter for filling farm-machinery orders.[1] The manifest advantages of centralizing the purchasing operations of the two organizations, and of combining the greater capital resources of the older company with the Alberta system of local distribution through coöperative elevators and shareholders' locals, were potent considerations leading to the amalgamation of the two farmers' companies. During the year 1916–17, when the necessary legal steps were being taken to consummate the merger, the operations of the two companies were coördinated through joint meetings of their respective directorates, and a large warehouse, was erected at Calgary to handle the supply business of the amalgamating concerns in Alberta territory.[2]

Coöperative Trading in Saskatchewan. — In Saskatchewan, coöperative trading developed along distinctive lines. Here local coöperative purchasing associations appeared before the establishment of any provincial trading "central." Under the Agricultural Co-operative Associations Act, passed in 1913, largely in accordance with representations made by the Saskatchewan Grain Growers' Association, Grain Growers' locals or other local farmers' groups might become incorporated for coöperative trading or marketing purposes, under supervision of the provincial Commissioner of Co-operation and Markets.[3] Over a hundred such associations were registered in the following year, a few forming coöperative stores, but most of them operating as local purchasing associations.[4] Such enterprises were naturally not welcomed by local merchants, and wholesale houses, under pressure from the latter, frequently refused to supply the coöperative associations. It was recognized that little progress could be made in this direction unless the farmers possessed a central wholesale organization of their own.

Although the Saskatchewan Co-operative Elevator Company

[1] G. G. G. Co., 1915, p. 12; 1916, p. 13.

[2] A. F. C. E. Co., 1917, pp. 15, 20; G. G. G. Co., 1917, p. 15.

[3] Stat. of Sask., 3 Geo. V, c. 62, 1913.

[4] *First Annual Report of Commissioner of Co-operation and Markets*, Regina, 1914.

was empowered under its charter "to do all things incidental to the production, storing and marketing of grain," its directorate had found it more expedient to concentrate its resources upon the extension of elevator locals and the development of its grain marketing business, than to emulate the Grain Growers' Grain Company and the Alberta Farmers' Company in undertaking coöperative supply as a subsidiary enterprise. The former of these was, indeed, doing a growing amount of business with its shareholders and with coöperative associations in Saskatchewan. It lacked, however, any organic connection with the latter, and it was strongly felt by many of the Saskatchewan Grain Growers' locals that they should have a central supply agency of their own, whose operations they would control directly and whose earnings should accrue to themselves instead of to an extra-provincial company. It was also urged by some of the delegates at the Saskatchewan Grain Growers' Association convention in 1914 that a common trading interest would be more effective in strengthening the relations between the association and its locals, than the mere continuation of the educational, protective, and welfare activities to which effort had hitherto been confined. At this convention a definite decision was made to enter the field of coöperative trading, and the directors were instructed to take immediate steps toward the organization of a trading department, to act as a central purchasing agency for any locals of the association, or for similar bodies incorporated under the provisions of the Agricultural Co-operative Associations Act.[1]

Trading Policy of Saskatchewan Grain Growers' Association. — In accordance with the nature of its origin, the Trading Central of the S. G. G. A. adopted from the outset the policy of selling only to organized local groups. In this it differed from the Grain Growers' Grain Company, whose organization at this time was not based on local units, and whose Co-operative Department supplied goods to individual farmers direct, as well as to local associations. The trading operations of the Saskatchewan Association differed also from those of the Grain Growers' Company in that they were initiated with virtually no capital. In establishing

[1] *G. G. Guide*, Feb. 13, 1914.

the Trading Department the Saskatchewan directors placed to its credit $1000 from the general funds of the association. Inasmuch, however, as the early trading operations of the association were almost exclusively on a commission basis, and deliveries made to locals for cash only, the department was able to finance its business with a minimum of capital. The turnover for the six months during which the Trading Department was in operation in 1914 amounted to $300,000, on which it was claimed that purchasing members, in obtaining their supplies at wholesale prices, had saved not less than $75,000. As in the case of the Grain Growers' Company and the Alberta Co-operative, the principal commodities handled consisted of flour and feed, coal, apples, binder twine, building and fencing materials.[1] As was to be expected, considerable antagonism was aroused among retailers by the association's trading activities. The Retail Merchants' Association, indeed, called upon it members to refuse to buy from any wholesale firm which sold to Grain Growers' locals or farmers' coöperative societies.[2] The attempted boycott was neutralized to a considerable extent, however, by the ability of the Central to secure many of its supplies through the Grain Growers' Company. The very opposition of the regular trade served to stimulate the association to greater enterprise, and its members to firmer support.

It early became evident, however, that if the trading operations of the association were to be developed on an effective basis, wider powers and greater capital must be secured. Although the S. G. G. A. had been incorporated by special act of the provincial legislature in 1908,[3] it had not been empowered to carry on trading operations, or to make the financial commitments necessary to such undertaking. If the Association's Trading Department was to develop as the wholesale agency of local coöperative associations, it was desirable that its capital should be furnished by these constituent units, and that they should share directly in its man-

[1] *G. G. Guide*, Feb. 13, 1914.

[2] "We have asked every wholesaler in the Dominion, by letter, what he thinks of coöperative societies, and if he sells to them, we will cease doing business with him." E. M. Trowern, Secretary, Retail Merchants' Association, quoted in *G. G. Guide*, July 23, 1913.

[3] Stat. of Sask., 8 Edw. VII, c. 36, 1908.

agement and in its earnings. On the other hand, the Agricultural Co-operative Associations Act made no provision for financial participation by local societies in any wholesale trading body. With a view to bringing about more complete trading and financial affiliation between these societies and the Saskatchewan Grain Growers' Association, special legislation was enacted during 1915. Under this, the act incorporating the S. G. G. A. was amended to authorize that body "to carry on the business of wholesale procurers, shippers and dealers in agricultural supplies, including therein livestock, all goods, wares, merchandise, lumber, building materials, fencing, machinery, implements, tools, and commodities ordinarily used in agriculture." To this end it was further empowered to secure capital through selling debentures, which, however, could be issued or transferred only to members of the association, and to societies incorporated under the Co-operative Associations Act, or members thereof. Debenture holders might be admitted to such participation in the management of the association as should be considered advisable. Provision was further made for optional distribution of the net profits of the association's business "amongst the members, debenture holders, customers or employees of the association on the co-operative plan, rateably or otherwise, as may seem expedient." [1] Collateral amendments to the Co-operative Associations Act made it legal for societies or Grain Growers' locals incorporated under it, to invest their funds in securities issued by the S. G. G. A., and "to enter into any arrangement for joint purchase, sharing of profits, union of interests, coöperation, joint adventure, or reciprocal concession" with that body. Coöperative societies, so far as their transactions in farm supplies were concerned, were authorized to sell only to their shareholders and to members of the S. G. G. A., and to make sales only for cash.[2]

Trading Relations of the Saskatchewan Grain Growers' Association and the Grain Growers' Grain Company. — The intent of these legislative changes of 1915 was thus to provide the legal means by which the hundreds of Grain Growers' locals through-

[1] Stat. of Sask., 5 Geo. V, c. 36, 1915.

[2] Stat. of Sask., 5 Geo. V, c. 37, 1915.

out the province might become incorporated as coöperative bodies and jointly finance the operations of the S. G. G. A. Central, which should function as a provincial supply agency. A considerable number of farmers and farmers' locals in Saskatchewan were already buying supplies, however, through the Co-operative Department of the Grain Growers' Company. Obviously the S. G. G. A. could not develop its full possibilities as a provincial co-operative wholesale agency if the Winnipeg company continued to sell direct to individual farmers as well as to locals within Saskatchewan. On the other hand the Grain Growers' Company, with some 7000 shareholders in that province, was hardly disposed to withdraw its activities in that direction.[1] It will be recalled that it was at this period that federation of the various farmers' commercial organizations in Western Canada was being actively mooted and that these proposals contemplated the operation of the Grain Growers' Company as an interprovincial agency to purchase and manufacture supplies for the provincial organizations, as well as to conduct a joint terminal and export business.[2] Under such an arrangement the S. G. G. A., while procuring many of its staple lines through the Grain Growers' Company, would be the only distributing agency for coöperative purchases in Saskatchewan. A resolution instructing the executive to take action, "with a view to the consolidation of the business of the various farmers' organizations," had been adopted at the 1915 convention of the S. G. G. A.[3] Pending the issue of the negotiations among the organizations concerned, a *modus operandi* was agreed on between the Grain Growers' Company and the S. G. G. A. The latter undertook to buy its requirements as far as possible through the farmer company, while locals were to be encouraged to place their orders through the Saskatchewan Central. The company agreed to allow the association a percentage on all its sales in Saskatchewan, whether made through the Central or not. The latter in return was to allow the company the same commission on any sales it made independently.[4]

This arrangement was continued to the end of 1916. It proved,

[1] G. G. G. Co. 1915, p. 12.
[2] See *supra*, pp. 168, 169.
[3] *G. G. Guide*, Feb. 17, 1915.
[4] G. G. G. Co., 1916, p. 17.

however, of considerably greater financial advantage to the association than to the company.[1] In view of this result and of the withdrawal of the Saskatchewan representatives from the federation negotiations,[2] it was decided by the directors of the Grain Growers' Company not to renew the trading arrangement beyond 1916. Conditions reverted, therefore, to their former status with company and association each carrying on a supply business in Saskatchewan, along independent and differently organized lines.

Trading Negotiations with Saskatchewan "Co-op." — Shortly after the termination of the trading agreement between the S. G. G. A. and the G. G. G. Co., a proposal was made somewhat unexpectedly at the association convention in February, 1917, by Hon. George Langley, on behalf of the directors of the Saskatchewan Co-operative Elevator Company.[3] This amounted to an offer whereby the latter should take over the trading business of the association, finance it on its own resources, and utilize its 300 country elevators, with attached coal and flour sheds, as local co-operative distributing centres, after the plan of the Alberta Farmers' Co-operative Elevator Company. Discussion of this proposal in convention and in subsequent meetings of locals to which the matter was referred, and various conferences between representatives of association and "Co-op," serve to reveal a decided reluctance on the part of the former to relinquish its trading activities, as tending to weaken the relations between Central and locals, and to make the latter dependent on a wholesale agency which they did not own or control themselves. On the other hand, it became evident that Mr. Langley's announcement had been made somewhat prematurely, and that his views did not command the concurrence of other directors, who felt it inexpedient for the company to commit itself to such subsidiary undertaking, especially at a time when it was just entering into the terminal elevator

[1] After a year's operation it was found that the commissions allowed by the company to the association on its sales in Saskatchewan amounted to $29,489, whereas the commissions which it received from the association amounted to only $8,390. G. G. G. Co., p. 11.

[2] See *supra*, pp. 169, 170.

[3] Mr. Langley was a director of both the "Co-op" and the S. G. G. A., as well as Minister of Municipalities in the Saskatchewan government.

business. Under these conditions the negotiations proved inconclusive, and the report by the Trading Department presented at the 1918 convention of the S. G. G. A., showing a turnover 60 per cent greater than that of the previous year, confirmed most of the delegates in their desire to have the association continue its trading operations independently. Thus neither trading affiliation with the Grain Growers' Company, nor the transfer of its supply business to the Saskatchewan "Co-op," had proved acceptable, and the association committed itself to a policy of development independently of either of the farmers' companies.

In continuing its trading operations without outside affiliation, the Central of the S. G. G. A. sought to finance its business along the lines contemplated in the legislative amendments of 1915. Six per cent trading debentures were offered for subscription by incorporated local coöperative associations. As most of the locals required all their available capital for their own trading purposes, and as a great deal of educational effort was necessary in order to interest them in the financing of their Central, the response to the debenture offering was very limited. As the subscription instalment, moreover, was only 20 per cent, the actual cash realized was much more limited. At the end of 1916 only $5,111 had been paid on such subscriptions. Since the association at this period, however, bought largely on commission, while selling for cash, and since it received half the profits on all goods sold by the Grain Growers' Company in Saskatchewan, it had been able to build up its trading capital out of surplus earnings to a total of $48,235 at the above date.[1] At the end of 1917, a working capital of approximately $85,000 had been accumulated.[2] In its first five years of trading operations (1914–1918), the association had managed indeed to do a business of between five and six million dollars with a paid-up debenture capital, which, at the end of the period, amounted to less than $15,000.[3]

[1] S. G. G. A., *Executive Report*, 1916.

[2] *Ibid.*, 1917.

[3] Exclusive of Association Life Membership trust funds, which had been authorized by resolution as available for trading purposes. At the end of 1916 trading loans from this source amounted to $13,855. S. G. G. A., *Financial Statement*, 1918.

II. Expansion and Retrenchment

The first period of coöperative trading by Western Grain Growers, embracing the years 1912 to 1917, was characterized, as shown in the preceding section, by more or less experimental enterprises undertaken independently by the Grain Growers' Grain Company, the Alberta Farmers' Co-operative Elevator Company, and the Saskatchewan Grain Growers' Association. The first named, which enjoyed the strongest financial resources, had developed an interprovincial business which had expanded from the handling of feed and seed grain through its elevators to the carrying of general farm supplies, including machinery, distributed by mail order from central warehouses or through local company elevator agents. The Alberta Company had developed its business mainly in connection with its elevator locals, limiting itself for the most part to the handling of bulk commodities through elevator warehouses or to purchasing on commission for local groups. The Saskatchewan Grain Growers' Association had established its Trading Department as a wholesale supply agency for its locals, and other farmers' groups incorporated as coöperative societies under provincial legislation and supervision. Negotiations for trading affiliation, first with the Grain Growers' Company and then with the Saskatchewan "Co-op," had been abandoned, and the Association had definitely decided in 1918, to carry on its supply business independently, by internal financing.

The next two or three years were marked by greatly expanded trading operations by the amalgamated Grain Growers' and Alberta companies, and by the S. G. G. A. with a largely augmented debenture capital. This expansion was abruptly arrested under the conditions of the immediate post-war years, during which heavy losses were sustained and a general retrenchment imposed. Since 1922 readjustments have been effected, in which coöperative trading by Western Grain Growers' organizations has assumed more restricted forms, which give indication, however, of relative permanence.

Distributing Policies of United Grain Growers. — The amalgamation of the Grain Growers' Grain Company and the Alberta

Co-operative Elevator Company was followed by an ambitious expansion of the farm-supply business under the United Grain Growers, which involved development of a general mail-order service, "line" distribution of farm machinery, and large-scale sawmill operation. From each of these the company, under post-war deflationary conditions, was eventually forced to withdraw. In the year of coördinated operation preceding the formal amalgamation, the supply business of the senior company had amounted to $1,957,215 (of which farm machinery accounted for approximately one third), while the turnover of the Co-operative Department of the Alberta Company had totaled $1,519,984.[1] Expanding grain acreage, heavy crops in 1915, 1916, and 1917, and rising war-time grain prices were favorable to farmer demand, and in the first year of the united company (1917–18) sales of farm supplies reached a total of nearly $6,000,000, yielding a net profit of $71,456.[2] Instead of merely buying goods on a commission basis for purchasing associations, the company was now conducting a general catalogue business with individual farmers as well as with locals; and in addition to operating coal and flour sheds alongside its elevators, it was now maintaining heavily stocked distributing warehouses at Winnipeg (one for general supplies, and one for farm machinery), Calgary, Regina, Edmonton, and Saskatoon.[3] In so doing, the U. G. G. had committed itself to extensive capital investments, and assumed the risks of carrying large stocks purchased under the difficult conditions of war-time supply, and subject to the uncertain demand of farmers whose purchasing power depended almost entirely upon their crop returns. A less satisfactory period for carrying on a catalogue business could scarcely have been found than the years 1917–20, in which manufacturers generally were not in a position either to guarantee

[1] A. F. C. E. Co., 1917, p. 14; G. G. G. Co., 1917, p. 14.

[2] U. G. G., 1918, p. 36; 1919, p. 55.

[3] At the end of the 1917–18 business year, stocks carried in the company's warehouses were inventoried at $2,231,000. Overhead charges on warehouses and office space of the Co-operative Department at this peak period amounted to $58,000 annually. U. G. G. 1921, p. 64.

delivery or to quote prices in advance.[1] The company on the whole followed the practice of marking up stocks only when cost advances actually became effective, without accumulating a trading reserve against subsequent price declines.[2] In its efforts to extend its supply service and keep down prices to its farmers, the company was operating on narrow margins while carrying large risks.

The heaviest trading commitments of the U. G. G. were in connection with its farm-machinery business, which expanded rapidly after the amalgamation of 1917, reaching its peak in 1920, when the sales exceeded one and two thirds millions.[3] Although the company's departure from factory-to-farm handling of farm machinery to the carrying of wholesale stocks in district warehouses permitted the more expeditious filling of orders, whether for new machinery or spare parts, it still experienced a disadvantage in being in less direct contact with farmer customers or prospects than were the line companies through their local agents. The complicated mechanism of certain new forms of farm machinery generally calls for more explanation and demonstration than can be satisfactorily conveyed through the mail-order medium. It is a business in which the personal representative cannot ordinarily be eliminated, if the farmer's goodwill is to be developed and his patronage retained.

With a view to establishing such a contact and at the same time turning its local elevator connection to further account, the united company began to select a number of its elevator operators to act as local agents for U. G. G. machinery, as well as handling grain and bulk farm supplies. During 1919–20, 23 stock-carrying agencies were established in Alberta, 28 in Saskatchewan, and 6 in Manitoba. In addition, 24 local agents and demonstrators were

[1] The first catalogue that the Co-operative Department issued in 1916 had to be replaced within a few weeks by a supplementary one with generally advanced prices. G. G. G. Co., 1916, p. 15.

[2] U. G. G., 1921, p. 64.

[3] The Grain Growers' farm-machinery sales were reported as follows:

G. G. G. Co.		U. G. G.	
1914–15	$86,735	1917–18	$1,283,870
1915–16	329,132	1918–19	1,552,116
1916–17	676,024	1919–20	1,688,551

appointed to develop business with surrounding farmers without handling stocks themselves.[1] Three media of contact were thus established between the company's Farm Machinery Department and the farmer: (*a*) direct mail order through catalogue; (*b*) local retail agencies; (*c*) travelling representatives. While the two latter methods afforded greater service to the farmer, they also involved greater cost. Accordingly, with a view to making the price paid by the farmer correspond with the service received, discounts from the retail prices were given to farmers sending in mail orders, accompanied by cash, to the company's district warehouses. In this particular, U. G. G. practice differed from that of the principal line companies, which aimed to encourage farmers to buy exclusively through their local agents and at a uniform price.

It will be seen from the above that the Grain Growers' Company had found it necessary, as the outcome of experience and competition, to make frequent and material changes in its method of handling farm machinery, until by 1919 it was conducting it on lines which did not differ greatly from those followed by the regular companies. It suffered the obvious disadvantages, however, of possessing no assured control over its supply, or over the patterns and models it offered, although most of the equipment it sold bore U. G. G. brands. Moreover, legislation had been passed in the Prairie Provinces during the war period, which regulated closely the form of agreements of sales for farm machinery, and which required, among other things, that implement dealers should give a warranty that supplies of all repair parts for machines sold should be kept available within the province.[2] The question of guaranteeing repair parts for U. G. G. implements had been raised in the shareholders' meeting in 1919. Following this discussion, steps were taken by the directors to secure ownership or control of as many patterns as possible of implements handled by the company, so that, in the event of any of the makers concerned subsequently discontinuing their manufacture, the U. G. G. would be in a position to make arrangements for their reproduction elsewhere, and thus ensure a line of repairs.

[1] U. G. G., 1920, p. 55.

[2] Stat. of Sask., c. 28, 1915; Stat. of Alberta, c. 4, 1918, sec. 31.

Trading Embarrassments and Losses. — Under the irony of circumstances, the farm-supply commitments and service undertakings of the U. G. G. reached their peak at the very time when farmers' purchasing power became demoralized under the drastic agricultural deflation which set in during 1920. The unusually light crops of 1918 and 1919 had imposed heavy carry-overs of binder twine purchased at inflated prices, and seriously affected general machinery sales and collections in low-yield districts. The Farm Supplies and Machinery Department showed a net trading loss of $59,426 for 1918–19, with almost equally unfavorable results the following year, when a departmental deficit of $52,099 was reported.[1] These losses had been sustained in years of record grain prices. With the general deflation in agricultural prices which developed with the harvesting of the 1920 crop, — aggravated as it was by the disestablishment of the Canadian Wheat Board, and by the restrictive effects of the Fordney Emergency Tariff enacted the following spring at the instance of American farmers, — the position of the U. G. G. Co-operative Department became little short of disastrous. With no inducement to expand crop acreage, the demand for wire fencing, of which the company carried large stocks, virtually disappeared. Prices of machinery and supplies purchased at peak of cost had to be heavily reduced in order to obtain buyers and meet price-cutting competition. Inventories of carry-over stocks had to be written down drastically. The result showed a departmental loss for the year of $282,303. No trading reserve had been built up during the inflationary period to meet such contingencies, and the deficit had to be taken care of through the impairment of the company's general reserve. It was recognized now that a mistake had been made in supplying goods to farmers on narrow margins during the period of rising prices. "We have had," said President Crerar in his address at the 1921 shareholders' meeting, "a lesson in what would have been the proper course to have taken during the tremendous and rapid increase in prices during the war. All stocks should have been marked up as the prices went up, irrespective of what the goods cost, and the

[1] U. G. G. 1919, p. 55; 1920, p. 54.

profits taken and set aside to care for these losses when the prices came down. Unfortunately, our company did not follow this practice." [1]

The difficulties of the company in connection with the handling of farm machinery were further aggravated by its disabilities as an importer after the war. Fluctuations in Canadian-American exchange after 1919 had made import costs distinctly speculative.[2] Stricter regulations had also been issued under the Dumping Act,[3] and in 1920 the Dominion government imposed a sales tax, with 50 per cent higher rates on imports than on corresponding goods of domestic origin. Under these conditions, importation of farm equipment from the United States became virtually prohibitive.[4] Moreover, certain companies which had supplied the U. G. G. with implements were now forced to close down.[5] After 1920 the purchases of the Farm Supplies and Machinery Department were practically confined to the filling of actual orders. During 1921–22 sales showed a decline of 40 per cent over the preceding year. With further drastic writing down of inventories, the departmental loss for the year was shown as $219,200. Thorough consideration of the present and prospective situation led the company's directorate to the conclusion that it would be more expedient to lose patronage through not having goods to fill orders, than to continue purchasing at prices hopelessly out of line with those of the farmers' product. It was decided in 1922, therefore, to discontinue the farm-machinery business and most of the general catalogue lines.[6]

[1] U. G. G., 1921, p. 64.

[2] The Canadian dollar was quoted as low as 82 cents in New York in January, 1921.

[3] See Memorandum of U. G. G. to Minister of Customs, U. G. G., 1920.

[4] The additional cost in some instances was found to be as great as 45 per cent above factory prices, exclusive of freight charges. U. G. G., 1921, p. 65.

[5] Considerable pressure was brought to bear on the directors, from shareholders and customers, for the purchase or acquisition of a controlling interest in some implement-manufacturing plant in Canada. It was pointed out, however, that the only plants that might be acquired would not be capable of supplying anything like a complete range of machinery, and that liability for additional lines of repairs was not lightly to be assumed. U. G. G., 1921, p. 65.

[6] U. G. G., 1922, p. 12. Sufficient stocks of machinery repairs were maintained to fulfill the company's warranty to farmer purchasers.

Since 1922 the supply business of the U. G. G. has been conducted along substantially the same lines as those followed in the earlier years. That is to say, operations have been limited to the handling of such bulk commodities as coal, flour, and feed, binder twine, wire, fencing, and oils. These are supplied to purchasing associations and individual farmers on a mail-order basis through the company's offices and warehouses, or handled locally on a commission basis by company elevator agents. At the end of 1926, the U. G. G. operated 263 flour houses and commission warehouses, 234 coal sheds and 8 supplies sheds in connection with its country elevator system, and held an investment interest in the Echo Flour Mills and the Superior Feed Company.[1] Upon the above basis the Co-operative Supplies Department since 1922 has shown itself something more than self-supporting, its sales responding to the improvement in Western farmers' purchasing power, and its service apparently proving on the whole more satisfactory than when more ambitious undertakings were attempted.[2]

U. G. G. Experience in Lumber Supply. — In conducting its supply operations in general the Grain Growers' Grain Company had not sought to perform other than a middleman service. In the case of lumber, however, an ambitious attempt was made to undertake production as well as distribution. Reference has previously been made to the acquisition by the company in 1911, of an extensive timber limit in British Columbia, with a view to developing an independent source of supply of a material of which every farmer was a potential consumer, and in which the manufacturing process was relatively simple. Delay in completion of the Grand Trunk Pacific Railway, the outbreak of the war, and competing uses for the company's capital, had caused development of this property to be deferred until 1917, when amalgamation with the Alberta "Co-op" increased both the resources and the potential patronage of the united company. The construction of a modern sawmill, with drying kilns, lath mills, and shingle

[1] U. G. G., 1926, pp. 38, 39.

[2] "The company last season sold over 9,000,000 pounds of twine, while the handling of coal made the U. G. G. the largest single handler of this commodity in Western Canada." U. G. G., 1927.

mills, was internally financed by subsidiary investment in the U. G. G. Sawmills Limited, incorporated in 1918 with a capitalization of $600,000.[1] Development under war-time labor and supply conditions caused the original cost estimates to be more than doubled, and initial operation was attended by serious labor difficulties. Embarrassments arising out of excessive capital and operating costs were aggravated by disappointing demand conditions. Commencement of output by U. G. G. Sawmills coincided with the poor crop yields of 1918 and 1919 while the agricultural depression ushered in by 1920 discouraged farm building operations generally. Quite apart, however, from abnormal cost and market conditions, the method of distribution pursued by the U. G. G. was not proving as satisfactory as its directors had anticipated. It had been expected that, with a variety of timber on its limits and with complete sawmilling equipment, the company would be able to develop on a larger and more serviceable basis the business inaugurated by the Lumber Branch of its Farm Supplies Department, by making shipments to farmers or farmers' locals of complete carload orders of dressed lumber, shingles and lath direct from the mill. Thus farmers would be independent of outside sources of supply, and distributing costs would be reduced to a minimum. In cases where farmers were able to anticipate and estimate their requirements with precision, and to combine their orders, such a method of supplying lumber proved distinctly advantageous. In dealing with farmers as a whole, however, the working limitations of the direct system tended to outweight the potential advantages. Many farmers found difficulty in preparing accurate estimates of the kinds and quantities of lumber required for their particular building purpose without the personal assistance of an experienced builder or lumber dealer. If requirements were overestimated, the surplus supply could not be returned. If they were underestimated, the deficiency could not ordinarily be made good by mail order without much delay and disproportionate expense. Moverover, the plan of joint carload ordering involved not merely a concurrence of neighbors' requirements, but a highly developed degree of coöperation as well, since

[1] U. G. G., 1919, p. 21.

complications were quite likely to arise in the accounting and distribution of mixed shipments.

As a means of removing some of these obstacles to the direct method of lumber supply, the company had undertaken to prepare detailed estimates and specifications for farmers' building requirements. It was frequently found, however, that farmers so supplied used these estimates to make the local retail lumber dealer meet the company's prices. It was decided therefore, in 1920 to discontinue the services of the Lumber and Builders' Supplies Department.[1] In the case of lumber, as of farm machinery, experience demonstrated that the mail-order method of supply provided no general substitute for distribution through retail channels, however salutary its competition might prove. While the direct plan made it possible to effect savings for those who chose to buy by this method, it did so at the expense of certain services which most farmers insisted on having. The implications of this experience were quite appreciated by the directors, as reflected in the president's annual report for 1920:

> This enterprise (U. G. G. Sawmills) was undertaken with a view to getting in a position to ship carlots of lumber direct to farmers and farmers' associations, reducing thereby the expense of the middleman. It may as well be admitted that this method of operation offers very little promise of success, and your board is now inclined to the view that it will be necessary for the company to establish a number of retail yards at suitable points, where sufficient promise of success offers. If the company could rely on selling in carload lots, the problem would be easier, but experience has amply shown that it is very difficult to do this business.[2]

Logging and milling operations were carried on intermittently by the U. G. G. Sawmills from 1920 to 1925 whenever such offered any prospect of reducing overhead losses on a "shut-down" basis. Depressed conditions persisted in the western lumber business generally during this period with sellers' competition especially keen. A few retail yards were established in an experimental way by the company during 1924, but the loss of the greater part of the mill plant by fire in May, 1925, caused the directors to decide to liquidate the sawmill and lumber-supply business.[3]

[1] U. G. G., 1920, pp. 13, 55.

[2] U. G. G., 1920, p. 12.

[3] The financial results and the liquidation of U. G. G. Sawmills are further discussed below, pp. 331, 332.

Trading and Financial Policies of S. G. G. A., 1917–19. — While the trading commitments of the Saskatchewan Grain Growers' Association were less extensive than those of the United Grain Growers, its post-war embarrassments, in view of its more limited capital resources, were relatively more serious. After the termination of its trading relations with the Grain Growers' Company, the association had proceeded to develop a general supply business and to carry stocks as well as handle carload orders on a commission basis. A number of local coöperative societies were advancing from track-side distribution of collective carload purchases to the establishment of coöperative stores. The number of incorporated trading associations had also greatly increased.[1] With a view to making these coöperative societies independent of "boycotts" and "combines," as well as to widening the range by its service, the association, toward the end of 1917, opened a wholesale grocery and general supply branch in Winnipeg, which carried on a mail-order catalogue business similar to that of the United Grain Growers. It also undertook to handle farm machinery on its own account.[2] As local coöperative trading developed, the Central found itself pressed to establish general distributing warehouses within closer range of its patrons, and to assist local coöperatives by putting in stocks and supervising and standardizing their trading and accounting methods.

With a view to financing such expansion, the 1919 convention of the association adopted a proposal of the executive for the issue of half a million dollars of new debenture stock, which, instead of being sold merely to local associations,[3] should also be offered to farmer members generally, on an attractive investment basis.[4] In order that investors should have a measure of control over the

[1] By 1920, 337 agricultural coöperative societies had been registered in the province. *Report of Commissioner of Co-operation and Markets*, 1920.

[2] S. G. G. A., *Executive Report*, 1917.

[3] At the end of 1918 only $80,000 in debentures had been taken by locals, on which only 20 per cent had been paid up. An additional $17,000 had been credited, however, on account of patronage dividends. *Ibid.*, 1918.

[4] Claims of debenture stockholders were to rank prior to those of debenture-holding locals, and in addition to 6 per cent interest, they were to be entitled to a bonus of 2 per cent before any distribution of profits might be made on a patronage basis.

trading operations of the Central, provision was made for an annual trading convention of debenture holders and representatives of debenture-holding locals, at which a report should be rendered by the Central, and two representatives elected to the directorate of the association. Such provision involved a recognition, on the one hand, of the necessity of offering special inducements and protection to the contributors of capital, and on the other hand, of the desirability of making it possible for the general convention of the association to devote its attention more freely to those non-commercial activities for which it had been originally organized. Debenture stock to the amount of $60,000 was subscribed by delegates before the close of the 1919 convention.[1] The campaign for new capital was actively prosecuted during 1919, at a time when farmers were probably deriving the maximum real advantages from war prices. By the end of the year, a quarter of a million debenture stock had been subscribed and $138,000 paid up.[2]

Losses and Retrenchment 1919–22. — The year 1919 proved a critical one in the association's trading history. Events not altogether under the control of the Central determined that the newly acquired capital should be applied chiefly in replacing losses rather than in expanding the association's business. Up to the end of 1917 the Trading Department had been able to show an annual surplus, and to declare patronage dividends exceeding $17,000 for the four years, applied to deferred debenture payments. In the year 1918, however, a trading loss of $7,434 was incurred. This arose chiefly out of wholesale cancellation of binder twine orders by locals in crop-failure areas, necessitating the carrying over of something like a million pounds. In this important branch of its business, the association had been bearing the risk of ordering and carrying large stocks to ensure its members against harvesting embarrassments, and at the same time selling to its patrons on close margins. In a season of sub-normal requirements such as 1918, the Central had to bear the carry-over and depreciation charges (twine prices dropping nine cents a pound during the year) without the compensation of protective margins. In the

[1] *G. G. Guide*, Feb. 19, 1919. [2] S. G. G. A., *Executive Report*, 1919.

following year, with an almost equally low yield, twine prices declined another two cents a pound, and a loss of $44,624 on this line alone had to be carried to surplus account.[1]

Difficulty was also experienced in connection with the association's wholesale grocery and general supply house at Winnipeg. The patronage of local coöperatives was for the most part intermittent and uncertain. Coöperative stores generally lacked adequate trading capital, and were not usually in a position to place quantity orders unless given credit by the Central. The very success of the association in breaking down the wholesalers' boycott against coöperative societies proved prejudicial to its own business, since many locals, attracted by the immediate advantage of closer prices or easier terms offered by regular dealers, diverted their patronage from their own wholesale agency. In conducting its general catalogue business the association was exposed to the same abnormal conditions as the U. G. G., with the further disadvantage of more restricted distributing connections and much more limited capital resources. By the end of 1919, therefore, the Trading Department had found it necessary to discontinue issue of its catalogue, and instead of opening new warehouses in Saskatchewan the executive decided to close out the Winnipeg mail-order house. The losses on the twine and mail-order business for 1919 were of such proportions as not only to wipe out the surplus of $44,265 which stood on the books at the beginning of the year, but also to result in a capital impairment of $32,810. The newly subscribed debenture capital had, therefore, to be applied largely to taking care of losses instead of being available for expansion.

The Trading Department of the S. G. G. A. was thus in serious difficulties even before the setting in of the post-war deflation. Although during 1920 the Central confined its buying operations more or less exclusively to bulk commodities, and goods required for actual orders, its previous commitments in farm machinery and general supplies involved cumulative carrying charges, and drastic marking down of prices in order to dispose of such stocks.

[1] Whereas the Saskatchewan wheat crop had reached a total of 224,000,000 bushels in 1915, and 147,235,000 bushels in 1916, it amounted to only 92,500,000 bushels in 1918, and 96,000,000 in 1919.

In 1922 the association, like the U. G. G., found it expedient to close out its Farm Machinery Department. With inventory depreciation fully taken into account, the financial statement for 1922 showed a net loss of $31,064, bringing the total capital impairment to nearly $120,000 — equivalent to more than 60 per cent of the paid-up debenture stock.

Coöperative Trading Readjustments in Saskatchewan. — Since 1922 the Trading Department of the S. G. G. A., like the Co-operative Supplies Department of the U. G. G., has confined its operations to the handling of bulk supplies, such as coal and wood, flour and feed, lumber and millwork, posts and wire fencing, binder twine, oils, and so forth. In supplying these to local societies, the association has carried the minimum of stocks on its own account, forwarding carload orders as far as possible for direct shipment from mines, mills, or factories. In returning thus to its earlier basis of operation, the Trading Department has been able to show small annual surpluses, which by the end of 1926 had reduced the association's impairment of capital to $100,035.[1]

Wholesale coöperative trading in Saskatchewan is at the present time (1927) in a somewhat indeterminate status, owing to two recent developments within the province. One of these has been the steps taken by coöperative stores (which the Trading Department of the S. G. G. A. is not in a position to supply in any general way) and coöperative purchasing associations,[2] with the encouragement of the provincial Commissioner of Co-operation and Markets and the Secretary of the Co-operative Union of Canada, looking toward the establishment of a coöperative wholesale society of their own, on lines analogous to the English and Scottish Co-operative Wholesale Societies.[3] The other development has been the amalgamation — effected in July, 1926, after protracted negotiations — between the Sas-

[1] *Report S. G. G. A. Trading Department*, 1926. Under the terms of issue of S. G. G. A. trading debentures, no interest might be paid upon them, so long as any capital impairment remained to be made up.

[2] In 1926–27, there were 47 coöperative stores and 197 coöperative purchasing associations reported in Saskatchewan. *Report of Commissioner of Co-operation and Markets.*

[3] *Ibid.*, 1926–27, p. 42.

katchewan Grain Growers' Association and the Farmers' Union of Canada, under the name of the United Farmers of Canada, Saskatchewan Section, Limited.[1] The amalgamation agreement contemplated placing the Trading Department directly under the control of the debenture holders, "while maintaining a point of contact with the association." At the request of the coöperative trading associations of the province a conference was held early in 1927 between the Wholesale Committee of the former and a committee of trustees of the United Farmers of Canada looking toward the taking over of the latter's Trading Department by the coöperative trading associations, with assumption by the latter of conditional responsibility for the impaired capital of the S. G. G. A. debenture holders. While the trustees of the U. F. C. found themselves unable to accept this proposal, as not sufficiently safeguarding the interests of debenture holders, nor providing for direct purchase by members, they were instructed by the U. F. C. convention to which they rendered their report,[2] "to take immediate steps to separate the Trading Department from the educational organization, having due regard in so doing to the rights of debenture holders and creditors, and having in mind the principle of co-operative purchase by members." [3] While extended negotiations may still be necessary before an accommodation is reached which will satisfy mutually the interests of coöperative stores, local purchasing associations, U. F. C. lodges, and trading debenture holders, it is to be expected that the outcome will be a wholesale supply agency controlled directly by local trading societies, and functioning independently of the provincial farmers' association. Debenture holders are hardly likely to obtain return of their investment except through undetermined annual payments based on each year's earnings.

[1] *G. G. Guide.* An act to incorporate the new organization was passed the following year. Stat. of Sask., 17 Geo. V, c. 84, 1927.

[2] Report of U. F. C. Trading Department, in *Western Producer*, April 7, 1927.

[3] *Western Producer*, March 31, 1927.

III. Results of Coöperative Trading in Western Canada

It will be seen from the foregoing review that coöperative trading in Western Canada has been a form of producers' rather than of consumers' coöperation. The primary aim has been to reduce costs of farm production rather than to lower living costs. It has represented a reaction against what has been regarded as exploitation by manufacturers and merchants, on whom the farmer has been dependent for his supplies, as the organization of farmers' elevator companies and wheat pools was actuated by the desire to reduce or eliminate dependence on the "Elevator Combine" and Grain Exchange dealers. The promotion of wholesale coöperative trading has been undertaken, not by local societies acting collectively, but as a subsidiary enterprise of centralized farmers' organizations established for other purposes. With the Grain Grower's Grain Company and the Alberta Farmers' Co-operative Elevator Company, coöperative supply was carried on incidentally to the primary business of grain marketing and elevator operation. With the Saskatchewan Grain Growers' Association, the Trading Department developed as a commercial adjunct to the basic objects of protection, education, and mutual aid. In all cases, however, these enterprises were undertaken in response to widespread and repeated demands from shareholders or members, expressed both through locals and through general meetings.

Relations between Central and Local Bodies. — Of the three organizations which entered the field of coöperative supply in 1913–14 each exemplified a different organic and financial relationship between the central and local bodies. The Grain Growers' Grain Company, at the outset, conducted its supply business mainly with Grain Growers' or United Farmers' locals in the three provinces. Although the participating members of these local associations were also frequently shareholders of the company, the locals as such had no corporate investment in it, nor any direct voice in its trading policy. Its supply operations were financed from its paid-up capital and reserves accumulated from grain-handling profits. While quoting the lowest possible cash prices to locals, or to farmers purchasing on a mail-order basis, no patronage dividends were distributed. Any profits derived from the company's supply operations went into its general earnings, and all losses had to be met out of its general reserves. Except, therefore, that the company was owned entirely by farmers, and that a large proportion of its patrons were also its shareholders, its trading relations with locals were not essentially different from that of any other commercial company.

In the case of the Alberta Farmers' Co-operative Elevator Company the relationship was more direct. Its shareholders' locals purchased supplies through a company with which they were organically and financially identified, and obtained distribution through the coöperative elevator around which each was organized.[1] With the general extension of the Alberta plan throughout the United Grain Growers' organization after 1917, shareholders' locals engaged in coöperative buying were able to make direct representation, through their secretaries, or through delegates at the annual meetings. Here, however, trading operations and finances were only one of many enterprises reported on, and they were not discussed separately by those directly interested. The United Grain Growers' supply business thus showed a relatively high degree of centralization. It did not depend on its own locals directly or exclusively for either finance or patronage, and its commitments and its methods were proximately determined by the general directorate of the company. While these conditions gave the company's management greater freedom, they likewise imposed a greater assumption of risk.

In the case of the Saskatchewan Grain Growers' Association, the aim had been to have its Trading Department bear the same organic and financial relationship to the local coöperative associations as the English and Scottish Co-operative Wholesale Societies to their local coöperative stores. In Great Britain, however, the wholesale societies were the joint creations of a considerable

[1] The company also traded directly with U. F. A. locals at points where it did not maintain elevators. With a view to establishing closer relations between Central and locals, the company held a special conference at Calgary during 1917, between its Co-operative Department and secretaries of U. F. A. and A. F. C. E. Co. locals engaged in coöperative trading. A. F. C. E. Co., 1917, pp. 15, 16.

number of well-established local coöperative trading bodies whose members' support was ensured through share subscription and patronage dividend distribution. In Saskatchewan the Grain Growers' locals had not been organized originally for trading purposes. Legal incorporation for such objects had to be promoted to a large extent by the Central itself. Few of the local associations carried permanent stocks of their own or commanded funded trading capital. In most cases members merely combined for occasional carload orders distributed from track. A Central based on such constituents was obviously limited in the sources of its capital and handicapped by uncertainty and irregularity of patronage. Hence it was that the association found it necessary, in 1919, to appeal to individual farmer investors, and to delegate control largely to a separate trading convention of such subscribers. The weakness and instability of local trading societies was undoubtedly one of the chief limiting factors in the association's business development. It meant that the Central, with restricted capital, had to bear the risk of contracting for goods in advance, without an assured outlet or alternative channel of disposal.

Methods of Distribution. — Four different methods of coöperative supply were undertaken at one time or other by the companies and the association. The first was that of central purchasing on a commission basis, as followed originally by the Alberta Company and the S. G. G. A., and by the Grain Growers' Company in the first phase of its farm-machinery and lumber business. This involved merely the placing of assembled orders with manufacturers or established wholesalers for direct shipment to local groups, for which a purchasing commission was charged by the central office. The second method was that of carrying stocks of such staples as flour and feed, coal, posts and twine, in elevator warehouses, handled by company elevator agents who received a commission on their sales. The third form was mail-order supply, involving catalogue issues and maintenance of stocks of general supplies in central warehouses. The fourth and most ambitious method consisted in undertaking supply at the source, as in the case of the U. G. G. Sawmills. The first method involved the minimum capital commitment and risk assumption.

Its limitations lay in not permitting immediate delivery of orders, or direct contact with purchasers. The second method has, in general, proved a satisfactory adjunct to elevator operation, affording a supplementary use of country houses and personnel, and affording personal contact with patrons. The range of commodities capable of being handled in this way was limited, however, and its service was confined to farmers accessible to company elevator points. The third method was attempted under abnormal conditions, and the inventory losses sustained by the U. G. G. Co-operative Department and the Saskatchewan Trading Central were shared in greater or less degree by most business concerns at that period, especially those dependent on farmer patronage. Apart, however, from the complications of abnormal price fluctuations, the attempt to supply complete lines of general merchandise from central warehouses involved grave risks. Such diversified operations not only call for greatly enlarged capital investment, but also involve greater proportionate overhead costs than the handling of bulk lines.[1] Here, too, the farmers' trading departments were exposed to the direct competition of established wholesale and mail-order houses with greater capital resources, larger turnovers, and more extensive and diversified outlets. As to the method of supply at the source, the sawmill experience of the Grain Growers' Company served chiefly to bring home — under abnormal conditions, it is true — the risks and difficulties of even so relatively simple a form of manufacturing as lumber production, and to demonstrate that the most effective means of reducing the cost of supplies does not necessarily lie in attempting independent production. Had the directors of the U. G. G. acted on the reiterated requests and resolutions of shareholders, the company would have been involved in the manufacture of farm implements, and the operation of coal mines and flour mills as well as of sawmills.[2] While the latter experience was

[1] "Those branches of the business which have entailed proportionately the greatest outlay for accounting, correspondence, advertising, adjustments, credits, etc., have been those which were purchased by our members in small volume orders. The office expense on a fifty-dollar order was often as great as on a car of coal or flour." — S. G. G. A., *Executive Report*, 1920.

[2] U. G. G., 1921, p. 26.

a costly one, its significance appears to have been fully appreciated by directors and shareholders.

Coöperative Results. — Distribution of dividends on purchases is generally regarded as an essential feature of coöperative trading. No such dividends have ever been distributed by the Grain Growers' Company, while the only extent to which such policy was carried out by the S. G. G. A. was the crediting to debenture-holding locals during the years 1914–17 of patronage dividends of from 1 to 1¾ per cent (aggregating $17,000) on account of debenture subscriptions. While returns to patrons were out of the question during the years in which heavy departmental losses were sustained, and in which reserve and capital impairment had to be restored, the general absence of such distribution in more favorable years represented an adaptation to circumstances in Western Canada, rather than a compromise of coöperative principle.[1] The grain grower was interested primarily in getting his supplies at lower prices than those charged by local dealers. He was rarely prepared, like the British trade union coöperator, to pay the prevailing price to his coöperative agency, and await an uncertain, deferred refund on the amount of his season's purchases. If farmers, whether buying individually or collectively, were quoted lower prices by regular dealers, they were prone to divert their patronage to such sellers. In so far, therefore, as the company and the association found it necessary to offer immediate savings to farmers and farmers' purchasing associations, they reduced their capacity to distribute subsequent patronage dividends. Such surpluses as might be realized where goods were handled on such narrow margins, were in most cases utilized either for expanding supply services or replacing previous losses.

[1] The question of patronage was given serious consideration at the time of the amalgamation of the G. G. G. Co. and the Alberta "Co-op." A careful study was made of the Rochdale system as practised in European countries, and in 1918 an interprovincial committee was sent by the U. G. G. to investigate the experience of farmers' organizations in several American states in applying patronage distribution in connection with coöperative elevators and trading associations. In making its report, the committee expressed the view that "in planning for the future we should not allow our enthusiasm and admiration for the system practised in older countries to interfere with our changing the plan of operation so as to make it adaptable to Western conditions on the farm." U. G. G., 1918, pp. 58, 59.

Although wholesale coöperative trading operations as conducted in Western Canada resulted in a very considerable net curtailment of the reserves of the United Grain Growers and a 60 per cent impairment in the debenture capital of the S. G. G. A., and although no cash patronage dividends were ever distributed by either organization, very substantial benefits were undoubtedly realized in lowered cost of supplies, not merely to farmers buying through the company and the association, but also to growers purchasing from regular middlemen who were compelled to meet the competition of the farmer-owned agencies. While the indirect results of the latter's participation are not capable of any precise measurement, they have certainly had the effect of narrowing very appreciably and generally trading margins on such supplies as flour, coal, twine, lumber, and fencing materials. As in the case of grain marketing, the very existence, and the potential as well as the actual competition of farmer-owned middleman agencies, afford an alternative channel for obtaining farm supplies as well as selling farm products, which relieves the grower from exclusive dependence upon private dealers. At the same time, participation in the supply business has served to bring home to farmers the risks and difficulties of such operations, the value of middleman services, and the economic justification of protective margins and certain trade practices which the grain grower has been disposed to regard with suspicion.

Such appreciation has probably been most manifest in connection with the supply of farm machinery. The eight or nine years during which the Grain Growers' Company operated its Machinery Department was an abnormal period, in which losses were more or less inevitable even with older established concerns. Quite apart, however, from these trying circumstances, the Grain Growers' experiments demonstrated fairly conclusively that the spread between the factory prices and the farm prices of agricultural implements could not be substantially reduced without limiting the service to the farmer purchasers. They had found it necessary to follow the line companies in establishing district warehouses, local supply agents and demonstrators, between the factory and the farm, and as each middleman service was provided, an additional increment had to be made to the price. While the competition of the U. G. G. tended to narrow margins on farm implements and to offer substantial savings to farmers who found the mail-order plan satisfactory, more far-reaching benefits to Western grain growers in connection with farm machinery have been obtained through non-commercial methods. Provincial legislation regulating the sale of farm machinery, as secured by farmers' associations, have tended to remove legitimate grievances in connection with implement notes and supply of repair parts.[1] With their strong Progressive representation in the federal Parliament, Western farmers have also been able in post-war years to secure further tariff reductions on farm machinery,[2] and the restoration of pre-war freight rates on farm implements shipped from Eastern Canada.[3]

Conclusion. — Coöperative supply as conducted by Western Grain Growers' organizations has served three classes of purchasers — coöperative stores, coöperative purchasing associations, and farmers buying individually. The organization and operation of coöperative stores calls for much more capital and considerably greater coöperative solidarity, than the intermittent transactions of purchasing associations. In many cases the former have developed out of the latter, and there appears to be a growing feeling, particularly in Saskatchewan, that the carrying of continuous stocks and general lines is a coöperative consummation to be aimed at. With certain outstanding local exceptions, the record of coöperative trading societies in Western Canada has shown a high degree of mortality and instability, arising out of such causes as inadequate capital and membership, inexperienced management, faulty accounting, unreliable patronage, and lack of soli-

[1] See *supra*, p. 302.

[2] Under the budget of 1922 duties on reapers, binders and mowers were reduced from 12½ to 10 per cent. Under the tariff amendments of 1924 they were still further lowered to 6 per cent. Corresponding reductions were made on other farm implements, and the sales tax was removed both on implements and on materials entering into their manufacture.

[3] Through restoration of "Crow's Nest Pass Agreement" rates. *Can. Annual Review*, 1922, pp. 237–240.

darity among members.[1] Most of the societies were organized during the war, so that the period of operation has been an abnormal one, on the whole. Despite the ephemeral career of many of these local trading organizations, considerable real progress has been made in Saskatchewan, under the educational and promotive work of the Grain Growers' Association and the provincial Co-operation and Markets Branch, under whose auspices annual conferences of coöperative society managers and secretaries are held. As evidenced by recent conferences and negotiations, a sufficient number of coöperative societies appear to have demonstrated their stability and usefulness to warrant establishment of a wholesale agency of their own on Rochdale lines. While this will presumably be effected by taking over the Trading Department of the U. F. C., it will probably be developed eventually along interprovincial lines.[2]

On the whole the growth of coöperative stores in Western Canada is likely to be slow, and their importance limited. The difficulties of securing adequate trading capital where settlement is sparse, and farmers as a class are borrowers, the competition of mail-order houses as well as of better stocked local stores; widespread dependence on credit purchasing; the preference generally shown for immediate savings in the form of lower prices rather than the prospect of deferred and uncertain patronage dividends; the heterogeneity of a predominantly immigrant population: all these factors serve to make the organization of coöperative stores more difficult and their operation more precarious than in the older countries of Europe, where they have been developed by wage earners in urban centers, or by farmers living in village communities rather than on isolated farmsteads. The most advantageous form of coöperative trading by farmers in Western Canada will probably continue to lie in collective purchasing of bulk supplies, such as coal, flour, twine, oils, lumber, and fencing

[1] See lists of dissolutions of associations in annual reports of Commissioner of Co-operation and Markets. In 1919 the number of active associations reporting was 350. In 1926, the number had fallen to 258.

[2] Representatives of the Co-operative Buying Associations of Alberta and Manitoba attended the conference between the committees of the Co-operative Trading Associations of Saskatchewan and the U. F. C., referred to above, pp. 311, 312.

materials, in which the savings of carload shipment and direct handling can be realized. Whether these are distributed at track-side, or through farmers' elevators or coöperative stores, depends on conditions of local organization.

While the Coöperative Supplies Department of the United Grain Growers as conducted at present is coöperative in little more than name, its operations are of very considerable service and competitive benefit to farmers, and afford a means of supply through a farmer-owned agency to such farmers as prefer to order individually or are not members of associations identified with the projected Co-operative Wholesale Society. Although the wholesale supply business of the U. G. G. is not organized or operated on Rochdale lines, the company nevertheless has to its credit the record of having pioneered on a bold and extensive scale in the field of grain growers' coöperative supply, and of having by its services and competition done much to reduce the more palpable disabilities to which the Western farmer has been exposed as a buyer as well as a seller.

CHAPTER XVIII

BUSINESS RESULTS OF GRAIN GROWERS' COÖPERATIVE ORGANIZATIONS

I. Position of Farmers' Commercial Organizations in Canadian Grain Trade

Since the precarious launching of Partridge's little Grain Growers' Company in 1906, the evolution of grain-marketing enterprises by the farmers of Western Canada has been marked by four successive phases. In the first, from 1906 to 1911, the Grain Growers' Grain Company alone was in the field, functioning merely as a farmer-owned commission and grain-trading agency, operating on the Grain Exchange and engaging experimentally in the export business. The second phase, 1911–23, was characterized by the participation of grain growers in country and terminal elevator operation, as well as in commission handling, and in large-scale export trade. The institution on semi-public lines, of the Saskatchewan Co-operative Elevator Company in 1911, was followed in 1912 by the leasing of the Manitoba government elevator system to the Grain Growers' Grain Company, and in 1914 by the organization of the Alberta Farmers' Coöperative Elevator Company. With the amalgamation in 1917 of the two latter concerns, the field was occupied for the next six years by the two centralized and integrated farmers' companies, the United Grain Growers and the Saskatchewan "Co-op." The third phase, 1923–25, is marked by the advent of the provincial wheat pools, operating under handling arrangements with the farmer-owned and regular line elevator companies. The fourth phase is characterized by the entry of the pools themselves into subsidiary elevator operation, involving the absorption in 1926 of the Saskatchewan "Co-op" by the Saskatchewan Pool. At the present, therefore, there are eight separately incorporated farmers' grain-marketing institutions operating in Western Canada. Seven of these, embracing the three provincial pools with their respective elevator subsidiaries and their joint Central Selling Agency, form one unified system. The other, and the senior organization, the United Grain Growers, represents a continuation of the earlier type, operating, however, under special arrangements with the pool system and pursuing a modified coöperative policy of its own. During the crop year 1925–26 — the last in which the Saskatchewan "Co-op" functioned as a distinct organization — the pools and the two farmers' elevator companies together handled 258,000,000 bushels of grain,[1] equivalent to 56 per cent of the total grain inspections in Western Canada.[2]

In the present chapter an attempt is made to estimate and compare the commercial and financial results of the operations of the various farmer-owned grain-marketing institutions through the phases noted.

Record of Grain Growers' Grain Company, 1906–12. — During the half-dozen years in which the original Grain Growers' Grain Company operated purely as a grain-trading concern, without any elevators of its own, its capital requirements were relatively small, and its risks comparatively slight, once its position on the Grain Exchange had been reestablished. The rapid growth of its paid-up capital, and its investment relations with the Home Bank, greatly facilitated the financing of its Grain Exchange operations and permitted early entrance into the export business. Its earnings during this period were derived mainly from its selling commissions, augmented by profits from export shipments and the handling of street grain purchased at Manitoba government elevator points. While the company investment in the *Grain Growers' Guide* was not at this time a source of profit, it was of great value in keeping the company before the farmers as the champion of their right to participate in the grain trade. As the only farmers' grain company in the field at this time, it tended to attract the investment participation and patronage of all those growers who were anxious to terminate their dependence upon private middlemen agencies in the marketing of their grain.

[1] After making allowance for pool grain handled through U. G. G. and Saskatchewan "Co-op" elevators.

[2] For 1925–26 these amounted to 353,850,670 bushels of wheat and 107,220,000 bushels of coarse grains. *Canadian Grain Trade Year Book*, 1925–26.

The business results of the operations of the Grain Growers' Grain Company during this period are indicated by the following figures:

TABLE VI. RECORD OF G. G. G. Co., 1906–1912

	Capital paid-up (At end of year)	Grain Receipts (Bushels)	Profits	Dividends per cent
1906–07	$11,795	2,340,000	$790	7
1908–09	20,385	4,990,541	30,190	40*
1908–09	120,708	7,643,146	52,902	30*
1909–10	292,957	16,332,546	95,663	15
1910–11	492,062	18,845,305	69,575	10
1911–12	586,472	27,775,000	121,614	10

* Stock dividends.

The very circumstances which had prevented the carrying out of the original intention of paying patronage dividends reacted to the financial interests of the company, and indirectly, of growers themselves. Reinvestment of earnings in the company offered greater possibilities of economic return to farmers then minute individual distributions. The sound policy of the directors in applying the large profits of the second and third years to the payment of the uncalled portion of the subscribed capital, and in carrying large surpluses to reserve in succeeding years, served to place the company in a position where in the next period it could undertake upon its own resources the operation of both country and terminal elevators, and finance other enterprises in the interests of grain growers.

Competitive Position of Farmers' Elevator Companies. — In the first year of grain growers' participation in the elevator business (1911–12), the Saskatchewan Co-operative Elevator Company operated 46 country houses. In the following year its system had expanded to include 137 elevators, while the Grain Growers' Grain Company assumed the operation of 135 elevators leased from the Manitoba government. When the Saskatchewan "Co-op" was taken over by the Saskatchewan Pool in 1926, after fifteen years of successful operation, its elevator system embraced 451 country houses, with lakehead terminals, owned or leased, having a combined capacity of 15,000,000 bushels, and a 2,000,000 bushel transfer elevator at Buffalo. At the same date the United Grain Growers operated 382 country houses throughout the three Prairie Provinces, and terminals of 3,100,000 bushels capacity. Between them the two companies maintained elevators at 830 of the 1717 country elevator stations in Western Canada. Together they controlled almost 20 per cent of all country elevators, and over 28 per cent of the total lakehead storage.

The competitive position of the farmers' elevator companies in the grain trade of Western Canada is perhaps best indicated by the record of the proportion of total grain marketings handled by them from year to year.

TABLE VII. PERCENTAGE OF TOTAL GRAIN INSPECTIONS HANDLED BY FARMERS' ELEVATOR COMPANIES, 1912–26

(Millions of bushels)

Year	1	2	3	4	Year	1	2	3	4
1911–12.......	27.8	3.3	185	17.0%	1919–20	24.5	20.3	201	21.7%
1912–13.......	30.0	12.0	241	17.8	1920–21	36.6	28.0	283	23.2
1913–14.......	33.7	19.5	263	20.2	1921–22	31.5	37.3	315	21.8
1914–15.......	23.8	13.7	153	24.5	1922–23	32.9	42.9	380	20.0
1915–16.......	67.7	43.2	333	33.3	1923–24	47.2	51.8	504	19.7
1916–17.......	44.1	34.6	305	25.8	1924–25	30.9	30.6	310	19.8
1917–18.......	29.9	27.0	230	24.0	1925–26	43.0	52.6	460	20.8
1918–19.......	22.2	21.8	185	23.8					

Column 1. Handled by Grain Growers' Grain Co., 1911–17, and by Alberta "Co-op" (1914–17); United Grain Growers, 1918–26.
Column 2. Handled by Saskatchewan Co-operative Elevator Co.
Column 3. Total grain inspections, Western Division:
1901–17, Fiscal year ending March 31.
1918–24, Year ending Aug. 31.
1925–26, Year ending July 31.
Column 4. Percentage of grain inspections handled by farmers' companies.

Note. Columns 1 and 2 include grain handled through company country elevators, plus grain shipped over platform on consignment to company commission departments.— For the years 1924–25, and 1925–26, approximately half of the two companies' total handlings represented pool grain.

II. Business Policies and Financial Records of U. G. G. and Saskatchewan "Co-op"

The competitive status of the farmers' companies as a group in the Canadian grain trade having been noted, it is instructive to examine next their business records in comparison with one another during their parallel existence. While the economic results to Western grain growers of their operations are not to be measured merely by their financial records, the latter are significant, both as a business test of their respective policies, and as a measure of the direct returns to farmer shareholders. Although the corporate existence of the Saskatchewan Co-operative Elevator Company has been terminated, the liquidation of its assets, which is still in process, involves the distribution of the capitalized equity accruing to its shareholders from its fifteen years of operation, which thus have a retrospective as well as comparative significance.

Comparative Financial Results. — Table VIII shows the profits earned and dividends paid by the two companies during their parallel existence, the growth of their reserves, and the ratio of their profits to their paid-up capital and reserves.

The Grain Growers' Grain Company was already a strongly established concern when the Saskatchewan Co-operative Elevator Company was launched, and the amalgamation of the Alberta Co-operative with the former, in 1917, brought about a two-thirds increase in the assets of the united company.[1] While the earnings of both the farmers' companies have been subject to the variations inherent in a business where handling rates are fixed, and where the volume of turnover is primarily governed by nature's annual crop response, it will be seen that the Saskatchewan "Co-op" was able to show a more consistent earning record and an uninterrupted accumulation of reserves.

The superior financial record of the younger company is attributable mainly to two factors. In the first place, it enjoyed the very substantial advantage of being able to finance its aggressive elevator construction programme upon a 15 per cent paid-up

[1] See *supra*, p. 175.

TABLE VIII. FINANCIAL RECORD OF FARMERS' COMPANIES, 1912–26

Fiscal Year	*Grain Growers' Grain Co.* Profits	Reserve	1	2	*Saskatchewan "Co-op."* Profits	Reserves	1	2	3
1912	$121,614	90,000	18	10	52,461	....	30	6	$3.00
1913	164,332	162,575	20	10	168,987	51,727	60	8	3.00
1914	151,081	200,000	15	10	286,182	116,290	57	8	3.00
1915	226,963	340,000	19	10	133,746	286,834	17	8	2.00
1916	572,804	600,000	34	10	557,795	322,973	58	8	6.00
1917	607,899	601,662	32	10	350,753	612,436	23	8	2.50
	United Grain Growers Ltd.								
1918	441,760	1,500,000	13	10	124,811	979,831	6	8	...
1919	148,549	1,500,000	4	6	193,599	1,069,591	9	8	...
1920	463,675	1,750,000	16	8	224,989	1,233,119	9	8	5.00
1921	233,743	1,765,000	5.5	6	279,414	1,190,622	11	8	...
1922	118,350*	1,200,000	3	..	463,057	1,434,359	16	8	3.50
1923	532,171	1,200,834	13	8	442,212	1,624,095	13	8	2.00
1924	552,443	1,203,017	13.5	8	475,534	2,284,463	12	8	4.50
1925	418,574	1,203,182	10	8	377,872	2,378,439	8	8	...
1926	676,378	1,450,000	16.4	8	825,547	2,608,412	15	8	...

* Loss.

Column 1. Percentage net profits to paid-up capital and reserve.

Column 2. Cash dividends paid per cent.

Column 3. Stock dividends distributed from surplus.

Note. In the case of the U. G. G. the figures given are those of the parent company. The results of the operations of subsidiaries are shown only in so far as dividends paid by them enter into the earnings of the parent company, or as the latter's reserve has been augmented or impaired through the absorption of subsidiary surpluses or losses.

margin, thanks to the availability of Saskatchewan government loans.[1] This permitted it to take advantage of the rapid expansion of grain acreage in Saskatchewan resulting from the threefold conjuncture of rising immigration, rapid railway construction,

[1] See *supra*, p. 104. While the annual interest payments constituted a large item in the expenses of the Saskatchewan "Co-op," the rate was low—5 to 5½ per cent. The company, moreover, was saved the expense of marketing bonds of its own, and its interest payments on each loan were subject to progressive reduction, as the 5 per cent repayments of principal were made each year to the provincial treasury.

and the introduction of Marquis wheat.[1] Under these conditions the double earnings of elevator and commission department handlings bore an unusually high proportion to the shareholders' invested capital in the early years. Prior to 1916 the country elevators operated by the Grain Growers' Grain Company were practically limited to those leased from the Manitoba government.[2] Not only did these involve fixed charges of considerable magnitude, but they were located in a province in which the grain-growing acreage had become relatively stationary, and in which elevator competition was especially keen. Until the company was able, in 1916, to finance out of its own resources the construction and purchase of elevators in Saskatchewan, its participation in business from that province was limited mainly to the handling of platform consignments through its commission department and leased terminal.

Financial Results of U. G. G. Subsidiary Enterprises. — The second and more significant factor affecting the financial records of the two companies has been the difference in the business policies pursued. The Saskatchewan "Co-op" consistently concentrated its resources and efforts upon grain marketing,[3] whereas the Grain Growers' Company has engaged in various subsidiary enterprises, undertaken with a view to serving the economic interests of Western farmers, rather than to enhancing the profits of the company. As shown in the preceding chapter, the operation of the Farm Supplies and Machinery Departments, while yielding small profits during most of the war-time period, involved heavy deflationary losses, which resulted in a considerable impairment of the company's surplus, more than $150,000 being written down on this account alone in 1922.[4] Of the eight subsidiary concerns organized by the Grain Growers' Company, only two — the Grain Growers' Export Company Limited and the

[1] By 1908 the crop acreage of Saskatchewan exceeded that of Manitoba and Alberta combined.

[2] See *supra*, pp. 157, 158.

[3] The directors, it will be recalled, gave serious consideration at one time to undertaking the handling of farm supplies through their elevators, on behalf of the S. G. G. A. See *supra*, p. 297.

[4] U. G. G., 1921, p. 63; 1922, p. 16.

Grain Growers' Export Company, Inc. (New York) — have on the whole proved financially profitable to the parent company.[1] These export subsidiaries have, of course, been directly associated with the company's grain business, and were paralleled by similar organizations on the part of the Saskatchewan "Co-op."[2] The fortunes of the other six subsidiaries of the United Grain Growers may be appropriately considered at this point.

Public Press and Grain Growers' Guide. — The Public Press Limited, established in 1909, primarily to publish the *Grain Growers' Guide*, paid its first dividend only in 1920.[3] Although operating on a self-supporting basis during the difficult post-war period, it was not until 1926 that it was again able to contribute to the investment income of the parent company. It possesses one of the best-equipped commercial printing plants in Western Canada. The Grain Growers' Guide Publishing Company was incorporated as a distinct subsidiary of the Public Press Limited, with a view to separating the publication of the *Guide* from the general printing business, and placing both on a self-supporting basis. Up to that time the *Guide* had been annually subsidized by the parent company.[4] Since its separate incorporation, the *Guide* has been able on the whole to pay its way, although not constituting a source of profit to the main company. As the journal of the Grain Growers' Movement, and as an educational medium, the *Guide* is, however, an asset whose value cannot be measured by its financial earnings. Since its change in 1926 from a weekly to a semi-monthly journal, its circulation has greatly increased, being now in excess of 120,000.

[1] In 1914–15 the New York Export agency made a profit of $530,000 (G. G. G. Co., 1915, p. 23). Under conditions of war-time grain control in Canada and the U. S., the earnings of the export companies were more or less nominal (see *supra*, p. 160). In 1920, however, of $120,000 received by the parent company as dividends from investments in subsidiaries, $100,000 was contributed by the New York company (U. G. G., 1920, pp. 8, 15). In 1920–21 the profits earned by the two export subsidiaries amounted to $382,000 (U. G. G., 1921, pp. 12, 13).

[2] See *supra*, pp. 181–185.

[3] U. G. G., 1920, p. 11.

[4] The amount of money invested by the G. G. G. Co. in building up the *Guide*, and taking care of its losses up to that time, amounted to approximately $150,000. U. G. G., 1919, p. 18.

United Grain Growers' Securities Limited. — The United Grain Growers' Securities Limited, organized as a subsidiary in 1918, with a view to functioning as a farmers' real-estate, insurance, and trust company,[1] has for the most part failed to realize the expectations on which it was established, and until quite recently has been operated at a great loss. Its first enterprise, the handling of farm lands on a commission basis, was launched at an unfavorable time in a field where specialized competition was particularly active.[2] The Land Commission branch was finally closed out in 1920–21, having incurred a loss in each year of its operation.[3] The Insurance Department, in handling the writing of practically all insurance on the extensive properties of the United Grain Growers Limited and its subsidiaries, has been of some advantage to the company. As representative of several large insurance companies, the U. G. G. Securities, working largely through company elevator operators as local agents, has been steadily extending its insurance business with farmers, placing, though not itself underwriting, hail, fire, accident, health, and life policies.[4] Operating purely as an insurance agency, this subsidiary has been able to pay dividends to the parent company during the

[1] U. G. G., 1918, p. 26.

[2] The purpose in initiating a Land Department was to offer farm owners an alternative to selling their lands through private real estate dealers, who, in taking options on farm properties, were frequently able to obtain an undue portion of the selling price for themselves. The restriction on emigration from the United States arising out of the Military Draft law of 1917, the failure of agricultural immigration from Europe to develop after the Armistice, and the operations of the Soldier Settlement Board, followed by the decline in land values after 1920, afforded highly unfavorable market conditions for the development of a land commission business, in which the company lacked both direct local contact with farm owners and established connections with land seekers. The Land Department appears, however, to have been of considerable service to individual farm buyers and sellers. U. G. G., 1918, 1919, 1921.

[3] U. G. G., 1921, p. 15; 1922, p. 11.

[4] The Insurance Department developed out of the request of the U. F. A. in 1918 that the company should undertake to handle hail insurance in Alberta. Having secured a general insurance agency, the company found it advantageous to place its own policies through this branch of the Securities Company. An Investment Department was also operated for a short time, to handle investments and estates for farmers. U. G. G. 1921, p. 15.

past three years.[1] So far as the farmer is concerned, however, the U. G. G. Securities, on its present basis, would not seem to offer any distinctive service that may not be supplied equally well by reputable competing agencies.

United Grain Growers (British Columbia) Limited. — The United Grain Growers (B. C.) Limited represented a reorganization in 1918 of the agency which the Grain Growers' Grain Company had established at New Westminster, B. C., as far back as 1913.[2] While the parent company controlled the majority of the stock,[3] a number of shares were also held by British Columbia farmers. The coast subsidiary's business consisted chiefly in the handling of feed and general farm supplies required by British Columbia farmers. Only so far as it afforded an outlet for sacked grain and feed from Alberta was it a marketing agency. The United Grain Growers (B. C.) Limited was able to show small profits each year until 1920–21.[4] when reckless buying and credit extensions by the manager, in combination with the severe post-war depression on the Pacific coast, resulted in such serious losses that the United Grain Growers' directors — who had experienced considerable difficulty in effectively supervising a subsidiary located at such distance from headquarters — decided to dispose of this investment. As farmers' organizations in British Columbia with whom negotiations were conducted, were not in a financial position to take over the business, the property was sold in 1921 to a private concern at a fair value.[5] Inventory depreciation and bad debts made it necessary, however, for the parent company to apply $30,000 from general reserve to take up these losses.[6]

United Grain Growers' Sawmills, Limited. — The subsidiary which has proved most embarrassing financially to the parent company has undoubtedly been the U. G. G. Sawmills. The cir-

[1] U. G. G., 1925, p. 12; 1926, p. 11; 1927, pp. 32, 57.

[2] See *supra*, p. 156. U. G. G., 1918, p. 27. Following the reorganization the head office was moved to Vancouver, and branches established at twelve country points. U. G. G., 1919, p. 19.

[3] The parent company's investment in 1920 stood at $75,000, U. G. G., 1920, p. 15.

[4] U. G. G., 1918–20.

[5] U. G. G., 1921, pp. 18, 19.

[6] U. G. G., 1922, p. 16. The sum of $36,000 had also been written off against the agency in 1916. G. G. G. Co., 1916, p. 9.

cumstances connected with the acquisition and development of the company's British Columbia timber limit have been discussed elsewhere.[1] The investment in this enterprise, standing in 1920 at $850,000, represented expenditure under conditions of greatly inflated cost, and constituted an asset of highly non-liquid character. Mistakes made in the location of the mill site and logging railways,[2] labor difficulties, and the destruction of the greater part of the mill plant by fire in 1925, were merely local aggravations of the generally depressed conditions which have prevailed since 1920 in the Western Canadian lumber industry. Losses of varying proportions have been sustained in every year of operation by the U. G. G. Sawmills, and in 1922 the parent company's reserve was written down by $200,000 to take care of impairment in this investment.[3] Since the fire in 1925 the company has been engaged in working off existing stocks of logs and lumber. Although an independent appraisal in 1926 placed the salvage value of stocks and equipment at $100,000, the directors decided to write off the whole amount, namely, $650,000, at which the sawmill investment was carried in the company's books — such a step being made possible without reduction of reserve, through revaluation of other assets.[4] In reporting the liquidation of this subsidiary to the shareholders, President Crerar made the following obituary comment: "The heavy loss that has resulted from this venture, which was entered upon by the company many years ago in an effort to improve conditions surrounding the sale of lumber, simply emphasizes the need of the most careful consideration of any new ventures that may be undertaken, no matter what benefits they may seek to give in improving any set of conditions." [5]

Thus, of the various subsidiary departments and companies of the United Grain Growers, only those connected with its export business have been financially profitable on the whole. The *Grain Growers' Guide* had to be subsidized during the greater part of its career, and the U. G. G. Securities was frequently a source of loss,

[1] See *supra* pp. 305, 306.
[2] U. G. G., 1920, p. 12; 1925, p. 13.
[3] U. G. G., 1922, p. 16.
[4] U. G. G., 1926, pp. 27, 28.
[5] U. G. G., 1926 p. 12.

although at the present time both of these, along with the Public Press, are moderately remunerative and useful auxiliaries. The Farm Machinery Department and the U. G. G. Sawmills, and, to a lesser degree, the British Columbia subsidiary, — however serviceable they may have been, directly or indirectly, to farmer purchasers, — have constituted a serious drain upon the financial resources of the parent company, and have all had to be liquidated. While the full losses arising out of these subsidiary undertakings are not shown in the above table, their effect upon the financial position of the parent company is impressively disclosed in the figures for 1922, when, for the first and only time in its history, the Grain Growers' Company registered a loss on its combined operations, and when its reserve had to be written down to the extent of $565,000 to take care of operating losses and depreciation of subsidiary assets.[1]

The result is all the more significant when compared with the record of the Saskatchewan "Co-op" during the same period. At the outset of its corporate career on September 1, 1917, the United Grain Growers showed a combined reserve of $1,500,000, more than double that of the Saskatchewan Company at the same date (namely, $612,436). By the end of 1920 the former had been raised to $1,765,000. The readjustments of 1922 involved an impairment of fully one third, reducing it to $1,200,000, or $300,000 less than the amount shown by the amalgamated company in 1917, and nearly a quarter of a million dollars less than that of the Saskatchewan Company at the end of 1922. In other words, the reserve of the United Grain Growers at the close of the 1922 fiscal year was only four fifths of what it had been in 1917, while that of the Saskatchewan "Co-op" had been increased by 134 per cent within the same period. The grain handlings of the two companies showed a remarkably close correspondence during these years, so that the difference in financial showing may be almost entirely attributed to the policy of concentration upon grain marketing followed by the Saskatchewan "Co-op," in contrast with the

[1] This included appropriations of $200,000 on account of U. G. G. Sawmills; $153,218 on account of Farm Machinery and Supplies Department; $30,000 to the B. C. Agency; and $101,408 to Profit and Loss Account. U. G. G., 1922, p. 16.

policy of diversified coöperative enterprise pursued by the older company during a time when general economic conditions could scarcely have been less favorable to such undertakings. Had it not been for the consistent action of the directors in building up reserves out of earnings from the company's remunerative grain business, it is doubtful whether it would have survived the post-war losses arising out of its subsidiary commitments. As it is, the company has been able to rehabilitate its finances in an impressive manner, as reflected in the figures of the last five years. Although subject to competition from pool elevators, and although handling pool grain on a cost basis, the United Grain Growers was able in 1925–26 to show the largest profit in its history, amounting to $676,378.[1]

Present Financial Position of U. G. G. — In accordance with suggestions made at the annual meeting in 1925, an independent appraisal of the company's assets was obtained in 1926 from the Canadian Appraisal Company. The report rendered by the latter placed the value of the company's physical assets, in the form of elevators, warehouses, equipment, Public Press property, and so forth, at a figure $2,300,000 above that at which these were carried in the company's books. On the other hand it appraised the U. G. G. Sawmills property (on a salvage basis) at $550,000 below, and the company's real estate at $224,000 below, their book values; thus showing a net appreciation of $1,526,000. In the company's statement for 1926 the entire book value of the U.G.G. Sawmills (namely, $650,000) was written off, and real estate inventories reduced by $224,000. Other assets were written up by a corresponding amount, thus leaving an appraised surplus of over $1,400,000 as an "unbooked" asset.[2]

The condensed balance sheet below shows the consolidated position of the United Grain Growers Limited and its subsidiaries, as of August 31, 1926.

From the table it will be seen that the shareholders' equity amounts to apparently $4,125,000,[3] which is equivalent to $35.30

[1] U. G. G., 1926, p. 18.
[2] U. G. G., 1926, pp. 16, 17; 1927, p. 27, 28.
[3] Represented by paid-up capital, general reserve, and surplus at, say, $755,000.

Assets			
Current Assets		$4,349,991	
Capital Assets (after giving effect to adjustments noted)		7,101,501	$11,451,492
Liabilities			
Current Liabilities		2,176,400	
Capital Liabilities (outstanding bonds, mortgages and debentures)		2,006,906	
Capital Stock in Subsidiaries, not owned by U. G. G.		37,837	
Capital Stock:			
Amount subscribed	$3,238,125		
Amount unpaid	317,505	2,920,630	
Reserves:			
General Reserve	1,450,000		
Depreciation Reserves	2,054,550	3,504,550	
Surplus:			
Subject to taxation on current year's profits		805,179	$11,451,492

per share (par value $25.00) [1] on 116,825 fully paid-up shares outstanding, or, on the basis of Canadian Appraisal Company's valuation, $47.50 per share. The company's profits for 1925–26 were equivalent to $5.80 per paid-up share, which, if capitalized at 6 per cent, would give a value of $96.00 for each share. The thirty-five thousand odd shareholders of the United Grain Growers hold securities which, while not subject to speculative trading, represent to-day a substantial appreciation above investment cost.

Relation of Grain Growers' Company to Home Bank. — Discussion of the financial record of the United Grain Growers cannot well be concluded without reference to its corporate relations with the Home Bank. It will be recalled that in the second year of the career of the Grain Growers' Grain Company a considerable investment was made in the stock of the Home Bank,[2] and that for a time the company acted as agent for the sale of Home Bank shares to Western farmers.[3] As the Grain Growers' Company was

[1] Since 1911 the treasury price of the company's stock has been $30 per share, the premium (less selling costs) being applied to surplus.

[2] 350 shares were purchased in 1908, and 650 in 1909, making 1,000 in all held by the company. Evidence of T. A. Crerar before Royal Commission on Home Bank Affairs, Winnipeg, April 20, 1924.

[3] See *supra*, pp. 65, 66. At the time of the failure of the Home Bank, it had some 1,100 shareholders in Western Canada. (Evidence of T. A. Crerar, etc.)

not in the fortunate position of the Saskatchewan Co-operative in having its bank account guaranteed by a provincial government, it was of no small advantage to the young company to have its account with a bank in which two of its officers (Messrs. Crerar and Kennedy) were directors. The investment, moreover, represented a remunerative and thoroughly liquid asset.

The circumstances leading to the disastrous failure of the Home Bank need not be related here, as they were not connected in any way with the operations of the United Grain Growers. As a member of the western committee of the bank's directors which met separately at Winnipeg, Mr. Crerar became concerned over certain non-liquid head-office accounts as far back as 1914.[1] Despite repeated demands made by the western directors for a change in the general management, and despite representations made by them to the Minister of Finance in 1918, they found themselves unable to obtain the desired action on the part of the eastern directors.[2] In 1918 Mr. Crerar resigned his directorship, following his appointment as federal Minister of Agriculture.

Although the United Grain Growers had disposed of its Home Bank shares some years before the bank became insolvent,[3] and was not called on therefore to meet the shareholders' double liability, considerable criticism arose against Mr. Crerar from western shareholders (who in many cases were also U. G. G. shareholders) for his responsibility in connection with the sale of Home Bank stock to western farmers and with the direction of the bank's affairs. Evidence given before the Home Bank Commission suggests, however, that if the vigilance shown by Mr. Crerar, distantly removed as he was from the bank's head office, had been equalled by the other directors, its affairs might have had a somewhat different issue. At the 1924 meeting of the United Grain Growers' shareholders, a resolution was passed expressing the

[1] According to evidence given before the Royal Commission appointed to investigate the claims of Home Bank depositors for government relief.

[2] Evidence of T. A. Crerar before Home Bank Commission, Ottawa, May 5, 1924.

[3] U. G. G., 1918, p. 43. The shares were sold at 139$\frac{3}{8}$. They had been bought at 133. (Evidence of T. A. Crerar, etc.).

satisfaction of the delegates with the statement made by Mr. Crerar of the relations of himself and the company to the Home Bank.[1] While the United Grain Growers Limited was not involved financially in the failure of the Home Bank, and while Mr. Crerar's integrity in the matter has been upheld, the incident does not tend to support the expediency of organic identification between a farmers' company and private commercial or financial corporations whose policies and affairs it does not control.

Financial Policy of Saskatchewan "Co-op." — The outstanding feature in the financial history of the Saskatchewan Company was the extent to which it was able to build up its resources with a minimum of investment contribution from its shareholders. The 15 per cent subscription instalment ($7.50 per share) represents the only amount which any of its 28,000 shareholders were ever called upon to pay up. In the initial years this was possible chiefly by reason of the elevator loans of the Saskatchewan government, and of its guarantee of the company's liability to banks. A considerable part of the capital invested in the "Co-op's" terminal elevator was also loaned by the government. In the last ten years of the company's career, however, it was able to finance an increasing proportion of its physical, as well as its commercial, expansion upon its own resources through capitalization of earnings.

Of the various alternative forms of disposal of surplus earnings authorized under the company's charter,[2] the directors followed throughout the practice of allocating the annual net surplus after payment of 8 per cent cash dividend, equally between general reserve and "elevator reserve." From time to time the former was distributed in the form of stock dividends, applicable to the unpaid balances of stock subscribers. At the end of 1924, when the last stock dividend was distributed, the paid-up value of the shares of the original stockholders, who had invested $7.50 per share prior to April 1, 1912, stood at $42, or 84 per cent of par. Of the $2,446,200 paid-up capital shown on the company's final balance-sheet (July 31, 1926) only $794,198, or less than one

[1] *G. G. Guide*, Nov. 26, 1924, p. 4.

[2] See Appendix D, sec. 20.

third, represented cash contributed directly by shareholders.[1] At the same date the company's elevator reserve account stood at $2,608,412, being substantially in excess of paid-up capital. The "actual fair value" placed by the board of arbitration upon the company's assets sold to the Saskatchewan Pool Elevators Limited, was $11,059,310, this being nearly $2,000,000 in excess of the value at which they were carried in the company's balance sheet.[2] The total mortgage indebtedness due the Saskatchewan government amounted to $2,336,743,[3] thus leaving a shareholders' equity of $8,722,567, or nearly $8,000,000 more than the total cash invested by stockholders — a remarkable record.

In the winding-up act passed by the Saskatchewan legislature in March, 1927, a basis of distribution was authorized, whereby the equity was apportioned according to the paid-up value of the shares, or, in other words, according to the date of allotment. Under this arrangement holders of shares issued in the first year of the company's operation were entitled to $155.84 per share, and those issued in the last two years, $27.82 each, representing increments ranging from $148.34 to $20.32 per share. In anticipation of this distribution, a number of calculating individuals had managed to purchase shares from stockholders who were either ignorant of their true asset value or were anxious for immediate cash conversion. Some 4000 of the 105,843 shares outstanding were understood to have thus changed hands, although under the constitution of the company its shares could be held only by "agriculturists," and transferred only through the secretary with the approval of the directors.[4] Speculative purchasers had sought to protect themselves by having vendors of the shares subscribe to an assignment of all proceeds accruing to such shares in the liquidation of the company.[5] In the government's bill, how-

[1] This being the sum of initial payments of $7.50 on the 105,893 shares allotted.

[2] The valuation placed by the arbitrators on the company's assets was made up as follows: Country elevator system $5,114,874; Terminal plant, Port Arthur $4,084,833; Equipment, leased terminal, Port Arthur $53,922; Buffalo transfer elevator $1,534,200; Office property, Regina $271,481. Total: $11,059,310.

[3] At the end of 1923, the company's indebtedness to the Saskatchewan government stood at $3,346,855.

[4] Appendix D, sec. 3.

[5] *Financial Post*, March 11, 1927.

ever, it was provided that no one who acquired "Co-op" shares otherwise than in accordance with the company's by-laws, could collect anything from the liquidators, although (as amended in committee) purchasers were given a lien on the value of the shares to the extent of the actual consideration paid therefor.[1] Despite strong protests against this alleged violation of property rights, and despite a request from the company's shareholders that restriction on trading in the company's shares be removed upon the appointment of a liquidator, Premier Gardiner insisted that the bill merely carried into the liquidation of the Saskatchewan Co-operative Elevator Company the same principles and rules that had applied to it as a going concern.[2] Thus, as the act of incorporation had represented an unusual form of government assistance to a coöperative organization, so the winding-up act embodied a still more unusual exercise of parliamentary authority in the interests of its members. It ensured, however, that the capitalized financial results of this government-aided, but by no means government-dependent, enterprise should accrue to the Saskatchewan farmers whose participation had built it up.

III. Operating Results of the Wheat Pools

While the period during which the three provincial wheat pools have been in operation is a limited one in point of time, and an experimental one in point of policy and method, the results for the first three years are instructive, if not conclusive.

Table IX shows the volume and proportion of grain handled by the respective pools.

The marked increase in the proportional wheat handling of all three pools in 1925–26, and the addition by two of them of coarse grains pools, are indicative of the extent to which the pooling system commended itself to Western farmers on the basis of the initial results realised through the Central Selling Agency — favored as they were by the short world crop of that year. The more limited expansion reflected in the handling of the 1926 crop (despite a considerable accession of new contracts) [3] is a reflection

[1] Stat. of Sask., 17 Geo. V, c. 72, 1927. [2] *Western Producer*, March 10, 1927.
[3] See *supra*, p. 252.

TABLE IX. DELIVERIES TO POOLS, 1923–27

Wheat

		Delivered to Pool (Bus.)	Total Marketing in Province (Bus.)	Per Cent Total Deliveries Handled by Pools
1923 Crop	Alberta	34,218,980	131,614,410	26
1924 Crop	Alberta	23,027,492	59,393,000	38.8
	Saskatchewan	50,251,181	122,389,000	41.0
	Manitoba	8,440,214	32,290,000	26.0
	Three pools	81,670,305	214,072,000	38.0
1925 Crop	Alberta	45,167,110	93,218,094	48.5
	Saskatchewan	129,708,034	233,406,545	55.6
	Manitoba	12,488,000	32,028,476	39.0
	Three pools	187,463,144	358,653,115	52.4
1926 Crop	Alberta	44,282,139	89,147,363	48.5
	Saskatchewan	119,488,976	209,405,288	57.0
	Manitoba	16,208,625	41,130,795	40.0
	Three pools	179,979,740	339,683,446	53.0
		Coarse Grains		
1925 Crop	Saskatchewan	11,366,154	41,879,000	27.2
	Manitoba	13,795,000	47,648,000	29.0
	Two pools	25,161,154	89,527,000	28.0
1926 Crop	Saskatchewan	8,367,339	32,915,239	25.4
	Manitoba	12,965,969	43,284,632	30.0
	Two pools	21,333,308	76,199,871	28.0

of such diverse factors as: natural shrinkage from death or removal of earlier members; anti-pool propaganda of the Northwest Grain Dealers' Association; grade inducements offered by line companies; and the exceptionally heavy crop yield in Alberta, where the proportion of pool acreage is considerably less than in Saskatchewan. The competitive and price-stabilising influence of the pools benefit growers generally, a considerable proportion of whom will doubtless always prefer to retain their own freedom of action in marketing, rather than bind themselves to contractual commitments and deductions. Even if the pools' share of the total wheat marketing should fail to increase appreciably beyond one-half, it is sufficiently inclusive to afford greater opportunities for realising the economies of large-scale handling than are available to any of its competitors, and to permit a significant control over market deliveries.

Pool Payments and Market Prices. — Payments made to members for wheat delivered to the pools have been distributed in four instalments.[1] For the 1924 crop (an exceptionally short one) the total price realized by the Central Selling Agency on behalf of the three pools (after deducting its selling and administrative expenses) was equivalent to $1.66 per bushel (basis No. 1 Northern, Fort William, Vancouver).[2] For the 1925 crop (whose yield was 60 per cent higher than that of the previous year) the comparable price distributed was $1.45 per bushel, and for the 1926 crop $1.42.

TABLE X. WHEAT PRODUCTION AND POOL PRICES

Year	Wheat Production Western Canada	World Wheat Production	Average Pool Price No. 1 Nor.
1923	452,260,000 bus.	3,818,844,000 bus.	$1.01
1924	235,694,000 "	3,471,823,000 "	1.66
1925	382,959,000 "	3,919,431,000 "	1.45
1926	383,440,000 "	4,180,130,000 "	1.42

In statements and publications issued by the Northwest Grain Dealers' Association, it has been pointed out that the prices realized by the pools, even without the various deductions withheld from members' returns, were appreciably less than the average market prices for the years in question.[3] The prices usually quoted in such comparisons are the average of the daily closing cash or "spot" prices for No. 1 Northern on the Winnipeg Grain Exchange. These are officially given as $1.71¾ for 1924–25, and $1.51 for 1925–26, being respectively 5¾ cents and 6 cents above pool prices. An unweighted average of daily closing prices on the Exchange does not represent, however, an average of the prices received by growers. While figures showing the quantity of wheat

[1] The economic aspects of this method of payment are discussed below, pp. 370–374.

[2] Alberta Pool payments are based on the Vancouver position.

[3] See *Facts on Grain Marketing;* also address on "The Canadian Wheat Pool," by W. Sanford Evans, Oct. 19, 1926.

sold at various prices are not published by the Winnipeg Grain Exchange, some measure of correlation between marketing and market prices is indicated by the following table, showing the average daily closing cash prices and the volume of wheat shipped from country points for each month of the 1924–25 and 1925–26 crop years.

TABLE XI. AVERAGE WINNIPEG CASH PRICES AND WHEAT DELIVERIES

By Months

	1924–1925		1925–1926	
Month	1	2	1	2
August	1.43½	1,356	1.67½	3,791
September	1.42¼	36,061	1.37½	94,595
October	1.59½	65,137	1.27	60,758
November	1.64⅛	45,602	1.42¼	101,267
December	1.72¾	17,552	1.57	47,782
January	1.96¼	12,541	1.51½	13,683
February	1.96½	10,548	1.54¾	8,750
March	1.76⅜	8,428	1,48⅜	5,913
April	1.69	4,073	1.57	5,436
May	1.82⅜	3,380	1.53¾	5,650
June	1.71⅛	6,173	1.53¼	6,939
July	1.62⅛	3,749	1.58⅞	3,047
		214,601		357,610

Column 1. Average daily closing cash price, No. 1 Northern, for month.
Column 2. Railway shipments from country points (in thousands of bushels).
(Figures from Canadian Grain Trade Year Books, 1924–25, 1925–26.)

It will be seen from the above that over 68 per cent of the 1924 wheat crop marketings and over 70 per cent of the 1925 crop, were shipped from country points during the three months of September, October, and November, in each of which the average monthly price was below —— in some cases substantially below —— the pool price. In fact, daily closing prices rose above $1.66 on only five days during this quarter in 1924, and above $1.45 on only fourteen days during the same period in 1925.

While railway shipments during the autumn quarter do not afford a direct measure of farmers' sales, — inasmuch as they include farmers' stored grain and platform shipments forwarded to terminals and held for owners' selling instructions, — they do include much the greater part of the wheat sold during the year on street.[1] Street prices are based, not on Winnipeg cash quotations, but on the future of the month in which the purchase is hedged. October, November, and December futures are generally lower than fall cash prices,[2] and street prices are adjusted to them at varying spreads, depending mainly on shipping conditions and local competition.[3] In the case of pool wheat handled on "street" basis, the spread is fixed and uniform (usually 4 or 5 cents below the basic list price). It may be concluded, therefore, that while non-pool farmers who sold their wheat in the later months of these crop years were able in an undeterminable number of cases, to realize higher prices than pool members, the average price actually received by non-pool growers — especially those selling on street — was appreciably less. Where a non-pool farmer did hold his wheat to a later month when the price was above pool average, carrying charges at the rate of one cent a bushel a month would be deductible from his selling price. In the case of pool members, on the other hand, the declared price was that realized after providing for terminal carrying charges. In short, the pool's average price is an average obtained by actual selling of farmers' grain; whereas the average with which it is compared by the Northwest Grain Dealers' Association shows no relation to actual sales.[4]

[1] It is estimated that between 40 and 50 per cent of shipments during the fall months represent wheat sold on street.

[2] Thus for September, 1924, the average closing price for the October future was \$1.36½, for the November future \$1.37¼, and for the December future \$1.31⅞ while the average cash price was \$1.42¼.

[3] The spread is usually greatest in the late fall, reflecting the prospect of having to carry the wheat as bought, until reopening of lake navigation, or pay the higher all-rail shipment transportation costs to seaboard. See section on "Street Prices" in *Report of Grain Inquiry Commission*, 1925, pp. 10–19. A street price list sent out by the Northwest Grain Dealers' Association on November 19, 1926 gave a price of \$1.18 for No. 1 Northern at 14-cent freight points. At the same date the Winnipeg cash price (Fort William basis) was \$1.38⅞, thus showing a net spread of 12½ cents.

[4] By taking the weekly average of street prices for No. 1 Northern at 27-cent (per 100 lbs.) freight rate points, as quoted in the daily prices lists sent out by the Northwest and Western Grain Dealers' Associations, and by taking the volume of wheat delivered at country shipping points in each week of the year as a weighting coefficient, the Department of Publicity and Statistics of the Canadian Co-operative

It will be realized, of course, that the greater the proportion of total cash sales on the Winnipeg market handled by the Pool, the closer must be the correspondence between the average market price and its own average selling price. Whatever strengthening influence it may be able to exercise upon the market will necessarily be reflected in the prices realized by those selling outside the Pool. This will be most marked between the beginning of the calendar year and the beginning of the new crop year, when the greater part of the marketable supply is controlled by the Pool. The advantages to its own members lie chiefly in the assurance they enjoy: first, of receiving the averaged result of the season's trading, irrespective of the time or manner of delivering their grain; and second, of sharing in any savings in marketing or handling costs which the Pool may be able to realize.

Pool Deductions. — Any adequate comparison of the returns received by pool and non-pool growers necessarily involves consideration of the various deductions to which the payments of the former are subject.[1] The basic payments of $1.66 and $1.45 made by the Central Selling Agency in 1925 and 1926 respectively, represent the prices realized after providing for terminal carrying charges, selling costs, and administrative expenses of the Central Selling Agency.[2] The last-named item was equivalent to one third of a cent per bushel handled in 1924–25, and one fifth of a cent per bushel for the two subsequent years.

Wheat Producers arrived at the following average street prices paid by the grain trade, as compared with pool prices at similar points.

	1923–24	1924–25	1925–26	1926–27
Ave. Grain Trade Price	$0.74½	$1.43¾	$1.19¾	$1.17⅘
Pool Price	0.79¾	1.46	1.25⅛	1.22 1/20

—*The Truth about Grain Prices*—Can. Co-op. Wheat Producers, 1927.

It is to be noted, however, that the pool prices here given were subject to the deductions taken by the respective provincial pools.

[1] See statement of Northwest Grain Dealers' Association, *re* Pool Deductions. *Manitoba Free Press*, Nov. 18, 1926.

[2] For the pool year 1926–27, terminal elevation and storage charges aggregated $4,891,490. Of this amount approximately one half was paid to pool-owned terminal facilities, as was the sum of $629,023, representing improvements in grades through mixing operations in pool private terminals. — *Directors' Report*, Can. Co-op. Wheat Producers, 1926–27.

The above gross returns to pool members were subject to three sets of deductions: (*a*) initial deductions on account of freight and handling charges; (*b*) deductions on account of elevator and commercial reserves; (*c*) deductions on account of provincial pool operating costs. The first of these represent charges for getting the grain into selling position at terminals, which must be borne by pool and non-pool farmers alike. In two respects, however, the former stand in a different position. In the first place, the handling charge on pool street grain is fixed and uniform, whereas non-pool street sellers are subject to variable and usually much larger spreads.[1] In the second place, in so far as pool grain is handled through pool elevators in Saskatchewan and Manitoba, patrons are credited pro rata with the difference between the charges they pay and the ascertained cost of elevator operation. Thus in the case of pool members delivering street grain, or patronizing pool elevators, their net deductions on account of initial handlings are less than those of non-pool growers.

Deductions on account of elevator and commercial reserves stand obviously in a different class from those made to cover pool operating expenses. The former are in the nature of deferred credits or contractual investments. Receipts issued for elevator reserve deductions are in effect savings certificates upon which interest at 6 per cent is payable out of pool elevator revenues. The amounts credited to members on account of commercial reserve deductions represent their individual equities in the liquid assets of the pools. No contractual payment of interest on such deductions has been provided for, the matter being left to the action of delegates at annual pool meetings.[2] Commercial reserves are intended to provide working capital, funds which are not required by the provincial pools themselves during the fall months being loaned to the Central Selling Agency for financing initial

[1] Pool policy in relation to handling of street grain is discussed below, pp. 366, 367.

[2] Saskatchewan Wheat Pool Radio Broadcast, "Pool Deductions and Reserves," *Western Producer*, March 10, 1927. At the Saskatchewan Pool meeting in November, 1927, it was decided that interest on commercial reserve deductions, at a rate to be determined by the directors, should be credited to each grower, as in the case of elevator deductions. — *Western Producer*, Nov. 24, 1927.

payments to growers, thereby reducing to such extent the Central's bank borrowings. While wheat pool contracts authorize deductions not exceeding 1 per cent of receipts, for commercial reserve purposes, the actual amount deducted each year is decided by the delegates on recommendation of their directors. At the end of the 1926–27 pool year the commercial reserves accumulated by the three pools totaled $4,776,317, being distributed as follows: Alberta Pool, $934,780; Saskatchewan Pool, $3,362,937; Manitoba Pool, $478,600. Future deductions on this account are likely to be made for the purpose of retiring earlier-dated certificates, on a revolving plan, rather than for increasing the size of the commercial reserve.

TABLE XII. POOL DEDUCTIONS FOR ELEVATOR AND COMMERCIAL RESERVES

(Amounts per bushel in cents)

	Commercial Reserve	Elevator Reserve
Season 1923–24		
Alberta Pool	.61	Nil
Season 1924–25		
Alberta Pool, from wheat	.66	2.00
Saskatchewan Pool, from wheat	1.66	2.00
Manitoba Pool, from wheat	1.66	2.00
Season 1925–26		
Alberta Pool, from wheat	.145	2.00
Saskatchewan Pool, from wheat	.725	2.00
" " " oats	.237	1.00
" " " barley	.30	1.50
" " " flax	1.05	3.00
" " " rye	.442	1.50
Manitoba Pool, from wheat	Nil	1.371
" " " oats	.475	1.001
" " " barley	.602	1.251
" " " flax	2.10	2.00
" " " rye	.885	1.751
Season 1926–27		
Alberta Pool, from wheat	1.15	2.00
Saskatchewan Pool, from wheat	1.42	2.00
Manitoba Pool, from wheat	1.42	2.00

Pool Operating Costs. — The third class of deductions, those taken to cover pool operating expenses, represent the direct charge borne by farmers as a condition of having their grain marketed under the pooling system. It is a deduction which does not fall as such upon the non-pool farmer, even though he may benefit by the pools' competition and influence on the market. The outlays of the provincial pools are of two sorts: adjustments with country elevators, and pool operating expenses proper. The former include such items as carrying charges on pool street grain,[1] and adjustments on grades and freight on dockage.[2] These arise out of the anomalous nature of pool "street" grain, which instead of being grain sold on street, is grain in less than carload lots, handled by elevator companies for the pools under special conditions. These mean in effect that some of the additional costs and risks involved in the handling of such grain are borne by pool members as a whole, instead of being carried directly by those delivering street grain. It is in part due to this arrangement that the initial deductions taken from the latter at the time of delivery are less than the spreads to which non-pool street sellers are ordinarily subjected. The actual deduction sustained by pool members on account of such adjustments (which must be made with pool elevators as well as with elevator companies handling pool grain under contract) is substantially reduced through the accrual to the pools of patronage refunds of surplus earnings from pool terminal elevators. In the case of the Manitoba Pool these have been sufficient to absorb practically all the carrying charges.

Pool operating expenses proper include such items as office salaries and expenses, directors' fees and travelling expenses, costs of organization and publicity work, expenses of field service department, pool locals and annual meeting of pool delegates. A large part of the administrative expenses of the pools arise out of their complicated accounting operations, involving as they do the checking of many thousands of growers' participation certificates and individual accounts, distribution of checks to growers at each payment period, crediting of members' reserve deductions and

[1] These cover storage and insurance on pool street grain, with interest on initial payments made by elevator companies to members delivering such grain. In pool contracts with elevator companies, these inclusive charges are set at the basic rate of 1/30 cent per bushel per day, up to time of terminal delivery. See Appendix G, sec. 12.

[2] Appendix G, secs. 8a, 10.

interest thereon, and accounting with each elevator company handling pool grain. This work has been further complicated by the inclusion of coarse grain pools in Saskatchewan and Manitoba. As an offset to such operating expenses, certain pool revenues are applicable, such as contract fees,[1] and interest on loans to the Central Selling Agency from elevator or commercial reserves, together with general interest on deposits. The following items taken from the financial statement of the Saskatchewan Co-operative Wheat Producers for 1925–26 are indicative of the nature of pool operating expenses and revenues.

TABLE XIII. SASKATCHEWAN POOL EXPENSES, 1925–26

Adjustments with Elevator Companies:		
Carrying charges		$1,141,182
Reserve for freight on dockage, etc.		80,000
Reserve for grade adjustments		11,000
Total		1,232,182
Less Revenue		
1924 Adjustment account	78,113	
Profits from terminals	64,374	
Premium on Vancouver diversions	6,565	149,052
		$1,083,130
Pool Administrative Expenses:		
Head office expenses	567,502	
Country organization and canvassers' commissions	72,085	
Field Service Department	66,270	
Delegates' fees and expenses	20,590	
Publicity	11,600	738,047
Less Revenue		
Contract fees	59,261	
General interest	26,051	
Interest on Commercial Reserve	41,039	126,351
Net administrative expenses		$611,696
Add net adjustments		1,083,130
Total non-credit deductions from growers		$1,694,826

The above costs were distributed over 126,600,522 bushels of wheat and 11,435,690 bushels of coarse grains, and were equivalent, therefore, to 1.19 cents per bushel handled.

[1] These are membership fees (less canvasser's commission) paid by contract signers. See Appendix E, sec. 14.

The following table shows the operating costs for each of the pools for successive years, in fractions of cent per bushel.[1]

TABLE XIV. WHEAT POOL OPERATING COSTS

	Net Carrying Charges	Net Administrative Costs	Non-Credit Deductions
Season 1923–24			
Alberta Wheat Pool			.484
Season 1924–25			
Alberta Pool		.34	.34
Saskatchewan Pool	.12	.52	.64
Manitoba Pool	*	.597	.597
Season 1925–26			
Alberta Pool		.355	.355
Saskatchewan Pool	.84	.35	1.19
Manitoba Pool	.013	.616	.629
Season 1926–27			
Alberta Pool		.347	.347
Saskatchewan Pool	.99	.45	1.44
Manitoba Pool	.017	.786	.803

* Carrying charges amounting to .431 cents per bushel were absorbed by adjustment with Central Selling Agency.

The higher deductions taken by the Saskatchewan Pool, despite the greater volume of its turnover, are to be accounted for mainly by the return of its terminal profits in the form of patronage credits to shippers; whereas the Alberta and Manitoba Pools apply their share of such surplus as an offset to country carrying charges.

It will be seen from the above that the expense deductions borne by pool members constitute a relatively small unit charge. Such as they are, they represent the premium which pool farmers pay for beneficial participation in such system of marketing. In the case particularly of members delivering street grain, the increased returns, under conditions of fixed handling margins and pooled carrying charges and risks, may amount to several times the premium paid. Furthermore, where pool members are also patrons of pool elevators, they may ordinarily expect to participate in patronage returns exceeding the deductions made on

[1] Adapted from official figures, Can. Co-op. Wheat Producers.

account of pool operating expenses. Thus, while the latter amounted to 1.44 cents a bushel in the case of Saskatchewan Pool members for 1926–27, it was more than covered by the patronage distribution of 1¾ cents a bushel returned by Saskatchewan Pool Elevators.

CHAPTER XIX

COÖPERATIVE POLICIES AND RESULTS

I. Coöperative Policies of Farmers' Companies

It will be realized from the foregoing history of Grain Growers' organizations in Western Canada that coöperative policy has pursued various objectives and assumed different forms in accordance with the conditions of the time and the existing resources of the farmers' organizations. Coöperation in the broad sense, as defined by the veteran coöperator, H. W. Wolff, "is just a simple junction of forces among a number of persons more or less similarly situated and having a common object in view, for attaining that object." That object among agriculturists, as expressed by the same authority, is "to offer a means for profitably uniting forces for the avoidance of unnecessary expense, for the obtainment of better value for produce, and for the withstanding of oppression." [1]

Early Phases.—The Grain Growers' organizations of Western Canada have steadily pursued this object during the quarter-century of their existence, although both the point of attack and the attack formation have been shifted from time to time. In the initial phase the objective most definitely aimed at was "the withstanding of oppression," in which light the grain grower regarded the monopolistic practices of the railway and line elevator companies. Here the relief sought was the obtaining of regulative legislation and the securing of its enforcement. This was designed, on the one hand, to facilitate direct shipment by the producer to the central market, and on the other hand, to protect him where he had to make use of the country elevator. This involved, in the one case, the imposing of obligations upon railway companies, and in the other, upon elevator companies. Compulsory construction of loading platforms, and recognition

[1] H. W. Wolff, *Coöperation in Agriculture*, pp. 18, 19.

of the farmer shipper's right to car allotment on a parity with the elevator, were fought for and gained by the Grain Growers' Associations as a means of direct access to market. Statutory definition of the responsibilities of the elevator operator as warehouseman, establishment of maximum handling charges, and the setting up of a permanent government supervising agency, were the legislative and administrative remedies obtained through the enactment and successive amendments of the Manitoba Grain Act, as the means of protecting growers who were dependent upon the local elevator in the marketing of their grain. Coöperation at this period took the form of collective representations by the Grain Growers' Associations before the government and Parliament, and of action through the courts where deemed necessary. It did not involve at this stage any assumption of middleman functions by farmers themselves; it aimed merely at regulation of private middleman and transportation agencies in the interests of producers.

With the advent in 1906 of the Grain Growers' Grain Company, coöperation took the form of direct participation in the grain trade upon the central market. The very efforts made by Grain Exchange interests to wreck the farmers' company served, on the one hand to bring the Grain Growers' Associations to the defence of their commercial auxiliary in legislature and court, and on the other hand, to rally the patronage support of growers in the country. Here it was a fight "to withstand the oppression" of the organized grain trade as the farmer viewed it, and to uphold the right of producers to function as their own middlemen. While constrained to forego its original intention of distributing patronage dividends, the Grain Growers' Company pursued the two-fold coöperative objective of securing the fullest possible share of middleman margins for farmer shareholders, and of offering superior middleman service within the limits of the established marketing system. The inauguration of the company's Sampling and Claims Departments afforded additional service and protection to grain shippers, which competition tended to generalize. The financing of the *Grain Growers' Guide*, and the annual grants to provincial farmers' associations made possible by the company's grain profits, served, furthermore, to strengthen the influence and solidarity of the Grain Growers' Movement.

The next phase in the development of coöperative policy by Western farmers had its basis in the Grain Growers' united demand for government ownership and operation of elevators as public utilities. Out of that persistent agitation and the egregious failure of the Manitoba government elevator experiment, there evolved, on the one hand, the unique plan of government-aided coöperative enterprise embodied in the institution of the Saskatchewan and the Alberta Co-operative Elevator Companies; and on the other hand, the transition of the Grain Growers' Company from a farmers' grain commission agency to an integrated farmer-owned line elevator system. Henceforth growers could market their grain through their own elevators as well as consign them to their own selling agency on the central market.

Entrance into the field of elevator acquisition and operation involved, however, extensive capital requirements, and in this phase the securing of farmers' stock subscriptions was of basic importance. While in Saskatchewan and Alberta the greater part of the capital for elevator construction was supplied through the provincial treasuries, government loans were nevertheless conditioned on farmers' stock subscriptions equal to the capital cost. Thus the Saskatchewan and Alberta companies, as well as the Grain Growers' Company with its diversified enterprises, made concentrated efforts through aggressive activity by their organization departments, and through the payment of attractive dividends, to secure investment participation by the greatest possible number of farmers. At the same time, the companies followed the policy of reinvesting earnings as a means of financing the extension of their facilities, and in the case of the Saskatchewan "Co-op," of increasing members' equity in the enterprise through successive stock dividend distributions. It is this need of greater capital resources to finance the expansion of the companies' facilities and services to farmers that mainly explains why the distribution of patronage dividends was never carried out by the farmers' elevator companies during this period. It was felt, too, that the most effective assurance of farmers' patronage lay in the possession of a stock-owning interest. But it was as a shareholder, not as a patron, that the farmer participated in the earnings of the companies and exercised a voice in their control.

Coöperative Structure of Farmers' Elevator Companies. — The Saskatchewan "Co-op," and the United Grain Growers, however, were not joint stock companies in the ordinary sense. Their articles of incorporation provided that their stock should not only be issued exclusively to bona fide agriculturists, but also that it could be transferred only to such persons.[1] The number of shares which any individual might hold was definitely limited, and in no case did they entitle the holder to more than one vote. Under these circumstances there was no free trading in company shares.[2] The companies were interested in the allotment of new stock, not in the market movements of outstanding shares. Shareholders were organized into local units, which might not only make representations to the management regarding operation of their local elevator, but also forward resolutions and recommendations to the directors, or to the annual meeting. At the latter each local was represented by elected delegates whose expenses were paid out of company funds. Voting was on a delegate, not on a proxy, basis. The annual meetings of the farmers' companies were, indeed, unique affairs. They often extended over half a dozen or more sessions, attended by between 300 and 500 delegates. Scores of resolutions forwarded by locals passed through resolutions committees for discussion by the meeting. The directors' reports and financial statements, with auditors' reports, were presented in great detail, and subjected generally to close scrutiny and thorough discussion by delegates. These reports, with minutes of annual meetings, were subsequently issued in printed form to each shareholder. The annual meetings of the farmers' companies were, indeed, in the nature of conventions, in which free discussion and parliamentary formality were blended in an impressive manner. It would be difficult to find companies of comparable size where shareholders have participated more generally or intelligently in the conduct of affairs,

[1] See *supra*, p. 45; Appendix D, sec. 3.

[2] See *supra*, pp. 338, 339.

or where directors have rendered a more complete and public accounting of their stewardship. In all these respects the farmers' companies were essentially coöperative in their organization and control.

The Question of Patronage Dividends. — The principal respect in which the coöperative character of the farmers' companies has been challenged, and upon which the sentiment for pool organization has largely rested, was their failure to distribute earnings upon a patronage basis. The financial and administrative considerations which overruled the adoption of such policy in earlier years have been noted elsewhere.[1] The accounting difficulties, however, were not insuperable, as demonstrated by the handling-at-cost arrangements offered to the pools by the companies in 1925, and by the street-grain patronage dividend plan now in operation by the U. G. G. Nor were financial considerations altogether responsible for the decision of the U. G. G. to defer the application of such method after extended consideration in 1918,[2] or for the tabling of a patronage dividend resolution at the annual meeting of the Saskatchewan "Co-op" in 1923.[3] The course taken represented rather a choice between alternative coöperative policies. The alternative to patronage distribution is not necessarily the distribution of profits to those who have contributed capital. Where the return to capital is limited to a stipulated maximum rate, and where excess earnings are employed in extending the company's facilities and its service to farmers in general, and in making grants to farmers' non-commercial organizations and educational objects, as realized by the Saskatchewan "Co-op" and the U. G. G., it is a case of utilizing profits for the benefit of farmers in general, instead of for the personal advantage of those individuals who have been patrons of the company. The Saskatchewan "Co-op," it is true, steadily pursued the policy of distributing stock dividends; but the principal effect of this was to make it possible for a greater number of farmers to secure the establishment of local coöperative elevators with a minimum of capital contribution. As described in a preceding chapter, profits

[1] See *supra*, pp. 192–194.
[2] U. G. G., 1918, pp. 44–60.
[3] *Sask. Co-op. News*, Dec., 1923, pp. 6, 7.

that might have been distributed as patronage dividends by the Grain Growers' Company were applied to financing coöperative supply services as a means of reducing farmers' production costs. In such cases as these it is a question of the scope and method of coöperative distribution, rather than of capitalistic as opposed to coöperative policy.

Coöperative policy, again, involves consideration, not merely of the mode of distributing profits, but also of the size of margins from which profits are derived. The patronage dividend plan generally implies the charging of regular trade margins, from which the surplus realized is rebated to those from whom such margins have been taken by the company. Alternatively, the lowering of trade margins or the rendering of superior service for the same charge, while precluding the payment of patronage dividends, may not only yield direct and immediate advantages to patrons, but also tend through the influence of competition to generalize the advantages. While the farmers' companies charged the same or, in some cases, higher rates than the line companies for handling grain through their elevators, they provided facilities which growers especially desired, and they pursued the general policy of narrowing and equalizing the spread on street grain which they purchased. The provision of special bin storage had been demanded by the Grain Growers in their agitation for government ownership of elevators,[1] and in building their elevators with such facilities, the farmers' companies provided growers with the means of having their grain stored without loss of identity, and its sale effected on the basis of official grade and dockage determination. With the advent of the coöperative elevators, special bin handling tended to replace platform shipment in favor with carload shippers, since it afforded the same protection with greatly reduced labor.[2] Most of the coöperative elevators were also equipped with improved cleaners, thereby permitting farmers who so desired to have their screenings returned to them and freight on dockage saved.[3]

[1] See *supra*, p. 85.

[2] See *supra*, p. 80. See also "The Country Elevator," in *Sask. Co-op. News*, Sept., 1924.

[3] *Report of Royal Grain Inquiry Commission*, 1925, pp. 60–72.

Policy in Relation to Street Grain. — While provision of special binning and cleaning facilities affords a service of appreciable advantage to carload shippers, the majority of grain growers are sellers of street grain, on which the widest margins are ordinarily taken and from which the profits of line companies are mainly derived. One of the standing complaints of Western farmers has been the setting of street prices in accordance with lists sent out daily to all elevator points by the Northwest Grain Dealers' Association, based on closing future prices of the month in which purchases are hedged at the time.[1] Neither of the farmers' companies was a member of the Grain Dealers' Association, the country operators of each being governed in their buying by street price lists sent out independently by their respective head offices.[2] From the outset the Saskatchewan "Co-op" followed the policy of paying street prices above those sent out by the Grain Dealers' Association.[3] The report of the Turgeon Grain Inquiry Commission stated that evidence presented at certain of its hearings showed that the price-reporting committee of the association during certain periods of the year sent out two street price lists to local agents, one going to points where the Saskatchewan "Co-op" was established, the other to stations where the latter was not a competitor.[4] Both of the farmers' companies supported their application to the Board of Grain Commissioners for higher maximum country elevator handling rates primarily on the ground that losses incurred in handling special binned grain at rates that did not cover the actual cost of service meant the charging of larger spreads on street grain.[5] While the Saskatchewan "Co-op" was the only elevator company to apply the maximum tariff of 2½ cents on special binned grain authorized by the Grain Commissioners in 1922, such action was accompanied by advancing

[1] See *supra*, p. 31 n.

[2] Evidence of James Murray (U. G. G.) before Grain Inquiry Commission, March 11,1924. Evidence of F. W. Riddell (Sask. Co-op.), March 13, 1924.

[3] Statements of C. A. Dunning and Geo. Langley to S. G. G. A. Convention, 1912. *G. G. Guide*, Feb. 21, 28, 1912. Evidence of F. W. Riddell before Grain Inquiry Commission, Winnipeg, March 13, 1924.

[4] *Report*, p. 18.

[5] U. G. G., 1920, pp. 50, 51; see also "Who Pays the Loss on Handling Charges?" in *Sask. Co-op. News*, March, 1922.

its street prices two cents above the lists sent out by the Grain Dealers' Association.[1] The farmers' companies, moreover, followed the policy, not only of keeping their street prices in general above those of the line companies, but also of offering uniform street prices at all points having the same freight rate to terminals.[2] Line companies, on the other hand, generally vary street margins in accordance with local conditions of competition and car supply.[3] Since the two farmers' companies maintained elevators at approximately one half of the grain-shipping stations in the Prairie Provinces the influence of their competition and policy in raising street prices and reducing local disparities was far-reaching. Buying street grain on narrow and uniform margins obviously means reduced profits, and correspondingly limited prospects of paying large patronage dividends. If the real object of coöperation be the mutual benefit of those who are economically weak, it is quite arguable that such end may be served no less effectually by reducing marketing margins for producers at large, than by earning large dividends for company patrons through maintaining high margins. "It may be the deliberate policy of a coöperative society to avoid having a surplus to be distributed. And that policy may be deliberately adopted in order to confer the largest possible benefit on those whose patronage makes the enterprise a success." [4] Patronage dividends to members may indeed be earned at the expense of other farmers.[5]

[1] *Sask. Co-op. News*, March, 1922, p. 10. This policy was maintained by the company in its handling arrangements with the Saskatchewan Pool in 1924, under which it charged 2½ instead of 1¾ cents on handling special bin grain, but paid street prices one cent above those provided under pool contracts with elevator companies.

[2] See *supra*, p. 126. "Our policy is to pay the same price, adjusted according to freight rates, at all our elevators." Statement of U. G. G. before Grain Inquiry Comm., Winnipeg, March 10, 1924.

[3] "The [Sask.] company was obliged to pay the same prices for grain at all points taking the same freight rate, being a coöperative organization, while these fellows handed out a fine deal at odd points only, and farmers receiving the benefit of these special deals should remember that brother farmers elsewhere had to pay for it." Address of C. A. Dunning to S. G. G. A. Convention, 1916, *G. G. Guide*, Feb. 23, 1916.

[4] *Sask. Co-op. News*, Sept., 1921, p. 10.

[5] The U. G. G. committee that investigated farmers' elevators in the U. S. in 1918 reported that they found that "the payment of a coöperative dividend has a

The Saskatchewan Co-operative, at any rate, advisedly followed the policy of increasing returns to farmers selling their grain by wagonload, as an alternative to paying patronage dividends.[1] The company was doubtless influenced in this decision by the consideration that its undertakings had been financed to a large extent by public funds, and that the benefits of its operation and competition should, therefore, be generalized as far as possible.[2] In seeking to increase competitive returns to farmers at large, rather than to offer premiums to those patronizing it directly, the farmers' companies would seem to have chosen, not between co-operation and non-coöperation, but rather between the narrower and the broader applications of the coöperative idea.

Since the advent of the wheat pools, the U. G. G. has been led to carry out patronage distribution in respect to the handling both of pool grain and that of its individual patrons. Under arrangements made with the Alberta and Saskatchewan Pools, the difference between revenue from handling grain through the company's country and terminal elevators, and the ascertained costs (including therein rental at 6 per cent of appraised value) has been returned by the company to the pools proportionately to the number of pool bushels handled.[3] At the annual meeting of the company in 1924, a resolution was carried providing for payment of individual patronage dividends on street grain, if

tendency to encourage the locally owned elevators to buy on a very wide margin, as very few of them pay any coöperative dividend to non-shareholders, with the result that the profits from the non-shareholders' business are divided up among the shareholders on a pro rata basis." U. G. G., 1918, p. 52.

[1] "Our policy has been, instead of paying patronage dividends, — which perhaps in some years we were financially able to do, — to automatically pay patronage dividends by buying our grain at as high a price as we could possibly pay with any reasonable degree of safety." Evidence of F. W. Riddell before Grain Inquiry Committee, March 12, 1924.

[2] "Our organization was made possible only because of certain legislation and financial commitments of the whole of the province, and my view anyway has been, that that lays the company under obligation to all the people, and particularly to the producer of grain, chiefly because we have no facility for redeeming any obligations to the rest of the province other than that. That reduces the question of patronage dividends to the question of the price you pay for your commodity in the country elevators." *Ibid.*

[3] U. G. G., 1926, pp. 20–23; 1927, p. 40.

warranted by earnings. These proved insufficient to permit such payment in 1925, but in 1926 the U. G. G. paid its first patronage dividend on street grain, at the rate of one cent a bushel, involving a total distribution of $78,792. A return at the same rate, aggregating $76,972, has been made in 1927.[1]

United Grain Growers' Coöperative Policy in Livestock Marketing. — Although the U. G. G. has only begun to distribute patronage dividends on grain since the coming of the wheat pools, and although it has never made such returns in connection with its farm-supplies business, the company has for a number of years carried out a pooling policy in the handling of livestock. The coöperative livestock marketing operations of the Grain Growers' Company constitute in themselves a highly instructive study, which hardly lies, however, within the scope of the present work. Nevertheless, as one expression of the broad coöperative policy of the United Grain Growers, the main lines of development may be briefly noted here.

Under the amalgamation of the Grain Growers' Grain Company and the Alberta Co-operative in 1917, the subsidiary livestock operations which the latter had conducted since 1914, and which the former had inaugurated in 1916, were consolidated in the Livestock Department of the U. G. G., which operated on a commission basis in the stockyards of St. Boniface (East Winnipeg), Calgary, and Edmonton, and later, in the newly established coöperative stockyards at Moosejaw and Prince Albert, Saskatchewan. The method of operation at this stage corresponded to that followed by the old Grain Growers' Grain Company before it entered the elevator field. The U. G. G. Livestock Department simply represented a farmer-owned selling agency handling carloads of cattle, hogs, and sheep, instead of grain. Its operations differed from those of the Grain Commission Department, however, in that it dealt less with individual shippers than with local shipping associations, whose organization it sought to promote at times through a small field staff, and through coöperation with the Markets Branch of the Saskatchewan Department of Agriculture.

[1] U. G. G., 1926, p. 27; 1927, p. 40.

Following the drastic decline in livestock prices after 1920, and the embarrassing restriction of the American market under the Fordney Tariff, the U. G. G. undertook to make a number of export cattle shipments to Great Britain on a pool basis.[1] These experiments led to the extension of the pooling plan to general cattle marketing on a non-contract basis. Pool deliveries were sorted by the company's representatives at the stockyards into commercial grades, or separated for the feed lots, and uniform carloads were shipped to whatever markets in Canada, the United States, or Great Britain offered the most favorable demand at the time for each class of cattle. Pool shippers received on delivery an advance up to 70 per cent of the appraised market value of their stock, with a participation certificate showing the number, weight, and valuation of the animals delivered. At first, weekly settlements were made on participation certificates, but in July, 1923, the pool was placed on a yearly basis. Henceforth shippers received at delivery the full appraised value of their cattle as established on the local market, sharing at the end of the year in the profits realized by pool merchandising of uniform carloads in domestic, American, and overseas markets.[2] The gain to shippers lay not only in the small additional price realized through such arbitraging operations, but also in the stabilizing influence on local market prices (reflected in the appraisal value of their stock), arising out of the pool's action in forwarding primary deliveries to other markets, thus relieving local selling pressure.

In the operation of its cattle pool, the only profits received by the U. G. G. were those realized through its Commission Department,[3] all merchandising profits being rebated to shippers.[4] The extension of the pool's business depended primarily, however,

[1] U. G. G., 1921, pp. 60, 61.

[2] See *Co-operative Cattle Selling*, issued by U. G. G., 1924.

[3] Pool cattle deliveries passed through the Commission Department to the cattle pool. Hogs and sheep and non-pool cattle were of course handled by the former exclusively. U. G. G., 1924, pp. 48, 49, 55.

[4] Between Feb., 1923, and June, 1925, over 150,000 cattle were handled through the U. G. G. Cattle Pool, on which patronage dividends of $85,000 were distributed. *Report of U. L. G. to Sask. Livestock Pool Investigational Board, 1925.*

upon the organization and patronage of local livestock shipping associations. Meanwhile in Alberta, and later in Saskatchewan and Manitoba, the demand had arisen for the establishment of producers' livestock marketing associations, organized on a provincial, contract basis, along lines similar to the wheat pools. The Livestock Department of the U. G. G., while operating an interprovincial cattle pool, was after all merely a subsidiary department of a farmers' grain company, and had no organic relations with livestock producers, except as individuals might be shareholders of the company, or as local shipping associations might appoint company elevator agents as their shipping agents. A provincial livestock pool was organized in Alberta early in 1925, followed by steps in the same direction in Saskatchewan (where a Livestock Pool Investigational Committee was appointed by the S. G. G. A., acting with the Farmers Union), and in Manitoba, through the newly established Co-operative Marketing Board.

With a view to anticipating duplication of coöperative livestock organization, the directors of the U. G. G. had announced, at the annual meeting of the company in 1924, the decision to convert the Livestock Department into a separate subsidiary which should operate on a purely coöperative basis. The livestock commission profits of the year ended, instead of being taken into company revenue, were invested in the stock of the new subsidiary, incorporated as the United Livestock Growers Limited. With a view to the establishment of organic relations with local livestock shipping associations, the latter were invited to choose representatives to the directorate of the United Livestock Growers, either directly or through a provincial association, where such existed.[1] In 1925 an arrangement was made with the Alberta Co-operative Livestock Producers Limited, whereby the latter purchased a third interest in the U. L. G., and contracted to market its members' deliveries through that body. A proposal made by the U. L. G. to turn over the assets and organization to the three provincial livestock pools at the beginning of 1928 was agreed on in principle at a conference held in Regina in May, 1927. The Saskatchewan and Manitoba Co-operative Livestock Producers,

[1] Report of U. L. G., etc., pp. 4–6.

however, have since proceeded along independent lines, and at the annual meeting of the U. G. G. in December, 1927, the delegates decided, after listening to representatives of the provincial livestock pools, that the latter were not yet in a position to assure marketing facilities that would satisfactorily replace those of the U. L. G. They authorised their directors, therefore, to continue the operations of the U. L. G. on the Calgary, Edmonton and St. Boniface markets.[1]

The history of the livestock marketing activities of the United Grain Growers thus reveals an instructive evolution in coöperative policy. Beginning with a subsidiary livestock commission department, and promoting the organization of local coöperative shipping associations, the company experimented with different types of cattle pools, emanating in the organization of a non-profit subsidiary in the form of the United Livestock Growers.[2] Since the advent of the provincial livestock contract pools the U. G. G. has sought to prevent coöperative duplication, through various proposals, to the point of offering to withdraw from the field altogether, provided equivalent facilities would be assured by coördination of the three provincial pools. While complete assimilation of the two systems has not yet been realised, the U. G. G. has pursued, throughout, a policy of patient and generous accommodation. Whatever the outcome, the credit of pioneering and evolving an efficient and comprehensive plan of coöperative livestock marketing in Western Canada belongs to the United Grain Growers.

III. Coöperative Aspects of the Wheat Pools

The wheat pools in Western Canada, it has been shown, were the outcome of various related causes. They were born during the post-war agricultural depression, and represented an attempt, on the one hand, to reproduce as completely as possible, on a voluntary basis, the collective selling system identified with the operations of the Canadian Wheat Board; and on the other hand,

[1] *G. G. Guide*, Dec. 15, 1927, p. 40.

[2] Approximately $100,000 has been returned to producers by the U. G. G. cattle pool and the U. L. G. — U. L. G., 1927

to adapt to the marketing of grain in Western Canada the California plan of non-profit contract pooling, which it was felt represented a truer form of coöperation than that realized by the farmers' elevator companies. The promoters of the pools, in their appeals for farmer membership, have been inclined to depreciate the coöperative character, the achievements, and the officers of the farmers' companies. Extended negotiations initiated by the latter with a view to coördination of forces and resources broke down on the declared ground that the two represented fundamentally different systems of marketing.[1] In the case of the Saskatchewan "Co-op," the solution was found — after a period of lively recrimination — in its complete absorption by the provincial pool. While the U. G. G. has so far retained its identity and its elevator system, it has found it advisable to dispose of a number of its local elevators to the provincial pools, and is exposed to actual pool elevator competition at numerous points.

Pool Elevators and Farmers' Company Elevators. — The farmers' elevator companies came into existence as a coöperative alternative to farmer dependence upon the line elevator companies, acting together through the Northwest Grain Dealers' Association. The pools came into being as a means of affording growers an alternative to speculative marketing through the Grain Exchange, to which the operations of the farmers' companies had been competitively adapted. In the case of the pools, elevator acquisition and operation have been incidental to the primary business of contract wheat pooling. In the case of the farmers' elevator companies, grain trading was largely incidental to their investment in warehousing facilities. The farmer's patronage was expected to accompany his investment in the coöperative elevator. Under the pool system, the farmer becomes an investor in elevators in proportion to the volume of his pool deliveries. In the former case, he became identified with the farmer-owned marketing organization by signing a stock subscription form; in the latter by signing a marketing contract form, through the fulfilment of which he automatically acquires elevator reserve certificates as evidence of individual investment interest in pool

[1] See *supra*, p. 232.

elevators. In the operation of the latter, moreover, profits or surplus accrue to farmers, not as contributors of capital (as under the Saskatchewan "Co-op" plan of stock dividend distribution), but as contributors of elevator business. As noted elsewhere the form of such returns differs in each province.[1] In Saskatchewan they have been distributed as cash patronage dividends.[2] In Manitoba they are applied to building up the equity of member-patrons in their local elevators. In Alberta they are absorbed into general pool revenue, and to such extent lessen the deductions made from growers' returns on account of pool operating expenses. All three methods, however, contribute to increase members' net returns from their marketings, directly or indirectly.

While the pool elevator subsidiaries are "non-profit" organizations in the sense noted above, they are not "non-stock" institutions. Each is incorporated with authorised share capitalization, which becomes "paid-up" through the process of investing elevator reserve deductions. The visible difference between stock distribution in the new and the older farmers' elevator companies is that in the former the stock, apart from directors' qualifying shares, is held, not by individuals, but by the provincial pools, representing members as a whole. On the other hand, the issue of interest-bearing certificates on account of elevator reserve deductions or reinvested patronage shares, is a recognition of individual capital claims which remain valid whether or not the holder continues to be a pool member or patron. It is not likely that the transfer of such certificates will be permitted to other than agriculturists. And it is contemplated that when new pool elevator capital requirements are provided for, the earlier dated certificates will be retired under the revolving fund plan. In any case certificates carry no voting rights. The control remains with the pools as a whole through the common directorates of provincial pools and elevator subsidiaries. In the novel case of the Manitoba Pool elevators, as has been seen, the ownership

[1] See *supra*, pp. 259–262.

[2] In 1925–26 these amounted to $474,614, and in 1926–27 (with the taking over of the Saskatchewan Co-op. system) they totaled $1,372,538.

will eventually pass to the local elevator associations, although operation will continue to be centralized.[1] Under the pool system capital is a hired agent instead of the controlling factor. It is capital, moreover, which has neither been loaned by the government, nor, as yet, borrowed on the market, nor even subscribed by farmers, but which has been incidentally contributed by pool members through contractual deductions or deferred patronage returns.

Pool Policy in Relation to Street Grain. — It has been shown in the preceding section of this chapter how the farmers' companies, especially the Saskatchewan "Co-op," pursued policies designed to reduce spreads and remove local disparities in relation to street grain, with a view to improving the marketing position of those growers who are numerically greater and economically weaker than those shipping by carload. Under pool operation, the relative disabilities of the former are tending to be removed altogether. This is being brought about, first, through readjustments in "street" spreads, and second, through change in the price basis.

In the first place, under pool contracts with elevator companies and under pool elevator tariffs (except in Manitoba), the spread between the initial payments to members delivering "stored-to-grade" or special binned grain, and those delivering street grain is fixed and uniform for the season and for all points having the same freight rate.[2] Thus local and day-to-day fluctuations in spreads between street and track prices are eliminated. Furthermore, risks of grade losses and carrying charges on street grain, which under ordinary conditions are reflected in the spread, are absorbed by the pool as a whole, and adjusted in the final payments, so that these items are not borne directly by those delivering street grain.[3] In the case of the Manitoba Pool elevators, the spread has been eliminated altogether, the same handling charge being made for grain whether delivered in wagonload or carload lots. Under this plan, street grain, whether delivered by pool or non-pool patrons, is handled under graded storage tickets, so that the farmer with a small amount of grain to deliver or sell is able to market it upon the same basis as the carload shipper.

[1] See *supra*, pp. 254, 255. [2] See Appendix G, secs. 4, 5. [3] See *supra*, p. 347.

In the second place, under the pool system, the farmer no longer sells his grain on street. He merely delivers a fractional carload to the order of the pool. The price that he receives is not the competitive price for the day on which he sells, but the averaged price realized from the season's sales. As most street grain is ordinarily sold during the fall months when the price is usually below the season's average, the pool farmer with a few wagonloads to market stands to receive a somewhat higher final price than the regular street seller, although his complete returns will be deferred and the amount uncertain. While the farmers' companies accomplished much in reducing spreads on street grain, their spreads nevertheless had to be deducted from the same price basis as that followed by the line companies. It is the former street seller, indeed, who stands to derive the greatest advantage from pool participation, and herein is to be found probably the most substantial coöperative accomplishment of the pools.

Reduction of Spreads between Grades. — The pool method is serving not only to reduce the spreads between street and track prices, but also the spreads between different grades. While the price differentials on grades below No. 1 Northern that are taken by line elevators on purchased grain are based on current Grain Exchange prices, they must be sufficiently wide to cover the risks involved in handling such grades. These are greater, of course, in the case of lower grades and off-grades (which are demanded chiefly for mixing purposes, frequently involving preliminary hospital treatment) than in the case of contract grades (Nos. 1, 2, and 3). The wide and erratic price spreads between grades have always been a standing source of dissatisfaction among growers.

In the issue of initial payment lists by the pools, more or less arbitrary spreads between grades and sub-grades must necessarily be set. In the making of final pool payments, however, returns are made on the basis of the actual prices realised by the Central Selling Agency in the marketing of each separate grade.[1] Through

[1] The adjustment of these spreads is a somewhat complicated matter. In the final distribution of Manitoba Pool payments in 1926, adjustments were made on 188 distinct grades and sub-grades of wheat.

such adjustments growers are assured of receiving the full commercial value realised on whatever grades they may have contributed. The narrowing of discounts on lower grades which the pool method has tended to bring about, is a matter of very considerable concern to farmers, the quality of whose crop has been lowered by adverse weather or rust conditions.

The following table, as compiled by pool officials, affords a comparison of the average grade spreads contained in the daily price lists sent out by the Northwest Grain Dealers' Association (for seven months of the 1926–27 crop year) and the finally determined discounts on pool wheat of corresponding grades.[1]

TABLE XV. COMPARISON OF GRADE SPREADS ON POOL AND NON-POOL WHEAT

Grade	Average Discount Under No. 1 Northern for 1926 crop of non-Pool wheat taken from Northwest Grain Dealers' Price List	Pool's Discount Under No. 1 Northern for 1926 crop	Higher Price Paid for Pool Wheat
No. 4	21½¢	20½¢	1¢
No. 5	35¢	33¢	2¢
No. 6	49¢	44½¢	4½¢
Feed	62¢	55¼¢	6¾¢
Red Durum	20½¢	12¢	8½¢
Smutty	18¢	11½¢	6½¢
Rejected	19½¢	13¼¢	6¼¢
Tough	8½¢	7¢	1¼¢
Damp	19¼¢	14½¢	4¾¢

Coöperative Aspects of Pool Terminal and Mixing Operations. — The history of the Grain Growers' Movement in Western Canada has shown that one of the most persistent sources of farmers' suspicions and complaints has lain in the terminal and mixing operations of elevator companies. At one period, it will be recalled, this feeling had found expression in a sustained agitation for government ownership and operation of terminal elevators. Even under the intensified system of government supervision which has prevailed since the creation of the Board of Grain Commissioners in 1912, farmers have more or less generally persisted in the belief that terminal cleaning and mixing operations afford opportunities for gains in weights and grades at the expense of

[1] *The Truth about Grain Prices*, Can. Co-op. Wheat Producers, 1927.

producers.[1] While participation of the two farmers' companies in terminal operation served to modify the attitude of farmer-shareholders in this direction, it also brought forth criticisms that in the conduct of their terminal business the farmers showed no more consideration for the interests of producers (except as they might be shareholders) than did the regular companies.

Pool terminal elevators follow the established practices of the trade under the rules prescribed by the Grain Commissioners in respect to handling, cleaning, reconditioning, and mixing of grain, and they charge the regular tariffs.[2] It is in the mode of distributing the profits from gains in grades and weights that the operation of pool terminals differs from that of the U. G. G. and former Saskatchewan "Co-op." terminals. Under the pool system such surpluses are distributed among the respective provincial pools in proportion to the volume of grain which each has shipped to pool terminals. In Alberta and Manitoba such receipts are applied against carrying charges on pool grain in country elevators, thereby increasing the net returns to growers. In Saskatchewan they are directly returned to pool elevator patrons and platform shippers to pool terminals; that is, to those who have contributed the business from which the terminal profits have been derived. The pool system would thus appear to offer the most equitable and satisfactory solution of the vexed problem of mixing and

[1] See farmers' evidence presented to the Turgeon Grain Inquiry Commission in 1923-24; and *Report*, pp. 75–107, 185–186. See also report presented by H. W. Marsh of Pool Grading Committee to U. F. C. Convention in *Western Producer*, March 23, 1927. As a matter of fact, competition among terminal operators in recent years has led to the payment of certain bonuses on terminal deliveries which are at times reflected in street prices offered by country elevators deriving such bonuses. Premiums on diversions to private terminals may also be received by carload shippers through commission agents. Hospital and mixing operations also tend to improve the commercial demand for lower grades and off-grades.

[2] Pool Terminals Nos. 1, 2, and 3 (belonging to the Central Selling Agency) and No. 5 (belonging to the Saskatchewan Pool) are used as lakehead mixing and hospital elevators. While improvements in grades through such operations are reflected in the sales receipts of the Central Selling Agency, the amount of such gains is credited by the latter to the terminals concerned, whose profits are in turn prorated to the contributing pools. For 1926–27 the C. S. A. credited pool terminals with the sum of $629,023 on account of grade improvements. *Directors' Report*, Can. Co-op. Wheat Producers, 1926–27.

terminal overages, that is attainable from the standpoint of producers.

Significance of Pool Method of Deferred Returns. — While the pooling system makes it unnecessary for the farmer either to sell his grain locally to dealers buying at speculative margins, or to speculate as to when to ship his grain for sale on the central market, it does involve speculation by its members as to the amount of their final returns. Instead of receiving the discounted current spot price once for all, the contract holder obtains merely an instalment in accordance with the initial payment list announced for the season. While assured of getting the year's average price realized by the pool on the grade delivered, he does not know what that may finally amount to until after he has begun to deliver his next year's crop.

Grain Exchange interests have not failed to emphasize the waiting and uncertainty involved in the pool method of payment, and to call attention to the effective loss of interest which the pool member sustains upon his deferred payments.[1] Pressure of creditors and the need for ready cash after harvest is indeed probably the principal reason why many farmers have hitherto refrained from signing pool contracts, as well as the most frequent cause of contract evasions. The size of the initial payments made by the Central Selling Agency is limited by the obligation of the latter under its credit arrangements with the banks to maintain a 15 per cent margin between such payments and the current market price.[2] In the case of some of the lower grades,

[1] "It is hard for pool farmers to make financial plans, because they have no idea how much cash the Pool will pay them. All farmers necessarily have one great uncertainty, the yearly yield per acre, but pool farmers have in addition the uncertainties of three financial harvests in the year." — *Facts on Grain Marketing* (issued by Northwest Grain Dealers' Association), p. 28. See also bulletins issued Oct. 30 and Nov. 29, 1926.

[2] In commenting on the relatively small second interim payment made in July 1927, vice-president Brouillette of the Saskatchewan Pool stated: "It is of the very highest importance that [initial and interim] payments be not made so high as to imperil the financial safety or stability of the organization. It is not always wise to make payments to the full extent of its resources; and even if it is granted that the greatest possible service to the farmer implies giving him his money as soon as possible, it is equally important that over-eagerness in this respect be avoided." *Manitoba Free Press*, July 25, 1927.

particularly of coarse grains, the initial payments have at times been so small as to embarrass many members in meeting post-harvest obligations and current expenses.[1] To an increasing extent, however, creditors of pool farmers are showing a disposition to adjust themselves to the new system, by taking assignments of growers' participation certificates, or accepting them as security for credits, realizing that the farmers' total pool receipts are likely to exceed the proceeds from forced sale in the fall months.[2]

The pool system of periodic payments has also been characterized by the Grain Dealers' Association as "blocking natural circulation" and substituting "money dumping":

> Instead of the prompt natural return of the money as realized by the Pool it is distributed by dumping at intervals. . . . Last crop year $37,000,000 was dumped in March, another $37,000,000 in July, and some more millions in October. A large part of what will be dumped next March and July would already have been in circulation at this date if it were not for the Pool. . . . Money is worth more to farmers and merchants than it is to the Pool.[3]

According to this view, "natural circulation" consists in the heavy seasonal expansion in bank-note issue and credit currency during the crop-moving period, whereby grain buyers are enabled to make immediate cash payments to farmers marketing their grain. To a very large extent, the money received by grain growers at this season, after paying harvest help and thresher-

[1] In the fall of 1926 the Manitoba coarse grains pool found it necessary to make an additional "loan" of 10 cents a bushel on all oats delivered, to be repaid through application of interim payments from the C. S. A. See *Facts on Grain Marketing*, p. 24.

[2] In addressing the American Institute of Co-operation at Chicago, on June 23, 1927, President Burnell of the Manitoba Wheat Pool cited the case of a Manitoba Pool farmer who asked if he could be released from his contract in view of the fact that the initial payment on his low-grade wheat was only 40 cents, which he needed for his immediate expenses, while the mortgage company was pressing him for payment. If he sold on the open market, the elevator company would give him 60 cents. At the suggestion of the pool office, he arranged with the mortgagee to take his participation certificate and credit him with future payments, leaving him his initial payment to apply on current expenses. The total payments received from the pool amounted to 85 cents, while, if the farmer had sold on street, he would have received only 60 cents.

[3] *Facts on Grain Marketing*, p. 17.

men, is immediately turned over to banks, mortgage companies, implement dealers, and merchants, in liquidation of borrowing and purchases made upon crop security or expectations, necessitating usually a renewal of such commitments before the next harvest. Under the pool system of distribution, the initial payment on delivery is followed by a first interim payment at seeding time, and a second interim payment just before harvest, while the final distribution is made as soon as the returns from the year's merchandising can be adjusted for each grade.[1] The effect of this is to release very considerable cash distributions in the early spring and late summer, when ordinarily farmers find it necessary to borrow extensively from the banks for seeding and harvesting expenses. Under the new conditions pool farmers are thus financing through deferred returns from the previous year's crop, instead of by mortgaging the coming crop. This means that there is a more evenly distributed circulation of currency and less seasonal "money dumping" than where the grain growers' cash income is distributed mainly during the last quarter of the year. While the pool farmer has to forego the immediate use of the full value of his crop, and suffer a potential if not actual loss of interest on the money retained by the pool, he stands to benefit to something more than a compensating degree in at least three other directions. (*a*) Where borrowing at seeding or harvesting time is obviated or reduced, interest on such loans is saved. (*b*) The saving in interest on bank borrowings by the Central Selling Agency, as a consequence of its limited delivery payments, is reflected in lower selling-cost deductions. (*c*) Finally — and of chief significance — by accepting payments in instalments pool members may ordinarily expect to receive larger aggregate returns than by selling for cash in the fall, even taking into account interest on deferred payments.

While the pool method of crop financing involves considerable readjustment in the relations between farmers and farmers' creditors, the general result appears to be in the direction of greater

[1] Although the annual "cut-off" date for pool deliveries is July 15, the final payment in 1925, owing to a considerable carry-over, was not distributed until November.

credit mobility and financial stability. Although it tends to reduce the volume of bank loans to farmers, it makes for greater liquidity in such accounts.[1] The attitude of the chartered banks is indicated in the following statement made by Sir John Aird, president of the Canadian Bank of Commerce, at the shareholders' meeting on January 12, 1926:

> The marketing of the western wheat crop is now in part financed by the farmer's own funds. The proceeds of the sale of his grain are disbursed to him by instalments, and the partial distribution made in the spring provides him with funds for his seeding operations. The change makes for more orderly financing on the farmer's part, and is in this respect beneficial. Any loss which the banks thus experience will undoubtedly be more than made up to them in the long run by the increased prosperity of their customers.

The periodic distribution of the farmers' grain receipts tends not only to reduce the credit commitments of the pool farmers, but also to relieve the competitive pressure of creditors for liquidation of their respective claims at the time when — under other conditions — the grain grower obtained most, if not all, of his cash returns. It becomes more possible for him to distribute his obligations throughout the year. This makes for improved collections in grain-growing districts, and as such is meeting with favor by farmers' creditors generally. The attitude of the latter was thus expressed by a member of the Canadian Credit Men's Trust Association,[2] in addressing the national convention of the Association in August 1926:

> The farmers have been able to retire a considerable portion of their past-due indebtedness since the inception of the Pool. Prices have been stabilzed to a certain extent, and the farmer placed in a more favorable positi on from the loan companies' point of view. The implement companies are favoring the pool movement. Payments from the Pool are made at seasons of the year which enable the farmers to purchase equipment more or less on a cash basis, rather than on the customary long-term basis. It is the general belief that the system of marketing under the Pool has the effect of

---

[1] In addressing the International Wheat Pool Confeience at Kansas City, in May, 1927, Premier Gardiner of Saskatchewan, stated: "Thousands of farmeis have quit borrowing money at the bank since the pool started, and see in the pooling system a method that not only helps the farmer, but helps our bankers through more orderly financing."

[2] Mr. George S. Jarvis of Saskatoon.

placing business on a more solid basis, by giving the farmer money spread over the year. This is having the effect of increasing the cash sales and enabling merchants to operate at lower costs.

More orderly financing by the pool farmer thus tends to be an accompaniment of more orderly marketing by the pool selling agency. While the former was not the primary object of pool organization, it is proving to be an economic by-product of benefit, not merely to its members, but to Canadian business in general. It is, moreover, a coöperative result which the farmers' companies were not capable, by the very nature of their organization, of bringing about, however beneficial to growers their competitive participation may have been.

While the signing of a pool contract is a purely voluntary act, it involves very considerable self-limitations upon the individual liberty of action of the signer. It means foregoing the freedom of open marketing through alternative channels — which was the central object of the early legislative efforts of the Grain Growers' Associations and of the commerical activities of the farmers' companies — for long-term contract marketing through a single agency. It prevents the pool farmer from taking advantage of favorable market turns which may bring him greater returns than his averaged pool receipts. He agrees to await deferred payments of uncertain amount, instead of obtaining full cash payment when he needs it. He consents to annual deductions for elevators which he may not be able to patronize. These are the coöperative costs and limitations assumed as the condition of collective marketing. While they constitute a far-reaching test of coöperative faith and spirit, they have been accepted by most farmers in preference to the involuntary disabilities to which they feel themselves subject under the speculative competitive system.

CHAPTER XX

SOLIDARITY OF THE GRAIN GROWERS' MOVEMENT

I. Interrelations of Grain Growers' Organizations

In the quarter-century since the launching of the Territorial Grain Growers' Association at Indian Head at the end of 1901, the Grain Growers' Movement in Western Canada has evolved various types of organization in response to differing conditions and changing objectives. In most cases these organizations have been territorial counterparts, or functionally complementary to one another. In other cases they have been more or less competitive. The interrelations of these organizations involve the larger institutional aspects of Grain Growers' coöperation—of coöperation among coöperatives. The history of these relations has shown certain tendencies in the directions of disunity — involving assertions of provincialism or internal protest. On the other hand, it has revealed a remarkable degree of solidarity, manifested in various amalgamations, federations, or other forms of organic coöperation. Changes in name and form of organization have been frequent, but in almost every case these have been evolved from within. There has been one continuous and indigenous Grain Growers' Movement, not a series of ephemeral farmer movements spreading from various centres, such as have characterized the Middle West and Northwestern States of the American Union, where the Grange, the Farmers' Alliance, the Society of Equity, the Farmers' Union, the Non-Partisan League, and the like, have waxed and waned in more or less independent succession.[1] The interrelations of the different Grain Growers' organizations, the extent to which certain institutions have been fostered by others, the forms of interprovincial and interinstitutional coöperation evolved, the influences making for separatism

[1] See Hibbard, *Marketing Farm Products*, part II.

on the one hand and solidarity on the other, the progressive achievements in the direction of coöperative democracy — these constitute what may be described as the political economy of the Grain Growers' Movement. A retrospective consideration of these relations is undertaken in this final chapter, with a view to indicating the essential unity and continuity of the organized Grain Growers' activities described in the preceding chapters. Only through envisaging the movement as a whole can the significance of the agrarian history of Western Canada within the present century be properly appreciated.

Relations of Grain Growers' Associations and Companies. — Four types of organizations have arisen: the provincial farmers' associations, the farmers' grain and elevator companies, the provincial pool organizations, and coördinating institutions such as the Canadian Council of Agriculture and the Canadian Co-operative Wheat Producers. The original institution from which the others have more or less directly sprung was the Territorial Grain Growers' Association, initiated in December, 1901. Through its aggressive example and the efforts of its leaders, the Manitoba Grain Growers' Association was brought into being as a sister organization in 1903. While the Grain Growers' Grain Company was initiated by Partridge and some of the more active spirits of the Sintaluta local of the Territorial Grain Growers' Association, and while most of its original shareholders were members of the Grain Growers' Associations, no organic relation existed between the former and the latter. The associations had been organized as non-commercial institutions; and although a certain amount of support for the project of a farmers' grain company was found in the association conventions before which Partridge presented his plan in 1906, the policy was affirmed of keeping the Grain Growers' commercial enterprise organically and officially distinct from their legislative and educational activities. The decision taken at this time would seem to have been well advised. The history of various farmers' movements, such as the Grange, the Patrons of Industry, the Society of Equity and the Non-Partisan League, has served to demonstrate the disruptive tendencies arising from the assumption of business undertakings by protective or propagandist organizations.[1] Where the latter are the controlling bodies, divergences on questions of finance, management and business policy almost inevitably arise between the trading department and membership and the general organization.[2]

While the Grain Growers' Company was thus financially and corporately independent of the associations, the effective affiliation of the two was demonstrated by the aggressive action pursued by the Manitoba Grain Growers' Association before the courts and the legislature, with a view to securing the restoration of the farmers' company to trading privileges on the Grain Exchange.[3] More permanent evidence of such solidarity was afforded by the establishment and financing of the *Grain Growers' Guide* by the Grain Growers' Grain Company as the common organ of the three provincial associations, and by the subsidizing of the latter through annual "educational grants" out of company earnings. Such subsidies, it is to be noted, were unconditional, and did not carry with them any representation on the boards of the associations.

In the case of the Saskatchewan and the Alberta Co-operative Elevator Companies the relationship with the respective provincial farmers' associations was more direct and intimate than in that of the Grain Growers' Grain Company. While the plan of organization of the first named was formulated by a government-

[1] See Buck, *The Granger Movement*, chap. 7; Hibbard, *Marketing Agricultural Products*, chaps. 18, 20; Wood, *Farmers' Movements in Canada*, pp. 77–83, 118–119.

[2] "Wherever there is a propaganda organization on the one hand, and a business organization on the other, there are sure to be differences of opinion as to the relations between the two. Shall a large, general body, such as the Society of Equity or the Farmers' Union, have a controlling voice in the management of a business exchange, or in a creamery or cheese federation? The argument in favor of some measure of control usually centers in the question of unity of action. Without this there is danger that some business group, inspired in the first place by the general body, may later build up a constituency and affiliation of its own, and eventually sever substantially all connection with the parent society. The argument against such control is simple and direct. It is based on the proposition that butter must be handled by those interested in butter, cheese by those interested in cheese, and not by any group, however wise, whose main concern is less definitely focussed." Hibbard, *op. cit.*, p. 239. See also below, pp. 379, 380.

[3] See *supra*, pp. 53–55.

appointed commission, the majority of the commissioners were officers of the Saskatchewan Grain Growers' Association, and the provisions of the bill of incorporation were submitted to the association convention as well as to the provincial legislature. The directors of the Saskatchewan Grain Growers' Association were named in the incorporating act as provisional directors of the Saskatchewan Co-operative Elevator Company, so that the responsibility for the launching of the latter rested in effect with the association.[1] The organization three years later of the Alberta Farmers' Co-operative Elevator Company involved a similar sponsoring and promotive relationship on the part of the United Farmers of Alberta. With the organization, however, of the statutory minimum number of shareholders' locals, and with the holding of the first regular shareholders' meeting and the election of regular directors, the initiating responsibility of the associations came to an end. Henceforth the affairs of the companies were conducted by, and their policies shaped entirely upon the responsibility of, shareholders, acting within the terms of the acts of incorporation. Community of interest was based, not upon legal or organic connection, but upon the extent to which company shareholders were also association members. While election of the same individual to the directorate of both company and association was not uncommon, especially in Saskatchewan, such interlocking was the result, neither of constitutional provisions, nor of manipulation by means of share control or proxy voting, but of the action of the general delegate bodies. Although resting upon this informal basis, the relations of the S. G. G. A. and the Saskatchewan "Co-op" continued to be especially close. It was, indeed, largely in protest against the alleged domination of the former by the latter, through interlocking and interacting directorates and executives, and through the annual company grants to the association, that the Farmers' Union later came into being in Saskatchewan, resulting in the disappearance of the corporate identity of both the older organizations. The Grain Growers' Grain Company differed from the Saskatchewan and the Alberta Co-operative Elevator Companies,

[1] See Appendix D, sec. 1.

not merely in having been established as a farmers' grain selling agency instead of an elevator company, but also in the interprovincial instead of the provincial distribution of its stockholders and patrons. It bore no special relation to any provincial farmers' association, although in taking over the Manitoba government elevators, it assumed the operating responsibility for the system established by the Roblin administration in response to the demands of the Manitoba Grain Growers' Association.

The Grain Growers' associations and the farmers' grain companies thus represented organizations performing distinctive functions, but possessing a substantially common membership. The functions of the associations, organized on an occupational basis, were essentially protective and educational, aiming at the securing of legislation regarded as in the interests of grain growers, the promotion of coöperative enterprises, and the development of community social life. The functions of the companies were primarily to provide and operate farmer-owned facilities for the handling of grain, both at country points and the primary market. In the case of the Grain Growers' Company and the Alberta Co-operative, commercial operations were extended to include coöperative supply and livestock marketing. Both of these enterprises involved commercial relations with local organizations, consisting usually of association locals or shareholders' locals in the case of coöperative purchasing, and of livestock shipping associations in the case of the company livestock commission departments.

The only instance in which commercial operations were carried on directly by any provincial association in Western Canada was the wholesale supply business conducted by the Trading Department of the Saskatchewan Grain Growers' Association. While such undertaking was due in part to the policy of the Saskatchewan Co-operative Elevator Company in confining its operations to the handling of grain, it was also adopted in the expressed belief that the development of a trading interest would tend to bring about closer and more active relations between the local associations and the central body.[1] The central was seriously

[1] See *supra*, p. 293.

handicapped, however, by not possessing any capital of its own, and in its efforts to provide the services desired by local co-operative societies, it became necessary to sell debentures, first to incorporated associations, and later to individual farmers. This in turn necessitated the delegation of a measure of control to a separate debenture holders' trading convention. While the losses and capital impairment sustained by the trading department fell upon the debenture holders instead of upon the association itself, the prestige of the latter was considerably prejudiced by the outcome of its commercial commitments. It is significant that at the first convention of the amalgamated United Farmers of Canada, Saskatchewan Section, the directors were instructed to take steps for the separation of the trading department from the educational association. As indicated elsewhere, the prospective solution appears to lie in the transfer of the co-operative supply business from the trading department of the provincial association to a central wholesale society owned and controlled by the coöperative stores and purchasing associations — that is, by those directly interested, instead of by the general body of organized farmers.[1]

Inter-company Relations. — Between 1913 and 1917 four separate Grain Growers' commercial organizations were in the field. The Saskatchewan and the Alberta Co-operative Elevator Companies were established, each on a provincial basis. The Grain Growers' Grain Company operated interprovincially, conducting various subsidiary enterprises in addition to its main business of grain marketing and elevator operation. Besides the three grain companies, the Saskatchewan Grain Growers' Association, through its Trading Department, had entered the field of co-operative wholesale supply. During this period negotiations were initiated by the Grain Growers' Company, it will be recalled, looking toward the federation of these commercial organizations, with a view to avoiding duplication and rivalry, and to consolidating resources.[2] The proposed conversion of the Grain Growers' Grain Company, with its broad, federal charter, into a central farmers' company, selling the grain marketed through farmers'

[1] See *supra*, pp. 311, 312.

[2] See *supra*, pp. 163–166.

elevators in the three provinces, and conducting common terminal and export operations, involved a relationship among growers' provincial companies, similar in purpose, if not in form, to that subsequently realized through the Central Selling Agency of the wheat pools. Under the plan proposed in 1916, however, the reorganized G. G. G. Co. would have functioned as an interprovincial purchasing and supply agency, as well as a common selling agency for grain and livestock, and would also have carried on the publication of the *Grain Growers' Guide* and other enterprises, in the interests of Western farmers as a whole.

While offering potential advantages through coördination and centralized operation, and while favorable to more comprehensive undertakings in business coöperation, the scheme also carried with it the potential dangers and disadvantages of over-centralization and over-expansion, as realized to some extent in the subsequent career of the United Grain Growers. The objections which proved most effective, however, were sentimental and personal, rather than purely economic. The consummation of the proposed plan would indeed have involved a certain subordination in status and autonomy on the part of the Saskatchewan "Co-op," whose distinctive character and record of business progress were matters of no inconsiderable provincial pride in Saskatchewan. Apart from certain difficulties arising out of the financial association of the provincial government and the Co-operative Elevator Company, there was a strong reluctance to forego the independent marketing of grain, in the production of which Saskatchewan notably exceeded the other Prairie Provinces. There was a certain misgiving also as to the possibility of being committed to policies in the determination of which the company would exercise only a limited control. In the course of negotiations it further became evident that questions of personal preferment in the reorganization of management incidental to such a federation were also of no little weight in influencing the attitude of the Saskatchewan representatives.[1]

The outcome of the inter-company negotiations was the substitution of outright amalgamation between the oldest and the

[1] See *supra*, pp. 251–253.

youngest companies for federation of the three organizations. To the shareholders of the Alberta Company, which throughout its career had been more or less dependent on the Grain Growers' Company in its current financing, amalgamation brought enhanced investment security and enlarged services. For the shareholders of the Grain Growers' Company the terms of amalgamation involved coöperative reorganization through the formation of shareholders' locals and the substitution of delegate for individual and proxy voting. While the formation of the United Grain Growers thus constituted a consolidation of capital resources, it also represented a less capitalistic form of organization than that which had hitherto characterized the pioneer Grain Growers' Company.

For the next nine years the United Grain Growers and the Saskatchewan "Co-op" functioned independently but not competitively, the operations of the former being interprovincial in scope and diversified in character, and those of the latter being concentrated, both territorially and commercially. As the policy of both companies was not to build elevators at points already served by the other, no competition existed between them at country stations. On the other hand, their combined elevator systems represented farmer company competition with line companies at approximately one half the grain-shipping points in Western Canada. On the Grain Exchange, however, the two farmer-owned agencies traded independently, no attempt being made to act together in "feeding the market," or making joint export sales. Premier Dunning's proposal in 1922 that the export divisions of the U. G. G. and the Saskatchewan "Co-op" should be amalgamated, and function as a voluntary pool selling agency, as well as a joint export subsidiary for company grain, was welcomed by officers of the U. G. G., but declared unacceptable by the directors of the Saskatchewan "Co-op," who at that time were committed to the movement for reëstablishment of the Canadian Wheat Board.[1] Had consolidation of the three farmers' companies been effected in 1916–17, or had the subsequent proposals of Mr. Crerar and Mr. Dunning been realized, for co-

[1] See *supra*, pp. 205, 206.

operation between the U. G. G. and the Saskatchewan "Co-op" in the joint organization of a voluntary wheat pool, it is quite possible that an independent pool organization would not have been set up through the provincial associations.

Relations of Companies and Pools. — While one is tempted to speculate on the course the Grain Growers' Movement might have taken, had unification of the two companies been effected, the fact remains that the parallel existence of the U. G. G. and the Saskatchewan "Co-op" permitted the concurrent pursuit of different commercial and coöperative policies and enterprises upon which agreement would probably have been unattainable in a single organization. Consolidation would not conceivably have brought any greater advantages to farmers at country points, where the presence and participation of the coöperative companies yielded their most direct benefit to producers. It is very doubtful, moreover, whether the pooling system would have made any very great headway, had a voluntary non-contract, or revocable-contract pool been operated by the joint companies, concurrently with the continuation of their established method of grain handling. Coöperative pool marketing was likely to make greater progress under organizations created specifically for the purpose, and promoting it as a "cause," than under the auspices of vested concerns offering it as one of various alternative methods of marketing. It was more or less inevitable, however, that promotion under the former conditions should be marked by a tendency on the part of its advocates to disparage the coöperative character and achievements of the older farmers' organizations. The breakdown of the negotiations initiated by the latter with a view to the coördination of the pool marketing organizations and the company elevator systems was fundamentally attributable to the conviction on the part of the former of the incompatibility of the two systems of marketing. Pool marketing, to be effective, it was felt, required that the pools should possess elevators of their own, whose agents should not have a divided interest and responsibility, and in whose operation the non-profit principle could be more completely applied.[1]

[1] See *supra*, pp. 230–232.

While the clash of the older and newer forms of Grain Growers' coöperation was marked by considerable dissension and recrimination in Saskatchewan, the two organizations, so far as membership was concerned, were not mutually exclusive. A very large number of farmers were both shareholders of the Saskatchewan Co-operative Elevator Company and contract-holders in the Saskatchewan Co-operative Wheat Producers. It was in the hands of these growers, with their double interest, that solution of the problem of organic relationship really lay. Farmers' Union members showed their appreciation of this situation in carrying on their campaign of "boring from within" the shareholders' locals of the Saskatchewan "Co-op," with a view to bringing about a decisive vote of delegates for sale of the company's facilities to the provincial pool. The registering of such decision reflected, therefore, the conversion of a substantial majority of "Co-op" shareholders to pool principles of elevator control and operation. As an outcome of the transfer, the ownership of the "Co-op" elevators has been diffused among more than 83,000 growers, instead of among some 28,000 agriculturists in Saskatchewan, a very large number of farmers having both a purchaser's and a vendor's interest in the transaction. As a further result, the number of farmer-owned elevators in Saskatchewan has been increased from 500 to 750 or more, all of which (except the fifty or so retained by the U. G. G.) are under unified control. Thus, while more or less acrimonious campaigning and somewhat strained relations preceded the settlement, the outcome has been an emergence of Grain Growers' commercial and coöperative solidarity on a broader and more cohesive basis.

While the formation of the wheat pools through the provincial associations represented in part a coöperative protest of Western farmers against the policies and methods of their own grain companies, there is little doubt that the effective establishment of the former was dependent in a large measure upon the existence, experience, and resources of the farmers' companies. The operation of the pioneer Alberta Pool in 1923 would scarcely have been possible but for the far-reaching assistance extended by the United Grain Growers through their timely loans and proffered guarantees, the release of two of their senior officials, the administrative information and counsel freely rendered in conferences, and the prompt and favorable arrangements offered for handling Alberta Pool grain through U. G. G. elevators. Similar organization loans were made by the U. G. G. to the Manitoba Pool, and by both farmers' companies to the Saskatchewan Pool. Had it not been for the readiness of the two companies to handle pool grain on satisfactory terms, it is not improbable that the line companies, which could not be expected to welcome the advent of the pools, might have insisted on conditions which would have prejudiced, if not rendered impossible, the effective operation of the latter. Control of elevator facilities is of strategic importance in the Canadian grain trade, as the organized Grain Growers acutely realized in the early days of the movement. The strong position attained in this field during the preceding decade by the coöperative companies, with elevators at every second grain-shipping point on the prairies, and their sympathetic attitude toward the pooling experiment, gave the pool organizations a substantial initial advantage, where otherwise they might have been decisively handicapped. Although the pools are now building up extensive elevator systems of their own, this has been possible — under the deduction method of finance — only as the result of earlier operations where dependence had to be placed entirely upon existing elevator companies.

While the assistance rendered by farmer companies in the form of organization loans and preferential handling of pool grain through their elevators was of direct and obvious advantage to the pools, the latter were also the beneficiaries of the experience gained by the companies during their extended period of competitive operation in the grain trade. This has been gained, not merely through the transfer of former U. G. G. or "Co-op" officials to the service of the pools, but, perhaps even more significantly for an organization based on democratic control, through the knowledge of grain marketing, elevator operation, and corporation finance acquired by thousands of pool members as shareholders or delegates to annual meetings of the two companies. The pioneering work, the experiments, and the struggles of the latter produced a fund of experience and an appreciation of competitive realities to which the pools have largely fallen heir. This has tended to restrain over-sanguine commitments, and to ensure the observance of generally sound business methods. The commercial and financial experience and the technical knowledge of the grain trade acquired by the farmers' business organizations since the initiation of the Grain Growers' Grain Company some twenty years ago, constitute, indeed, one of the significant factors which help to account for the strong position of the Canadian wheat pools, in contrast to the failure of the United States Grain Growers, Incorporated, and to the ephemeral career of many of the wheat pools in American states.

Conclusion. — While separatist tendencies and internal dissensions have thus asserted themselves from time to time in the Grain Growers' Movement, especially in Saskatchewan, the continuity of the Western farmers' enterprises has been substantially maintained. It is notable that, where any Grain Growers' organization has passed out of existence, or where any commercial enterprise developed under Grain Growers' auspices has been transferred or disposed of, it has, in almost every case, been taken over by another farmer-owned organization. Thus the Manitoba government elevators, established in response to the agitation of the Manitoba Grain Growers' Association, were leased by the Grain Growers' Grain Company, and subsequently purchased by the U. G. G. When the Alberta Farmers' Co-operative Elevator Company was wound up as such, it was in connection with its amalgamation with the Grain Growers' Grain Company to form the United Grain Growers Limited. Similarly, the liquidation of the Saskatchewan Co-operative Elevator Company was incidental to the sale of its assets to the Saskatchewan Pool Elevators. Finally, the Trading Department developed by the S. G. G. A. is under negotiations for transfer to the Co-operative Wholesale Society of the Saskatchewan co-operative trading associations.[1] Except in the cases of the U. G. G. Sawmills, the Grain Growers' British Columbia Agency, and the farm-machinery departments of the U. G. G. and the S. G. G. A.

[1] See *supra*, pp. 311, 312.

Trading Central, no commercial enterprise initiated by the central Grain Growers' organizations has been liquidated, or disposed of to other than farmer-owned institutions.[1] Thus, while changes in name and form of organization have not infrequently taken place in accordance with changing conditions and policies, the enterprises themselves have been perpetuated under farmer control. In each case, moreover, the transfer has represented a more or less significant development in coöperative organization and policy.

II. Interprovincial Relations and Policies

The fourth type of Grain Growers' organization, as noted, consists of those agencies designed to coördinate or consolidate the various provincial bodies. While organization, whether of associations, companies, or pools, on a provincial basis, represented a natural adaptation to territorial and jurisdictional realities, the advantages of interprovincial action were realized at an early stage of the Grain Growers' Movement. This first found formal expression in the Interprovincial Council of Grain Growers' and Farmers' Associations, formed in 1907, primarily with a view to bringing united action to bear in the agitation for government ownership and operation of elevators.[2] Out of this conference body developed the more comprehensive Canadian Council of Agriculture, which, as organized in 1910, represented a national affiliation of the three prairie farmers' associations and the Dominion Grange in Ontario (later merged in the United Farmers of Ontario). The Council of Agriculture was conceived as an agrarian counterpart of the Canadian Manufacturers' Association and the Dominion Trades and Labor Council, which should seek to present the views and protect the interests of the farmers of Canada in the formulation of federal policies and legislation.

Political Activities of Council of Agriculture. — The memorable "Siege of Ottawa" at the end of 1910, by the deputation of 800 farmers marshalled by the Council of Agriculture, with the rally-

[1] As noted elsewhere, liquidations of farmers' local trading associations have been numerous. See *supra*, pp. 319, 320.

[2] See *supra*, pp. 81, 82.

ing aid of the *Grain Growers' Guide*, constituted a more or less spectacular demonstration of the solidarity of the farmers' movement.[1] Nor did it lack tangible results. The demands thus dramatically presented at the seat of government, and aggressively followed up in the general election of the ensuing year, found response in the negotiation by the Liberal ministry of the Reciprocity Pact with the United States; in the general revision of grain legislation embodied in the Canada Grain Act; in the institution of the Board of Grain Commissioners; and in the establishment of government terminal and interior storage elevators; together with the authorization of the Hudson Bay Railway as an additional grain route, and the designation of Calgary as a car-order point, for grain diversions to Pacific ports.

The reorganization of the Council of Agriculture in 1916 admitted to membership the farmers' commercial organizations, consisting of the Western coöperative grain companies, the *Grain Growers' Guide*, and the United Farmers' Co-operative Company of Ontario. Such inclusion was in conformity with the fact that the revenue of the Council was mainly derived from the annual grants of these commercial bodies.[2] As thus constituted, the Council functioned as a periodic conference-body of the executives of the various provincial associations and farmers' companies, with secretarial headquarters at Winnipeg. Matters of more or less exclusive interest to grain growers were generally dealt with in special meetings of the Western Section of the Council. In 1917 — a war-time federal election year — the Council drafted the so-called "Farmers' Platform," which was endorsed by the four provincial associations, and vigorously championed by the *Grain Growers' Guide*. This pronouncement contained declarations in favor of tariff reductions on farm supplies and the necessities of life, extension of Imperial Preference and renewal of Reciprocity negotiations with the United States, greater dependence on direct taxation for federal revenue, nationalization of railways, non-alienation of natural resources, women's suffrage,

[1] See *supra*, p. 137.

[2] Between 1910 and 1914 the Grain Growers' Company made grants to the C. C. A., aggregating $73,773.—U. G. G., 1924, p. 21.

provincial autonomy in liquor legislation, etc.[1] These declarations, it will be seen, were not limited to issues of direct class concern to grain growers, and the formulation and discussion of the Council's platform were indicative of a widening political interest and consciousness on the part of the organized farmers. A number of Grain Growers' leaders were elected to the federal Parliament in 1917, including President Crerar of the United Grain Growers and President Maharg of the Saskatchewan Grain Growers' Association, the former being appointed Minister of Agriculture in the Union government of Sir Robert Borden.

After the close of the World War, the political activities of the organized farmers became conspicuous, both in the provincial and federal fields, the agricultural deflation which set in during 1920 serving as a potent stimulus to such action. In the provincial field the United Farmers of Ontario were called on to form an administration as a result of the Ontario elections of 1919. Similar farmer governments were established by the United Farmers of Alberta in 1921, and by the United Farmers of Manitoba in 1923. In the federal elections of 1921 the Progressive Party, organized through the Council of Agriculture and led by Mr. Crerar, emerged as the second largest party in the new Parliament.[2] The political record and fortunes of the organized farmers in Canada cannot be treated in this study.[3] It is significant to observe, however, that since 1921 the agrarian group has virtually held the balance of power in federal politics, a position that has been effectively used in securing legislation favorable to agricultural interests. Probably the concession of most general advantage to Western grain growers was the statutory restoration in 1922 of the pre-war "Crow's Nest Pass" freight rates on grain and flour moving to the head of the lakes and on various westbound commodities, including farm implements.[4] Of far-reaching

[1] See N. C. Lambert, "Nationalizing a Farm Movement," *G. G. Guide*, June 26, 1918.

[2] The standing of the parties was as follows: Liberals 118, Progressives 65, Conservatives 50, Labor 2.

[3] See in this connection, L. A. Wood, *Farmer Movements in Canada;* Wm. Irvine, *The Farmer in Politics.*

[4] Since 1922 freight rates on grain in Western Canada have averaged about two

benefit to Alberta grain growers have been the successive reductions in the mountain differential on grain and flour moving to Pacific ports, and the construction of government terminal elevators at Vancouver, Edmonton, and Prince Rupert.[1] As a result Alberta wheat producers, who formerly occupied the position of greatest disadvantage in relation to transportation and market,[2] now enjoy a preferred status as to freight costs, with the further substantial advantage of shipping through ports open throughout the year, in contrast to the seasonal grain rush to the head of the lakes before the close of navigation.[3] In relation to federal tariff policy, the political influence of the agrarian bloc has been effective, not only in preventing post-war rate increases during a period when the tariff of practically every other country has been more or less substantially raised, but also in obtaining further downward revision of duties on agricultural implements, and a drastic reduction of those on motor vehicles.[4] The introduction of federal agricultural credit legislation, the general revision of the Canada Grain Act (following the investigation of the Turgeon Commission), and the resumption of construction operations on the Hudson Bay Railway, were other measures brought about more or less directly in response to the persistent representations of the organized farmers through the Council of Agriculture, their provincial associations, their various organs, and their parliamentary spokesmen.

thirds the rates for corresponding distances in the U. S. — See H. C. Wallace, "The Wheat Situation." *U. S. D. A. Yearbook*, 1923, pp. 110–113.

[1] In a comprehensive judgment issued by the Board of Railway Commissioners in Sept., 1927, following extended investigations and hearings under special terms of parliamentary reference, the Crow's Nest rate basis was made applicable to grain moving to Pacific ports for export, and existing inequalities on branch lines in prairie territory were removed. At the same time the rate over the National Transcontinental to the port of Quebec was cut in half — an adjustment long urged by Western grain growers.

[2] See *supra*, pp. 118, 119.

[3] The initial payment price lists of the Alberta Wheat Pool are scheduled on Vancouver basis, so that the saving in freight rates, as compared with the Fort William basis, accrues directly and fully to the grower.

[4] Under the budget of 1922, the duties on reapers, binders, and mowers were reduced from 12½ to 10 per cent and under the tariff amendments of 1924, to 6 per cent. Corresponding reductions were made on other farm machinery. In the budget of 1926 the tariff on motor cars and trucks was reduced from 35 to 20 per cent.

Realization of the need of careful investigation and the compilation of comprehensive and authoritative data as a basis for effective presentation of farmer demands or objections before parliamentary committees or government commissions, led to the establishment of an Economic Research Department by the Council of Agriculture in 1923. Studies made by the staff have been chiefly in the field of banking and agricultural credits, the tariff, taxation, and transportation, on the basis of which, memoranda regarding legislation or judgments on such matters have been presented by the Council's economist at Ottawa before special committees of the Commons and Senate, and such semi-judicial bodies as the Board of Railway Commissioners and the recently formed Tariff Commission. The expenses of this department have been provided for through the annual grants of the farmers' companies and the *Grain Growers' Guide.*

The Council of Agriculture and the Wheat Pools. — During the period of war-time control of the grain trade, representatives of the Council of Agriculture constituted one quarter of the membership of the Board of Grain Supervisors which fixed the price and controlled the movements of the 1917 and 1918 crops.[1] The order-in-council constituting the Canadian Wheat Board in 1919 was a direct embodiment of the plan of compulsory government marketing, drawn up and submitted to the Minister of Trade and Commerce by the Council, three of whose representatives were members of the Board, including the vice-chairman, F. W. Riddell.[2] The persistent but ineffectual efforts of the Council to secure the reëstablishment of the Wheat Board have been discussed elsewhere; likewise its failure to bring into operation a voluntary, interprovincial pool, although a detailed plan for such was drawn up by the Council's Wheat Pool Committee in 1920.[3] Lack of success in the latter direction was due to a complex of causes: persistence of farmer leaders in the hope of Wheat Board reëstablishment, lack of unanimity among the membership of the Council, failure of the two farmers' companies to act together in the formation of a joint pool selling agency, doubt as to the possibility of securing contracts covering the 60 per cent of crop

[1] See *supra*, p. 195. [2] See *supra*, p. 196. [3] See *supra*, pp. 200, 201.

acreage regarded as essential to effective operation, and the attitude of criticism and suspicion toward the leaders and policies of the coöperative companies maintained by many of the more radically minded farmers. The root difficulty lay in the necessity of securing the concurrence in principle and detail of too many bodies as a preliminary to pool organization. Pool marketing first became a reality in Western Canada through the independent action of the United Farmers of Alberta, whose executive had become impatient over the lack of progress in Council pool conferences. In the provincial associations were found the autonomy of action, the driving force, and the local ramifications necessary to effective organization compaigns, each province vying with the other. Interprovincial coöperation in the formation of the Central Selling Agency was the sequel, not the antecedent, of provincial pool organization.

The Canadian Co-operative Wheat Producers, Limited, with its tripartite directorate, interlocking with those of the three provincial pools, represents the most recent form of interprovincial coördination evolved by the Grain Growers' organizations. It stands entirely apart from the Council of Agriculture. While its functions are highly specialized, it constitutes the most highly organized and the most harmonious form of interprovincial cooperation yet attained by Western Grain Growers. The new wine of coöperative pooling has demanded new bottles. Since the formation of the pools independently of the Council, the prestige of the latter has manifestly declined. This has been further influenced by the waning of the Progressive Party, and the rise of the Farmers' Union.

The United Farmers of Canada. — As previously observed, the emergence of the Farmers' Union in Saskatchewan, under conditions of post-war agricultural distress represented a radical reaction against what were regarded by its leaders as the conservative policy of the Saskatchewan Grain Growers' Association, and its domination by the Co-operative Elevator Company through the medium of interlocking directorates and double-office-holding, and by virtue of the financial dependence of the association upon the annual grants of the company. The constitution of the

Union, indeed, contained specific declarations against multiple office-holding and long-term elections.[1] Pool marketing was a conspicuous feature in Farmers' Union policy, and Aaron Sapiro was invited to Saskatchewan by its executive, with a view to the organization of a contract wheat pool, independently of either the S. G. G. A. or the Saskatchewan "Co-op." While the Union was led, largely through Mr. Sapiro's counsel, to join hands with the S. G. G. A. in the organization of an inclusive provincial pool, its leaders were opposed to marketing affiliation with the Saskatchewan "Co-op," and pursued an aggressive campaign designed to bring about the taking over of the latter as part of the Saskatchewan pool elevator system.

While the decision of the "Co-op" shareholders to accept the pool's offer of purchase made possible the consolidation of the two groups of farmers' elevators, Saskatchewan farmers were still divided between the two rival associations — the S. G. G. A. with its quarter-century of continuous existence, and the Farmers' Union with its policy of more or less radical departure. The desirability of amalgamating these two bodies in the interests of provincial solidarity was recognized on both sides, and a joint committee was appointed early in 1926 to work out a basis of union. Considerable difficulty was experienced, however, in reconciling conflicting policies and personalities. The Farmers' Union was organized as a national body, with a number of lodges in Manitoba and Alberta, as well as in Saskatchewan where its main strength lay. Its leaders were opposed to affiliation with the Council of Agriculture, supported as it was by the farmers' commercial organizations. After several months of study and conference the amalgamation committee drew up a basis of union and set of by-laws, which in July, 1926, were separately submitted to conventions of the two associations meeting concurrently in Saskatoon. As in the case of the conventions, under similar circumstances, of the Alberta Farmers' Association and the Canadian Society of Equity, in Edmonton, in 1909,[2] the separate sessions culminated in the march of

[1] Constitution of the Farmers' Union of Canada, Articles 5, 27, 28.

[2] See *supra*, pp. 116, 117.

the delegates of one body to the convention hall of the other, where amid mass cheering and formal handshaking by leaders, the nuptials of the two rival associations were dramatically consummated.

Upon the whole, the principles and policies of the Farmers' Union prevailed in the adoption of the constitution of the new organization which, it was agreed, should be known as the United Farmers of Canada, Saskatchewan Section, Limited. As implied in the name, national organization was contemplated. Members of Farmers' Union lodges in Manitoba and Alberta were to be attached to the new body, pending the formation of separate provincial sections of the United Farmers of Canada, with which it was hoped the United Farmers of Manitoba and the United Farmers of Alberta might be merged. Other principles of the Farmers' Union were embodied in by-laws providing that there should be no interlocking of the United Farmers of Canada directorate with those of other farmers' organizations; that no office should be held by the same person continuously for more than two years; that the association should not ally itself with any political party, or contribute funds thereto; and that no gratuitous financial assistance should be accepted from any commercial organization.[1]

The United Farmers of Canada and the Council of Agriculture. — The United Farmers of Canada, Saskatchewan Section, which was formally incorporated by special act of the Saskatchewan legislature in January, 1927,[2] has not seen fit to continue the former membership of the S. G. G. A. in the Council of Agriculture. With the passing of the Saskatchewan "Co-op," the Council is, therefore, without any representation at present from the most highly agriculturalized province in the Dominion. The leaders of the newly amalgamated associations in that province appear to favor a nationally organized "United Farmers of Canada," with constituent provincial sections, financed by a per capita levy upon all members, as a substitute for the Council of Agriculture, which they regard as being dominated by the commercial organizations through which it has been subsidized.

[1] *G. G. Guide*, Aug. 1, 1926.

[2] Stat. of Sask., 17 Geo. V, c. 84.

While the continuation of a national agrarian organization is highly desirable from the standpoint of Western farmers, inasmuch as the chief economic handicaps to which grain growers have been exposed in relation to the tariff, transportation, and banking, are matters of federal jurisdiction, the form of such interprovincial organization is a more debatable issue. The Council of Agriculture has been merely a conference of executive officers of its constituent bodies, each organized independently for specific provincial or commercial purposes. The project of a national United Farmers of Canada, with provincial sections, implies the adoption of a uniform constitution, and a much greater degree of centralization than that represented by the Canadian Council of Agriculture. Any such attempt to bring about organic uniformity among provincial farmers' organizations would be more likely to raise difficulties and differences than to achieve greater solidarity. The various provincial associations have grown up indigenously and autonomously, adapting their organization, policies and activities to the special conditions and problems in their respective provinces. This has made for greater vitality and permanence, and the richer growth that springs from organic responsibility and freedom to experiment. Solidarity rests on free and intelligent coöperation rather than on uniformity, and a federal council composed of officers of affiliated organizations would seem to offer a more effective and less costly medium of interprovincial action than a national convention of a Dominion-wide association.

Notwithstanding these considerations, a reorganization of the Canadian Council of Agriculture would appear to be called for, in view of the advent of the wheat pools, the disappearance of the Saskatchewan "Co-op," the emergence of the new amalgamated association in Saskatchewan, and the existence of separate provincial farmers' organs alongside the *Grain Growers' Guide*. In such reorganization it would probably prove most satisfactory to have the constituent bodies limited to provincial farmers' associations. The wheat pools are organized exclusively for co-operative marketing purposes, and possess a most effective agency of interprovincial coördination in the Canadian Co-operative Wheat Producers. The United Grain Growers, which fostered and aided so many enterprises and organizations in the Grain Growers' movement, does not now command the same prestige among farmers as before the advent of the pools. While stronger than ever financially, it stands somewhat apart from the newer coöperative organizations, especially since the absorption of the Saskatchewan Company. The *Grain Growers' Guide*, moreover, no longer speaks as the organ of the provincial associations. Since the central aim of the Council of Agriculture is to protect the interests of agriculturists and to give organized expression to farmer-citizenship in the federal field, as the various associations seek to do in their respective provincial spheres, it is logical that it should be composed of these bodies, preferably without separate representation of the farmers' commercial organizations whose membership is more or less coextensive with that of the associations.

While the part played in the Canadian Council of Agriculture by the United Grain Growers, and the leadership in the Progressive Party occupied by its president, have been instrumental in securing benefits of no slight importance for Western farmers as a whole, they have also exposed the company to political opposition and criticisms both without and within the farmers' ranks, which have more or less reacted to its disadvantage as a coöperative business institution. Thus, in a statement issued by the directors of the U. G. G. in 1921, it was claimed that confidential information supplied by the company to an audit investigation of terminal elevator returns made for the federal government in 1918, as well as to a parliamentary committee on the cost of living in 1919, had been employed by government partisans in discrediting the U. G. G. in the election campaign of 1921.[1] In the appointment of the Hyndman Grain Inquiry Commission in the same year the government, it was further asserted, was actuated by a desire to incriminate the farmers' company rather than to investigate the need for a general revision of grain legislation.[2] The hearing by the Commission of charges against the

[1] See "Why the Company Took Out the Injunction," U. G. G., 1921, pp. 85, 86.

[2] Newspaper comments at the time of the appointment of the commission

U. G. G., without giving the latter an opportunity of being represented, was made the basis of an application for an injunction to restrain the Commission in its investigations. Similar applications were made by other Grain Exchange firms, resulting in the granting of a restraining injunction, and the discontinuance of the Commission's inquiries.[1] While the incident probably reacted more to the disadvantage of the government than of the company, it was indicative of the more or less inevitable results of engagement in political activity by a commercial organization. Such participation also afforded a basis for internal criticism from farmers who disapproved of the identification of the U. G. G. with private Grain Exchange firms in the injunction proceedings, and who were disposed to question the motives of the company's leaders. It was a factor in the reaction against the farmers' companies, and it is significant that the constitutions of the Farmers' Union and the United Farmers of Canada contained declarations against political alliances or financial contributions.

In confining itself, as do the pools, to the field of coöperative business, the U. G. G. stands to follow the line of greatest advantage as an institution. While in the past its resources and leadership have been a highly important factor in securing federal recognition of farmers' claims, such efforts are likely to be best carried on in the future through the provincial associations themselves, working together through their national council. The chief disabilities under which Western grain growers have labored in the past in respect to marketing, transportation, credit, and the tariff, have been largely removed, in so far as they are matters of legislative solution or government regulation. While vigilance and unity of action will always be needed if farmers' interests are to be duly considered in the determination and execution of public policies, the maintenance of such solidarity rests primarily with the farmers' non-commercial associations. In federal matters directly affecting the farmers' business organizations, their case may be presented before the appropriate

hinted at "Revelations that would split asunder the organised farmers of the West." *Ibid.*, p. 86.

[1] *Ibid.*, pp. 87, 88.

parliamentary committee or government commission by their own representatives, as by the pools in connection with the Campbell Amendment to the Grain Act.[1] While the activities of the Council of Agriculture in the past have been largely dependent on the grants from the farmers' companies, its future financial needs can probably be taken care of by assessments or contributions from the constituent associations in proportion to membership, as the American Federation of Labor and the Dominion Trades and Labor Council are financed by their affiliated unions.[2]

With the absorption of the Saskatchewan "Co-op" by the Saskatchewan Pool Elevators, with the amalgamation of the Saskatchewan Grain Growers' Association and the Farmers' Union, with the admirable coördination of the three provincial wheat pools through the Canadian Co-operative Wheat Producers, and with the prospective conversion of the Trading Department of the U. F. C. into an interprovincial Co-operative Wholesale Society, the interorganic and interprovincial relations of the Grain Growers' institutions are being reëstablished on a basis which appears to combine the advantages of functional specialization and territorial autonomy with coöperative coördination and conscious solidarity. While names have been changed, constitutions recast and relationships readjusted, the continuity and cohesion of the Grain Growers' Movement has been essentially maintained through the quarter-century or more of its history.

[1] See *supra*, pp. 263–265.

[2] In this connection, it may be noted that the U. F. C., Saskatchewan Section, has adopted the device of providing for payment of the membership fee of $5 (of which $3.50 goes to the central office, and $1.50 to the local lodge) through members' requisition on wheat pool payments. *G. G. Guide*, April 4, 1927.

CHAPTER XXI

CONCLUSION

Nature of Economic Results of Grain Growers' Coöperation. — There are three conceivable ways in which the economic returns of the producers of agricultural staples may be improved: namely, by reduction of marketing margins, by an increase in the market price, or by lowered costs of production. In each case a larger residuum accrues to the producer.

The organized Grain Growers of Western Canada have concentrated their efforts chiefly upon reducing the spread between the final selling price of wheat and the price received by the grower. Since the beginning of the Grain Growers' Movement, much has been accomplished in this direction, partly through recourse to government action, but mainly through coöperative marketing participation. The fixing of maximum handling charges by the Board of Grain Commissioners, and the general scaling down and equalization of freight rates on grain for export, have accrued to the advantage of grain growers in general. Provisions written into the Grain Act at the instance of Grain Growers' associations, with a view to giving producers direct access to the central market, enabled carload shippers to sell on the basis of primary instead of country market prices, and of initial grading by government inspectors instead of by elevator agents. Competition of farmer-owned elevators at country points served to reduce substantially the customary spreads on street grain, while returning to farmer-shareholders a portion of handling profits in the form of cash or stock dividends. Under the pool system of non-profit operation and direct selling, the farmer is receiving in effect the competitive world price, less the actual cost of handling, transportation, and selling. The advantage to producers lies not only in the direct return of that portion of marketing margins which constitutes the middleman's profit, but also in further reduction of marketing costs through the potential economies of large-scale, centralized selling.

The attainable savings under coöperative grain pooling are distinctly more limited, however, than in the case of farm products in which trading is less highly organized and less closely regulated. Under the combined influence of active competition, risk insurance through hedging, Grain Exchange rules, and Grain Commissioners' tariffs and regulations, middleman margins have been reduced within narrow limits in the Western Canadian grain trade. While wider spreads generally prevailed in the local marketing of street grain, the policy and participation of the farmers' companies had been effective in substantially narrowing these at competing points, before the advent of the pools. Some saving in selling expenses is possible under pool marketing, through elimination of hedging costs, through the making of direct sales, and through large-scale chartering of shipping space. Reduction in unit marketing costs depends chiefly, however, on the concentrated volume of wheat and coarse grains handled through the Central Selling Agency. On the other hand, the securing and maintenance of such volume has involved considerable outlay for promotional and educational work and permanent field service, while the pool system of accounting and distribution of payments entails additional expense. The net reduction in marketing costs is likely, therefore, to prove comparatively small. The Canadian Wheat Pool plan does make it possible, however, for its members, whether delivering a single wagonload or several carloads of grain, to receive the full pooled commercial value of their product, in final markets, less the lowest attainable marketing costs.

The pool elevator system also serves to bring the pool farmer's aggregate returns somewhat closer to the final selling price of his grain. Not only has it virtually removed the differential on the handling of street grain, but it also returns elevator operating surpluses to members, either in the form of patronage credits (as with the Saskatchewan and Manitoba Pool Elevators) or as offsets to pool operating expenses (as in the case of the Central Selling Agency's terminals and the Alberta Pool Elevators). Thus pool grain is marketed at cost, in relation both to elevator handling and to selling. So far the volume of grain handled through pool elevators has been substantially above the general average of the trade, thus making possible lower unit costs and substantial surpluses. The situation may easily become less favorable, however, if pool directorates, in response to insistent minority demands, undertake the construction of new elevators at points where the contract acreage does not adequately justify it, or where local elevator accommodation is already more or less redundant. Some subsidence of the initial patronage interest of members may be expected in the case of pool elevators, as of coöperative company elevators, farmer loyalty not always being proof against the inducements of higher grades or special consideration that may be offered by line elevator agents. Careful consideration by the pool management of each new local commitment, as well as the maintenance of superior service, is necessary if pool elevator ownership and operation are to be effective as a means of improving the net returns of members.

Economic Limits of Pool Marketing. — While many pool members, recalling, or reminded of, the record wheat prices associated with the operation of the Canadian Wheat Board, have signed pool contracts in the expectation that pool selling would be effective in raising the price of their wheat; and while the average prices realized since the inception of the pools have indeed been considerably higher than those of either the pre-war period, or of the four years preceding pool operation, it is generally recognized by responsible pool leaders that such changes have been the outcome of broad international causes rather than of the action of the Canadian Pool itself. Although Canada since the War has become the largest national exporter of wheat in the world, contributing in recent years about 40 per cent of the world's export surplus, her production is less than 12 per cent of the world total. It is the latter rather than the former proportion which is the more significant in determining the price which Canadian wheat can command in world markets. Any increase in European production involves a diminished demand for Canada's surplus, even if that of other competing export countries shows no increase. Any rise in price, whether due to natural or manipulated scarcity, serves to set in motion forces which tend to generate a decline from such level. Recourse will be had to substitute starch foods in the form of rye and potatoes in continental European countries, or of rice and millet in Asiatic countries. At the same time the higher price serves to call forth larger production of wheat itself, whose supply is probably the most widely distributed geographically, and the most sensitive to price movements, of all staple agricultural products.[1] The hard spring wheat of the Canadian prairies, it is true, is more or less a premium wheat, because of its high gluten content and its sale on government grade certificate. European millers use it, however, chiefly for blending purposes, and any appreciable advance in such premium through restricted supply tends to bring about a reduction in the proportion of Canadian wheat used in the blend.[2]

The Canadian Wheat Pool exercises no control whatever over the physical volume of Canadian wheat. It is bound to market whatever quantity may be delivered to it by its members, under conditions of international competition. It may, indeed, exercise a measure of control over the market movement of its wheat. It may refrain from selling at times when prices appear to be depressed under seasonal or temporary influences, and release its holdings more freely when prices show a firmer tendency. It may exercise a certain stabilizing influence on the market, through being less vulnerable to the risks of forced selling, and through the alternative outlets afforded by its overseas sales connections. It cannot risk, however, holding back any substantial portion of its season's deliveries, in the face of a new crop of anything like normal proportions, and of the impatience of its members over unduly deferred final settlements. It may succeed in making Canadian millers purchase their wheat at prices more closely in line with world-market quotations, and it may narrow competition among sellers of Canadian wheat to overseas millers. But it cannot count on disposing of its surplus to the latter except at prices which will meet the competition of substitute wheat and substitute starch foods.

Possibilities of International Pool Organization. — Realizing the

[1] See speech on *International Grain Marketing*, by Dr. Robert Magill, at Winnipeg, July 20, 1926. Circulated by Northwest Grain Dealers' Association.

[2] See *Report of Royal Grain Inquiry Commission*, 1925, pp. 168–182.

limited price-controlling power of the producers of a single wheat-exporting nation, certain pool enthusiasts have advocated joint action by producers' pools in the principal competing countries as the next objective in coöperative organization. The possibilities of such international action have indeed been discussed at two international wheat pool conferences, organized largely under Canadian initiative. The first was held at St. Paul, Minnesota, in February, 1926, and the second at Kansas City, Missouri, in May, 1927. At the latter gathering which was attended by delegates from pool organizations in various states of the American Union and the Australian Commonwealth, and from Soviet Russia, in addition to Western Canada, the following resolution was passed:

> As soon as practicable, the wheat producers of the chief exporting countries of the world should look toward coördination of their coöperative program. This must be preceded by thorough organization of the producers of wheat in each country on a permanent basis, and such organization must control a substantial percentage of the wheat grown in these countries When these conditions are met, then international coördination will give the wheat growers the same control over the marketing of their crop already possessed by other industries and will materially assist in putting agriculture in its rightful place among the other industries of the world.[1]

While some measure of informal coördination of selling policy may be sooner or later attained among wheat producers' national pools, the possibilities of either the formation or the effectiveness of a world wheat pool are decidedly slight. Where the physical supply itself is not under control, no system of quota assignment can be attempted, as in the case of industrial cartels. No division of markets is practicable, moreover, with such a commodity as wheat, of which different varieties and grades from different countries are desired in the same market, and frequently blended in the same mill. Any concerted attempt to realize a minimum selling price is subject to the unalterable necessity on the part of each pool of disposing of its holdings before the advent of the new crop. Nor are the members of any national pool likely to be willing to entrust the selling of their surplus to an agency responsible

[1] Report of conference proceedings in *Grain Growers' Guide*, May 6, 1927; *The Scoop Shovel*, May, 1927.

to any other producing interests but their own. The various harvest periods at which the crops of winter and spring wheat regions, and of the north and south temperate zones become available, constitute moreover a certain natural marketing sequence which minimizes the need for any international marketing control. Dumping of wheat, so far as it exists, is to be found among producers rushing their grain after harvest to primary markets in their own country, rather than among exporters shipping to world markets (except in cases where consigned cargoes may have to be thrown on the open market on arrival in port). Even when national pools are established in other exporting countries on lines similar to the Canadian Coöperative Wheat Producers, coördination among them is not likely to be carried beyond the pooling of information and the adoption of common selling policies.

These limitations were not ignored by delegates at the Kansas City Conference. Various speakers deprecated the idea of seeking to organize any world pool with a view to raising prices to consumers.[1] The conference was primarily inspirational and educational, consisting largely of an exchange of experiences, and the attention of the delegates was concerned with the extension of coöperative marketing among wheat producers in the countries represented, rather than upon pool organization on international lines. The continuation proceedings of the conference consisted in the reappointment of an international committee, with instructions to take steps toward the establishment of a permanent international bureau, to serve "as a clearing house for statistical information and matters relating to the development of international coöperation." [2]

[1] Thus President H. W. Wood of the Alberta Pool declared: "If this means the merging of all coöperative wheat-selling into one pool unit, under some kind of central management, then I am unalterably opposed to it, because I do not believe it is practicable to do so." *Scoop Shovel*, May, 1927, p. 42. See also speech of L. C. Brouillette and G. W. Robertson. *Ibid.*, pp. 4, 32.

[2] "After all, the immediate problem is not actually international selling. Is not the first step the establishing of the proper basis from which international coördination can develop? Such a bureau would devote itself exclusively to assisting in building up the general pooling idea, and through its personnel could help to build on a strong foundation the various units of this great movement." —Address of G. W. Robertson.

The Outlook. — At the present time the wheat pools command the more or less enthusiastic support of the majority of farmers in Western Canada. The improved prices on wheat markets since the inception of the Canadian Co-operative Wheat Producers are popularly associated with, even if not directly attributed to the operations of the Central Selling Agency. The aggressive educational work carried on both by the provincial associations and by the pools have not been unfruitful. The new coöperation has indeed become a veritable religion among prairie farmers. Under the initiative and auspices of the provincial associations the contract-pool marketing method is being applied, not merely to wheat and coarse grains, but also to livestock, dairy products, and eggs and poultry, while a new impetus has been given to the coöperative purchasing movement.[1] Anticipatory steps taken during the present year toward securing advance signatures to wheat and coarse grain contracts for the new period beginning with the 1928 crop, give general assurance of the continuation of the pooling system under conditions of more inclusive as well as more intelligent support.[2] The initial problems of securing efficient managerial services, of creating a central selling organization, of establishing satisfactory credit relations with the banks, of making suitable handling arrangements with established elevator companies, and of financing the acquisition of independent elevator facilities, of working out the administrative details and the technique of pool payments and credit adjustments — these have been handled, on the whole, with a notable absence of miscalculation or misjudgment. With the experience of the initial years, with a highly developed selling organization, with substantial reserves, with an extensive and expanding subsidiary elevator system, and with a membership generally advanced in coöperative education, the pools should enter the next period of operation under distinctly favorable conditions.

[1] The extension of coöperative marketing is being appreciably aided by the application of the unclaimed Canadian Wheat Board surplus of $534,200, which was distributed proportionately to the three Prairie Provinces in 1925, as statutory trust funds devoted primarily to research and education in coöperative marketing.

[2] In Saskatchewan, more than 50 per cent of the crop acreage was signed up for the new period during the summer of 1927, without any intensive campaign.

While the pooling system thus gives evidence of becoming established as a stable institution in Western Canada, the history of the Grain Growers' Movement as a whole, as well as of farmers' movements elsewhere, prepares one to expect possible reactions in the future. The enthusiasm which has attended the launching of the wheat pools is likely to show a subsidence such as followed the demonstrative loyalty accorded the Grain Growers' Grain Company in its initial years, and the class-conscious support enjoyed by the coöperative elevator companies prior to the post-war depression. While the counter-propaganda conducted by the Northwest Grain Dealers' Association appears to have the effect of rallying growers to the support of the pools rather than of diverting their loyalty,[1] the farmer is less resistant to considerations of preferential treatment or greater convenience which may be offered by private dealers under pressure of competition. Any improvement in primary market prices or street prices which may be brought about through the influence of the pools cannot be confined to pool members. There will always be a minority of individualistic farmers who, while not opposed to the pools, are unwilling to assume contract obligations, and who prefer to act on their own marketing judgment. Even in the case of those who have signed contracts, the pools must inevitably encounter in greater or less degree a disposition to evade such obligations, or an unwillingness to renew them, on the part of farmers who, owing to circumstances or temperament, may prefer immediate, if discounted, cash payment to deferred, if possibly larger, aggregate returns. Any failure on the part of the pools to fulfill the expectations held out, and any mistake of judgment or change of policy on the part of their officers, are bound to be capitalized to the full by private grain interests in the struggle for competitive survival. So long as the pools undertook merely to concentrate the sale of their members' wheat, under handling contract arrangements with

[1] A characteristic rejoinder to the anti-pool propaganda as contained in such pamphlets as "Facts about Grain Marketing," and "Why the Hurry?" (these being collections of leaflets, and radio broadcasts issued by Northwest Grain Dealers' Association) is to be found in the bulletin, *The Alberta Pool and the Grain Trade,* issued by the Department of Education of the Alberta Co-operative Wheat Producers.

the established elevator companies, the regular trade was not unduly disturbed by their operation. With their entry, however, into large-scale elevator acquisition, at both country and terminal points, and with the passing of the Campbell Amendment to the Grain Act, the very existence of the private elevator companies is threatened. A merger of the latter is not unlikely to be realized before the expiration of the present pool period, with a view to enabling them to compete more effectively with the pool system.[1] Competition on such a basis would probably mean, for the time being, still narrower handling margins and greater service for farmers in general. If it should have the effect, however, of bringing about the disintegration of the pools, prairie grain growers would find themselves confronted by an even more powerful elevator combine than that which first stimulated them to coöperative organization. The real test of pool solidarity and adaptability would appear, therefore, to lie in the next few years. It is a test, however, which the experience and confidence gained through a quarter-century of successful business coöperation, in the face of more or less open opposition, well prepare the organized Grain Growers to meet.

While the pool marketing organization as now established does not necessarily represent the final development of Grain Growers' coöperation in Western Canada, it does appear to offer a system which, in combination with the highly effective facilities evolved by traders' coöperation, and the governmental protection and regulation exercised through the Board of Grain Commissioners, the Inspection Department, and the Board of Railway Commissioners permits the prairie grain grower to realize the full commercial value of his product at minimum marketing costs. Under these conditions the possibilities of further improvement in the economic position of the Canadian grain grower would seem to lie mainly in the direction of lowering production costs. Having assumed middleman functions from point of production to point of consumption, the coöperative producers can no longer with any

[1] A merger of private elevator companies jointly controlling more than half the country elevators in Western Canada is reported to be in process of organization at the present time (October, 1927). *Financial Post*, Oct. 14, 1927.

appearance of justice attribute the responsibility for inadequate returns to the practices of private dealers and speculation. Although wheat production in Western Canada generally is carried on under conditions of more or less marked comparative advantage in relation to other countries,[1] the possibilities of increasing yields, of minimizing production risks and of reducing individual production costs through the application of agronomical science and through further research, are incalculable. With the passing of the old days of free or cheap land, with the impairment of virgin soil fertility, and with the spread of rust and other grain pests, the prairie farmer's attention needs to be concentrated increasingly upon questions of seed selection and tillage, of improvements in grades and yields, and of reduction in dockage percentages. Extractive methods must be abandoned, and a greater and more diversified return must be derived from the farm acreage than that represented by a more or less speculative annual crop of wheat alone. Coöperative purchasing of farm supplies also needs to be further developed as a means of lowering production costs, as coöperative selling aims to reduce marketing costs. It is somewhat significant of the growing realization on the part of Western grain growers of the importance of more scientific production, as well as of more economical marketing, that the Saskatchewan Grain Growers' Association on receiving the sum of $284,200 in 1925 as the province's share of the unclaimed surplus of the Canadian Wheat Board, created the Saskatchewan Agricultural Research Foundation, whose funds should be devoted to research in plant and animal diseases, as well as in coöperative marketing.[2] Nor is it without significance that the columns of the Grain Growers' Guide have steadily tended to become less fully occupied with agrarian propaganda and Grain Growers' organizational news, and increasingly devoted to matters of agricultural technique and farm management, and to the broader issues of a citizenship.

Moral Results of Grain Growers' Coöperation. — While farm

[1] See H. S. Patton, "The Changing Equilibrium in the World's Wheat Trade," *Papers on the World's Wheat Trade.*

[2] See Statutes of Sask., 16 Geo. V, c. 60, 1926.

management is essentially a matter of individual initiative and action, it is likely to be more intelligently and confidently directed where the farmer plays a part in the marketing as well as in the production of his commodities. His morale as a producer is consciously elevated when, instead of being compelled to accept the middleman's prices and terms, or leave his products unsold, he is able, by coöperation with his fellow producers, to sell through his own agency on a basis of marketing equality. The self-respect which accompanies farm ownership is enhanced when he becomes joint-owner in a large-scale commercial organization, and receives an income as an investor as well as a producer. The achievements of prairie farmers in building up two of the largest and most successful elevator companies in Western Canada, followed by the organization and operation of an interprovincial wheat pool which has become the largest single grain-marketing agency in the world, have not only made the participating grain growers conscious of being business men, but have also revealed to them that by coöperation they can engage in "big business" on an even larger scale than that realized by vested commercial interests. Furthermore, through their provincial associations and the Council of Agriculture, Western farmers have participated in the passing of important federal as well as provincial legislation. Not only have Grain Growers' leaders been elevated to major ministerial portfolios in the national government, but in three provinces the farmers' associations have been called on to assume the responsibilities of actual administration, and in two of the three cases the farmers' governments have been returned to power on their records.

The farmer's morale does not depend merely on prices, but also on the social recognition he receives from other classes in the community. The Grain Growers' Movement has had a double moral effect. It has served to raise the status of the farmer as a commercial producer and as a citizen, not only in his own eyes, but also in the regard of the community at large. At the same time actual participation in large-scale business and finance, and in the responsibilities of government, have exercised a certain sobering, educative effect, which has tended to make the attitude of Western farmers as a class toward other economic groups and institutions less one of suspicion and antagonism, and more one of intelligent accommodation. Agricultural coöperation is essentially a form of intensified group competition, aiming at the realization of a more even balance of economic power in relation to other occupational groups. While such result is socially desirable, and while occupational self-respect and security can only be attained by coöperation within the group, it does not mark the ultimate goal of coöperation. Such an idea was appropriately the theme of a notable address given at the Farmers' Union convention in 1925 by the veteran Partridge of Sintaluta, — idealist, and pioneer organizer of the Grain Growers' Movement,—when he said to the assembled Saskatchewan farmers:

> Coöperation, to an agricultural population, is the primary step towards that true coöperation which will embrace the various elements of society. The type of coöperation that I ultimately hope to see is the coöperation of all those who live and desire to live by useful labor, whether of hand or brain — the coöperative commonwealth. If you content yourselves with mere vocational coöperation, it seems to me that you stop short of the ideal that will really be effective in changing human relationships and making them satisfactory.

APPENDICES

APPENDIX A

STATISTICS

I. Wheat Production, Prices and Exports in Western Canada, 1908–1927

Source: Dominion Bureau of Statistics

Year	Prairie provinces			Average Cash Price for Oct.[1] cents	Exports of Wheat and Flour[2] 1000 Bushels
	Acreage 1000 Acres	Production 1000 Bushels	Average Yield per Acre		
1908	5,624	91,853	16.4	98.5	52,487
1909	6,878	147,482	21.7	96.9	56,958
1910	7,867	110,167	14.0	95.9	63,529
1911	9,991	208,366	20.9	100.6	59,523
1912	10,011	204,280	20.4	90.4	81,291
1913	10,036	209,262	20.9	80.5	113,311
1914	9,335	140,958	15.1	112.2	142,171
1915	13,868	360,187	26.1	93.7	94,199
1916	14,363	242,314	16.9	174.4	186,546
1917	13,619	211,953	15.6	221.0	223,060
1918	16,125	164,436	10.3	224.4	195,082
1919	17,750	165,544	9.4	215.0[3]	83,233
1920	16,841	234,138	14.0	231.9	117,862
1921	22,181	280,098	12.7	115.5	156,291
1922	21,223	375,194	17.7	100.7	169,853
1923	20,880	452,260	21.2	97.7	261,096
1924	21,066	235,694	11.2	159.5	309,587
1925	20,943	382,959	18.3	127.0	241,396
1926	21,897	383,440	17.5	143.5	295,062
1927	21,425	418,992	19.6	144.1	294,162

[1] Average of daily closing Winnipeg cash prices for No. 1 Northern, basis Fort William — Port Arthur.

[2] For fiscal year ending March 31. Flour exports converted into bushels at rate of 1 barrel of 196 lbs. = 4½ bushels.

[3] Exclusive of participation certificates, redeemed at 48 cents.

II. Turnover of Western Wheat Pools, 1923–1927

Volume of Wheat Handled

1000 Bushels

Crop	Alberta Pool	Saskatchewan Pool	Manitoba Pool	Total Pool	Wheat Inspections	Per cent Pool Wheat
1923....	34,219	....	....	....	257,197	13.3
1924....	23,027	50,203	8,440	81,670	214,390	38.1
1925....	45,160	129,600	12,488	187,248	352,510	53.1
1926....	44,287	119,460	16,208	179,955	335,500	53.6

Value of Turnover [1]

000 omitted

Crop	Alberta Pool	Saskatchewan Pool	Manitoba Pool	Total Turnover	Average Pool Price No. 1 Nor.
1923.........	$40,647	....	....	$40,647	1.02
1924.........	35,042	$77,021	$12,133	124,197	1.66
1925.........	60,590	181,423	23,769	265,782	1.45
1926.........	53,902	164,878	29,269	248,049	1.42

[1] Being the sums turned over to the respective pools by the Central Selling Agency, after deducting all selling and terminal costs and central administrative expenses.

APPENDIX B

CHRONOLOGY OF GRAIN GROWERS' MOVEMENT

Figures in brackets are page references in text to events chronicled.

1869. Acquisition of Hudson's Bay Territory by Dominion of Canada.
1870. Creation of Province of Manitoba.
1876. First eastern shipment of wheat from Western Canada (via Minnesota). (7)
1883. Completion of Canadian Pacific Railway between Lake Superior and Winnipeg. C. P. R. builds first lakehead terminal at Fort William. (130)
1884. First shipment of wheat from Western Canada to Europe.
1886. Inauguration of federal grain inspection at Winnipeg and Port Arthur. (27)
1887. Organization of Winnipeg Grain and Produce Exchange.
1889. Creation of Western Grain Standards Board. (27)
1899. Creation of Manitoba Inspection District. (28)
1899. Appointment Royal Commission on Shipment of Grain. (21)
1900. Manitoba Grain Act passed. (23–25)
1901. (Dec.) Initiation of Territorial Grain Growers' Association. (33)
1902–03. Shipping amendments to Manitoba Grain Act. (34, 38)
1902. C. P. R. car allotment case. (35)
1903. Organization of Manitoba Grain Growers' Association. (37)
1903. Incorporation of North West Grain Dealers' Association. (31)
1905. Creation of Provinces of Saskatchewan and Alberta.
Formation of Alberta Farmers' Association. (115)
1906. Territorial Grain Growers' Association becomes Saskatchewan G.G.A.
Appointment second Royal Grain Inquiry Commission. (42)
1906. (Jan.) Preliminary organization of Grain Growers' Grain Co. (45)
(Sept.) Grain Growers' Grain Co. commences operations under Manitoba charter. (47, 48)
(Nov.) Suspension of G. G. G. Co. by Council of Winnipeg Grain Exchange. (50)
1907. Trial of Grain Exchange councillors on complaint of M. G. G. A. (53, 58)
(Apr.) Conditional reinstatement of G. G. G. Co. to trading privileges on Grain Exchange. (55)
(July) Election of T. A. Crerar to presidency of Grain Growers' Company. (63)
Organization of Interprovincial Council of Grain Growers' and Farmers' Associations. (82)

1908. Reorganization of Winnipeg Grain Exchange as voluntary association. (60)
General revision of Manitoba Grain Act following report of Millar Grain Commission. (133 f.)
(June) First issue of Grain Growers' Guide. (70)

1908–09. Interprovincial negotiations between Grain Growers' Associations and Western Premiers *re* government ownership of elevators. (82 f.)

1909. Amalgamation of Alberta Farmers' Association and Canadian Society of Equity to form United Farmers of Alberta. (116)

1910. Inauguration of Manitoba government elevator system. (84)
Appointment of Saskatchewan Elevator Commission under chairmanship of Dr. R. Magill. (98)
(Feb.) Organization of Canadian Council of Agriculture. (137, 387)
(Dec.) Agrarian "Siege of Ottawa." (137)

1911. (Mar.) Incorporation by statute of Saskatchewan Co-operative Elevator Co. (102)
Federal incorporation of Grain Growers' Grain Co. (154)
Incorporation of Grain Growers' Export Co. (148)

1912. Lease of Manitoba government elevators to Grain Growers' Grain Company. (95)
Entry of G. G. G. Co. into terminal operation. (148)
Canada Grain Act passed. Creation of Board of Grain Commissioners. (104 f.)

1913. Statutory incorporation of Alberta Farmers' Co-operative Elevator Co. (120 f.)
Agricultural Co-operative Associations Act passed in Saskatchewan. (292)
Organization of Co-operative Supply Department of G. G. G. Co. (285)

1914. Organization of Trading Department of Saskatchewan Grain Growers' Association. (292 f.)

1915. Incorporation of Grain Growers' Export Co. (New York) Inc. (159)

1915–16. Negotiations for federation of farmers' companies. (163 f.)

1916. Reorganization of Canadian Council of Agriculture to include farmers' commercial organizations. (388)

1917. Drafting of "Farmers' Platform" by Council of Agriculture. (388)
Amalgamation of G. G. G. Co. and Alberta Co-operative Elevator Company to form United Grain Growers Limited. (170 f.)
Construction of first farmer-owned terminal elevator by Saskatchewan "Co-op." (179 f.)
Establishment of Board of Grain Supervisors for wartime wheat control. (195)

1918. Incorporation of U. G. G. Securities Ltd. (330)
Incorporation of U. G. G. Sawmills Ltd. (305)

1919. Establishment of Canadian Wheat Board by federal government. (196)

1920. Refusal of federal government to renew powers of Canadian Wheat Board. (198)

Drafting of plan for voluntary wheat pool by Council of Agriculture. (200 f.)

Incorporation of Saskatchewan Co-operative Export Co. (182)

Organization through Council of Agriculture of Progressive Party under leadership of T. A. Crerar. (389)

1921. (July) Formation of farmers' government under Hon. Herbert Greenfield by United Farmers of Alberta. (389)

U. G. G. takes out injunction to restrain Hyndman Grain Inquiry Commission. (396)

(Dec.) Election of 65 Progressives to federal parliament. (389)

(Dec.) Organization of Farmers' Union at Saskatoon. (213 f.)

1922. Closing out of farm machinery business by U. G. G. (304)

Enabling legislation for reëstablishment of Wheat Board passed by federal parliament and by legislatures of Saskatchewan and Alberta. (203 f.)

Formation of Farmers' government under Hon. John Bracken by United Farmers of Manitoba. (207)

Restoration of Crow's Nest Pass freight rates on wheat. (389)

1923. Appointment of fourth Royal Grain Inquiry Commission under Mr. Justice Turgeon.

Establishment of U. G. G. Cattle Pool. (361)

Rejection by Manitoba legislature of Wheat Board Bill. (208)

(June) Abandonment of provincial efforts for Wheat Board reestablishment. (208)

(July) Abandonment of project of voluntary wheat pool under auspices of Council of Agriculture for separate provincial pools. (211)

(Aug.) Initiation of wheat pool campaigns in Alberta and Saskatchewan. (213 f.)

(Oct.) Alberta Wheat Pool commences operations. (217 f.)

1924. (Jan.) Incorporation of Manitoba Co-operative Wheat Producers. Ltd.

(Aug.) Organization of Central Selling Agency (Canadian Co-operative Wheat Producers). (221)

(Sept.) Saskatchewan and Manitoba Wheat Pools commence operations. (219 f.)

Acquisition of Pool Terminals Nos. 1, 2 and 3, by Central Selling Agency. (229)

Incorporation of United Livestock Growers Ltd. (362)

1925. (Feb.) Incorporation of Saskatchewan Pool Elevators Ltd. (230)

(Mar.) Incorporation of Manitoba Pool Elevators Ltd. (232)

(Apr.) Failure of negotiations for coördination of wheat pools and farmers' elevator companies. (232 f.)

(Sept.) Incorporation of Alberta Pool Elevators Ltd. (239)

(Oct.) Proposal by Saskatchewan Pool to purchase elevators of Saskatchewan "Co-op." (243)

1925. (Dec.) Completion of Saskatchewan "Co-op." transfer elevator at Buffalo. (186)

Initiation of coarse grains pools by Saskatchewan and Manitoba Co-operative Wheat Producers. (224 f.)

General revision of Grain Act, following report of Turgeon Grain Inquiry Commission.

1926. (Feb.) International Wheat Pool Conference at St. Paul.

(Apr.) Decision of Saskatchewan "Co-op" shareholders to sell assets to Saskatchewan Pool. (235)

1926. (July) Amalgamation of S. G. G. A. and Farmers' Union as United Farmers of Canada, Saskatchewan Section, Ltd. (393 f.)

(Aug.) Transfer of assets of Saskatchewan "Co-op" to Saskatchewan Pool Elevators at arbitrated valuation of $11,059,310. (236)

(Dec.) Proposal of provincial pools to purchase elevators of U. G. G. rejected by shareholders. (241)

1926. Liquidation of U. G. G. Sawmills. (332)

1927. U. G. G. undertakes construction of 5,000,000-bushel terminal at Fort William. (243)

Alberta Wheat Pool leases government terminal elevators at Vancouver and Prince Rupert.

(Mar.) Winding up of Saskatchewan Co-operative Elevator Co. (237)

(Apr.) Campbell amendment to Grain Act passed. (263 f.)

(May). International Wheat Pool Conference at Kansas City. (403 f.)

APPENDIX C

CHARTS OF GRAIN GROWERS' ORGANIZATIONS

I. United Grain Growers Limited

Amalgamation of Grain Growers' Grain Co. (1906–17) and Alberta Farmers' Co-operative Elevator Co. (1913–17)

Capital Authorized	$5,000,000
Capital Subscribed	3,239,250
Capital Paid-up Aug. 31, 1927	2,979,078
Reserve Fund, Aug. 31, 1927	1,500,000

Subsidiaries. (See pages 328–332)

Company	Incorporated	Paid-up Capital
1. Grain Growers' Export Co., Ltd.	1911	$390,000
2. Grain Growers' Export Co., Inc. (N. Y.)	1915	350,000
3. Public Press, Ltd.	1909	210,000
Grain Growers' Guide Publishing Co.	1918	....
4. U. G. G. Securities, Ltd.	1918	100,000
5. U. G. G. Sawmills, Ltd.[1]	1919	850,000
6. United Livestock Growers, Ltd.	1924	20,000

Organization and Distribution of Shareholders. (*January 1, 1926*)

Province	Shareholders' Locals	Number of Shareholders
Manitoba	101	9,200
Saskatchewan	83	9,000
Alberta	155	16,300
British Columbia	8	1,000
Total	347	35,500

[1] In process of liquidation.

II. Canadian Council of Agriculture

Organized 1910; reorganized 1916. (See p. 388)

Constituent Organizations

A. *Provincial Farmers' Associations.*[1]

1. United Farmers of Manitoba (1921).
   (Manitoba Grain Growers' Association 1903–20).
2. Saskatchewan Grain Growers' Association (1906).[2]
   (Territorial Grain Growers' Association, 1902–05).
3. United Farmers of Alberta (1909).
4. United Farmers of Ontario (1914).

B. *Provincial Farm Women's Associations (Women's Section).*[3]

5. United Farm Women of Manitoba.
6. Saskatchewan Grain Growers' Association, Women's Section.
7. United Farm Women of Alberta.
8. United Farm Women of Ontario.

C. *Farmers' Companies.*[4]

9. United Grain Growers, Limited (1906).
10. Saskatchewan Co-operative Elevator Company (1911–26).
11. United Farmers Co-operative Company (Ontario) (1914).

D. *Farmers' Organ.*[4]

12. Grain Growers' Guide (1908).

[1] The United Farmers of British Columbia (organized in 1917), and the United Farmers of New Brunswick (organized 1918) were also members of the Council of Agriculture during the short period of their existence which terminated in 1921.

[2] Since the amalgamation of the S.G.G.A. and the Farmers' Union in 1926 to form the United Farmers of Canada, Saskatchewan Section Ltd., Saskatchewan has not been represented in the Council of Agriculture. (See p. 394.)

[3] The Women's Section of the Council was organized in 1925.

[4] The farmers' commercial companies and the Grain Growers' Guide were admitted to membership in the Council under the reorganization of 1916. (See p. 517.)

III. The Wheat Pool Structure

(See pp. 355–359, 369–374; also Appendix F.)

Alberta Co-operative Wheat Producers

7 Districts, each electing one director to Pool Board.
70 Sub-districts, each electing one Pool delegate.
260 Locals, each having up to 5 directors.

Alberta Pool Elevators, Ltd.

Authorized capital $600,000.
Stock held by Alta Co-op. Wheat Producers.
Directorate identical with Pool Board.
157 Country elevators (end of 1927).
Lease of government terminal elevators at Vancouver and Prince Rupert.

Saskatchewan Co-operative Wheat Producers

16 Districts, each electing one director to Pool Board.
160 Sub-districts, each electing one Pool delegate.
1050 Local pool committees.

Saskatchewan Pool Elevators, Ltd.

Authorized capital $100,000.
Directorate identical with Pool Board, each director holding one share.
730 Country elevators (end of 1927).
Saskatchewan Pool Terminals, Ltd.

Manitoba Co-operative Wheat Producers

7 Districts, each electing one director to Pool Board.
90 Constituency "locals," each electing one or more Pool delegates.
450 Pool shipping committees.

Manitoba Pool Elevators, Ltd.

Authorized capital $100,000.
Directorate identical with Pool Board.
58 Local co-operative elevator associations (end 1927), chartered under Manitoba Co-operative Associations Act.

Canadian Co-operative Wheat Producers, Ltd. (*Central Selling Agency*)

Capital $150,000, one-third being subscribed by each provincial pool.
9 Directors, three elected by each provincial pool.
Offices at Winnipeg, Fort William–Port Arthur, Calgary, Vancouver, Toronto, Montreal, New York, London, Paris.
Connections with 28 selling agencies in 15 countries.
Controls Pool Terminals Nos. 1, 2, 3.

APPENDIX D

AN ACT TO INCORPORATE THE SASKATCHEWAN CO-OPERATIVE ELEVATOR COMPANY, LIMITED

(In which Amendments are Incorporated)

[*Assented to March 14, 1911.*]
[*Amended, 1912, 1913, 1915, 1917.*]

HIS Majesty by and with the advice and consent of the Legislative Assembly of Saskatchewan enacts as follows:

1. *Interpretation.* In this Act the term "local" unless the context otherwise requires means the body of shareholders who support an elevator organized and established at any point in the province and the term "local board of management" means the board of managers elected at any such local according to the provisions of this Act.

INCORPORATION, POWERS, ETC.

2. *Incorporation.* John A. Maharg, of Moose Jaw; Charles A. Dunning of Beaverdale; Fred W. Green, of Moose Jaw; Allen G. Hawkes, of Percival; James Robinson, of Walpole; Dr. T. Hill, of Kinley, all in the Province of Saskatchewan and all such persons as shall become shareholders of the company shall be and are hereby declared to be a body corporate and politic under the name and style of "The Saskatchewan Co-operative Elevator Company, Limited," with power to construct, acquire, maintain and operate grain elevators within Saskatchewan, to buy and sell grain and generally to do all things incidental to the production, storing and marketing of grain.

3. *Capital stock.* The capital stock of the company shall consist of such amount as shall from time to time be fixed by the Lieutenant Governor in Council and shall be divided into shares of fifty dollars each to be held only by agriculturists:

Provided that no person shall hold more than twenty shares and no assignment or transfer of any share shall be valid unless approved by the directors.

4. *Powers.* The company shall have power to acquire by purchase or otherwise and to hold any interest in real or personal property which the directors may deem requisite for the purposes of the company and to dispose of the same or any part thereof.

5. *Head office.* The head office of the company shall be at Regina in the Province of Saskatchewan or at any such other place in Saskatchewan as the directors may from time to time determine by bylaw.

6. *Provisional directors.* Until directors are elected as hereinafter provided the aforesaid John A. Maharg, of Moose Jaw; Charles A. Dunning, of Beaverdale; Fred W. Green, of Moose Jaw; A. G. Hawkes, of Percival; James Robinson, of Walpole; Dr. T. Hill, of Kinley, all in the Province of Saskatchewan, shall be the provisional directors; and they or a majority of them are

hereby empowered to take subscriptions for shares and to receive payments thereon, to organize locals, to make all necessary payments for costs and expenses incident to the sale of shares and the organization of locals and generally to perform all acts and things necessary for the organization of the company.

7. *Commencement of business.* The company shall not commence business until twenty-five locals have been organized as hereinafter provided.

8. *First general meeting.* As soon as the conditions for the commencement of business as set out in the next preceding section have been complied with, the provisional directors shall call the first general meeting of the company at the head office of the company by giving twenty days' notice of the holding of such meeting to each shareholder; such notice to be given by registered letter; and at the said meeting a board of directors comprised of nine duly qualified shareholders shall be elected who shall be paid such remuneration as the meeting may determine.

9. *Directors.* At the first general meeting of the company three directors shall be elected for three years, three for two years and three for one year and thereafter a sufficient number of directors shall be elected each year to fill the vacancies occurring on the board; and all directors elected annually subsequently to the first general meeting shall hold office for three years.

(2) The company in general meeting may by a resolution which shall receive a two-thirds majority of the delegates voting thereon remove any director before the expiration of his period of office and may subsequently by an ordinary resolution appoint another person in his stead, the person so appointed shall hold office during such time only as the director in whose place he is appointed would have held the same if he had not been removed.

10. *Persons entitled to vote.* The persons entitled to vote at the first general meeting and at all subsequent general meetings of the company shall be the shareholders who have been elected delegates by the locals for that purpose under the provisions of section 14 hereof; each delegate shall have one vote; and excepting as provided in this section no shareholder shall vote at any meeting of the company on account of any shares held by him or otherwise and all acts done by a majority of the delegates at any meeting of the company shall be deemed to be the acts of the company.

11. *Powers of directors.* The business of the company shall be managed by the directors who may affix the seal of the company and make all contracts on behalf of the company and may exercise all such powers of the company as are not by this Act required to be exercised by the company in general meeting or as are not conferred by bylaw of the company upon the local boards of management and any other powers not contrary to the provisions of this Act which may be conferred upon them by bylaw of the company.

Locals

12. *Locals.* Any number of shareholders may request the directors to establish a local at any railway shipping point in the province.

13. *Conditions of establishment of locals.* The directors shall not without the consent of the Lieutenant Governor in Council establish any local unless it appears to their satisfaction that the amount of shares held by the sup-

porters of the proposed local is at least equal to the value of the proposed elevator, that fifteen per cent. of the amount of such shares has been paid up and that the aggregate annual crop acreage of the said shareholders represents a proportion of not less than 2,000 acres for each 10,000 bushels of elevator capacity asked for.

14. *Annual meeting.* Upon the establishment of a local and annually thereafter upon a date to be fixed by bylaw of the company a meeting of the supporters of the said local shall be held at which all matters pertaining to the management, operation and maintenance of the elevator shall be reviewed and discussed and a local board of management consisting of five duly qualified supporters shall be elected to hold office until their successors are appointed; and at the said meeting there shall be elected from among the supporters of the local three delegates or such other number of delegates as the company may by bylaw determine to attend the general meetings of the company.

15. *Voting.* Unless otherwise provided by bylaw of the company at all meetings of the supporters of any local each shareholder shall have one vote for each share held by him:

Provided that no person shall have more than five votes.

16. *Powers of local board.* The local board of management shall have such powers and duties as shall be determined from time to time by bylaw of the company or as may be delegated to them by the directors.

Finance

17. *Finance.* It shall be the duty of the directors to make provision for keeping an accurate account of all the business and financial transactions of the company and for that purpose all books, records, forms and methods of accounting shall be submitted to the Provincial Treasurer and Provincial Auditor for approval before being adopted.

18. *Financial year.* The financial year of the company shall end on the thirty-first day of July in each year, on which date the books and accounts of the company shall be closed and balanced.

19. *Audit by Provincial Auditor.* It shall be the duty of the Provincial Auditor to arrange for a continuous audit of the accounts and inspection of the books and records of the company. Such audit and inspection shall be under the supervision of the Provincial Auditor, and the cost and expenses thereof shall be paid by the company.

20. *Disposition of moneys received by the company.* (1) Out of the moneys received by the company as a result of the operation of the elevators under its control there shall first be paid all charges for operation and maintenance including salaries.

(2) If after the said charges are paid there remains a surplus on hand at the end of the financial year the company may at its discretion pay out of such surplus to each shareholder whose shares were allotted prior to the first day of April of such financial year a dividend of not more than ten per cent. upon the paid up capital.

(3) If after the said dividends, if any, are paid there remains a balance on hand the company may at its discretion distribute:

(*a*) To the shareholders of the company such sums as may be fixed by the company but not exceeding fifty per cent. of such balance on a co-operative basis, each shareholder being entitled to receive such sum hereunder as shall be fairly and equitably proportionate to the volume of business which he has brought to the company; or

(*b*) To the supporters of locals such sums as the company may fix but not exceeding fifty per cent. of such balance on the basis of the aggregate relative net financial results of the respective locals; or

(*c*) To the shareholders and supporters of locals partly according to each of the schemes of distribution provided for in clauses (*a*) and (*b*) of this subsection such sums as the company may fix but not exceeding on the aggregate fifty per cent. of such balance;

(*d*) Or in lieu of any or all of the payments authorised under this or the next preceding subsection as aforesaid it may apply such surplus or balance to the extent of fifty per cent. thereof for the general purposes of the company or in making provision for the same;

(*e*) Or it may apply such surplus or balance to the extent of fifty per cent. thereof in liquidation or part liquidation of the unpaid balance of the capital stock of the company, an equal proportionate payment being made upon all shares allotted prior to the first day of April in the financial year during which such surplus was earned.

(4) Should there remain a surplus on hand after all payments and disbursements are made as provided in the next preceding subsection of this section, such surplus shall be set apart in a separate account to be styled "The Elevator Reserve Account," which account may be drawn upon by the company from time to time for the purpose of purchasing grain, and at the close of the grain season any sum so taken and invested shall be replaced in the account out of the company's funds:

Provided that the funds in such account may be employed for such other purposes not inconsistent with this Act as may be approved by the Lieutenant Governor in Council.

21. *Restriction upon next preceding section.* The provisions made in the next preceding section for the payment of dividends, the distribution of surplus moneys and the creation of a reserve fund shall not be put into effect unless and until all moneys then due and payable to the government under this Act have been paid.

22. *Moneys to be deposited in chartered bank.* All moneys received by the company or any of its officers on behalf of the company shall be deposited forthwith in such chartered bank or banks as the directors may determine and shall be paid out under regulations to be framed by the directors by cheques signed by the president and treasurer of the company or such officers as may be appointed by the directors for the purpose.

23. *Security by officers of the company.* The treasurer of the company and each of its officers, employees or servants whose duty it is to receive or handle moneys on behalf of the company shall before entering upon the duties of their office furnish a bond or covenant of some guarantee company to be named by the directors to secure the due accounting by them for all moneys that come into their hands which bond shall in each case be in such form

and for such amount as shall be approved by the directors or such other officers as are appointed by the board of directors for that purpose and the directors shall pay the premiums for such guarantee bonds out of the funds of the company.

GOVERNMENT ASSISTANCE

24. *The Lieutenant Governor may make loan to the company.* The Lieutenant Governor in Council is hereby authorised from time to time and on such terms and conditions as may be agreed on with the company to loan to the company for the purpose of aiding in the acquisition or construction, extension or remodelling of any local elevator a sum not to exceed eighty-five per cent. of the estimated cost of the said elevator or such extension or remodelling of any such elevator as may from time to time be considered advisable or necessary by the directors.

(2) *Raising funds for loans.* For the purpose of raising the funds required for loans under this section the Lieutenant Governor in Council may authorise the Provincial Treasurer from time to time to issue securities of the province; and the sums required shall be raised as provided by The Saskatchewan Loans Act and shall form part of the general revenue fund of Saskatchewan.

25. *Terms of repayment and security therefor.* Any sums loaned to the company by virtue of the next preceding section shall be repayable in twenty equal annual instalments of principal and interest, the first of such instalments to be due and payable on the thirty-first day of August in the second year next following the granting of the loan and shall be secured by a mortgage or mortgages upon the said elevator and any interest in real or personal property which the company may hold and use in connection with the said elevator.

25*a*. All elevators, property or uncalled capital stock of the company and every interest which the company may have therein intended under this Act or by any agreement between the company and the government to be transferred to the government as security for any loan or advance made under the authority of this Act or any other Act to the company by the government shall pending the execution of such transfer or transfers be charged with the payment of all moneys which may have been or may hereafter be advanced upon any such loan pursuant to the terms of any agreement relating thereto between the government and the company and the company may not without the consent of the Lieutenant Governor in Council first obtained dispose of the same save subject to any charge so created as aforesaid.

26. The form and terms of the mortgages and of any other evidences of debt which may be given by the company on account of any such said loan, the times and manners in which the sums loaned shall be paid to the company and the disposition of all moneys loaned shall be such as the Lieutenant Governor in Council may approve.

26*a*. *Payment of expenses of organization.* It shall be sufficient for the purposes of this Act and *The Chattel Mortgage Act* if any chattel mortgage or other instrument given by the company to the province or to any minister on behalf of the province by way of security for any advance made to the company under the authority of this Act be without any affidavit of execution or of *bona fides* or without a detailed description of the chattel property charged thereby filed in the office of the registrar of joint stock companies and such mortgage or other instrument shall have priority from the date of such filing over all executions, transfers, mortgages or other incumbrances or charges or dispositions of any sort affecting the same property or any part thereof and shall from the date of the filing thereof as aforesaid be and remain in full force and effect without renewal until discharged or satisfied.

27. *General powers of the Lieutenant Governor in Council.* The Lieutenant Governor in Council shall have power to pay to the provisional directors of the company any sum not exceeding the amount granted by the Legislature for that purpose which may be required to cover the expenses incurred in the organization of the company and of locals; any sums so paid to the provisional directors shall be expended in such manner as may be approved by the Lieutenant Governor in Council and all such expenditures shall be subject to the audit of the provincial auditor.

27a. *Guarantee to provincial treasurer.* Subject to the approval of the Lieutenant Governor in Council and upon such terms and conditions as may be fixed by him the Provincial Treasurer may enter into an agreement with the company and with any person, bank or corporation to guarantee the repayment of moneys advanced to the company for purposes authorized by this Act, with interest, and the company may secure the government against loss through such guarantee in such manner or form as the Lieutenant Governor in Council may approve.

General

28. *General powers of Lieutenant Governor in Council.* The Lieutenant Governor in Council shall have power to make all provisions not inconsistent with this Act which may be required for the better carrying out of the purposes of the Act.

Bylaws

29. *Powers to make bylaws.* The company may from time to time make such bylaws not contrary to law or inconsistent with this Act for the administration, management and control of the property and business of the company and for the conduct in all particulars of the affairs of the company as are considered necessary or expedient for carrying out the provisions of this Act according to the true intent and meaning thereof.

30. *Power to borrow money.* The company shall have power to borrow money for the purpose of carrying out the objects of its incorporation and to hypothecate, pledge and mortgage its real and personal property, rights and assets and to sign bills, notes, contracts and other evidences of or securities for money borrowed or to be borrowed by the company for the purposes aforesaid.

The board of directors may exercise these powers when duly authorised thereto by bylaws of the company.

Agreements

31. *Variation of agreements.* Where the company has hitherto made or shall hereafter make an agreement with the government of Saskatchewan or with any person, bank or corporation or with the government and any person, bank or corporation, the terms of such agreement may be altered or varied with the consent of all the parties thereto.

32. *Agreements to be laid before Legislature.* The provincial treasurer shall lay before the Legislative Assembly within fifteen days of the opening of the annual session in each year copies of all agreements entered into by the government with the company or with any person, bank or corporation for the advance of money to the company, for the guarantee of any advance or for the indemnification of the government against its liability under any such guarantee.

APPENDIX E

TEXT OF GROWER'S CONTRACT
ALBERTA CO-OPERATIVE WHEAT PRODUCERS, LIMITED

Agreement

THIS AGREEMENT made this day of , A.D. between ALBERTA CO-OPERATIVE WHEAT PRODUCERS, LIMITED, a body corporate formed under "The Co-operative Associations Act," of the Province of Alberta, with its head office at Calgary, in the Province of Alberta, hereinafter called "The Association," of the First Part, and the undersigned, a person concerned in the production of wheat in the Province of Alberta and in the marketing of the same, hereinafter called "The Grower," of the Second Part.

WHEREAS, the undersigned Grower desires to co-operate with others concerned in the production of wheat in the Province of Alberta and in the marketing of the same, hereinafter referred to as Growers, for the purpose of promoting, fostering and encouraging the business of growing and marketing wheat co-operatively and for eliminating speculation in wheat and for stabilizing the wheat market; for co-operatively and collectively handling the problems of Growers and for improving in every legitimate way the interests of Growers in the Province of Alberta and for other pertinent purposes;

AND WHEREAS, the Association has been formed under "The Co-operative Associations Act" of the Province of Alberta with full power to act as agent, factor, mercantile agent and attorney in fact, to handle wheat produced and delivered to it by its members, and with such further powers as are set forth in its Memorandum of Association;

AND WHEREAS, the Grower is desirous of becoming a member of the Association and of entering, together with other Growers, into this Contract with the Association;

AND WHEREAS, this Agreement, although individual in expression, is one of a series either identical or generally similar in terms between the Association and Growers of wheat in the Province of Alberta, and shall constitute one Contract between the several Growers of wheat in the Province of Alberta signing the same and this Association:

NOW THIS AGREEMENT WITNESSETH that, in consideration of the premises and in consideration of the covenants and agreements on the part of the Association as hereinafter set forth, and in consideration of the execution of this Agreement, or one similar in terms, by other Growers of wheat in the Province of Alberta, and in consideration of the mutual obligations herein set forth, the Parties hereto hereby agree to and with each other as follows:

1. It is expressly provided and agreed that, if by the fifth day of September, A.D., 1923, signatures by Growers of wheat and the owners, purchasers, share-crop purchasers, tenants, lessors and lessees of land, whose wheat acreage taken as a whole shall be equal to Fifty per cent. (50%) of the acreage in wheat in the Province of

Alberta in the year 1922, shall not have been secured to this Agreement, or an Agreement similar in terms, the Association shall notify every subscriber hereto thereof before the eighth day of September, A.D., 1923, by notice mailed to him at the address noted below and the Grower shall have the right to withdraw his signature hereto by written notice to the Trustees of the Association at its head office at Calgary, in the Province of Alberta, between the eighth day of September, A.D., 1923, and the twenty-second day of September, A.D., 1923, and, upon such notice being received by the said Trustees, this Agreement shall be deemed to be, and shall be, cancelled, rescinded and of no force nor effect in so far as the Grower sending such notice is concerned. If all signatures are not then withdrawn, the Association may, in its discretion, proceed to carry out and give effect to the terms of this Agreement without notice to the Growers and this Agreement shall be binding in all its terms upon each and all of the Growers who have not given notice as last hereinbefore provided for or the Association may, upon notice to the Growers who have entered into this Agreement, declare this Agreement at an end and, upon notice being mailed to the Growers at their several addresses noted on this Agreement, or one similar in terms, to this effect, then this Agreement shall be deemed to be, and shall be, cancelled, rescinded and of no force nor effect; and, in such last mentioned event, the Association shall have its accounts audited by a chartered accountant whose reports shall be filed at the head office of the Association and shall be open for inspection at all reasonable times by any Grower who has executed this Agreement and the funds of the Association then on hand shall, after deduction of the expenses of or incidental to the formation and organization of the Association and all other proper expenses up to the date of distribution, be distributed pro-rata among the Growers who have executed this Agreement and paid moneys to the Association in accordance with its terms as hereinafter set forth. If the necessary signatures to this Agreement, as hereinbefore specified, have been secured on or before the fifth day of September, A.D., 1923, then this Agreement shall be binding in all its terms upon this Association and upon all of the Growers executing this Agreement.

2. It is expressly provided and agreed that, for all matters of acreage, bushelage, percentages or signatures and for all statements of fact in connection therewith and for determining whether or not by the fifth day of September, A.D., 1923, signatures by Growers of wheat and the owners, purchasers, share-crop purchasers, tenants, lessors and lessees of land, whose wheat acreage taken as a whole equals Fifty per cent. (50%) of the acreage in wheat in the Province of Alberta in the year 1922, have been secured to this Agreement, or an Agreement similar in terms, the Trustees of the Association shall be the sole judges and a written statement signed by the chairman appointed by the Trustees of the Association shall be deemed to be, and shall be, conclusive evidence thereof with or without notice to the Grower.

3. The Association agrees to act as agent, factor, mercantile agent and attorney in fact for the Grower to receive, take delivery of, handle, store, transport, market, sell and otherwise dispose of the wheat produced and delivered to it by the Grower, excepting only registered seed wheat.

4. The Grower convenants and agrees to consign and deliver to the Association or its order at the time and place designated by the Association all of the wheat and the warehouse or storage receipts covering it produced or acquired by or for him in the Province of Alberta, except registered seed wheat, during the years, 1923, 1924, 1925, 1926 and 1927.

5. It is agreed that the Association will, in its discretion, whenever and wherever possible receive and take delivery of the Grower's wheat at the Grower's most convenient delivery point.

6. The Grower hereby appoints the Association his sole and exclusive agent, factor and mercantile agent within the meaning of "The Factors Act" of the Province of Alberta and also as his attorney in fact for the purposes hereinafter set forth with full power and authority in its own name, in the name of the Grower or otherwise to transact such business, and take such action as may be necessary, incidental or convenient for the accomplishment thereof, coupling such appointment with a direct financial interest as the common agent, factor and mercantile agent and attorney in fact of Growers hereunder and without power of revocation for the full term hereof: —

(*a*) To receive and take delivery of, handle, store, transport, market, sell and otherwise dispose of the wheat produced and delivered to it by the Grower in whatsoever way and at such time and place as the Association shall in its judgment determine to be to the best advantage of all of the Growers who have executed this Agreement, or an Agreement similar in terms.

(*b*) To mingle and mix the wheat received by the Association from any Grower with wheat of like kind and grade delivered to the Association by other Growers and, in its discretion, clean, condition, blend or process the same, subject always to the laws for the time being in force governing the same.

(*c*) To borrow money in the name of the Association and on its own account on the wheat delivered to it or on any warehouse or storage receipt or grain receipt or on any accounts for the sale thereof or on any drafts, bills of lading, bills of exchange, notes or acceptances, orders, or on any commercial paper delivered therefor and to exercise all rights of ownership without limitation and to pledge in its name and on its own account such wheat or receipts or accounts or drafts, bills of lading, notes, acceptances, orders or other commercial paper as collateral therefor. The Association shall have the right to apply the money so received pro-rata among the Growers who have executed this Agreement and delivered wheat to it or to use the said moneys for any proper association purpose or activity deemed by the Association to be in the best interests of its members.

(*d*) To pay or retain and deduct from the gross returns from the sale of the wheat delivered to it by the Growers the amount necessary to cover all brokerage, advertising, taxes, tolls, freights, elevator charges, legal expenses and all other proper charges such as salaries, fixed charges and general expenses of the Association and, in addition, the Association may deduct such percentage, not exceeding One per cent. (1 %) of the gross selling price of the wheat as it shall deem desirable as a commercial reserve to be used for any of the purposes or activities of the Association.

(*e*) To settle any and all claims for damages or otherwise which may occur in connection with the handling of the Grower's wheat during transit or otherwise or that may arise in connection with the exercise of any of the powers or authority herein granted.

(*f*) To deduct from the gross returns from the sale of wheat handled by the Association for the Growers who have executed this Agreement or, upon first obtaining the consent in writing of any group of Growers, a sum out of each Grower's proper proportion thereof not exceeding Two cents (2¢) per bushel and to invest the same, in the discretion of the Trustees of the Association, in shares of the capital stock of any Company or Association (formed or to be formed), whether promoted, owned or controlled by the Association or not, which Company or Association is formed for the erection or acquisition by purchase, lease or otherwise of grain elevators and which Company or Association has entered into a contract or contracts with the Association to handle the wheat of its members under the control and direction of the Association, and for such purpose to apply for and enter into all necessary and incidental contracts on behalf of and in the name of the Grower for the purchase of such shares of the capital stock of any such company.

(*g*) To take exclusive possession and control of the Grower's wheat crop and to harvest and market the same according to the terms of this Agreement or at its option to take any legal action to obtain possession thereof or to have a Receiver appointed with power to take exclusive possession and control of the said wheat crop and deliver the same to this Association as hereinbefore provided or otherwise to dispose of the same as a Court having jurisdiction in that behalf may direct, in the event of the Grower failing to fulfil on his part the provisions of this Agreement or any of them or failing to deliver his wheat crop as herein provided. If possession of such wheat shall be taken by the Association by reason of such breach of contract on the part of the Grower, the Association shall be entitled to retain out of the proceeds derived from the sale thereof, in addition to the sums heretofore provided for, all additional expenses incurred in connection therewith.

7. Any unused balance of reserves and surpluses shall stand in the name of the Association and be owned by the members and shall, when in the opinion of the Trustees a distribution should be made or upon a dissolution of this Association, be divided in the same proportions in which it was contributed by the members.

8. Notwithstanding anything hereinbefore contained, the Grower may retain wheat for his own seed and feed and may, upon first receiving a permit in writing from the Association, dispose of wheat for seed or feed directly to any farmer who is a neighbor and a member of the Association. All other seed wheat, except registered seed wheat, shall be sold by and through the Association only.

9. The Grower expressly covenants and agrees that he will not (save as herein permitted) sell or otherwise dispose of any of the wheat produced or acquired by him in the Province of Alberta during the life of this Agreement to any person or persons, firm or corporation other than this Association.

10. The Grower expressly warrants that he has not heretofore mortgaged or pledged or charged or granted a lien on or contracted to sell, market, consign or deliver any of his said wheat to any person, firm or corporation except as noted at the end of this Agreement. Any wheat covered by such existing contracts shall, subject to any agreement or arrangement with all interested parties, be excluded from the terms hereof for the period and to the extent noted.

11. It is agreed that the Grower may, subject to the terms of this Agreement and subject to any law in force for the time being, mortgage or pledge his interest in his wheat crop but, in such event, the Grower shall forthwith notify the Association and the Association shall, in its discretion, be at liberty to pay off or take over or assume the indebtedness under such mortgage or pledge and to take delivery of the Grower's crop and to deduct from all moneys which become payable to the Grower by the Association a sum equal to the amount which the Association has paid out or agreed to pay with respect to such mortgage or pledge.

12. The Association shall, so soon as practicable after the delivery of wheat to it by the Grower, make an advance to the Grower at such rate per bushel according to grade, quality and place of delivery as, in the discretion of the Association, it shall deem proper and the Association agrees that, subject to any laws in force for the time being, it will, in its discretion, from time to time pay over to the Grower as funds are available from the sale of the crop of each season, his proportion of the proceeds of all wheat of like variety and grade sold by the Association in each season for the Growers who have executed this Contract, less all deductions which the Association is entitled to make pursuant to the provisions of this Contract and less all advances made by the Grower and less all handling and other proper charges of every description whatsoever including the costs of maintaining the Association and of transporting, handling, grading, storing, selling and marketing such wheat and of other proper activities.

13. The Grower convenants and agrees to, and hereby does, apply for one (1) share out of the Ordinary Shares in the capital stock of the Association and agrees to pay to the Association the par value thereof, namely, the sum of One Dollar ($1.00). The Association covenants and agrees to accept the said application and to allot to the Grower one (1) share of stock out of the Ordinary Shares in the capital stock of the Association.

14. The Grower covenants and agrees to pay the further sum of two dollars ($2.00) to defray the expenses of organization, to carry on field service and educational work and other proper activities of the Association.

15. The Grower covenants and agrees, as and when requested by the Association or any officer, agent or servant thereof, to make application from time to time for railway cars for the shipment of his wheat pursuant to the provisions of "The Canada Grain Act" and to perform such other acts and execute such document as the Association may require in connection with the handling of the Grower's wheat.

16. The Association may sell the said wheat to millers, brokers or others, within or without this province, at such time and upon such conditions and terms as it may deem fair and advisable.

17. The Association may sell all or any part of the wheat delivered to it by its members, pursuant to this Contract through any agency or by joining with any agency for the coöperative marketing of wheat of the Provinces of Alberta, Saskatchewan and Manitoba, or of other provinces or groups of provinces or of the Dominion or of other countries, under a term contract or otherwise, and under such conditions as will serve the joint interests of the Growers and the Association

is hereby authorized and empowered to transfer to and confer upon any such agency (formed or to be formed) all of the powers, rights and privileges of this Association under this Contract and any proportionate or other expenses connected therewith shall be deemed marketing costs, provided always that nothing herein contained shall authorize the Association to sell through or join with any such agency or to exercise the authority and powers last hereinbefore mentioned or to enter into any Contract with any such agency whereby any of the deductions authorized by this Contract are increased in any amount whatsoever.

18. The Grower hereby authorizes the Association to enter into any contract for such consideration and on such terms and conditions as it may deem advisable and profitable for the inspecting, grading, handling, elevating, storing. warehousing and shipping of the wheat covered hereby, or any portion thereof, and for the use of the security thereof as collateral within the general purposes of this agreement by the Association.

19. This Agreement shall be binding upon the Grower, his personal representatives, successors and assigns, during the period hereinbefore mentioned, as long as he raises wheat, directly or indirectly, or has the legal right to exercise ownership or control of any thereof, or any interest therein, or of any land on which wheat is grown during the term of this Contract.

20. From time to time each year the Grower will mail to the Association as requested a statement of his expected acreage of wheat for that year and its condition on the forms provided for that purpose by the Association.

21. Inasmuch as the remedy at law would be inadequate and inasmuch as it is now and ever will be impracticable and extremely difficult to determine the actual damage resulting to the Association, should the Grower fail so to deliver all of his wheat, the Grower hereby agrees to pay to the Association for all wheat delivered, sold, consigned or marketed by or for him or withheld other than in accordance with the terms hereof, the sum of Twenty-five Cents (25¢). per bushel as liquidated damages for the breach of this Contract, all parties agreeing that this Contract is one of a series dependent for its true value upon the adherence of each and all of the contracting parties to each and all of the said Contracts.

22. The Grower agrees that, in the event of a breach by him of any material provision hereof, particularly as to delivery or marketing of any wheat other than through the Association, the Association shall, upon proper action instituted by it, be entitled to an injunction to prevent further breach hereof, and other equitable relief, according to the terms of this Agreement; and the Association and the Grower expressly agree that this Agreement is not a contract for personal services or demanding exceptional capacity or talents; and that this is a Contract of agency coupled with financial interest under special circumstances and conditions and that the Association cannot go into the open markets and secure wheat to replace any which the Grower may fail to deliver; and that this Contract will be the proper subject for the remedy of specific performance in the event of a breach thereof.

23. Any deduction or allowance or loss that the Association may make or suffer on account of inferior grade, quantity, quality or standard, or condition at delivery, shall be charged against the Grower and deducted from his net returns hereunder.

24. The Association may make rules and regulations and provide inspectors to standardize the quality, method and manner of handling, sacking and shipping of such wheat; and the Grower agrees to observe and perform any such rules and regulations prescribed by the Association and to accept the grading established or grading done by the Association, and which shall, subject to any law in force for the time being, be conclusive.

25. The Grower appoints the Association, its Trustees and each of them its officers, agents and servants, his agent and attorney in fact to make, execute and take delivery of all contracts that may be required to be entered into pursuant to the provisions of "The Canada Grain Act" on his behalf and in his name, place and stead, which Contracts and all moneys payable in respect thereof are hereby assigned to the Association; and to receive accounts and to receive payment of all moneys payable to the Grower under such Contract in full settlement for such Contract or otherwise, all in his name, place and stead, and to account and settle for any moneys so received by crediting the same to the Grower on the books of the

Association, which moneys, less all deductions as herein provided, shall be distributed pursuant to the provisions of this Agreement. Such receipt of payment and giving of credit on the books of the Association as aforesaid shall be deemed to be and shall be a proper accounting for and settlement in full for all such Contracts.

26. The Association may establish selling, statistical or other agencies in any place in the world and the Association may act in any of the businesses of the Association through or by means of agents, brokers, sub-contractors or others.

27. The Grower agrees that notwithstanding anything hereinbefore contained, if, for any reason, it should, in the opinion of the Association, become impracticable or impossible to carry into effect the terms and provisions of this agreement as hereinbefore set forth with respect to the 1923 wheat crop, the Association is hereby authorized and empowered to make any arrangements that it may consider desirable for the coöperative marketing of the said wheat crop.

28. Notwithstanding anything hereinbefore contained, the Association will, by notice given in a newspaper in the cities and the principal towns of Alberta, to be selected by the Association, fix the date at which it will commence operations and until such date the Grower or Growers may sell or otherwise dispose of his or their wheat, if accompanied by actual delivery of the same, and the Association shall not be bound to accept delivery thereof or be otherwise liable in respect thereto. This Agreement shall remain in full force, effect and virtue notwithstanding that the Association may not be able to commence operations in time to handle any of the 1923 crop.

29. The parties agree that there are no oral or other conditions, promises, covenants, representations or inducements in addition to or at variance with any of the terms hereof and that this Agreement represents the voluntary and clear understanding of both parties fully and completely.

In Witness Whereof the Grower has hereunto set his hand and seal and the Association has hereunto affixed its seal under the hand of its proper officer in that behalf, the day and year first above written.

APPENDIX F

TEXT OF AGREEMENT BY PROVINCIAL WHEAT POOLS FORMING THE CENTRAL SELLING AGENCY

THIS AGREEMENT made this Twentieth day of August A.D. 1924.

BETWEEN:

THE ALBERTA CO-OPERATIVE WHEAT PROCUCERS, LIMITED,
SASKATCHEWAN CO-OPERATIVE WHEAT PRODUCERS, LIMITED
and MANITOBA CO-OPERATIVE WHEAT PRODUCERS, LIMITED,
hereinafter called the "ASSOCIATIONS,"

OF THE FIRST PART,

and

CANADIAN CO-OPERATIVE WHEAT PRODUCERS, LIMITED,
hereinafter called the "COMPANY,"

OF THE SECOND PART,

WITNESSETH:

WHEREAS the Associations are Wheat Marketing Associations organized on a non-profit basis and operate in the respective Provinces of Alberta, Saskatchewan and Manitoba under standard marketing contracts with their producer members for the purposes of marketing the wheat of their said members on a co-operative basis and for the purpose of promoting, fostering and encouraging the business of growing and marketing wheat co-operatively and eliminating speculation in wheat and stabilizing the wheat market;

AND WHEREAS it is provided in the said marketing contracts that the Associations may sell all or any part of the wheat delivered to them by their respective members through any agency or by joining with any agency for the purpose of marketing the wheat of the said Provinces, under a term contract or otherwise, and under such conditions as will serve the joint interests of the producers; and the Associations are thereby authorized and empowered to confer upon any such agency all of the rights, powers and privileges of the Associations under the said marketing contracts;

AND WHEREAS the Associations are of the opinion that the interests of their members will be best served and the aims and objects of the Associations promoted by the sale of the wheat of their members through such an agency and for such purpose have caused the Company to be formed.

NOW THEREFORE, in consideration of the premises and of the execution of this Agreement by each and every of the Associations and of the mutual and individual obligations herein set forth and the reliance of each of the Associations upon the other Associations for complete performance of all the provisions hereof, and in consideration of the covenants and agreements on the part of the Company herein set forth, it is hereby mutually agreed by and between the Associations and each of them and the Company as follows:

1. Until otherwise mutually agreed the number of holders of common stock in the company shall be limited to twelve (12) and such stock holders shall consist of the three Associations, Parties of the First Part, and nine persons, of whom three shall be nominated by each of the said Associations. Each of the persons so nominated must be a member of the Association by which he is nominated and each of such persons shall hold one share only of the common stock of the Company. Each of the said Associations agrees to subscribe and does hereby subscribe for four hundred and ninety-seven (497) shares of common stock of the Company, and agrees to pay therefor the sum of forty-nine thousand, seven hundred (49,700) dollars, as follows: ten (10) per cent on allotment and the balance subject to call by the Directors of the Company.

(*a*) At all meetings of the Company, each Association shall be represented by the individual stockholders nominated by it as aforesaid, and each of said individual shareholders shall, in accordance with the by-laws of the Company, be entitled to one (1) vote. Should any of such individual stockholders be absent from any meeting of the shareholders or directors of the Company, his or their vote or votes shall be cast by a shareholder present at such meeting and nominated by the Association which nominated the absent shareholder or shoreholders.

(*b*) The nine (9) individual stockholders shall form the Board of Directors of the Company.

(*c*) An executive committee shall be appointed consisting of three (3) members of such Board of Directors, one of which three members shall be nominated by each of the Associations for membership on such Executive Committee, which Committee shall for the time being, and as provided in the resolution of appointment, or by the By-laws of the Company, have and exercise all or any powers of the Directors in the management of the business and affairs of the Company.

(*d*) Each Association hereby approves of and agrees to abide by the by-laws of the Company.

2. Each Association hereby transfers to and confers upon the Company all of the powers, rights and privileges of the Associations under its contract with the growers, and hereby appoints and constitutes the Company its sole and exclusive agent and attorney-in-fact for the purposes hereinafter set forth, with full power and authority in its own name or in the name of the Association, at its option, to transact such business and take such action as may be necessary, incidental or convenient for the accomplishment thereof, coupling such appointment with a direct financial interest as the common agent and attorney of all the associations hereunder, and without power of revocation for the full term hereof:

(*a*) To receive and take delivery of, handle, transport, store, market, sell and otherwise dispose of the wheat delivered to it by the Association or at the order of the Association in whatsoever way and at such time and place as the Company shall in its judgment determine to be to the best advantage of all the members of the Association.

(*b*) To mingle and mix the wheat received from the Association with wheat of like kind or grade delivered to the Company by another Association.

(*c*) To borrow money in the name of the Company and on its own account on the wheat delivered to it or on any warehouse or storage receipt or grain receipt or on any account for the sale thereof or on any drafts, bills of lading, bills of exchange, notes or acceptances, orders, or on any commercial paper delivered therefor, or any documents of or evidencing title thereto, delivered therefor, and to exercise all rights of ownership without limitations and to pledge in its name and on its own account such wheat or receipts or accounts or drafts, bills of lading, notes, acceptances, orders or other commercial paper or documents of or evidencing title, as collateral therefor; also to sign, endorse, assign, negotiate, discharge, surrender, sell, dispose of or otherwise deal with all and every such documents and instruments, and the proceeds thereof.

(*d*) To pay or retain and deduct from the gross returns from the sale of all wheat received by the Company, all moneys borrowed under the provisions of this Agreement, with interest and all other proper charges and expenses thereon and the amount necessary to cover brokerage, advertising, taxes, tolls, freights, warehouse charges, legal expenses, and all other proper charges, such as salaries, fixed charges and general expenses of the Company.

3. The Associations agree to advance to the Company by way of loan from time to time as and when requested by the Board of Directors of the Company, such moneys as may in the judgment of such Board of Directors be required to carry on the operations of the Company, and such advances shall be contributed by the Associations in equal proportions, or in such other proportions as may from time to time be mutually agreed upon by the Parties hereto.

4. Subject to the terms hereof, the Associations covenant and agree with the Company and with each other to deliver to or to the order of the Company all the wheat and the warehouse or storage receipts covering it, which is delivered to or to the order of each of them under the said marketing contracts with their respective members from and after the 16th day of July, 1924. The Company agrees to act as agent, factor and attorney-in-fact for the Associations, to receive, take delivery of, handle, store and to market, sell and otherwise dispose of, at the best price obtainable under market conditions, the wheat delivered to it by the Associations. The Company shall as soon as practicable after each delivery of wheat to it by an Association, make an advance to the Association of such rate per bushel according to grade, quality and place of delivery, as, in the discretion of the Company, it shall deem proper, and the Company agrees that it will, in its discretion, from time to time pay over to the Associations, as funds are available from the sale of the crop of each season, their respective and proper proportions of the proceeds of the wheat sold by the Company in each season for the Associations, less all deductions (which the Company is entitled to make pursuant to the provisions of this Contract, and less all advances made to the Associations, and less all other deductions) hereinbefore authorized.

5. Wheat shall be deemed to be delivered to the Company within the meaning of this Agreement, so as to render the Company accountable therefor, only when the bills of lading, warehouse receipts, shipping bills therefor, or other documents of or evidencing title thereto, shall have been transferred, properly endorsed by the Association to the Company.

6. The Company agrees that it will give full and proper attention to the development of the Western route for the shipment of wheat and the development of Oriental markets for same and that it will keep true and correct account of any and all sales made basis Vancouver, including sales to mills made on such basis, and that it will from time to time account to and pay over to such Association delivering grain sold by the Company basis Vancouver for the benefit of all the members thereof, any increase in price or premium derived from such sales over and above sales made the same date basis Fort William.

7. (*a*) The Associations severally and collectively hereby transfer to and confer upon the Company all powers, rights and privileges granted them by their respective marketing contracts and involved in the handling, storing, warehousing, grading, transporting, financing and marketing of the wheat delivered to it under this Agreement.

(*b*) The rights, powers and authority conferred by the Associations on the Company under the terms of this Agreement shall be exercised in pursuance of and in conformity with the provisions of the standard marketing agreements of the respective Associations with their grower members, copies of which Agreements are attached hereto and made a part hereof.

8. (*a*) For the purpose of defining generally the field of activity of the Company, it is agreed that the departments of service hereunder mentioned and described may be established, maintained and administered by the Company, viz:

1. Local sales (for delivery and use within the Province).
2. Sales domestic and export.
3. Finance.
4. Transportation beyond terminal points.
5. Statistics and information.
6. Field service (supervising the provincial field service and supervising publicity).
7. Terminal elevators and warehouses (handling of problems of receiving grain outside of the Province).
8. Grading.
9. General Counsel.

10. Office systems (creating systems for respective provincial offices for efficiency for audits).

(*b*) For the purpose of defining generally the field of activity of the Associations it is agreed that the departments of service mentioned and described hereunder may be established, maintained and administered by the Associations:

1. Field service (membership, local publicity).
2. Elevators and warehouses (within the Province).
3. Local counsel (enforcement of membership contracts).
4. Relations with elevators.
5. Office management (actual administration).
6. Transportation to terminals.

(*c*) Notwithstanding anything in this Agreement contained, and to remove any possiblity of doubt, it is hereby declared and agreed that the Associations shall retain control of all deliveries of grain by their producer members, and shall directly receive and take delivery of all grain consigned and delivered by their respective producer members. All such grain delivered by producer members to their respective Associations shall, by such Associations, be thereupon delivered to the Company.

9. It is expressly understood and agreed by the parties hereto that, subject to the provisions of the contracts entered into between the Associations and their respective producer members, and in so far as the Associations are empowered under the provisions of said contracts to transfer title to the Company, absolute title to the wheat covered by this Agreement shall pass to and vest in the Company for all purposes upon delivery of the wheat to the Company or to any warehouse, elevator or carrier to the order of the Company or upon delivery to the Company of the warehouse receipts, representing said wheat and that all documents of title including bills of lading, covering such wheat shall be made in the name of the Company or to its order, at the time of delivery to or to the order of the Company.

Provided that nothing herein is intended to prevent any of the said Associations from pledging its wheat before delivery to the Company for money borrowed by such Association.

10. It is expressly understood that the Company may grant any Association permission to make local sales of wheat in its own territory, provided that duplicate records of such sales are forwarded to the Company.

11. The Associations hereby agree that the decisions of the Company on all matters pertaining to marketing, handling, grading, pro-rating, deductions and distributions within the powers conferred upon it by this Agreement shall be conclusive.

12. Each Association agrees that in the event of a breach by it of any material provision hereof, particularly as to delivery of the wheat other than to or through the Company, the Company shall, upon proper action instituted by it, be entitled to an injunction to prevent further breach hereof, and to such other equitable relief as the Courts may deem proper; and the Company and each of the Associations expressly agree that this Agreement is not a contract for personal services or demanding exceptional talent or capacity; and that this is a contract for the handling of wheat under special circumstances and conditions and will cause the Associations to set up a large group of experts and to have an extensive organization for the purpose of carrying out the provisions hereof, and that the primary purpose of adjusting the supply of wheat to the true demand for wheat as against speculative and manipulative demands can only be attained upon full performance of this contract and complete delivery of wheat by the said Associations.

13. (*a*) Inasmuch as the remedy at law would be inadequate, and inasmuch as it now is and ever will be impracticable and extremely difficult to determine the actual damage resulting to the Company should any Association fail to deliver all of its wheat as provided in this Agreement, each Association hereby agrees to pay to the Company, for the Associations actually performing their obligations hereunder, for all wheat delivered, sold, consigned, marketed or withheld by or for it other than in accordance with the terms hereof, the sum of ten (10) cents per bushel as liquidated damages for the breach of this Agreement. All moneys received by the Company as liquidated damages from any Association under the provisions hereof

shall be payable to and shall be paid to the Associations other than that from which such liquidated damages have been received, and such payment to the aforesaid Associations shall be made in proportion to the quantities of wheat delivered by them respectively to the Company throughout the year in which such liquidated damages are so received and paid. Any moneys received by an Association from the Company as liquidated damages recovered under the provisions hereof shall be considered as and counted among the proceeds of such Association.

(*b*) It is understood and agreed that neither the Associations as a group nor the Company desire to secure the above mentioned sum of ten (10) cents a bushel for liquidated damages as a profit or a penalty but that their and each of their desire is to secure the delivery of the wheat hereinbefore referred to as essential for the attainment of the purpose of the Company, and that the above mentioned statement of liquidated damages represents the best estimate obtainable over a period of time and covering all grades of wheat, to compensate the loyal Associations for the actual loss which is likely to be suffered by them through the inability of the Company to handle the large volume of wheat and thereby to keep the general markets from being overloaded or unduly depressed.

14. A complete audit of the business and books of the Company shall be made by certified chartered accountants at least once a year and additional audits shall be forthwith made upon the written request attested by the corporate seals of two of the Associations and copies of such audits and reports shall be presented to each Association and each Association, through its properly accredited representatives, shall have the right to examine the books of the Company at any reasonable time.

15. This agreement shall come into effect on the day and the date hereof and shall continue in full force and effect for a period of time sufficient to complete the handling of the 1924, 1925, 1926 and 1927 crops of wheat that may be delivered to the respective Associations and shall not apply to any crops thereafter; provided, however, that any Association may withdraw from this Agreement by three (3) months' notice in writing delivered at the office of the Company prior to the first day of July in any year, and upon delivery of such notice such Association shall cease to be bound by the terms of this Agreement on and after the 15th day of July in the said year.

APPENDIX G

TEXT OF HANDLING CONTRACT BETWEEN SASKATCHEWAN CO-OPERATIVE WHEAT PRODUCERS LIMITED AND ELEVATOR COMPANIES

Memorandum of Agreement

BETWEEN

, hereinafter called "The Company"

— and —

SASKATCHEWAN CO-OPERATIVE WHEAT PRODUCERS LIMITED, hereinafter called "The Pool."

It is agreed between the parties as follows:

1. The Company will, at any elevator owned or controlled by it in Saskatchewan accept delivery of wheat from any Pool contract holder, hereinafter called "The Grower," on terms and conditions enumerated hereunder, and will deliver it to the Pool at terminal points or mills in the Western Inspection Division, unless otherwise mutually agreed, as requested by the Pool, limited only by the availability of cars in which to make shipment.

2. For the purpose of description, the three methods of handling wheat through country elevators are divided into three classes:

Class A. — Special bin wheat.
Class B. — Street wheat.
Class C. — Stored to grade wheat.

In respect to these classes respectively the Company agrees to handle the Grower's wheat on behalf of the Pool according to his preference, as follows:

Class A. In quantities of one or more carloads, to special bin and preserve the identity until the wheat is delivered at a terminal point or mill in the Western Inspection Division, according to government grades and dockage. The Company will forward such wheat to the terminal point in its proper order as soon as the Grower secures a car or cars.

Class B. In quantities of less than carload lots, commonly termed street wheat, to grade and make the initial cash payment to the Grower on behalf of the Pool by issuing a cash ticket which shall not be deemed to be a purchase or sale of the said street wheat at prices to be agreed upon between the Company and the Pool.

The Company agrees also, wherever it finds it possible to do so, to handle any individual Grower's wheat as follows:

Class C. In quantities of one or more carloads, to store according to a grade agreed upon between the Company's elevator agent and the Grower. The Company will forward this wheat to a terminal point as soon as the Grower secures a car or cars.

3. In handling wheat in any of the three above-named classes, the Company will use its own credit and monies, and country paymasters arrangements, to furnish advances to Growers at any time after the wheat is delivered at its elevator and elevator tickets are issued. In the case of Classes A and C, the Company will make advances on a reasonable basis to meet the immediate requirements of the Grower until such time as his grain is delivered to the Pool at terminal points. In the case of Class B, the Company will make the initial payment hereafter set out for the street wheat on behalf of the Pool, and will carry this wheat at the rate hereinafter provided until it is delivered to the Pool at terminal points.

A. The Pool agrees that the Company may hypothecate wheat of Class B to its bank or banks in accordance with the bank's usual form under Section 88 of the Bank Act as security only for the advances actually made on such wheat, if such hypothecation is required by the bank as a condition of the bank loaning to the Company the money for the financing of Pool wheat.

4. In handling wheat in Class A and C the Company will collect from the Grower its regular elevator handling and storage charges, and a service charge of three-quarters ($\frac{3}{4}$) of a cent per bushel, also interest on advance if made, and in return will furnish the Grower with regular country elevator services, will keep the grain fully insured, will bill out cars, check government inspection, pay railway freight charges, government inspection and weighing fees and any other proper charges incurred on behalf of the Grower. The Company will assume liability for collecting from the Railway Company for wrecked or leaky cars. It will also secure terminal warehouse receipt for such wheat and will deliver these documents promptly to the Pool, collecting from the Pool full initial cash payment that is coming to the Grower from the Pool, and will promptly remit balance due to the Grower over and above the advance that may have been made and other proper charges. The Company will also make up and forward to the Grower his "Grower's Certificate." The Company will, in fact, perform and render all services needed by the Grower in delivering his wheat to the Pool at any terminal point or mill in the Western Inspection Division, and will turn it over to the Pool at such points, in such position that it is immediately available to the Pool for direct sale or export.

5. In handling wheat in Class B the Company agrees to make initial payment for the Pool by cash ticket (which can be immediately cashed by the Company's paymasters) to the Grower, at a figure that shall be the initial cash payment determined by the Pool, as set forth in schedule hereto annexed applicable to Class B wheat, or less if notified in writing by the Pool, basis terminal elevators Fort William, after deducting the proper freight charges and a sum not to exceed on Numbers One, Two and Three Manitoba Northern five cents (5c) per bushel, and on all other grades not to exceed six cents (6c) per bushel, plus in the case of all grades any fraction of a cent less than one-half ($\frac{1}{2}$c) per bushel which may arise when deducting the freight rate per bushel from the initial cash payment as determined. (The application of the deduction of this fraction of a cent as agreed on is set forth in Schedule "B" attached, based on initial payment of one dollar per bushel in

store, Fort William.) It is agreed that if the character of any crop warrants it, a further deduction on tough or commercial grades, which shall be mutually satisfactory, and agreed upon shall be made.

6. The Pool agrees to pay the Company the full initial cash payment at terminals as soon as warehouse receipts, or in the case of Vancouver shipments, bills of lading for the street wheat are delivered to the Pool (the margin between this price paid by the Pool to the Company and the price paid at country points for this street wheat being retained by the Company as payment for services rendered).

7. The Pool agrees that in the event of its changing during the year, the spreads between grades as determined in its initial cash payment, it will accept delivery from the Company of all street wheat received by the Company as aforesaid on the spreads as previously fixed, at the spreads on which the Company has based its initial cash payment.

8. The Company further agrees to make a daily report to the Pool of the Class B wheat received at each of its elevators, to secure cars for, and ship this wheat forward to terminal points specified by the Pool in the Western Inspection Division, for the Pool, in equal turn with its own street grain according to the date it has been received into its elevator. The Company also agrees to deliver to the Pool at terminal points the full amount in bushels for which cash tickets for such street wheat have been issued, and to pay freight on dockage and terminal cleaning charges on such street wheat. The Company agrees to supply the Pool daily with a list of cars of Pool street wheat and Pool special binned wheat billed each day to Fort William or Port Arthur.

8 (a). The Company also agrees to deliver to the Pool at terminal points the full amount of bushels for which cash tickets for such street wheat have been issued, and to pay freight on dockage and terminal cleaning charges on such street wheat as contains less than 3% of dockage. On all street wheat containing 3% or more dockage the Pool will pay to the Company the freight on dockage and terminal cleaning charges, less an allowance covering the average value of the screenings. The application of this 3% dockage provision on the Pool street wheat from each of the Company's elevators shall be determined as follows:

At the end of each season during the life of this contract, the total number of cars of street wheat shipped from each of the Company's elevators which at inspection contained 3% dockage or over shall be definitely ascertained and proportionately allocated between the Company and the Pool according to the percentage of graded wheat shipped from each of the Company's elevators on behalf of the Company and the Pool, and on the percentage so determined as Pool wheat, the Pool will pay to the Company the differential already referred to in this paragraph.

9. The Company further agrees to assume the risk of grade on this Class B wheat and to deliver to the Pool at terminal points on basis of government grades and dockage, accepting payment at the Pool fixed cash payment price for the particular grade delivered. The Company agrees to ship from each country elevator as nearly as possible the same quantities and grades that were received from the Growers at such country elevator, and agrees not to

substitute wheat from other shipping points without the consent of the Pool. The Pool agrees to accept wheat from substitute points when requested where it can do so without loss.

10. It is mutually agreed that a cash settlement for the total over or under delivery of any grade of this street wheat by the Company to the Pool shall be made at the end of the season at the original spreads fixed by the Pool. The Company also agrees to deliver to the Pool as nearly as possible quantities of each grade of such street wheat equal to the quantities for which they have issued Growers' Certificates, and nothing in this contract is to be construed as obligating the Pool to accept any one grade instead of any other grade except in reasonable amounts such as might be accounted for by losses of grade.

11. The Company further agrees to insure and keep insured, at its own expense, this street wheat, at basis Fort William spot values.

12. The Pool agrees to pay the Company a carrying charge on this street wheat amounting to one-thirtieth (1/30) of a cent per bushel per day, said carrying charge to commence on the date of mailing or delivery to the Pool of the regular daily report form reporting this wheat to have been received at the Company's elevator, and to continue until the date the Pool pays the Company for such wheat inclusive. In the event of the Company not shipping this Pool street wheat in its proper turn and at the first opportunity that cars are available, unless so requested by the Pool, then the Pool is not liable for payment of the carrying charge accrued and unpaid on this or any other Pool street wheat the Company may then have in the elevator from which the Company has failed to make shipment in its proper turn. Should the Pool's initial payment cash ticket price at cents ( ) rate points Fort William be seventy cents (70c) or over, the Pool agrees to pay graduated scale of carrying charges as per Exhibit "D" attached.

13. The Company agrees that as part of this carrying charge of one-thirtieth of a cent per bushel per day is remuneration for carrying this wheat in its elevators only until transportation is available, unless otherwise requested by the Pool, its failure to ship as agreed upon shall cause it to forfeit its claim to the carrying charge accrued and unpaid on this or any other Pool street wheat then in the particular elevator from which the Company, has failed to make shipment of wheat in its proper form.

14. The Pool agrees that the Company, if at any time it needs space in its elevators, shall have the right to ship forward to terminal points any wheat mentioned in Classes A, B, and C and to demand that the Grower shall secure car or cars according to his turn on the car order book at its discretion, after notifying the Pool of its desire to do so. The Pool further agrees that during the first three months of the crop season, taken from September 1st in each year, all wheat shall be forwarded to terminal points or mill elevators at points in the Western Inspection Division as soon as possible after its delivery at the Company's elevators.

15. The Pool agrees that all Pool wheat of whatever class forwarded to terminal points shall be handled through any elevator that the Company desires.

16. The Company agrees that it will, wherever it is reasonably possible, without detriment to its own business, store and carry any wheat in Classes A, B, and C in its elevators if so desired by the Pool.

17. The Pool agrees to pay to the Company upon receipt of proper statements, the carrying charges accrued and due to the Company as at the 15th and last day of each month.

18. The Pool agrees that it will pay to the Company the determined upon initial cash payment immediately upon delivery by the Company to the Pool of terminal documents for any wheat forwarded through the Company to the Pool.

19. The Company agrees that at the time of issuing cash tickets it will also issue to the Grower a "Grower's Receipt" in a form determined by the Pool.

20. The Pool agrees that in the event of its desiring the Company to perform any services not specified in this Agreement, special remuneration will be mutually decided upon, and the Pool will pay such remuneration to the Company. The Company agrees that if it can reasonably do so it will render such additional services.

21. The Pool agrees to instruct each Grower that when he delivers his wheat to any elevator of the Company, he, the Grower, must — no matter in what manner he wants his wheat handled — advise the Company's elevator agent that it is Pool wheat. The Pool further agrees that any failure of the Elevator Company to handle Grower's wheat upon the terms outlined in this Agreement consequent on the failure of the Grower so to notify the Company's elevator agent, shall absolve the Company from responsibility for the resultant failure to carry out the terms of this agreement.

22. The Pool agrees to supply all special stationery and forms not usually used in the Company's business, but necessary for use by the Company in carrying out this Agreement.

23. It is mutually agreed between the Pool and the Company that any failure on the part of either of them in carrying out the terms of this Agreement, which failure is the result of occasional inadvertence on the part of their employees, shall not be construed as being a breaking of any clause of the Agreement by the Pool or the Company.

24. It is mutually agreed that the price shown on the attached exhibits marked "A" and "B" are the Pool initial cash payment prices at terminal points and at country elevator points respectively, as referred to in this Agreement.

25. The Company agrees to handle this business to the best of its ability so as to assist and help the Pool in every way to secure efficient and satisfactory results for the Grower, and hereby agrees that in the conduct of its business it will not in any way discriminate between Growers who are members of the Pool and those who are not.

26. The Pool agrees to always maintain a reasonable margin between the amount of initial advance which has been paid upon street wheat on hand in elevators or in transit and the market value and that in event of said margin being less than ten cents (10c) per bushel the Pool agrees to return to the Company a portion of the initial cash payment previously made sufficient

to maintain the margin of ten cents. The Pool further agrees that in the event of the above margin of ten cents (10c) a bushel not being maintained, the Company may, after delivery to the office of the Canadian Co-operative Wheat Producers, Limited, 10th Floor Electric Railway Chambers, Winnipeg, before the hour of 3 o'clock on Saturdays and before the hour of 5 o'clock on other days, of a notice of their intention to sell such wheat on a day four days from the date of delivery of such notice, unless the 10 cent margin has in the meantime been restored, sell such wheat in the open market for future delivery basis any specified grade or grades during trading hours on such day, and at such sale the Company itself may purchase the actual amount of wheat at the market price, and a record of such sale or purchase shall be immediately given to the representative of the Canadian Co-operative Wheat Producers, Limited, on the said trading floor; provided always that the Pool may, by submitting instructions in writing from the Canadian Co-operative Wheat Producers, Limited, require the Company to sell all or any portion thereof at any time prior thereto; and provided also that the Company may in its uncontrolled discretion distribute the sale of the said wheat over a period of more than one day after the said fourth day. Nothing herein contained shall in any way take away from or change any rights of any bank under any hypothecation agreement.

27. This Agreement shall be deemed to be in force and to be binding on the parties hereto until September 1st, 1925.

28. It is hereby agreed that the Company may at any time, if in the interest of its business it is considered expedient so to do, upon two weeks notice in writing to the Pool, close any of its said elevators, and the Company shall not be bound to carry out the terms of this Agreement with respect to any such elevators during such time as they shall remain closed.

29. It Is Hereby Agreed that these presents and everything herein contained shall respectively enure to the benefit of and be binding upon the parties hereto, their successors and assigns respectively.

30. The form of contract entered into between the Pool and the Grower is hereto attached, marked "C."

31. The Pool covenants and agrees to deliver to the Company any information which it receives as to any lien charge or claim against the wheat of the Pool members whose addresses are shewn as being in the neighborhood of any point where the Company has an elevator.

APPENDIX H

TEXT OF AGREEMENT BETWEEN LOCAL CO-OPERATIVE ELEVATOR ASSOCIATION AND GROWER UNDER MANITOBA POOL ELEVATOR PLAN

Agreement

THIS AGREEMENT made this........................day of........................A.D. 192 .... between..........................Co-operative Elevator Association Limited, a body corporate with its head office at the shipping point hereinafter named, hereinafter called "the Association" of the First Part, and the undersigned, who resides in the vicinity of the shipping point, hereinafter called "the Grower" of the Second Part.

WHEREAS the Grower is, or is about to become a member of Manitoba Co-operative Wheat Producers Limited (hereinafter referred to as "the Pool") and desires to co-operate with other members of the Pool who reside in the same vicinity, in acquiring by lease, and in the operation of a grain elevator at the shipping point for the handling of Pool grain;

AND WHEREAS the Association has been incorporated for the purpose aforesaid, and proposes to enter into an Agreement with Manitoba Pool Elevators Limited (hereinafter referred to as "Pool Elevators") for the leasing and operation of an elevator for Pool grain at the shipping point;

AND WHEREAS the Grower is or is desirous of becoming a member of the Association and wishes to enter, together with other growers, into this Agreement with the Association;

AND WHEREAS this Agreement, although individual in expression, is one of a series either identical or generally similar in terms, between the Association and a number of members of the Pool who reside at or in the vicinity of the shipping point, and shall constitute one contract between the several persons signing the same and this Association;

AND WHEREAS the undersigned Grower and each of the other persons signing this or a similar agreement with the Association, have heretofore entered into contracts (or a contract) with the Pool for the delivery to the Pool of grain produced or acquired by them, upon the terms and conditions in the said contracts (or contract) set forth.

NOW THIS AGREEMENT WITNESSETH that in pursuance of the premises and in consideration of the mutual covenants and Agreements herein contained and of the execution of this Agreement, or one similar in terms, by a number of other members of the Pool who reside at or in the vicinity of the shipping point, the parties hereto hereby agree as follows:

1. Wherever the term "grain" is used in this Agreement, it shall mean and include all grain mentioned in the contracts (or contract) heretofore entered into as aforesaid between the undersigned Grower and the Pool. Wherever the term "shipping point" is used in this Agreement it shall mean ....in the Province of Manitoba.

2. The Grower covenants and agrees that during the period or periods mentioned in the contracts (or contract) entered into as aforesaid between the Grower and the Pool, he will, as and when required by the Association, deliver to the Association at the elevator acquired or to be acquired by it as aforesaid at the shipping point, all the grain which, by the terms of said contracts (or contract) he has agreed to consign and deliver to the Pool. The Grower further expressly covenants and agrees that he will not (save as herein permitted) during the said periods, or any of them, deliver any of the said grain to any person or persons, firm or corporation other than the Association. It is acknowledged and agreed that the provisions of this section constitute a material provision of this Agreement, and that in the event of a breach of said provisions or any of them by the Grower, subsection 3 of Section 26 of "The Co-operative Associations Act" shall apply to such breach.

3. Grain shall be deemed to be delivered to the Association within the meaning of this Agreement only when the same is actually in the possession of the Association in its elevator at the shipping point aforesaid.

4. The Association covenants and agrees to receive delivery of such grain and to consign and re-deliver same to the Pool, in accordance with the requirements of the contracts (or contract) entered into as aforesaid between the Grower and the Pool.

5. The Grower agrees to pay to the Association, as and when required by it, his proportionate share, computed on an annual bushelage basis, of the total cost to the Association of acquiring, maintaining and operating the said elevator. It is agreed that in computing such total cost, the Association shall be entitled to include:

(*a*) Annual sum for depreciation, equivalent to at least 10% of the cost of the elevator.

(*b*) An annual rental equivalent to 7% of the cost of such elevator, less proper deductions from such cost from year to year on account of depreciation.

(*c*) Taxes, fire insurance (both on building, grain and other contents) rental on lease of site, expenses incurred in repairing and maintaining the said elevator in a good state of repair, Workmen's Compensation and any other charges imposed by law.

(*d*) Salaries, wages and allowances to officers, employees and directors.

(*e*) Legal expenses incurred either in connection with the incorporation and organization of the Association or otherwise.

(*f*) The Association's proportionate share of cost of general superintendence and control by Pool Elevators.

(*g*) The cost of all licenses and bonds required under the provisions of "The Canada Grain Act."

(*h*) Any other cost or expense to which the Association may be subject under the terms of its Agreement with Pool Elevators.

(*i*) Any other cost or expense which the Directors of the Association may, in their discretion, consider necessary to incur in the interests of the Association and its members.

It is further agreed that notwithstanding anything in this Agreement contained, the annual payment to be made by the Grower to the Association on each bushel of Pool grain shall not be less (but may be more) than two (2) cents, and that any balance of the annual payment which may remain after making provision for the various costs and expenses above referred to, shall be paid and applied by the Association on account of moneys which it has agreed or shall agree to pay under the terms of the lease covering the elevator acquired or to be acquired by the Association.

It is agreed that the amount payable by the Grower under the provisions of this section shall bear the same proportion towards the total costs of the Association as the amount of Pool grain produced or acquired by the Grower bears to the total amount of grain handled by the Association in the same year.

6. It is understood and agreed that the obligation of the Grower to pay to the Association the moneys herein agreed to be paid, shall be absolute and that the Grower shall not be relieved in any degree from his said obligation by any neglect or failure on his part to deliver his grain to the Association in accordance with the provisions of this Agreement.

7. The business of the Association shall be conducted on a non-profit basis and the Grower shall not be charged with anything on account of profits.

8. Should the Association, in the exercise of its discretion, not require payment of the whole or any part of the moneys payable to it by the Grower under the terms hereof, prior to or at the time of the receipt by the Grower of his initial payment from the Pool, the Grower shall make and deliver to the Association such order or assignment of moneys accruing to him through his interim or final payment, as is required by the Association for the purpose of ensuring to it payment of the moneys to which it is so entitled from the Grower.

9. The Grower covenants and agrees as and when requested by the Association or any officer, agent or servant thereof, to make application from time to time for railway cars for the shipment of his grain, pursuant to the provisions of "The Canada Grain Act" or any other similar Act which may hereafter during the period of this Agreement, come into force, and to perform such other acts and execute such documents as the Association may require in connection with the handling of the Grower's grain.

10. The Grower covenants and agrees to, and hereby does, apply for one (1) share in the capital stock of the Association and agrees to pay to the Association the par value thereof, namely: the sum of One (1) Dollar. The Association covenants and agrees to accept the said application and to allot to the Grower one (1) share in the capital stock of the Association.

11. This Agreement shall be binding upon the Grower, his personal representatives, successors and assigns, during the period or periods hereinbefore mentioned, so long as he or any member of his family residing with him raises grain directly or indirectly in the vicinity of the shipping point, or has the legal right to exercise ownership or control of any thereof, or any interest therein or of any land on which Pool grain is grown during the said periods.

12. Should it happen that the Grower, having hauled grain to the shipping point, and having the same ready for delivery to the Association, finds himself unable to make such delivery because of the inability of the Association to receive it, then and in such event, the Grower, after notifying the Association of his intention, and receiving written permission to do so, may deliver such grain, as Pool grain, to an elevator other than that operated by the Association. In such event, the Grower shall immediately discontinue hauling grain until such time as the Association shall again be in a position to receive it, unless otherwise authorized by the Association.

13. It is distinctly understood and agreed that neither this Agreement nor anything herein contained shall affect the contracts (or contract) entered into by the Grower with the Pool, or shall relieve the Grower in any degree from his obligation to carry out and perform all the covenants and agreements in the said contracts (or contract) contained and on the part of the Grower therein agreed to be performed. It is further understood and agreed that this Agreement is entered into without prejudice to the said contracts (or contract) between the Grower and the Pool and to the rights of the parties to said contracts (or contract) thereunder. It is further understood and agreed that should any inconsistency arise between the provisions of this Agreement and the provisions of the contracts (or contract) between the Grower and the Pool, the Grower shall be bound to comply with the provisions of the contracts (or contract) with the Pool.

14. The parties agree that there are no oral or other conditions, promises, covenants, representations or inducements in addition to or at variance with any of the terms hereof, and that this Agreement represents the voluntary and clear understanding of both parties fully and completely.

APPENDIX I

SOURCES AND REFERENCES

THE material contained in the study has been derived mainly from five classes of sources:

(*a*) Governmental, including federal and provincial statutes, sessional papers, departmental reports, etc.

(*b*) Documents and publications of grain growers' and farmers' organizations, including constitutions and by-laws, annual reports, official organs, pamphlets, etc.

(*c*) General reference, consisting of books, bulletins and pamphlets dealing with grain growing and the grain trade, agricultural marketing and coöperation, and farmers' movements.

(*d*) Periodicals, including agricultural and coöperative journals, newspapers, and special articles in sundry periodicals.

(*e*) Personal interviews and correspondence with officers of Western farmers' organizations, government and grain trade officials, editors, farmers, etc.

The following list indicates the principal published sources and references consulted:

I. FEDERAL AND PROVINCIAL STATUTES

1. *Statutes of Canada:*
   - (*a*) Respecting the Grain Trade,
     - General Inspection Act, 37 Vic. (1874), c. 45; R. S. C., 1886, c. 99.
       - Amendments: 1889, c. 16; 1891, c. 48; 1899, c. 25.
     - Grain Inspection Act, 4 Edw. VII (1904), c. 15.
       - Amendments: 1908, c. 36.
     - Manitoba Grain Act, 63–64 Vic. (1900), c. 39.
       - Amendments: 1902, c. 19; 1903, c. 33; 1908, c. 45.
     - Canada Grain Act, 2 Geo. V, 1912, c. 27.
       - Amendments: 1913, c. 21; 1914, c. 33; 1915, c. 10; 1916, c. 6; 1919, c. 40; 1919 (2), c. 6; 1920, c. 37.
       - Reënacted 1925, c. 33.
       - Campbell Amendment, 1927, c. 41.
   - (*b*) Respecting Canadian Wheat Board,
     - Act to confirm powers of Canadian Wheat Board, 9–10 Geo. V (1919) (2), c. 9.
     - Continuing Act, 10–11 Geo. V (1920), c. 40.
     - Enabling Act, 12–13 Geo. V (1922), c. 14.
   - (*c*) Respecting Grain Growers' Grain Co. and United Grain Growers, Ltd.,
     - Act of Incorporation, G. G. G. Co., 1 Geo. V (1911), c. 80; amended, 1915, c. 73.
     - Amendments to permit re-organization as United Grain Growers, Ltd., 1917, c. 79; 1918, c. 74.

(*d*) Respecting Western Freight Rates,

Act to confirm Crow's Nest Pass Rate Agreement, 60 Vic. (1897), c. 5.

Amendment to Railway Act suspending Crow's Nest Pass rates, Railway Act, 1919, sec. 325, sub-sec. 5.

Restoration of Crow's Nest Pass rates on wheat and flour, 12–13 Geo. V (1922), c. 41.

Act generalizing Crow's Nest Pass rates throughout Western territory, 15–16 Geo. V (1925), c. 52, sec. 1.

2. *Statutes of Manitoba:*

Act respecting Winnipeg Grain and Produce Exchange, 7–8 Edw. VII (1908), c. 89.

Act respecting Grain Growers' Grain Company, 9 Edw. VII (1909), c. 89; amended 1910, c. 96.

Act respecting a System of Government Grain Elevators, 10 Edw. VII (1910), c. 27.

Amendments, 1912, c. 26; 1917, c. 38.

Co-operative Associations Act, 6 Geo. V (1916), c. 23.

Amendments, 1921, c. 10.

Act to incorporate Manitoba Co-operative Wheat Producers, Ltd., 14 Geo. V (1924), c. 130.

Act respecting Marketing and other Co-operative Associations, 15 Geo. V (1925), c. 8.

An Act respecting the Investment of the Surplus Moneys of the Canadian Wheat Board received by the Government of Manitoba and the use of the Income therefrom (Wheat Board Money Trust Act), 16 Geo. V (1926), c. 58.

3. *Statutes of Saskatchewan:*

Incorporation of Saskatchewan Grain Growers' Association, 8 Edw. VII (1908), c. 54.

Amendment to permit co-operative trading, 1915, c. 36.

Incorporation of Saskatchewan Co-operative Elevator Co., Ltd., 1 Geo. V (1911), c. 39; amended 1912, 1913, 1915, 1917, 1920.

Confirmation of agreements with company, 1912–13, c. 42; 1919, c. 86; 1921, c. 76.

Re financing of terminal elevators, 1919–20, c. 58.

Agricultural Co-operative Associations Act, 4 Geo. V (1913), c. 52.

Amendments *re* relations with S. G. G. A., 1915, c. 37.

Municipal Hail Insurance Act, 5 Geo. V (1915), c. 22.

Act respecting sale of Farm Implements, 5 Geo. V (1915), c. 28; amended 1917, 1920.

Canadian Wheat Board (Additional Powers, Saskatchewan) Act, 13 Geo. V (1922), c. 22.

Act for Relief of Creditors, 13 Geo. V (1923), c. 21.

Act to incorporate Saskatchewan Co-operative Wheat Producers, Ltd., 14 Geo. V (1924), c. 66.

Act respecting Co-operative Marketing Associations, 16 Geo. V (1925–26), c. 37.

An act to incorporate the Saskatchewan Agricultural Research Foundation, 16 Geo. V (1925–26), c. 60.

Act empowering Saskatchewan Co-operative Elevator Co. to sell assets, 16 Geo. V (1925–26), c. 2.

Act confirming sale by Saskatchewan Co-operative Elevator Co. to Saskatchewan Pool Elevators, Ltd., 17 Geo. V (1927), c. 71.

Act winding up Saskatchewan Co-operative Elevator Co., 17 Geo. V (1927), c. 72.

Act to incorporate United Farmers of Canada, Saskatchewan Section, Ltd., 17 Geo. V (1927), c. 84.

4. *Statutes of Alberta:*

Incorporation of Alberta Farmers' Co-operative Elevator Co., Ltd., 4 Geo. V (1913), c. 13.

Amendment to permit amalgamation, 1917, c. 29.

Act to "wind up" company, 1918, c. 23.

Co-operative Associations Act, 4 Geo. V (1913), c. 12.

Act respecting Powers of Canadian Wheat Board, 12 Geo. V (1922), c. 2.

Incorporation of Alberta Co-operative Wheat Producers, Ltd., 14 Geo. V (1924), c. 7.

Amendment to permit government loans for local elevators, 1925, c. 28.

Wheat Board Money Trust Act, 16 Geo. V (1926), c. 5.

II. Government Documents and Reports

A. *Dominion of Canada:*

1. *House of Commons Debates, re* Grain Legislation and Canadian Wheat Board; especially years 1899–1900, 1903–04, 1908, 1911–12, 1919–25.

Senate Debates, *re* Grain Legislation and Canadian Wheat Board; especially 1911 (Grain Bill), 1926–27 (Campbell Amendment).

2. *Sessional Papers:*

Report of Royal Commission on Shipment and Transportation of Grain in Manitoba and N. W. T., 1899–1900; Sess. Papers 81–81b, 1900.

Report of Royal Commission on the Grain Trade, 1906–07; Sess. Paper 59, 1907.

Report of Royal Grain Inquiry Commission, 1923–24; Sess. Paper 35, 1925.

Report of Canadian Wheat Board, 1919–20. Sess. Paper 54, 1921.

Proceedings of Special Committee of House of Commons to Inquire into Agricultural Conditions, 1923.

Report on Agricultural Credit by H. M. Tory; Sess. Paper 142, 1924. Supp. Report, S. P. 152, 1925.

3. *Periodic Reports:*

Annual Reports of Board of Grain Commissioners, Dept. of Trade and Commerce, 1913–1926.
Annual Report on Grain Trade of Canada, Dept. of Trade and Commerce, Internal Trade Branch.
Annual Reports, Dept. of Agriculture, Ottawa.
Monthly Bulletin of Agricultural Statistics, Dominion Bureau of Statistics.
Canada Year Books, Dominion Bureau of Statistics. (*Statistical Year Book of Canada*, 1889–1904. Present title since).
Reports of Decennial Census of Canada, 1871–1921.
Census of Population and Agriculture of Prairie Provinces, 1916, 1921, 1926.

B. *Province of Manitoba:*

Report of Manitoba Elevator Commission; Sessional Papers 13, 15, 16, 18, 1911; No. 24, 1912.

C. *Province of Saskatchewan:*

Report of Elevator Commission of Saskatchewan, Regina, 1910.
Report of Grain Markets Commission of Saskatchewan, 1914.
Report to Government of Saskatchewan on Wheat Marketing by James Stewart and F. W. Riddell, 1921.
Reports of Co-operative Organization Branch, Dept. of Agriculture, 1914–20.
Reports of Co-operation and Markets Branch, 1921–1926.

III. Documents of Grain Growers' Organizations

1. *Grain Growers' Guide, Winnipeg, 1908–1927* (weekly to end of 1925; semi-monthly since), contains summarized annual reports and convention proceedings of Western farmers' associations, companies and pools.

2. *United Grain Growers, Limited:*

Annual Reports, Grain Growers' Grain Company, 1907–1917.
Annual Reports, United Grain Growers, Limited, 1918–1927.
Special Reports, included in above.

1916. Report on Amalgamation of Farmers' Companies.
Brief to Customs Department on Importation of Agricultural Implements.

1918. Report of Committee appointed to visit United States' Farmers' Organizations with special reference to Co-operative Trading.

1921. Charges against the Company.
"Why the Company took out the Injunction against the Grain Inquiry Commission."
Report on Voluntary Wheat Pool.

1923–24. Reports on Cattle Pools.
1923–27. Reports on relations with Wheat Pools.

Minutes of Annual Meetings, 1918–1926.

Charter and By-laws.

Prospectus of Grain Growers' Grain Company: "What Co-operation has done for Western Farmers" (n. d.).

"Farmers in Business for Ten Successful Years, 1906–1916."

"The Organized Farmer in Business," 1919.

"Terminal Tariffs and Overages," 1919.

"Co-operative Cattle Selling," 1924.

"United Livestock Growers, Limited"—Report to Saskatchewan Livestock Pool Investigational Board, June, 1925.

"Record of U. G. G. on Question of Pool Marketing," November, 1925.

Livestock Marketing News (monthly), 1923–1926.

Evidence of C. Rice-Jones before Special Committee of Commons on Cost of Living. Ottawa, June, 1919.

Evidence of T. A. Crerar before Royal Commissioner on Home Bank Affairs, Winnipeg, April 20, 1924; Ottawa, May 5, 1924.

Evidence of J. R. Murray before Royal Grain Inquiry Commission, Winnipeg, March 10 and 12, 1924.

3. *Saskatchewan Co-operative Elevator Company, 1911–1926.*

Annual Reports, 1911–1926.

Delegate's Handbooks (annual).

By-laws.

"The Saskatchewan Co-operative Elevator Act Explained."

Souvenir Booklet in connection with visit of agricultural editors of United States. Regina, August, 1925.

Saskatchewan Co-operative News, Regina, 1916–1926. Monthly organ of Company, containing director's reports, proceedings of annual meetings, financial statements, etc.

Special articles: "Co-operation Misconstrued" (September, 1921); "Cost of Handling Grain" (February, 1922); "Who Pays the Loss on Handling Charges?" (March, 1922); "The Company's Subsidiaries" (Feb., March, April, Sept., 1924); "The Country Elevator" (Sept., 1924); Text of Saskatchewan Pool offer to purchase, and director's comment thereon, April, 1926); "Record of Negotiations of the Farmers' Companies with the Pools during 1925" (January, 1926).

News Bulletins, Field Service Dept., 1924–25.

Evidence of F. W. Riddell before Royal Grain Inquiry Commission, Winnipeg, March 13–14, April 29, 1924.

Evidence of J. A. Maharg, before Royal Grain Inquiry Commission, Winnipeg, April 29, 1924.

Text of award of Board of Arbitrators *re* valuation of company's assets, Western Producer, Aug. 8, 1926.

4. *Alberta Farmers' Co-operative Elevator Company.*
   Minutes of Annual Meetings, Calgary, 1913–1917.
   Annual Reports in *Grain Growers' Guide.*

5. *Territorial Grain Growers' Association,*
   Reports and Proceedings, 1902–1906, in *Manitoba Free Press*, etc.

6. *Saskatchewan Grain Growers' Association:*
   Executive Reports, 1906–1925.
   Delegates Handbooks.
   Constitution and By-laws.
   Pamphlets: "How to Form Incorporated Locals"; "What Every Grain Grower Requires to Know" (1916); "The S. G. G. A. — Its Origin and Growth" (1923).
   Catalogues and Circulars of Trading Dept.
   Reports of annual meetings and organization news in S. G. G. A. section, *Grain Growers' Guide*, 1909–1923; *Western Producer*, 1924–1926.
   Report of Joint Committee on Amalgamation with Farmers' Union, *Western Producer*, July 21, 1927.

7. *Farmers' Union of Canada:*
   Constitution and By-laws.
   Annual reports and proceedings, 1922–27, in *Grain Growers' Guide*, *The Progressive* (1923), and *Western Producer* (1924–27).

8. *United Farmers of Canada, Saskatchewan Section, Ltd.:*
   Official reports, proceedings and organization news in *Western Producer* (1926–27).

9. *Manitoba Grain Growers' Association:*
   Annual Reports and Proceedings, 1903–1920.
   "Review of Negotiations that led to Government Ownership and Operation of Elevators in Manitoba and Causes of Failure," Winnipeg, 1911.

10. *United Farmers of Manitoba:*
    Annual Reports and Proceedings, 1921–1927, in *Grain Growers' Guide; Scoop Shovel*, 1925–27.

11. *Alberta Farmers' Association:*
    Annual Reports and Proceedings, 1905–08, in *Edmonton Bulletin*, etc.

12. *United Farmers of Alberta:*
    Constitution and By-laws.
    Annual Reports and Proceedings, and official organization news in U. F. A. Section, *Grain Growers' Guide*, 1909–1921; *The U. F. A.*, Calgary, official organ (semi-monthly) since 1921.

13. *Canadian Council of Agriculture:*
    Constitution and By-laws.
    Reports and Proceedings, 1910–1927, in *Grain Growers' Guide.*
    Memorial to federal government *re* Grain Terminals, etc., Dec., 1910.
    "The Farmers' Platform," 1916.
    "Nationalizing a Farm Movement" in *Grain Growers' Guide*, June 26, 1918.
    Memoranda of C. C. A. Research Department, *i. e.*, Banking, Agricultural Credit, Freight Rates, Tariff, Taxation, etc.
    Report of Wheat Pool Committee, *Grain Growers' Guide*, Dec. 15, 1920.
    Memorials to federal government re Canadian Wheat Board, 1919, 1920, 1922, 1923.

14. *Alberta Co-operative Wheat Producers, Limited:*
    Memorandum of Association, By-laws, August, 1923.
    Growers' Contract.
    Handling Agreement with Elevator Companies.
    Annual Reports and Proceedings and official organization news in *The U. F. A.* (1923–1927).
    Publications of Department of Education and Publicity: *Wheat Pool Lectures* (April, 1927); *The Alberta Pool and the Grain Trade* (May, 1927); *Alberta Wheat Pool Rally* (June, 1927); *Canvasser's Hand-book* (June, 1927). *Pooling Alberta Wheat* (Jan. 1928).

15. *Alberta Pool Elevators, Limited:*
    Articles of incorporation, 1925.
    Operating reports and official news in *The U. F. A.* 1925–27.

16. *Saskatchewan Co-operative Wheat Producers, Limited:*
    Articles of association, 1923.
    Growers' Wheat Pool and Coarse Grains Pool contracts.
    Handling agreement with elevator companies.
    Annual Reports and Proceedings, and official organization news in *Western Producer*, 1924–27.
    Handbook No. 1, 1926.
    Handbook No. 2, Feb., 1927.
    Handbook No. 3, July, 1927.

17. *Saskatchewan Pool Elevators, Limited:*
    Articles of incorporation, 1925.
    Operating reports and official news in *Western Producer*, 1925–27.
    Offer to purchase assets of Saskatchewan Co-operative Elevator Co., *Western Producer*, March 25, 1926.
    Offer to prepay balance of purchase price to liquidators, *Western Producer*, June 16, 1927.

18. *Manitoba Co-operative Wheat Producers, Limited:*
    Articles of association, 1924.
    Growers' Wheat Pool and Coarse Grains Pool contracts.

Handling agreement with elevator companies.
Annual Reports and Proceedings, and official organization news in the *Scoop Shovel*, 1925–27.

19. *Manitoba Pool Elevators, Limited:*
Articles of incorporation, 1925.
Agreement between co-operative elevator associations and growers.
Operating reports and official news in the *Scoop Shovel.*

20. *Canadian Co-operative Wheat Producers, Limited:*
Agreement forming the Central Selling Agency, 1924.
Articles of incorporation.
Directors Annual Reports 1925–27.
Canadian Wheat Pool Year Book, 1925.
Press statements, etc., of Department of Publicity and Statistics.
"The Truth about Grain Prices," 1927.
A. J. McPhail, "History and Accomplishments of the Canadian Wheat Pool," *Proceedings of Third National Coöperative Marketing Conference,* Washington, January, 1915.
C. H. Burnell, "Wheat Pool Experiences and Prospects," *Proceedings of American Institute of Coöperation,* Chicago, June, 1927.
Addresses of A. J. McPhail, C. H. Burnell, and H. W. Wood at International Wheat Pool Conference, Kansas City, May, 1927.
Proceedings of International Wheat Pool Conference, St. Paul, Feb., 1926.
Proceedings of International Wheat Pool Conference, Kansas City, May, 1927.

IV. General Works

A. *Grain Growing and the Grain Trade:*
Bracken, John. *Crop Production in Western Canada.*
Buller, A. H. R. *Essays on Wheat,* N. Y., 1919.
Chambers, E. J. *The Unexploited West,* Dept. of the Interior, Ottawa, 1914.
Dondlinger, P. T. *The Book of Wheat,* N. Y., 1912.
Edgar, William. *Story of a Grain of Wheat.*
Innis, H. A. *History of the Canadian Pacific Railway,* London, 1923.
Mavor, James. *Report to the Board of Trade on the North-West of Canada,* London, 1904.
Piper, C. B. *Principles of the Grain Trade of Western Canada,* Winnipeg, 1915.
Rutter, W. P. *Wheat Growing in Canada, the United States and Argentina,* London, 1911.
Shortt, A. and Doughty, A. G. (editors). *Canada and Its Provinces,* Edinburgh, 1914–1916.
vol. 17. Skelton, O. D. Economic History of Canada, 1867–1911.
vol. 20. Dafoe, J. W. Economic History of Prairie Provinces.
Smith, J. G. *Organized Produce Markets.* London, 1922.

B. *Agricultural Marketing and Coöperation:*

Boyle, J. E. *Agricultural Economics*, Philadelphia, 1921.
Carver, T. N. *Principles of Rural Economics*, Boston, 1911.
Faber, Harald. *Coöperation in Danish Agriculture*, London, 1918.
Fay, C. R. *Coöperation at Home and Abroad*, London, 1920.
Hibbard, B. H. *Marketing Farm Products*, N. Y., 1919.
Holyoake, G. J. *History of Coöperation*, London, 1906.
Huebner, G. G. *Agricultural Commerce*, N. Y., 1924.
Macklin, Theo. *Efficient Marketing for Agriculture*, N. Y., 1921.
Powell, G. H. *Coöperation in Agriculture*, N. Y., 1917.
Smith-Gordon, L. E. P. and Cruise O'Brien. *Coöperation in Many Lands*, Manchester Coöperative Union, 1919.
Webb, Sidney and Beatrice. *The Consumers' Coöperative Movement*, London, 1921.
Weld, L. D. H. *Marketing of Farm Products*, N. Y., 1916.
Wolff, H. W. *Coöperation in Agriculture*, London, 1914.

C. *Grain Growers' Movement:*

Chipman, G. F. *The Grain Growers' Movement in The Prairie Provinces of Canada*, London, 1914.
Irvine, William. *The Farmer in Politics*, Toronto, 1921.
Mackintosh, W. A. *Agricultural Coöperation in Western Canada.* (Queen's University Studies), Kingston, 1924.
Moorhouse, Hopkins. *Deep Furrows*, Toronto, 1917.
Wood, L. A. *Farmers' Movements in Canada*, Toronto, 1924.
Canadian Annual Review, Toronto, 1905–1926, *passim.*

V. BULLETINS AND PAMPHLETS

Bawlf, W. R. *The Marketing of Canadian Grain Under War Conditions*, Winnipeg, 1918.
Black, J. D. and Price, H. B. *Coöperative Central Marketing Organization* (Univ. of Minnesota, Agr. Exp. Sta. Bul. No. 211), St. Paul, 1924.
Boyle, J. E. *The Law of Supply and Demand and the Wheat Market*, Ithaca, N. Y., 1921.
Chipman, G. F. "The Siege of Ottawa," *Grain Growers' Guide*, Winnipeg, 1911.
Clark, W. C. *The Country Elevator in the Canadian West* (Bulletin of Departments of History and Political and Economic Science in Queen's University), Kingston, 1916.
Evans. W. Sanford. *The Canadian Wheat Pool*, Winnipeg, 1926.
Filley, H. C. *Coöperative Elevators* (Nebraska College of Agriculture. Ext. Bul. 64), 1921.
Food Research Institute, Stanford University: *Wheat Studies.*
Vol. I, No. 6. *Farm Costs of Wheat Production in the North American Spring Wheat Belt.*
No. 8. *Canada as a Producer and Exporter of Wheat.*

Vol. II, No. 3. *A National Wheat Growers' Coöperative.*
No. 5. *Price Spreads and Shipment Costs in the Wheat Export Trade of Canada.*
Vol. III, No. 1. *American Importation of Canadian Wheat.*
No. 2. *The World Wheat Situation 1925–26.*

Hammatt, Theo. D. *Marketing Canadian Wheat* (U. S. Department of Commerce, Trade Information Bul. 251), Washington, 1924.

MacGibbon, D. A. *Traffic Routes for Canadian Grain,* University of Alberta Press, 1926.

Mackintosh, W. A. *The Canadian Wheat Pools* (Bul. No. 51 of Depts. of History and Political and Economic Science in Queen's University), Kingston, 1925.

Magill, Robert. *Grain Inspection in Canada,* Dept. of Trade and Commerce, Ottawa, 1914.

Magill, Robert. *International Grain Marketing,* Winnipeg, 1926.

McHugh, J. G. *Modern Grain Exchanges,* Chamber of Commerce, Minneapolis, 1922.

Northwest Grain Dealers' Association, Winnipeg, 1926–27.
Facts on Grain Marketing.
Why the Hurry?
Serious Charges made by Pool Director.
Bulletin Series, "For Your Information."

Patton, H. S. *Papers on the World's Wheat Trade,* University of Alberta Press, Edmonton, 1925.
I. *A Century and a Quarter of Wheat Prices.*
II. *The Changing Equilibrium in the World's Wheat Trade.*

Powell, G. H. *Fundamental Principles of Coöperation in Agriculture,* University of California Exp. Sta., Circular 222.

Sapiro, Aaron. *Coöperative Marketing,* Chicago, American Farm Federation Bureau, 1920.

Surface, F. M. *International Competition in the Production of Wheat for Export* (U. S. Dept. of Commerce, Trade Information Bul. 210), Washington, 1924.

Weld, L. D. H. *Coöperative Marketing of Grain in Western Canada,* Univ. of Minnesota, Studies in the Social Sciences, No. 4, St. Paul, 1915.

U. S. Dept. of Agriculture Bulletins:
No. 371. Humphrey, J. R. and Kerr, W. H., *Patronage Dividends in Coöperative Grain Companies,* 1916.
No. 937. Mehl, J. M., *Coöperative Grain Marketing: A comparative Study of Methods in U. S. and Canada,* 1921.
No. 718. Doty, S. W. and Hall, L. D., *Coöperative Live Stock Shipping Associations,* 1916.
No. 1106. Hulbert, L. S., *Legal Phases of Coöperative Associations,* 1922.
No. 1144. Jesnera, O. B., *Coöperative Marketing* (Farmers Bulletin).
No. 1302. Elsworth, R. H., *Development and Present Status of Farmers' Coöperative Business Organizations,* 1924.

VI. Periodicals

1. *Special Articles:*

Chipman, G. F. et al, "History of the Grain Growers," *Grain Growers' Guide*, June 26, 1918.

Colquette, R. D. "Pools Complete Another Year's Activities," *Grain Growers' Guide*, Nov. 1, 1926.

"The Livestock Pools," *Grain Growers' Guide*, Oct. 1, 1927.

Fay, C. R. "Agricultural Coöperation in the Canadian West," *Annals of American Academy of Political and Social Science*, May, 1923.

Hull, J. T. "The Story of the Wheat Pools," *Grain Growers' Guide*, Sept. 24, Oct. 1, 1924.

James, C. C. "Canadian Wheat History," *Grain Growers' Guide*, June 7, 1916.

MacGibbon, D. A. "Grain Legislation Affecting Western Canada," *Journal of Political Economy*, March, 1912.

Patton, H. S. "Canadian-American Reciprocity," *Quarterly Journal of Economics*, August, 1921.

Warbasse, J. P. "The Coöperative Movement," *New Republic*, Aug. 31, 1921.

"The Wheat Pools of Western Canada," (ed.) *Economist* (London), Feb. 13, 1926.

"Coöperative Marketing of Wheat in Western Canada," (ed.) *Board of Journal and Commerce Gazette* (London), Jan. 21, 1926.

2. *Agricultural, Grain Trade and Coöperative Periodicals:*

Agricultural Gazette, Dept. of Agriculture, Ottawa (to 1924).

Monthly Bulletin of Agricultural Statistics, Dominion Bureau of Statistics, Ottawa.

Agricultural Coöperation, Bureau of Agricultural Economics, Washington.

International Review of Agricultural Economics, International Institute of Agriculture, Rome.

Agricultural and Industrial Progress in Western Canada (monthly), Canadian Pacific Railway, Montreal.

Grain Trade News (weekly), Winnipeg.

The Northwestern Miller, Minneapolis.

The Canadian Co-operator (monthly), Co-operative Union of Canada, Brantford, Ontario.

Coöperation (monthly), Coöperative League of America, New York.

Grain Growers' Guide (weekly; semi-monthly since 1926), 1908, Winnipeg

Saskatchewan Co-operative News (monthly), 1916–1926, Regina.

The U. F. A. (semi-monthly), 1922, Calgary.

The Scoop Shovel (monthly), 1925, Winnipeg.

The Nor'west Farmer (semi-monthly), Winnipeg.

The Farm and Ranch Review (semi-monthly), Calgary.

The Saskatchewan Farmer (semi-monthly), Regina.

3. *Newspapers:*

Manitoba Free Press, Winnipeg.
Regina Leader.
Saskatoon Star.
Western Producer (formerly *The Progressive*), Saskatoon.
Edmonton Bulletin.
Calgary Herald.
Financial Post, Toronto.

VII. Miscellaneous

Winnipeg Grain Exchange: Constitution, By-laws, Rules and Regulations.

Winnipeg Grain Exchange: Annual reports.

Canadian Grain Trade Year Book, W. Sanford Evans Statistical Service, Winnipeg.

Western Canada Grain Grades and Elevator Tariffs (annual), Dawson Richardson Publications, Winnipeg.

Report of Secretary of Agriculture to President on the Wheat Situation, U. S. Dept. of Agriculture Year Book, 1923.

Great Britain, Royal Commission on Wheat Supplies, Report, Cmd. 1544, 1921.

International Economic Conference, Geneva, 1927. Document C. G. I. 14, "The Part played by Coöperative Organizations in the International Trade in Wheat," etc.

Proceedings of National Coöperative Marketing Conferences, 1923–26. National Council of Farmers' Coöperative Marketing Association, Washington.

Proceedings of American Institute of Coöperation, 1925–27.

INDEX

INDEX

Bei Fragen zur Produktsicherheit wenden Sie sich bitte an:
If you have any questions regarding product safety,
please contact:

Walter de Gruyter GmbH
Genthiner Straße 13
10785 Berlin
productsafety@degruyterbrill.com